BEIJING & SHANGHAI

1ST EDITION

Where to Stay and Eat
for All Budgets

Must-See Sights
and Local Secrets

Ratings You Can Trust

Fodor's Travel Publications   New York, Toronto, London, Sydney, Auckland
www.fodors.com

FODOR'S BEIJING & SHANGHAI

Editors: Emmanuelle Morgen, Deborah Kaufman

Editorial Production: Tom Holton

Editorial Contributors: Collin Campbell, Caroline Liou, Keming Liu, Kristin Rattini, and Guy Rubin

Maps: David Lindroth, Ed Jacobus, *cartographers;* Bob Blake and Rebecca Baer, *map editors*

Design: Fabrizio La Rocca, *creative director;* Moon Sun Kim, *cover designer;* Guido Caroti, *art director;* Melanie Marin, *senior picture editor*

Production/Manufacturing: Colleen Ziemba

Cover Photo: (Forbidden City, Beijing): Jeffrey Aaronson / Network Aspen

First Edition

ISBN 1–4000–1339–9

ISSN 1553–1171

SPECIAL SALES

This book is available for special discounts for bulk purchases for sales promotions or premiums. Special editions, including personalized covers, excerpts of existing books, and corporate imprints, can be created in large quantities for special needs. For more information, write to Special Markets/Premium Sales, 1745 Broadway, MD 6-2, New York, New York 10019 or e-mail specialmarkets@randomhouse.com.

AN IMPORTANT TIP & AN INVITATION

Although all prices, opening times, and other details in this book are based on information supplied to us at press time, changes occur all the time in the travel world, and Fodor's cannot accept responsibility for facts that become outdated or for inadvertent errors or omissions. So **always confirm information when it matters,** especially if you're making a detour to visit a specific place. Your experiences—positive and negative—matter to us. If we have missed or misstated something, **please write to us.** We follow up on all suggestions. Contact the Beijing & Shanghai editor at editors@fodors.com or c/o Fodor's at 1745 Broadway, New York, New York 10019.

PRINTED IN THE UNITED STATES OF AMERICA

10 9 8 7 6 5 4 3

DESTINATION BEIJING & SHANGHAI

The Heart of the Dragon and the Head of the Dragon: China's two greatest cities represent, on one hand, the country's mystical cultural heritage, and on the other hand, its bright, new future, fueled by an increasingly powerful economy. In Beijing you can walk beneath the red flags of Tiananmen Square, climb the endless steps of the Forbidden City, and behold the majestic Summer Palace at dusk. The country's capital is like a gigantic museum, and it captures the essence of China. At the other end of the spectrum is Shanghai, a growing financial center. In the 1920s the city was infamous for its gambling, gangsters, and opium dens; today citizens, international businesspeople, and tourists stroll along wide, newly paved sidewalks beneath gleaming skyscrapers. As different as they are, Beijing and Shanghai share some essential Chinese traits. Both have ancient temples and modern high-rises, the ubiquitous family-style restaurants, and early-morning markets thriving with shoppers.

Tim Jarrell, Publisher

CONTENTS

Index 245

Maps

CloseUps

ABOUT THIS BOOK

RATINGS	Orange stars ★ denote sights and properties that our editors and writers consider the very best in the area covered by the entire book. These, the best of the best, are listed in the **Fodor's Choice** section in the front of the book. Black stars ★ highlight the sights and properties we deem **Highly Recommended**, the don't-miss sights within any region. It goes without saying that no property pays to be included. Use the index to find complete descriptions.
SPECIAL SPOTS	**Pleasures & Pastimes** and text on chapter-title pages focus on types of experiences that reveal the spirit of the destination. Also watch for **Off the Beaten Path** sights. Some are out of the way, some are quirky, and all are worth your while. When the munchies hit, look for **Need a Break?** suggestions.
TIME IT RIGHT	Check **On the Calendar** up front and chapters' **Timing** sections for weather and crowd overviews and best days and times to visit.
SEE IT ALL	Use Fodor's **Great Itineraries** as a model for your trip. Either follow those that begin the book, or mix itineraries from several chapters. In cities, **Good Walks** guide you to important sights in each neighborhood; ☞ indicates the starting points of walks and itineraries in the text and on the map.
BUDGET WELL	Hotel and restaurant price categories from ¢ to $$$$ are defined in the opening pages of each chapter—expect to find a balanced selection for every budget. For attractions, we always give standard adult admission fees; reductions are usually available for children, students, and senior citizens. Look in **Discounts & Deals** in Smart Travel Tips for information on destination-wide ticket schemes. Want to pay with plastic? **AE, D, DC, MC, V** following restaurant and hotel listings indicate whether American Express, Discover, Diners Club, MasterCard, or Visa are accepted.
BASIC INFO	**Smart Travel Tips** lists travel essentials for the entire area covered by the book; city- and region-specific basics end each chapter. To find the best way to get around, see the transportation section; see individual modes of travel ("Car Travel," "Train Travel") for details.
ON THE MAPS	**Maps** throughout the book show you what's where and help you find your way around. Black and orange numbered bullets ❶❶ in the text correlate to bullets on maps.
BACKGROUND	We give background information in the course of explaining sights as well as in **CloseUp** boxes and in **Understanding Beijing & Shanghai** at the end of the book. To get in the mood, review the suggestions in **Books & Movies**. The **glossary** can be invaluable.

FIND IT FAST	Within the Beijing and Shanghai chapters, sights are grouped by neighborhood. Where to Eat and Where to Stay are also organized by neighborhood—Where to Eat is further divided by cuisine. The Nightlife & the Arts and Sports & the Outdoors sections are arranged alphabetically by entertainment type. Within Shopping, a description of a city's main shopping districts is followed by a list of specialty shops grouped according to their focus. The Side Trips chapters explore the regions around Beijing and Shanghai.
DON'T FORGET	Restaurants are open for lunch and dinner daily unless we state otherwise; we mention dress only when there's a specific requirement and reservations only when they're essential or not accepted—it's always best to book ahead. Hotels have private baths, phone, TVs, and air-conditioning and operate on the European Plan (a.k.a. EP, meaning without meals), unless stated otherwise. We always list facilities but not whether you'll be charged extra to use them, so when pricing accommodations, find out what's included.
SYMBOLS	

Many Listings

★ Fodor's Choice
★ Highly recommended
⊠ Physical address
✢ Directions
⌂ Mailing address
☎ Telephone
🖷 Fax
⊕ On the Web
✉ E-mail
🎫 Admission fee
☉ Open/closed times
▶ Start of walk/itinerary
Ⓜ Metro stations
🖃 Credit cards

Outdoors

⛳ Golf
⛺ Camping

Hotels & Restaurants

🏨 Hotel
🛏 Number of rooms
♨ Facilities
🍽 Meal plans
✕ Restaurant
⌅ Reservations
🏛 Dress code
⃠ Smoking
🍺 BYOB
✕🏨 Hotel with restaurant that warrants a visit

Other

☾ Family-friendly
🛈 Contact information
⇨ See also
⊠ Branch address
☞ Take note

China

ALTAI MTS.

KAZAKHSTAN

KIRGHIZSTAN

TIEN SHAN

TARIM BASIN

Ürümqi

TAJIKISTAN

AFGHANISTAN

TAKLA MAKAN

XINJIANG

GANSU

INN

MONGOLIA

(JAMMU AND KASHMIR)

KUNLUN SHAN

QINGHAI

Xining

PLATEAU OF TIBET

TIBET

HIMALAYAS

Yarlung Zangbo

Lhasa

Nu (Salween)

Lancang

SICH

NEPAL

BHUTAN

Kunming

BANGLA-DESH

YUNNAN

INDIA

MYANMAR (BURMA)

Bay of Bengal

THAILAND

L

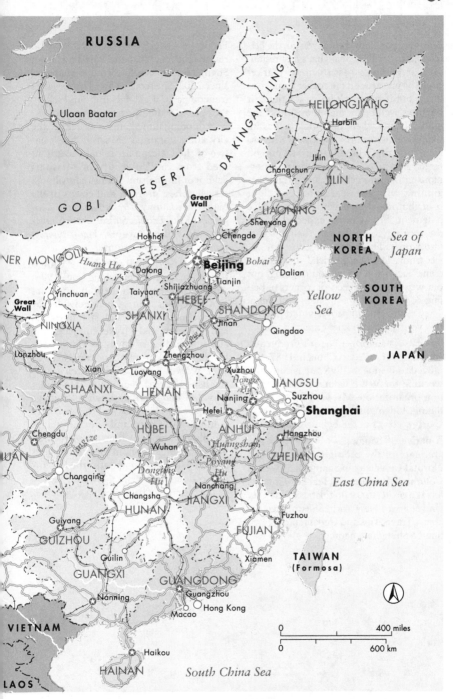

ON THE ROAD WITH FODOR'S

The more you know before you go, the better your trip will be. Shanghai's best restaurant or Beijing's best open-air market could be just around the corner from your hotel, but if you don't know it's there, it might as well be on the other side of the globe. That's where this book comes in. Our focus is on providing you with information that's useful, accurate, and on target. Every day Fodor's editors put enormous effort into getting things right, beginning with the search for the right contributors—people who have objective judgment, broad travel experience, and the writing ability to put their insights into words. There's no substitute for advice from a like-minded friend who has just come back from where you're going, but our writers, having seen all corners of Beijing & Shanghai, are the next best thing. They're the kind of people you'd poll for tips yourself if you knew them.

Caroline Liou, a former Fodor's production editor, first traveled to China in 1987. She moved to Beijing in 1998 and is currently working for WWF China, the conservation organization. Ms. Liou updated the dining, lodging, shopping, nightlife, and sports sections of the Beijing chapter.

A native of Baoding, Dr. Keming Liu is a graduate of the prestigious East China Normal University in Shanghai as well as Columbia University's Teacher College. She is a professor of linguistics at the City University of New York. She updated the Smart Travel Tips and Understanding Beijing & Shanghai chapters.

Freelance writer Kristin Baird Rattini, who revised the Shanghai and Side Trips from Shanghai chapters, has lived in Shanghai since 2002. She remains awed by the city's frenetic pace of change and humbled by the reminder that the current wave of expats flooding into Shanghai is neither the city's first, nor its last. Ms. Rattini is a native of the Chicago area, and she graduated from the University of Missouri School of Journalism. She has contributed travel stories, profiles, and essays to the magazines *Family Circle, National Geographic Kids, People, Sunset, that's Shanghai,* and United Airlines' *Hemispheres,* among other publications.

Guy Rubin, originally from the United Kingdom, has lived in Beijing since 1996. After recovering from spells in industries as disparate as management consultancy and the entertainment industry, five years ago he co-founded a travel company specializing in luxury tours to China. Mr. Rubin's travel articles have appeared in *City Weekend* and *Capital Views,* two English-language magazines in Beijing; *Citylife Chiangmai,* an English-language magazine in Thailand; and the Web sites culturaltravels.com and chinanow.com. His photographs of China have appeared in several publications in the United States and Italy. Mr. Rubin updated the Exploring section of the Beijing chapter, as well as the Side Trips from Beijing chapter.

WHAT'S WHERE

As you navigate in and around Beijing and Shanghai, remember the Chinese words for directions: north is *bei*; south is *nan*; west is *xi*; east is *dong*; and middle is *zhong*. Street signs in cities are marked in both Chinese characters and pinyin (romanized Chinese).

Beijing

Beijing is in northeastern China about 120 mi inland from the Gulf of Bohai. The Liao, Jin, Yuan, Ming, and Qing dynasties all chose Beijing as their capital, for close to 2,000 years of imperial presence, and the city was destroyed and rebuilt numerous times. While the narrow, winding streets in the old neighborhoods recall imperial times, the wide avenues and huge blocks in the newer parts of the city reflect the principles of communist China, and are laid out so that the individual feels small in comparison to "order." The Forbidden City is at the heart of Beijing and is surrounded by the city's municipal districts.

Forbidden City. A 200-acre walled maze of interlocking halls, gates, and courtyard homes built to house the emperor, his family, and his court subjects in the 15th century, the Forbidden City stands at the center of Beijing. Its entrance is Tiananmen Gate, the Gate of Heavenly Peace.

Dongcheng District. Immediately east of the Forbidden City, Dongcheng is home to Beijing's "downtown" area. Most of the district is modern, with wide avenues and tall buildings, although a few historic parks, homes, and temples, including the Lama Temple, form pockets of tranquility.

Chaoyang District. Chaoyang stretches east and north of Dongcheng. Here you'll find Beijing's diplomatic neighborhood, populated with international embassies; the Sanlitun area, crowded with bars and nightclubs; several outdoor markets and upscale shopping malls; and a slew of upscale, high-rise hotels.

Chongwen District. South of Dongcheng and southeast of the Forbidden City, Chongwen is where to find Beijing's spectacular Temple of Heaven and the Ancient Observatory.

Haidian District. In the northwestern corner of the city, the Haidian District is where you'll find the Summer Palace, as well as numerous parks and gardens.

Xicheng District. On the west side of the Forbidden City, Xicheng is where to get lost among Beijing's old hutong alleyways and to take long walks by Qianhai and Houhai lakes.

Xuanwu District. Also known as the Muslim Quarter, Xuanwu, southwest of the Forbidden City, has Beijing's oldest and largest mosque, as well as the Buddhist Temple of the Source of Law, buried deep in a quiet hutong. The district has an even mix of old and new, developed neighborhoods.

Side Trips from Beijing

In Chapter 2, we suggest day trips to several historical sights of note within a few hours' drive of Beijing. The best way to reach these sights is to hire a car and driver, or sign on with a bus tour. The staff at your hotel can help arrange your tour; and we list tour operators and travel services agencies under "Smart Travel Tips A to Z" in the Side Trips from Beijing chapter.

The Great Wall. You can see long stretches of the Great Wall at several points outside of Beijing. The segment closest to the city, about one hour's drive (60 km or 37 mi) northwest of downtown, is at Badaling. Because of its proximity to the city, it's also the most popular segment to visit. You have to travel farther to get to the Great Wall at Mutianyu, 90 km (56 mi) northeast of downtown, but it's worth it—this is where to get the most awe-inspiring views of the wall. Adventure-seekers should head for the hiking trails at the farthest and least developed of the Great Wall visiting areas: Simatai, 120 km (74 mi) northwest of the city.

The Ming Tombs. The famous tombs of 13 Ming emperors rest near Changping, 48 km (30 mi) northwest of Beijing, en route to the Great Wall at Badaling.

Fahai Temple and Jietai Temple. Both great Buddhist temples are west of the city. Fahai is actually within the city limits, in Shijingshan District, about 20 km (12 mi) 12 mi from downtown. Jietai is in Mentougou County, 35 km (22 mi) west of downtown.

Marco Polo Bridge. Beijing's 12th-century bridge is in the city's Fengtai District, 16 km (10 mi) southwest of Guanganmen Gate.

Zhoukoudian Peking Man Site. This extensive paleontological site is 48 km (30 mi) southwest of Beijing.

Yunju Temple. Yunju, home to some 14,000 tablets carved with Buddhist scripture, is 75 km (47 mi) southwest of Beijing in Fangshan County.

Eastern Qing Tombs. Five emperors, 14 empresses, and 136 imperial concubines are laid to rest at this enormous burial site 125 km (78 mi) east of Beijing in Zunhua County. The two- to three-hour drive to the tombs is one of the most rewarding side trips you can make.

Shanghai

Shanghai is on the eastern coast of China, 1,461 km (908 mi) south of Beijing. The city is divided into east and west sides by the Huangpu River. As the most Westernized city in China after Hong Kong, Shanghai is on the cutting edge of China's race for modernization. Almost a quarter of the world's construction cranes stand in this city of 14 million; often it feels like half of those are on the street you happen to be walking down. On the other hand, architectural remnants of a strong colonial past survive along the charming, winding, bustling streets that make this city undeniably and intimately Chinese.

Puxi. Literally "west side of the river," Puxi covers the Huangpu District, including all of the old city and downtown Shanghai west. The Bund (Waitan) stretches along five riverfront blocks of Zhongshan Dong Yi Lu between Jinling Lu and Suzhou Creek. Farther west, the former French Concession is in the Luwan and Xuhui districts.

Pudong. Meaning "east side of the river," Pudong is Shanghai's newest area of development. This is where to find the city's, and the world's, tallest skyscrapers and biggest businesses.

Hongkou District. Hongkou and neighboring Yangpu District, where thousands of Jewish refugees made their homes during World War II, are on the west side of the river north of Suzhou Creek.

Hongqiao Development Zone. Pudong's alter ego, this area outside the Ring Road to the west has been built up with office buildings, hotels, and commercial shopping centers.

Side Trips from Shanghai
China's eastern provinces are the most densely populated and industrialized regions in the country. They are also home to some of China's most heavily visited spots.

Suzhou. In Jiangsu province, Suzhou, with its renowned gardens, is about 1½ hours west of Shanghai by train.

Zhouzhuang. This lovely 12th-century town known for its numerous waterways is a 90-minute bus ride west of Shanghai.

Hangzhou. The city of Hangzhou is a two- to three-hour drive southwest of Shanghai in Zhejiang province.

GREAT ITINERARIES

Beijing in 5 Days

Day 1. Start at **Tiananmen Square**, the heart of modern China and the entry point to the spectacular **Forbidden City**. Explore the former imperial palace to your heart's content. In the afternoon, take a guided pedicab ride through a hutong, a mazelike neighborhood, to the **Drum Tower**. Have Peking duck for dinner, perhaps at the **Quanjude Peking Duck Restaurant**, south of Tiananmen Square.

Day 2. Head straight for the vast grounds of the **Temple of Heaven**, one of Beijing's most important historical sights. If you have time in the morning or early afternoon, take in the **Lama Temple** and the nearby **Temple of Confucius**, too. Save two or three hours in the afternoon for shopping at **Beijing Curio City** and **Silk Alley** in the Chaoyang District. Have dinner in the Sanlitun area.

Day 3. Set aside Day 3 for a trip to the **Ming Tombs** and the **Great Wall** at Mutianyu, where a Japanese gondola offers a dramatic ride to the summit. Bring a brown-bag lunch.

Day 4. For an enjoyable day trip closer to Beijing, walk around Kunming Lake at the rambling **Summer Palace**, and then spend a few hours at the nearby **Old Summer Palace**, an intriguing ruin. In the evening, plan to see a **Peking opera** performance or hit the clubs in the Sanlitun embassy area.

Day 5. On Day 5 hire a car and visit the spectacular **Eastern Qing Tombs**, where a "spirit way" lined with carved stone animals and unrestored templelike grave sites rest in a beautiful rural setting. Wear walking shoes and bring a lunch. The drive takes five hours round-trip, so depart early.

Shanghai in 5 Days

Day 1. Begin your first day in **Yu Garden**, and take a walk through the old city streets and markets surrounding it. Next, head to **the Bund** for a waterfront stroll and a look at some of Beijing's grandest historic buildings. Segue down **Nanjing Lu**, Shanghai's busiest street. For dinner, the exceptional M on the Bund offers good views of the river and the Bund lit up at night.

Day 2. Head back to Nanjing Lu and make your way to the **Shanghai Museum**. If you have time before or after the museum, stroll by the **People's Square** for some people-watching or swing over to the **Bird and Flower Market**. In the afternoon take a cab north to **Jade Buddha Temple**. That night you can take a relaxing cruise along the Hangpu River.

Day 3. Make a trip to Pudong in the morning, and go to the top of the **Jinmao Tower** for a bird's-eye view of the city. Relax on the riverfront promenade, and after lunch take the **Bund Tourist Tunnel** back to Puxi. In the afternoon, spend some time walking around the former **French Concession** for a view of old Shanghai and the city's new chic stores. In the evening, catch a show of the Shanghai acrobats.

Day 4. On Day 4 take a bus or train from Shanghai to **Suzhou** to see the town's renowned gardens.

Day 5. Visit **Zhouzhuang** on Day 5 for a glimpse of life in China's water towns.

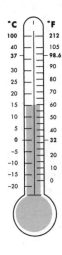

The best time to visit Beijing and Shanghai is early fall. The weather is at its best in September and October, with a good chance of sunny days and mild temperatures. Winters are cold and rainy, and the rain continues through early spring. Late April through June is pleasant, but come July the days are hot and excruciatingly humid. Although temperatures can be scorching, summer is the peak tourist season, and hotels and transportation can be very crowded. Book several months in advance if possible for summer travel.

Avoid the three national holidays: Chinese New Year, which ranges from mid-January to mid-February; Labor Day holiday, the first week of May; and National Day, the first week of October. Hundreds of millions of Chinese travel during these weeks, making the crowds at tourist sites unbearable.

Climate

What follows are average daily maximum and minimum temperatures in Beijing and Hong Kong.

⏹ Forecasts **Weather Channel Connection** ☎ 900/932–8437, 95¢ per minute from a Touch-Tone phone.

BEIJING

Jan	34F	1C	May	81F	27C	Sept.	79F	14
	14	–10		55	13		57	14
Feb.	39F	4C	June	88F	31C	Oct.	68F	20C
	18	–18		64	18		43	6
Mar.	52F	11C	July	88F	31C	Nov.	48F	9C
	30	–1		70	21		28	–2
Apr.	70F	21C	Aug.	86F	30C	Dec.	37F	3C
	45	7		68	20		18	–8

SHANGHAI

Jan	46F	8C	May	77F	25C	Sept.	82F	28C
	33	1		59	15		66	19
Feb.	47F	8C	June	82F	28C	Oct.	74F	23C
	34	1		67	19		57	14
Mar.	66F	19C	July	90F	32C	Nov.	63F	17C
	40	4		74	23		45	7
Apr.	66F	19C	Aug.	90F	32C	Dec.	53F	12C
	50	10		74	23		36	2

ON THE CALENDAR

Most of China's holidays are calculated according to the lunar calendar and can vary by as much as a few weeks from year to year. Check with the CITS for specific dates.

WINTER	
December 25, January 1	**Christmas and New Year's Day** are becoming an excuse for the Chinese to exchange cards, buy decorations (made in China), and eat out banquet style.
February	**Chinese New Year,** China's most important holiday, follows the lunar calendar and falls in early to mid-February. Also called Spring Festival, it gives the Chinese an official three-day holiday to visit family and relatives, eat special meals, and throw firecrackers to celebrate the New Year and its respective Chinese zodiac animal. Students and teachers get up to four weeks off, and many others consider that the festival runs as long as a month. It is a particularly crowded time to travel in China. Many businesses reduce their hours or close altogether. Tickets and hotel rooms may be hard to find.
February and March	The **Spring Lantern Festival** marks the end of the Chinese New Year on the 15th day of the first moon. Colorful paper lanterns are carried through the streets, sometimes accompanied by dragon dances.
SPRING	
May 1	**International Labor Day** is a busy travel time, especially if the holiday falls near a weekend.
SUMMER	
June	**The Dragon Boat Festival,** on the fifth day of the fifth moon, celebrates the national hero Qu Yuan, who drowned himself in the third century in protest against the corrupt emperor. Legend has it that people attempted to rescue him by throwing rice dumplings wrapped in bamboo leaves into the sea and frightening fish away by beating drums. Today crews in narrow dragon boats race to the beat of heavy drums, and rice wrapped in bamboo leaves is consumed.
FALL	
October 1	**National Day** celebrates the founding of the People's Republic of China. Tiananmen Square fills up with flowers, entertainment, and a hefty crowd of visitors on this official holiday.
October	**Mid-Autumn Festival** is celebrated on the 15th day of the eighth moon, which generally falls in early October. The Chinese spend this time gazing at the full moon and exchanging tasty moon cakes (so named because they resemble the full moon) filled with meat, bean paste, sugar, and other delectable surprises.

PLEASURES & PASTIMES

Antiques Markets Chairman Mao alarm clocks, calligraphy scrolls, porcelain, jade pieces, valuable coins, old Chinese locks, and a great number of fake antiques are spread carefully on tables that line the streets of Beijing and Shanghai on a weekly and sometimes daily basis. Ask around for the date and time of the antiques market in your area and be mindful of rip-offs when you arrive. If you are seriously searching for antiques, it's best to get a local who speaks English to bargain for you while you wait unseen for the right price.

Restaurants Dining in China is best enjoyed in large groups so you can sample a variety of dishes. Menus are usually divided into appetizers, meats, vegetables, seafood, soups, and so on. It's best to order from each category so you dine in true Chinese style—dishes at your elbows, across the table, in front of you, stacked up, and sometimes even on the ledge behind to make room for the next round.

Beijing and Shanghai are known for their own unique cooking styles and specialties, but you can also find regional Chinese cuisine on specialty menus in both cities. Indeed, there are generally four regional categories of food found across the country.

Northern, or Mandarin, cuisine is characterized by fine cutting and pure seasoning, providing dishes with strong garlic, ginger, and onion flavors. Peking duck, served with pancakes and *hoisin* sauce, and Mongolian hotpot are native to this region. An abundance of steamed bread (*mantou*) and flat pancakes are sold on the street and make good snacks.

Southern, or Cantonese, cooking is famous for dim sum, an eating experience found mainly in Hong Kong, Guangdong province, and some larger cities with an overseas contingent. Bite-size dumplings, wonton, rice noodle dishes, sesame seed buns filled with bean paste, and a variety of other tasty snacks are pushed around on carts among patrons. Cantonese cooking tends to be the lightest and least oily of the four regional categories, though it can be just as exotic, with snake, turtle, monkey, rabbit, and a host of other animal and reptile specialties finding their way onto the menus.

Eastern, most notably Shanghainese, food is notorious for its heavy use of oil, though the freshest seafood, from hairy crabs to snails to shark's fin soup, are served in this region. Chicken and seafood dishes are simmered, boiled, or braised in their own juices, enhancing the natural flavors. Some wonderful *baozis* (steamed white bread filled with either vegetables, pork, or black bean paste) are sold on the streets of most cities and towns scattered throughout the region.

The spiciest of the four categories, Sichuan cooking loves to use that Chinese peppercorn and will keep you slugging back bottles of purified water. Chengdu is famous for its snacks, a variety of small dishes both hot and cold, served all day. Tea-smoked duck, marinated for more than 24 hours, peels right off the bone and melts in the mouth. Sichuan hotpot restaurants have become so popular they are popping up as far away as Beijing.

Note that even fancy Chinese restaurants are often quite affordable by Western standards. Most sizable hotels serving foreigners have a Western as well as a Chinese kitchen.

Early Morning
At 6 in the morning, no matter where you are in China, everyone is up and outside buying their daily vegetables, fruits, meats, eggs, and noodles in the local market. Vendors are out steaming, frying, boiling, and selling breakfast snacks to people on their way to work. Men and women practice tai chi in parks, along rivers, and in some unlikely places—the steps of a movie theater, an empty alley, the side entrance of a hotel—whenever the sun rises. Early morning in China is when the cities, towns, and villages come alive and should be experienced as much as possible, as every place has a different way of doing "business."

Wandering
Wandering and sometimes getting lost in either Beijing or Shanghai will reveal an inner logic to the city you are visiting. Here is where you get to experience China without a frame of propaganda around it. Encounter charming alleyways that twist behind major streets, hidden outdoor markets, friendly, responsive locals gesturing unintelligible messages, dramatic shifts from poverty to riches, and wild displays of the new and the old.

Outside the city, budget time for hiking. Explore the Thirteen Ming Tombs or the Eastern Qing Tombs on foot and picnic in the ruins (a tradition among Beijing's expatriate community since the 1920s). Most upscale hotels offer elegant boxed lunches. If you've hired a car to the Great Wall, consider venturing a bit farther into the countryside where farming villages await. Don't be surprised when local farmers invite you into their homes for a rest and some tea.

FODOR'S CHOICE

The sights, restaurants, hotels, and other travel experiences are our writers' and editors' top picks—our Fodor's Choices. They're the best of their type in and around Beijing and Shanghai; you will find all the details in the chapters that follow.

LODGING

$$$$	**China World, Beijing.** Marble and gold everywhere characterize this luxury hotel on one of Beijing's premier shopping streets. The hotel is part of the China World Trade Center, which includes a mall with 200 stores.
$$$$	**Grand Hyatt, Shanghai.** The world's tallest hotel, the Grand Hyatt offers spectacular views of Shanghai from Pudong, the city's financial district.
$$$$	**The St. Regis, Beijing.** Visiting dignitaries and celebrities stay at the St. Regis, where opulence—and prices—know no limits. This is where to go if you really want to splurge.
$$$–$$$$	**Shangri-La, Hangzhou.** On the site of a former Buddhist temple, this hotel is surrounded by 40 acres of camphor and bamboo trees. Many of the formal rooms overlook a lake.
$$$–$$$$	**Sheraton Hotel, Suzhou.** A pagoda lobby and traditional-style buildings help this hotel blend in with its surroundings in historic Suzhou.
$$$	**Grand Hyatt, Beijing.** You may never want to leave the incredible pool area, with its serene waterfalls, "virtual sky" ceiling, and Olympic-size swimming pool, but the Forbidden City is just a short walk away.
$$$	**Peninsula Palace, Beijing.** With ultramodern facilities, including plasma-screen TVs, and top-notch service, this hotel takes the cake as the classiest hotel in Beijing.
$$–$$$	**Red Capital Residence, Beijing.** This is your chance to stay in an exquisitely restored traditional courtyard home once frequented by red capitalists in the 1950s.

BUDGET LODGING

$–$$	**Ramada Plaza, Shanghai.** This classy hotel with a soaring atrium and statues of Greek gods is in the middle of the action right on Nanjing Road.
¢	**Lüsongyuan, Beijing.** A traditional wooden entrance leads to five courtyards, all a part of this excellent hostel, which also has its own restaurant.

RESTAURANTS

$$$$ | **Mei Fu, Beijing.** Delicate preparations of Shanghainese cuisine are served on antique wooden tables beside little waterfalls in this lovely restaurant on Houhai Lake.

$$$–$$$$ | **The Courtyard, Beijing.** This elegant retreat serves a fusion of Chinese and Continental cuisines before a view of the Forbidden City.

$$$–$$$$ | **Green T. House, Beijing.** Owned by celebrity chef Jin R., Green T. is the city's chicest restaurant of the moment, serving creations so artistic, you almost don't want to eat them.

$$$–$$$$ | **Red Capital Club, Beijing.** Step back into the days of the Cultural Revolution at this decadent restaurant in a restored courtyard near the homes of former national leaders. Extravagant meals are served banquet-style.

$$–$$$$ | **M on the Bund, Shanghai.** This chic rooftop restaurant serves sophisticated cuisine with hints of Mediterranean and Middle Eastern influences. The view and adjacent lounge draw a hip crowd.

$–$$$ | **Meilongzhen, Shanghai.** Dating from 1938, Meilongzhen serves outstanding Sichuanese food in traditional surroundings.

BUDGET RESTAURANTS

$ | **Lao Hanzi, Beijing.** Head to this casual restaurant in the Houhai Lake bar area for delicous smoked duck, salt-coated shrimp, and baked fish.

¢–$ | **Bao Luo, Shanghai.** Celebrity chef Jean Georges Vongerichten has called Bao Luo his favorite restaurant in Shanghai for its super-fresh ingredients and authentic Chinese cooking. Expect serious crowds.

¢–$$ | **Simply Thai, Shanghai.** First-rate spring rolls, samosas, curries, and fried rice, plus tables on a patio, bring crowds to this low-key restaurant.

GARDENS

Humble Administrator's Garden, Suzhou. Anything but humble, these elaborate gardens contain a collection of 700 bonsai trees among other botanical marvels.

Master of the Nets Garden, Suzhou. With ponds, pavilions, and a tiny stone bridge, this perfect little garden offers a serene and beautiful escape.

Yu Garden, Shanghai. The garden built in the 16th century, creates an atmosphere of peace amid the clamor of the city, with rocks, trees, dragon walls, bridges, and pavilions.

STREETS & SQUARES

The Bund, Shanghai. A waterfront boulevard lined with beautiful art deco buildings and souvenir stands, the Bund is where to get a taste of Shanghai's animated street life.

People's Square, Shanghai. The city's main square is a social center surrounded by important sights and museums.

Tiananmen Square, Beijing. The world's largest public square and the scene of several notorious political clashes, Tiananmen Square is at the entrance to the Forbidden City and at the heart of modern China.

RUINS & HISTORICAL SITES

Evening Sunlight at Thunder Peak Pagoda, Hangzhou. A perfect reproduction of a 10th-century pagoda guards an active archaeological site and numerous treasures, including a miniature silver pagoda containing what is said to be a lock of the Buddha's hair.

The Great Wall at Simatai. Built by successive dynasties over two millennia, the wall is a collection of many defensive installations that extends some 4,000 km (2,500 mi) from the East China Sea to Central Asia.

The Eastern Qing Tombs, east of Beijing. Although it takes the better part of a day to visit this site 78 miles east of Beijing, the experience of walking among these ancient, elaborate tombs is absolutely worth it. Take a picnic and take your time exploring the site.

MUSEUMS

Shanghai Museum. China's best museum houses an incomparable collection of art and artifacts, including paintings, sculpture, ceramics, calligraphy, furniture, and fantastic bronzes.

Zhang Residence, Zhouzhuang. This expansive, 15th-century courtyard home is filled with Ming-era furniture, musical instruments, and games. Don't miss the master bedroom upstairs.

PALACES

The Forbidden City, Beijing. Home to 24 emperors and two dynasties for 500 years, the 200-acre compound is filled with halls, courtyards, and lesser buildings, all stained imperial vermilion, decorated with gold on the outside, and furnished with exquisite screens, thrones, paintings, and more.

The Summer Palace, Beijing. Imperial families escaped summer heat in airy pavilions among trees and man-made lakes in this 18th-century garden retreat on the northwest fringe of the city.

TEMPLES & MONASTERIES

Lama Temple, Beijing. Join the monks and pilgrims at this beloved temple decorated with fine scrolls, carvings, and statues.

Temple of Heaven, Beijing. The Temple of Heaven holds the blue-roof Hall of Prayer for Good Harvests and the round altar where the emperor conducted sacrifices.

Temple of the Soul's Retreat, Hangzhou. Beside this large, fourth-century temple, you can see 338 Buddhist figures carved by monks into the limestone of the mountain.

SHOPPING

Dongtai Lu Antiques Market, Shanghai. Wheelers and dealers peddle antique and reproduction ceramics, jade, furnishings, and curios at this colorful market.

Panjiayuan Market, Beijing. Hundreds of open-air stalls have antiques, bric-a-brac, rugs, jewelry, and clothes for sale.

Shanghai Museum Bookshop, Shanghai. Quality art and gifts, such as pearls, porcelain, and glossy coffee-table books are sold here.

Silk Alley Market, Beijing. The city's most popular market for clothing, this is where to find designer and knock-off North Face jackets, Esprit sportswear, and cashmere (real and faux) wraps.

NIGHTLIFE & THE ARTS

Cotton Club, Shanghai. This dark and smoky jazz and blues club is the number one live-music venue in Shanghai.

The Door, Shanghai. Head to the Door for a truly eclectic experience: contemporary interpretations of traditional Chinese music played in a room filled with antique furniture and modern accents.

Huguang Guildhall, Beijing. Beautifully restored, the city's oldest Peking opera theater still stages traditional performances nightly.

SMART TRAVEL TIPS

AIR TRAVEL

In 2004 transportation officials in China and the United States signed an agreement to expand air service between the two countries, adding 84 passenger flights per week to the existing service over the next six years. Within mainland China all carriers are regional subsidiaries of the Civil Aviation Administration of China (CAAC). Reservations and ticket purchases can be made in the United States through travel Web sites and other agencies. In China you can make reservations through local China International Travel Service (CITS) offices (⇨ Visitor Information) in most cities.

Flying is more expensive in China than it is in the United States, but the standards of service are not as high. You can make reservations for domestic flights at your hotel travel desk, but some routes fill up quickly, so it's best to book in advance.
🛪 Reservations **U.S.-China Travel Service**
☎ 800/332-2831.

BOOKING

When you book, look for nonstop flights and remember that "direct" flights stop at least once. Try to avoid connecting flights, which require a change of plane. Two airlines may operate a connecting flight jointly, so ask whether your airline operates every segment of the trip; you may find that the carrier you prefer flies you only part of the way. To find more booking tips and to check prices and make online flight reservations, log on to www.fodors.com.

CARRIERS

Air Canada has daily flights to Beijing and Shanghai from Vancouver and Montréal. Air China flies nonstop to Beijing and Shanghai from New York and the west coast of the United States. You can choose to stop in Beijing and board a later flight to Shanghai with one single ticket. Cathay Pacific flies to Beijing via Hong Kong. China Eastern and China Southern airlines serve both international and domestic routes. Both airlines fly from China to the west coast of the United States.

Japan Airlines and All Nippon fly to Beijing via Tokyo. Northwest and United both have service to Beijing from the United States, and United has a nonstop flight to Shanghai from Chicago.

▐ To & From China Air Canada ☎ 888/247-2262, 800/361-8071 TTY ⊕ www.aircanada.com. **Air China** ☎ 800/982-8802 in New York, 800/986-1985 in San Francisco, 800/882-8122 in Los Angeles ⊕ www.airchina.com. **All Nippon** ☎ 800/235-9262 ⊕ www.fly-ana.com. **Cathay Pacific** ☎ 800/233-2742 ⊕ www.cathaypacific.com. **China Eastern** ☎ 626/583-1500, 310/646-1849, or 800/200-5118 in Los Angeles, 415/982-5115 or 650/875-2367 in San Francisco ⊕ www.ce-air.com. **China Southern** ☎ 888/338-8988 ⊕ www.cs-air.com/en. **Japan Airlines** ☎ 800/525-3663 ⊕ www.japanair.com. **Northwest** ☎ 800/225-2525 ⊕ www.nwa.com. **United** ☎ 800/241-6522 ⊕ www.ual.com.

▐ Within China Air China ☎ 800/982-8802 in New York, 800/986-1985 in San Francisco, 800/882-8122 in Los Angeles ⊕ www.airchina.com. **China Eastern** ☎ 626/583-1500, 310/646-1849, or 800/200-5118 in Los Angeles, 415/982-5115 or 650/875-2367 in San Francisco ⊕ www.ce-air.com. **China Southern** ☎ 888/338-8988 ⊕ www.cs-air.com/en. **China Southwest Airlines** ☎ 028/8666-8080 in China ⊕ www.cswa.com/en. **Shanghai Airlines** ☎ 800/620-8888 ⊕ www.shanghai-air.com.

CHECK-IN & BOARDING
Always **find out your carrier's check-in policy.** Plan to arrive at the airport about two hours before your scheduled departure time for domestic flights and 2½ to 3 hours before international flights. You may need to arrive earlier if you're flying from one of the busier airports or during peak air-traffic times. To avoid delays at airport-security checkpoints, try not to wear any metal. Jewelry, belt and other buckles, steel-toe shoes, and keys are among the items that can set off detectors.

Assuming that not everyone with a ticket will show up, airlines routinely overbook planes. When everyone does, airlines ask for volunteers to give up their seats. In return, these volunteers usually get a several-hundred-dollar flight voucher, which can be used toward the purchase of another ticket, and are rebooked on the next flight out. If there are not enough volunteers, the airline must choose who will be denied boarding. The first to get bumped are passengers who checked in late and those flying on discounted tickets, so get to the gate and check in as early as possible, especially during peak periods.

Always **bring a government-issued photo ID** to the airport; even when it's not required, a passport is best.

CUTTING COSTS
The least expensive airfares to China are priced for round-trip travel and must usually be purchased in advance. Airlines generally allow you to change your return date for a fee; most low-fare tickets, however, are nonrefundable. It's smart to call a number of airlines and check the Internet; when you are quoted a good price, book it on the spot—the same fare may not be available the next day, or even the next hour. Always check different routings and look into using alternate airports. Also, price off-peak flights, which may be significantly less expensive than others. Travel agents, especially low-fare specialists (⇨ Discounts & Deals), are helpful.

Consolidators are another good source. They buy tickets for scheduled flights at reduced rates from the airlines, then sell them at prices that beat the best fare available directly from the airlines. (Many also offer reduced car-rental and hotel rates.) Sometimes you can even get your money back if you need to return the ticket. Carefully read the fine print detailing penalties for changes and cancellations, purchase the ticket with a credit card, and confirm your consolidator reservation with the airline.

When you fly as a courier, you trade your checked-luggage space for a ticket deeply subsidized by a courier service. There are restrictions on when you can book and how long you can stay. Some courier companies list with membership organizations, such as the Air Courier Association and the International Association of Air Travel Couriers; these require you to become a member before you can book a flight.

Many airlines, singly or in collaboration, offer discount air passes that allow foreigners to travel economically in a particular country or region. These visitor passes usually must be reserved and purchased before you leave home. Information about passes often can be found on most airlines' international Web pages, which tend to be aimed at travelers from outside the carrier's home country. Try searching for "pass" within the carrier's Web site, or ask your travel agent.

F Consolidators **AirlineConsolidator.com** ☎ 888/468-5385 ⊕ www.airlineconsolidator.com; for international tickets. **Best Fares** ☎ 800/880-1234 or 800/576-8255 ⊕ www.bestfares.com; $59.90 annual membership. **Cheap Tickets** ☎ 800/377-1000 or 800/652-4327 ⊕ www.cheaptickets.com. **Expedia** ☎ 404/728-8787 or 800/397-3342 ⊕ www.expedia.com. **Hotwire** ☎ 866/468-9473 or 920/330-9418 ⊕ www.hotwire.com. **Now Voyager Travel** ✉ 45 W. 21st St., Suite 5A, New York, NY 10010 ☎ 212/459-1616 🖷 212/243-2711 ⊕ www.nowvoyagertravel.com. **Onetravel.com** ⊕ www.onetravel.com. **Orbitz** ☎ 888/656-4546 ⊕ www.orbitz.com. **Priceline.com** ⊕ www.priceline.com. **Travelocity** ☎ 888/709-5983, 877/282-2925 in Canada, 0870/876-3876 in the U.K. ⊕ www.travelocity.com.

F Courier Resources **Air Courier Association/Cheaptrips.com** ☎ 800/280-5973 or 800/282-1202 ⊕ www.aircourier.org or www.cheaptrips.com; $34 annual membership. **International Association of Air Travel Couriers** ☎ 308/632-3273 ⊕ www.courier.org; $45 annual membership. **Now Voyager Travel** ✉ 45 W. 21st St., Suite 5A, New York, NY 10010 ☎ 212/459-1616 🖷 212/243-2711 ⊕ www.nowvoyagertravel.com.

F Discount Passes **All Asia Pass**, Cathay Pacific, ☎ 800/233-2742, 800/268-6868 in Canada ⊕ www.cathay-usa.com or www.cathay.ca.

ENJOYING THE FLIGHT

State your seat preference when purchasing your ticket, and then repeat it when you confirm and when you check in. For more legroom, you can request one of the few emergency-aisle seats at check-in, if you're capable of moving obstacles comparable in weight to an airplane exit door (usually between 35 pounds and 60 pounds)—a Federal Aviation Administration requirement of passengers in these seats. Seats behind a bulkhead also offer more legroom, but they don't have under-seat storage. Don't sit in the row in front of the emergency aisle or in front of a bulkhead, where seats may

not recline. On local carriers within China, be prepared for less legroom and smaller seats.

Ask the airline whether a snack or meal is served on the flight. If you have dietary concerns, request special meals when booking. These can be vegetarian, low-cholesterol, or kosher, for example. It's a good idea to pack some healthful snacks and a small (plastic) bottle of water in your carry-on bag. On long flights, try to maintain a normal routine, to help fight jet lag. At night, get some sleep. By day, eat light meals, drink water (not alcohol), and **move around the cabin** to stretch your legs.

FLYING TIMES

The flying time to Beijing is between 20 and 24 hours from New York, including a stopover on the West Coast or in Tokyo; from 17 to 20 hours from Chicago; and 13 hours direct from Los Angeles or San Francisco.

HOW TO COMPLAIN

If your baggage goes astray or your flight goes awry, complain right away. Most carriers require that you **file a claim immediately.** The Aviation Consumer Protection Division of the Department of Transportation publishes *Fly-Rights*, which discusses airlines and consumer issues and is available online. You can also find articles and information on mytravelrights.com, the Web site of the nonprofit Consumer Travel Rights Center.

F Airline Complaints **Aviation Consumer Protection Division** ✉ U.S. Department of Transportation, Office of Aviation Enforcement and Proceedings, C-75, Room 4107, 400 7th St. SW, Washington, DC 20590 ☎ 202/366-2220 ⊕ airconsumer.ost.dot.gov. **Federal Aviation Administration Consumer Hotline** ✉ for inquiries: FAA, 800 Independence Ave. SW, Washington, DC 20591 ☎ 800/322-7873 ⊕ www.faa.gov.

RECONFIRMING

Check the status of your flight before you leave for the airport. You can do this on your carrier's Web site, by linking to a flight-status checker (many Web booking services offer these), or by calling your carrier or travel agent. Always confirm international flights at least 72 hours ahead of the scheduled departure time. When flying within China or departing from China on an international flight, you risk losing your seat if you fail to confirm 72 hours ahead of departure time.

AIRPORTS

Among the airports you're most likely to fly into on your trip to Beijing and Shanghai are Beijing Capital International Airport (PEK); Hong Kong International Airport (HKG), also known as Chek Lap Kok; Shanghai's Hongqiao International Airport (SHA); and Shanghai's Pudong International Airport (PVG). All of these airports are centrally located, with easy access to city centers.

It's best to arrive at the airport 2 hours before an international flight, and 1 to 1½ hours before a domestic flight. You'll have to complete a yellow health form and have it stamped at the temperature check station before proceeding to the check-in counter. Be sure to keep some yuan for the departure tax—Y90 for international flights, Y50 for domestic flights—which you must pay before proceeding through customs and security.

🚩 Beijing Capital International Airport ☎ 010/6456-3604. **Hong Kong International Airport** ☎ 852/2181-0000. **Hongqiao International Airport** ☎ 021/6268-8918 Ext. 2 for 24-hr airport information. **Pudong International Airport** ☎ 021/3848-4500 Ext. 2.

BIKE TRAVEL

Bike travel is popular in major cities, but it takes a skilled biker to navigate the chaotic city streets and bumpy country alleys. In China, few observe traffic rules, and bicyclists must be particularly vigilant about their own safety. When biking be sure to **yield to motorists** and **watch carefully before crossing intersections.**

Beijing has wide bike lanes that are separate from regular traffic, which makes bike riding a bit safer. A bicycle is an interesting way to cover large portions of Shanghai, especially its backstreets, at your own pace.

Bikes can be rented just about everywhere in Beijing, although your hotel and CTS (the government tourism office) are usually the best places to rent or inquire.

When renting, you must show ID and pay a deposit. You usually pay an hourly fee, but you will get better rates if you rent a bicycle for a half or full day. Try to rent bikes through a travel agency that provides insurance and emergency aids. Always check that the brakes are in good working order. It's also prudent to **park your bike at guarded parking spaces** to avoid theft; just lock your bicycle next to others in a bike lot and pay the attendant. Bike-repair shops are common.

Biking independently beyond Beijing and Shanghai is not a good idea, as foreigners are not permitted in many cities and can be penalized by the police for trespassing. It's better to join a bike tour. The U.S. company Backroads arranges bike tours in various parts of China, including the Beijing area. Bike China Adventures has a tour that takes in Beijing and the Great Wall; a link on the company's Web site takes you to stories about cyclists' adventures in China. Discover China organizes bike tours that start in Hong Kong and go through Guangdong and Guangxi provinces and beyond, with extensions available for tours of Beijing, the Great Wall, and more.

🚩 Tour Operators Backroads ⊠ 801 Cedar St., Berkeley, CA 94710-1800 ☎ 800/462-2848 ⊕ www.backroads.com. **Bike China Adventures** ⊕ www.bikechina.com. **Discover China** ⊠ 3625 Keating St., Suite 8, San Diego, CA 92110-1913 ☎ 619/294-4535 ⊕ trips.discover-china.org.

BIKES IN FLIGHT

Most airlines accommodate bikes as luggage, provided they are dismantled and boxed; check with individual airlines about packing requirements. Some airlines sell bike boxes, which are often free at bike shops, for about $20 (bike bags can be considerably more expensive). International travelers often can substitute a bike for a piece of checked luggage at no charge; otherwise, the cost is about $100. Most U.S. and Canadian airlines charge $40–$80 each way.

BUS TRAVEL

China's best bus service is generally for short distances within city boundaries, as opposed to long-distance travel. But Greyhound Canada Transportation Corporation and the New National Express Group Company, a transportation company in China, signed contracts in October 2002 to develop a bus network in China. A line between Beijing and Shanghai is expected to begin operation in time for the 2008 Olympics. Passengers can expect to ride in environmentally friendly, zero-emission, hydrogen-powered buses, which are already being tested on the Beijing avenues.

Express buses, equipped with lavatories and snacks, run the 1,296 km (804 mi) between Beijing and Shanghai. These buses are cheaper than plane or train travel between the two cities, plus there's no need to purchase tickets in advance, and the buses take you right to the downtown areas of both cities. The travel time is much longer, however; it takes about 15 hours to make the trip.

For intracity travel, be aware that buses in China are extremely crowded, and that drivers rarely speak English.

CTS or your hotel can arrange bus tickets and provide bus schedules. You can also buy tickets in advance from the bus station. Bus stations generally only have schedules in Chinese and rarely have English-speaking staff. Be prepared to pay cash for your ticket. Reservations are generally not necessary.

🚌 **Beijing Hua Tong Enterprise** ✉ No. 16 West Small Zone, Wenzhou Economic & Technology Developing Area, Beijing ☎ 577/8652–8888. **Shanghai Long Distance Transport Co.** ✉ 258 Hengfeng Lu, Shanghai ☎ 021/6317–3912.

BUSINESS HOURS

Note that almost all businesses close for Chinese New Year (sometime in mid-January–February) and other major holidays.

BANKS & OFFICES

Most banks and government offices are open weekdays 9–5, although some close for lunch (sometime between noon and 2). Bank branches and CTS tour desks in hotels often keep longer hours and are usually open Saturday mornings. Many hotel currency-exchange desks stay open 24 hours.

MUSEUMS & SIGHTS

Most temples and parks are open daily 8–6. Museums are generally open 9–4 six days a week, with Monday being the most common closed day. Other tourist sights are typically open daily 9–5.

PHARMACIES

Pharmacies are open daily from 8:30 or 9 AM to 6 or 7 PM. Some large pharmacies stay open until 9 PM or even later.

SHOPS

Shops and department stores are generally open daily 9–7; some stores stay open even later in summer, in popular tourist areas, or during peak tourist season.

CAMERAS & PHOTOGRAPHY

The Chinese love cameras and will be glad to take your picture—some may even want to be in them. However, you should always ask before taking pictures of people. Remember that at some religious sites photography is not allowed, and you risk a fine and/or camera seizure if you try to sneak a photo.

The *Kodak Guide to Shooting Great Travel Pictures* (available at bookstores everywhere) is loaded with tips.

🌐 Photo Help **Kodak Information Center** ☎ 800/242–2424 ⊕ www.kodak.com.

EQUIPMENT PRECAUTIONS

Don't pack film or equipment in checked luggage, where it is much more susceptible to damage. X-ray machines used to view checked luggage are extremely powerful and therefore are likely to ruin your film. Try to ask for hand inspection of film, which becomes clouded after repeated exposure to airport X-ray machines, and keep videotapes and computer disks away from metal detectors.

CAR RENTAL

Renting a car in China is not advisable, and in many cases is not possible without a Chinese driver's license. In Beijing or Shanghai, you *can* rent a car, but only for driving within each city. International tourists are forbidden from driving between cities. Because of dangerous driving conditions, difficult parking, a lack of English signage, and the complexity involved in renting a car, it's better to hire a car with a driver for the day. Avis and Hertz rental cars in Beijing and Shanghai come with chauffeurs. The cost for a car and driver is reasonable by Western standards, usually Y500 to Y800 ($60 to $100) per day for an economy vehicle. In China check with your hotel concierge or local CTS office about hiring a car.

F Major Agencies **Avis** ☎ 800/331-1084, 800/ 879-2847 in Canada, 0870/606-0100 in the U.K., 02/ 9353-9000 in Australia, 09/526-2847 in New Zealand ⊕ www.avis.com. **Hertz** ☎ 800/654-3001, 800/263-0600 in Canada, 0870/844-8844 in the U.K., 02/9669-2444 in Australia, 09/256-8690 in New Zealand ⊕ www.hertz.com.

INSURANCE

When driving a rented car you are generally responsible for any damage to or loss of the vehicle. You also may be liable for any property damage or personal injury that you may cause while driving. Before you rent, see what coverage you already have under the terms of your personal auto-insurance policy and credit cards.

REQUIREMENTS & RESTRICTIONS

In China your own driver's license is not acceptable. An International Driver's Permit is available from the American or Canadian Automobile Association, or in the United Kingdom, from the Automobile Association or the Royal Automobile Club. Foreigners are generally forbidden from driving between cities.

CAR TRAVEL

Car travel in China, even when you're in the passenger seat, can be frightening. Cars speed to pass one another on one-lane roads, constantly blaring their horns. Taxis and pedicabs pass within inches of each other at intersections. Lanes and traffic rules seem ambiguous to those not accustomed to the Chinese style of driving. Because of these challenges, it is recommended that you hire a car and driver rather than attempt to drive a car yourself.

Taxi driver identification numbers can be used to report bad behavior or bad driving, and thus tend to inspire more care. Many taxi drivers are also held liable for the condition of their vehicles, so they are less likely to take dangerous risks.

RULES OF THE ROAD

Driving is on the right in mainland China. Traffic in the cities can move slowly, but pay attention nonetheless. Many street signs are in pinyin as well as Chinese characters.

CHILDREN IN CHINA

Beijing and Shanghai have parks, zoos, and frequent performances involving acrobats, jugglers, and puppets. Check with the CTS office in most cities for activities or tours. Most large international hotels have baby-sitting services and may even offer special activities, though services may not be on a level with those in the West. Fees range from Y30–Y50 for the first hour, Y25–40 for each subsequent hour, plus a transportation fee of Y30–Y50 if the baby-sitter stays past 11 PM. However, travel can be rugged and familiar foods hard to find, and there are health risks and sanitation problems. It's not advisable to take children on trips outside Beijing and Shanghai.

If you are renting a car, don't forget to arrange for a car seat when you reserve. For general advice about traveling with children, consult *Fodor's FYI: Travel with Your Baby* (available in bookstores everywhere).

FLYING

If your children are two or older, ask about children's airfares. As a general rule, infants under two not occupying a seat fly at greatly reduced fares or even for free. But if you want to guarantee a seat for an infant, you have to pay full fare. Consider flying during off-peak days and times; most airlines will grant an infant a seat without a ticket if there are available seats. When booking, confirm carry-on allowances if you're traveling with infants. In general, for babies charged 10% to 50% of the adult fare you are allowed one carry-on bag and a collapsible stroller; if the flight is full, the stroller may have to be checked or you may be limited to less. Experts agree that it's a good idea to use safety seats aloft for children weighing less than 40 pounds. Airlines set their own policies: if you use a safety seat, U.S. carriers usually require that the child be ticketed, even if he or she is young enough to ride free, because the seats must be strapped into regular seats. And even if you pay the full adult fare for the seat, it may be worth it, especially on longer trips. Do **check your airline's policy about using safety seats during takeoff and landing.** Safety seats are not allowed everywhere in the plane, so get your seat assignments as early as possible.

When reserving, request children's meals or a freestanding bassinet (not available at all airlines) if you need them. But note that bulkhead seats, where you must sit to use the bassinet, may lack an overhead bin or storage space on the floor.

PRECAUTIONS

If you're traveling with a child, be sure to take a generous supply of Pepto-Bismol tablets, antibiotics such as Cipro, rehydration salts for diarrhea, motion sickness tablets, Tylenol, and vitamins. Children, like adults, will need some time to adjust to China's food, so be sure all food is thoroughly cooked. Boiled water is fine for children to drink; soybean milk, juices, and bottled mineral water are also available.

SIGHTS & ATTRACTIONS

Places that are especially appealing to children are indicated by a rubber-duckie icon (🐥) in the margin.

SUPPLIES & EQUIPMENT

Formula, baby food, and disposable diapers are readily available in supermarkets.

COMPUTERS ON THE ROAD

Most hotel business centers have computers with up-to-date software and Internet access, but the service can be pricey. High-end hotels that serve foreigners generally have in-room data ports, but be prepared for very slow dial-ups. For your laptop, bring a surge protector and a 220-volt adapter and power converter. **Carry several types of adapters** in case the Asian one (with diagonal prongs slanting inward) doesn't fit.

CONSUMER PROTECTION

Whether you're shopping for gifts or purchasing travel services, **pay with a major credit card** whenever possible, so you can cancel payment or get reimbursed if there's a problem (and you can provide documentation). If you're doing business with a particular company for the first time, contact your local Better Business Bureau and the attorney general's offices in your state and (for U.S. businesses) the company's home state as well. Have any complaints been filed? Finally, if you're buying a package or tour, always consider travel insurance that includes default coverage (⇨ Insurance).

🔢 **BBBs Council of Better Business Bureaus** ✉ 4200 Wilson Blvd., Suite 800, Arlington, VA 22203 ☎ 703/276-0100 🖷 703/525-8277 ⊕ www.bbb.org.

CUSTOMS & DUTIES

When shopping abroad, keep receipts for all purchases. Upon reentering the country, **be ready to show customs officials what you've bought.** Pack purchases together in an easily accessible place. If you think a duty is incorrect, appeal the assessment. If you object to the way your clearance was handled, note the inspector's badge number. In either case, first ask to see a supervisor. If the problem isn't resolved, write to the appropriate authorities, beginning with the port director at your point of entry.

IN AUSTRALIA

Australian residents who are 18 or older may bring home A$400 worth of souvenirs and gifts (including jewelry), 250 cigarettes or 250 grams of cigars or other tobacco products, and 1,125 ml of alcohol (including wine, beer, and spirits). Residents under 18 may bring back A$200 worth of goods. Members of the same family traveling together may pool their allowances. Prohibited items include meat products. Seeds, plants, and fruits need to be declared upon arrival.

🔢 **Australian Customs Service** 🖉 Regional Director, Box 8, Sydney, NSW 2001 ☎ 02/9213-2000 or 1300/363263, 02/9364-7222 or 1800/020-504 quarantine-inquiry line 🖷 02/9213-4043 ⊕ www.customs.gov.au.

IN CANADA

Canadian residents who have been out of Canada for at least seven days may bring in C$750 worth of goods duty-free. If you've been away fewer than seven days but more than 48 hours, the duty-free allowance drops to C$200. If your trip lasts 24 to 48 hours, the allowance is C$50. You may not pool allowances with family members. Goods claimed under the C$750 exemption may follow you by mail; those claimed under the lesser exemptions must accompany you. Alcohol and tobacco products may be included in the seven-day and 48-hour exemptions but not in the 24-hour exemption. If you meet the age requirements of the province or territory through which you reenter Canada, you may bring in, duty-free, 1.5 liters of wine *or* 1.14 liters (40 imperial ounces) of liquor *or* 24 12-ounce cans or bottles of beer or ale. Also, if you meet the local age requirement for tobacco products, you may bring in, duty-free, 200 cigarettes and 50 cigars. Check ahead of time with the Canada Customs and Revenue Agency or the Department of Agriculture for policies regarding meat products, seeds, plants, and fruits.

You may send an unlimited number of gifts (only one gift per recipient, however) worth up to C$60 each duty-free to Canada. Label the package UNSOLICITED GIFT—VALUE UNDER $60. Alcohol and tobacco are excluded.

🛂 Canada Customs and Revenue Agency ✉ 2265 St. Laurent Blvd., Ottawa, Ontario K1G 4K3 📠 204/983-3500, 506/636-5064, 800/461-9999 in Canada ⊕ www.ccra.gc.ca.

IN CHINA

You can generally bring anything into China for personal use that you plan to take away with you when you leave; you should have no trouble bringing in cameras, video recorders, GPS equipment, laptops, and the like. Firearms, drugs, plant materials, animals, and many food items are prohibited. China is very sensitive about printed matter deemed seditious, such as religious, pornographic, and political items, including newspaper articles and books on Tibet. Customs officials are for the most part easygoing, and visitors are rarely searched. It's not necessary to fill in customs declaration forms, but if you carry in a large amount of cash, say several thousand dollars, you should declare it upon arrival.

On leaving, you're not allowed to take out any antiquities dating to before 1795. Antiques from between 1795 and 1949 must have an official red seal attached.

IN NEW ZEALAND

All homeward-bound residents may bring back NZ$700 worth of souvenirs and gifts; passengers may not pool their allowances, and children can claim only the concession on goods intended for their own use. For those 17 or older, the duty-free allowance also includes 4.5 liters of wine or beer; one 1,125-ml bottle of spirits; and either 200 cigarettes, 250 grams of tobacco, 50 cigars, *or* a combination of the three up to 250 grams. Meat products, seeds, plants, and fruits must be declared upon arrival to the Agricultural Services Department.

🛂 New Zealand Customs ✉ Head office: The Customhouse, 17–21 Whitmore St., Box 2218, Wellington 📞 09/300–5399 or 0800/428–786 ⊕ www.customs.govt.nz.

IN THE U.K.

From countries outside the European Union, including China, you may bring home, duty-free, 200 cigarettes, 100 cigarillos, 50 cigars, 100 cigarillos, or 250 grams of tobacco; 1 liter of spirits or 2 liters of fortified or sparkling wine or liqueurs; 2 liters of still table wine; 60 ml of perfume; 250 ml of toilet water; plus £145 worth of other goods, including gifts and souvenirs. Prohibited items include meat products, seeds, plants, fruits, and dairy products.

🛂 HM Customs and Excise ✉ Portcullis House, 21 Cowbridge Rd. E, Cardiff CF11 9SS 📞 0845/010–9000 or 0208/929–0152 advice service, 0208/929–6731 or 0208/910–3602 complaints ⊕ www.hmce.gov.uk.

IN THE U.S.

U.S. residents who have been out of the country for at least 48 hours may bring home, for personal use, $800 worth of foreign goods duty-free, as long as they haven't used the $800 allowance or any part of it in the past 30 days. This exemption may include 1 liter of alcohol (for travelers 21 and older), 200 cigarettes, and 100 non-Cuban cigars. Family members from the same household who are traveling together may pool their $800 personal exemptions. For fewer than 48 hours, the duty-free allowance drops to $200, which may include 50 cigarettes, 10 non-Cuban cigars, and 150 ml of alcohol (or 150 ml of perfume containing alcohol). The $200 allowance cannot be combined with other individuals' exemptions, and if you exceed it, the full value of all the goods will be taxed. Antiques, which U.S. Customs and Border Protection defines as objects more than 100 years old, enter duty-free, as do original works of art done entirely by hand, including paintings, drawings, and sculptures. This doesn't apply to folk art or handicrafts, which are in general dutiable.

You may also send packages home duty-free, with a limit of one parcel per addressee per day (except alcohol or tobacco products or perfume worth more than $5). You can mail up to $200 worth of goods for personal use; label the package PERSONAL USE and attach a list of its contents and their retail value. If the package contains your used personal belongings, mark it AMERICAN GOODS RETURNED to avoid paying duties. You may send up to $100 worth of goods as a gift; mark the package UNSOLICITED GIFT. Mailed items do not affect your duty-free allowance on your return.

To avoid paying duty on foreign-made high-ticket items you already own and will take on your trip, register them with Customs before you leave the country. Consider filing a Certificate of Registration for laptops, cameras, watches, and other digital devices identified with serial numbers or other permanent markings; you can keep the certificate for other trips. Otherwise, bring a sales receipt or insurance form to show that you owned the item before you left the United States.

For more about duties, restricted items, and other information about international travel, check out U.S. Customs and Border Protection's online brochure, *Know Before You Go.*

🛈 **U.S. Customs and Border Protection** ✉ for inquiries and equipment registration, 1300 Pennsylvania Ave. NW, Washington, DC 20229 ⊕ www.cbp.gov ☎ 877/287-8667, 202/354-1000 ✉ for complaints, Customer Satisfaction Unit, 1300 Pennsylvania Ave. NW, Room 5.2C, Washington, DC 20229.

DISABILITIES & ACCESSIBILITY

Facilities for people with disabilities are not widespread, but more and more government-run businesses are providing ramps for people who use wheelchairs and "dotted" pavements for people with vision impairments.

Mobility International USA, which has led several group tours to China, can provide information for people with disabilities who wish to visit the country. The Society for Accessible Travel & Hospitality has information on traveling to China, and can refer you to tour operators that specialize in trips for travelers with disabilities.

🛈 Resources **Mobility International USA** ✉ 45 W. Broadway, Eugene, OR 97405 ☎ 541/343-1284 for phone and TTY ⊕ www.miusa.org. **Society for Accessible Travel & Hospitality** (SATH) ✉ 347 5th Ave., Suite 610, New York, NY 10016 ☎ 212/447-7284 🖷 212/725-8253 ✎ sathtravel@aol.com ⊕ www.sath.org.

RESERVATIONS

When discussing accessibility with an operator or reservations agent, ask hard questions. Are there any stairs, inside *or* out? Are there grab bars next to the toilet *and* in the shower/tub? How wide is the doorway to the room? To the bathroom? For the most extensive facilities meeting the latest legal specifications, opt for newer accommodations. If you reserve through a toll-free number, consider also calling the hotel's local number to confirm the information from the central reservations office. Get confirmation in writing when you can.

TRANSPORTATION

Buses in China do not accommodate people with disabilities, and subway and train stations have long, steep concrete staircases.

F Complaints **Aviation Consumer Protection Division** (⇨ Air Travel) for airline-related problems. **Departmental Office of Civil Rights** ⊠ for general inquiries, U.S. Department of Transportation, S-30, 400 7th St. SW, Room 10215, Washington, DC 20590 ☎ 202/366-4648 🖷 202/366-9371 ⊕ www.dot. gov/ost/docr/index.htm. **Disability Rights Section** ⊠ NYAV, U.S. Department of Justice, Civil Rights Division, 950 Pennsylvania Ave. NW, Washington, DC 20530 🖷 ADA information line 202/514-0301, 800/ 514-0301, 202/514-0383 TTY, 800/514-0383 TTY ⊕ www.ada.gov. **U.S. Department of Transportation Hotline** 🖷 for disability-related air-travel problems, 800/778-4838 or 800/455-9880 TTY.

TRAVEL AGENCIES

In the United States, the Americans with Disabilities Act requires that travel firms serve the needs of all travelers. Some agencies specialize in working with people with disabilities.

F Travelers with Mobility Problems **Access Adventures/B. Roberts Travel** ⊠ 206 Chestnut Ridge Rd., Scottsville, NY 14624 ☎ 585/889-9096 ⊕ www.brobertstravel.com ⊘ dltravel@prodigy. net, run by a former physical-rehabilitation counselor. **Flying Wheels Travel** ⊠ 143 W. Bridge St., Box 382, Owatonna, MN 55060 ☎ 507/451-5005 🖷 507/451-1685 ⊕ www.flyingwheelstravel.com.

DISCOUNTS & DEALS

Be a smart shopper and compare all your options before making decisions. A plane ticket bought with a promotional coupon from travel clubs, coupon books, and direct-mail offers or purchased on the Internet may not be cheaper than the least expensive fare from a discount ticket agency. And always keep in mind that what you get is just as important as what you save.

DISCOUNT RESERVATIONS

To save money, look into discount reservations services with Web sites and toll-free numbers, which use their buying power to get a better price on hotels, airline tickets, even car rentals. In addition to U.S. travel Web sites and the hotels' own sites, it pays to browse several Asian hotel discounters that offer online deals. A few of the more reputable sites are Sino Hotel, CTRIP, and Asia Hotels, which has independent traveler reviews for most hotels in its database. Also try calling the hotel's local toll-free number (if one is available) rather than the central reservations number—you'll often get a better price—and ask about special packages or corporate rates. Like most things in China, hotel rates are negotiable.

When shopping for the best deal on hotels and car rentals, look for guaranteed exchange rates, which protect you against a falling dollar. With your rate locked in, you won't pay more, even if the price goes up in the local currency.

F Airline Tickets **Air 4 Less** 🖷 800/AIR4LESS; low-fare specialist.

F Hotel Rooms **Accommodations Express** 🖷 800/ 444-7666 or 800/277-1064 ⊕ www.acex.net. **Asia Hotels** ⊕ www.asiahotels.com. **CTRIP** 🖷 800/820- 6666 in China ⊕ www.ctrip.com. **HotelClub** 🖷 410/ 576-8584 ⊕ www.hotelclub.net. **Hotels.com** 🖷 800/246-8357 ⊕ www.hotels.com. **Sino Hotel** 🖷 866/652-2041 ⊕ www.sinohotel.com. **Steigenberger Reservation Service** 🖷 800/223-5652 ⊕ www.srs-worldhotels.com. **Turbotrip.com** 🖷 800/473-7829 ⊕ www.turbotrip.com. **Vacation-Land** 🖷 800/245-0050 ⊕ www.vacation-land.com.

PACKAGE DEALS

Don't confuse packages and guided tours. When you buy a package, you travel on your own, just as though you had planned the trip yourself. Fly/drive packages, which combine airfare and car rental, are often a good deal. In cities, ask the local visitor's bureau about hotel and local transportation packages that include tickets to major museum exhibits or other special events.

EATING & DRINKING

In China, chopsticks are the utensil of choice. The Chinese generally like to eat family style, with everyone sitting at a round table (which symbolizes union and perfection), burrowing their chopsticks into a common dish. It's considered bad manners to point or play with your chopsticks, or to place them on top of your rice bowl when you're finished eating (place the chopsticks horizontally on the table or plate). It is acceptable, however, to shovel rice into your mouth, to talk with your mouth full, and to stand up to reach for food across the table from you. Don't hesitate to spit bones directly onto the table: putting your fingers in your mouth is bad manners.

If you're invited to a formal Chinese meal, be prepared for great ceremony, many toasts and speeches, and a grand variety of elaborate dishes. Your host will be seated at the "head" of the round table, which is the seat that faces the door; it's differentiated from the other seats by a napkin shaped as a crown. The highest guest of honor will be seated to the host's right, the second highest guest of honor to the host's left. Don't start eating until the host takes the first bite, and then simply serve yourself as the food comes around. Be sure to **always let the food touch your plate before bringing it up to your mouth**; eating directly from the serving dish without briefly resting the food on your plate is considered bad form. It is an honor to be served by the person sitting next to you (though as a guest, you are not expected to do the same).

The restaurants we list are the cream of the crop in each price category.

MEALS & SPECIALTIES
Do try as many different kinds of foods as you can; food is an integral part of Chinese culture. Color, smell, taste, shape, sound, and serving vessels are all important aspects of the food being served. Vegetables are the main ingredients. Chinese food can be loosely divided into Northern and Southern styles. Food in northern China is based on wheat products and is often quite oily, with liberal amounts of vinegar and flavorful spices such as garlic. Meat and vegetable dumplings, noodles, and filled buns are common. The cuisine in southern China is known for its use of fresh ingredients and liberal doses of hot spices; remember you can always request a dish to be more or less spicy. Rice and rice by-products form the foundation of meals.

If you're craving Western food, rest assured that Beijing and Shanghai have plenty of American fast-food chains. Most higher-end restaurants have a Western menu, but don't expect the food to taste like it does back home.

MEALTIMES
Lunch in China is usually served in restaurants between 11 and 2, dinner from 5 to 10. Unless otherwise noted, the restaurants listed in this guide are open daily for lunch and dinner. Restaurants and bars catering to foreigners may stay open 24 hours or close briefly in the wee hours.

RESERVATIONS & DRESS
Reservations are always a good idea; we mention them only when they're essential or not accepted. Book as far ahead as you can, and reconfirm as soon as you arrive. (Large parties should always call ahead to check the reservations policy.) We mention dress only when men are required to wear a jacket or a jacket and tie.

WINE, BEER & SPIRITS
Among the beers you'll find in China are Tsingtao, China's emperor of beers, and some international brews. Fruit wines, which are quite sweet and at times sparkling, are not commonly served at restaurants, where you're more likely to find spirits and other alcoholic beverages. The most famous brand of Chinese liquor is Moutai, a distilled liquor with an elegant aroma, mellow flavor, and pleasant aftertaste. Always ask for local brands when dining or purchasing liquor in China, as each place has its own local prizewinner. For example, Beijing Erguotou is the most popular white spirit in Beijing due to its affordable price, pure taste, and solid reputation.

ELECTRICITY
The electrical current in China is 220 volts, 50 cycles alternating current (AC); wall outlets come in a variety of configurations to fit two- and three-pronged round plugs, as well as two-pronged flat sockets. To use electric-powered equipment purchased in the United States or Canada, bring a converter and several types of adapter (the better hotels often supply standard adapters for electrical appliances).

If your appliances are dual-voltage, you'll need only an adapter. Don't use 110-volt outlets marked FOR SHAVERS ONLY for high-wattage appliances such as blow-dryers.

Most laptops operate equally well on 110 and 220 volts and so require only an adapter. You may also want to bring a power-surge protector.

EMBASSIES & CONSULATES

⚡ Australia Australian Consulate ✉ 22F, CITIC Sq., 1168 Nanjing Xilu, Jingan District, Shanghai 200041 ☎ 021/5292-5500 ⚱ 021/5292-5511. **Embassy of Australia** ✉ 21 Dongzhimenwai Dajie, Chaoyang District, Beijing 100600 ☎ 010/6532-2331 ⚱ 010/6532-6718.

⚡ Canada Canadian Consulate ✉ Tower 4, Suite 604, Shanghai Center, 1376 Nanjing Xilu, Jingan District, Shanghai 200040 ☎ 021/6279-8400 ⚱ 021/6279-8401. **Canadian Embassy** ✉ 19 Dongzhionenwai Dajie, Chaoyang District, Beijing ☎ 010/6532-3536 ⚱ 010/6532-4972.

⚡ New Zealand New Zealand Consulate ✉ Qihua Dasha, 15th floor, 1375 Huaihai Zhonglu, Xuhui District ☎ 021/6471-1108 ⚱ 021/6431-0226. **New Zealand Embassy** ✉ 1 Donger Jie, Ritanlu, Chayang District, Beijing 100600 ☎ 010/6532-2732 or 010/6532-2733 ⚱ 010/6532-4317.

⚡ United Kingdom British Consulate ✉ Suite 301, Shanghai Center, 1376 Nanjiing Xilu, Jingan District, Shanghai 200040 ☎ 021/6279-7650 ⚱ 021/6279-7651 ✉ Visa and Consular Sections, Suite 715, Shanghai Center, 1376 Nanjing Xilu, Jingan District ☎ 021/6279-8130. **British Embassy** ✉ 11 Guanghua Lu, Chaoyang District Beijing 100600 ☎ 010/6532-1061 ⚱ 010/6532-1937.

⚡ United States United States Consulate ✉ 1469 Huaihai Zhonglu, Xuhui District, Shanghai 200031 ☎ 021/6433-6880, 021/6433-3936 for after-hours emergencies ⚱ 021/6433-1576. **United States Embassy** ✉ 3 Xiushui Beijie, Chaoyang District, Beijing 100600 ☎ 010/6532-3431 Ext. 229 or 010/6532-3831 Ext. 264 ⚱ 010/6532-2483.

EMERGENCIES

If you lose your passport, contact your embassy immediately. Embassy officials can advise you on how to proceed in case of other emergencies. The staff at your hotel may be able to provide a translator if you need to report an emergency or crime to doctors or the police. Most police officers and hospital staff members don't speak English, though you may find one or two people who do. Ambulances generally offer just a means of transport, not medical aid, so take a taxi to the hospital.

⚡ Ambulance ☎ 120. **Fire** ☎ 119. **Police** ☎ 110.

ENGLISH-LANGUAGE MEDIA

NEWSPAPERS & MAGAZINES

China's media is by no means independent of government control, although widespread changes have been proposed within the Communist Party to provide greater autonomy. China's main English-language newspaper, a version of the *People's Daily* (⊕ http://english.peopledaily.com.cn) that shares some of the same content but has original articles for the Western readership, is no exception to the rule of heavy government censorship. Its Chinese version is the most influential and authoritative newspaper in China, with a heavy inclination toward voicing the views of the Party. The English version is slightly more open to non-Party news and ideas and tends to be more progressive. The free English-language *City Weekend* (⊕ www.cityweekend.com.cn), *That's Beijing*, and *That's Shanghai*—with information on restaurants, events, and cultural venues—are available in hotel lobbies and at bars. Xianzai (⊕ www.xianzai.com) sends out e-mail newsletters on weekly events and special hotel, flight, and restaurant offers; you can sign up for the Beijing or Shanghai edition on the Web site.

Foreign magazines and newspapers, including *USA Today*, the *International Herald Tribune*, the *South China Morning Post*, and Asian editions of the *Wall Street Journal* and *Newsweek*, are available at kiosks in large international hotels.

RADIO & TELEVISION

Most Western hotels have satellite TV, with CNN, BBC, ESPN, and HBO in addition to the standard Chinese stations. The government-run CCTV has eight channels offering extensive English programming, from international affairs to TV news magazines, sports, and entertainment.

You can listen to music on Beijing Music Radio 97.4 FM and Shanghai East Radio 101.7 FM (with English-language music programs at 2 PM–3 PM and 8 PM–9 PM). Voice of America (www.voanews.com) can be heard in China, but be prepared for interruptions by the government at the slightest political provocation or because of tension between the United States and China.

ETIQUETTE & BEHAVIOR

Be respectful and try not to get upset if things go wrong, especially when reserving tickets and hotel rooms. Be friendly but stern if you are having difficulties—raising your voice and threatening will only embarrass you in front of the Chinese, who feel that "face" is extremely important. It helps to learn a few words of Chinese, even if all you can say is thank you (shee-yeh shee-yeh) and hello (nee how). If you are stared at, simply smile back or treat it humorously. Playing with chopsticks is a sign of bad manners. Bowing the head and pressing the hands together is a sign of deep gratitude. Handshaking is the common greeting, but don't shake women's hands too firmly. Try to keep an open mind about anything that seems initially appalling, whether it's dog meat or Chinese toilets. The Chinese are generally a gracious people who will reciprocate kindness.

For guidelines on dining etiquette, *see* Eating & Drinking.

GAY & LESBIAN TRAVEL

China is still a conservative country when it comes to outward displays of affection. Although it's not unusual to see Chinese couples walking arm-in-arm in the bigger cities, Western couples, whether heterosexual or homosexual, may want to refrain from even these mild gestures. Homosexuality is not illegal but is considered a perversion or mental illness or, at the very least, improper behavior. There is a growing underground gay scene in Shanghai and other major cities, but discretion is wise.

∃ Gay- & Lesbian-Friendly Travel Agencies **Different Roads Travel** ✉ 8383 Wilshire Blvd., Suite 520, Beverly Hills, CA 90211 ☎ 323/651-5557 or 800/429-8747 (Ext. 14 for both) 🖷 323/651-5454 ✍ lgernert@tzell.com. **Kennedy Travel** ✉ 130 W. 42nd St., Suite 401, New York, NY 10036 ☎ 212/840-8659 or 800/237-7433 🖷 212/730-2269 ⊕ www.kennedytravel.com. **Now, Voyager** ✉ 4406 18th St., San Francisco, CA 94114 ☎ 415/626-1169 or 800/255-6951 🖷 415/626-8626 ⊕ www.nowvoyager.com. **Skylink Travel and Tour/Flying Dutchmen**

Travel ✉ 1455 N. Dutton Ave., Suite A, Santa Rosa, CA 95401 ☎ 707/546-9888 or 800/225-5759 🖷 707/636-0951; serving lesbian travelers.

HEALTH

Beijing and Shanghai both have English-speaking doctors. The best way to find one is to ask your hotel concierge; if that doesn't work, try the local Public Security Bureau. There are modern hospitals, but if you become seriously ill or are injured, it's best to try to fly home, or at least to Hong Kong, as quickly as possible. Check for medical coverage with your health insurer before you go.

Pneumonia and influenza are common among travelers returning from China; many health professionals recommend inoculations before you leave. Be sure you're well rested and healthy to start with.

Do *not* buy prescription drugs in China unless absolutely necessary, as the quality control is unreliable.

FOOD & DRINK

The major health risk in China is traveler's diarrhea, caused by eating contaminated fruit or vegetables or drinking contaminated water. So watch what you eat. Avoid ice, uncooked food, and unpasteurized milk and milk products, and **drink only bottled water,** which is widely available, or water that has been boiled for several minutes. Tap water in major cities like Beijing and Shanghai is safe for brushing teeth. Mild cases may respond to Imodium (known generically as loperamide) or Pepto-Bismol, both of which can be purchased over the counter. Drink plenty of purified water or tea—chamomile is a good folk remedy. In severe cases, rehydrate yourself with a salt-sugar solution—½ teaspoon salt and 4 tablespoons sugar per quart of water.

OVER-THE-COUNTER REMEDIES

Most pharmacies carry over-the-counter Western medicines and traditional Chinese medicines.

HOLIDAYS

National holidays include January 1 (New Year's Day), two days in mid-January to February (Chinese New Year, also called

Spring Festival), March 8 (International Women's Day), May 1 (International Labor Day), May 4 (Youth Day), June 1 (Children's Day), July 1 (anniversary of the founding of the Communist Party of China), August 1 (anniversary of the founding of the Chinese People's Liberation Army), and October 1 (National Day—founding of the Peoples Republic of China in 1949).

INSURANCE

The most useful travel-insurance plan is a comprehensive policy that includes coverage for trip cancellation and interruption, default, trip delay, and medical expenses (with a waiver for preexisting conditions).

Without insurance you'll lose all or most of your money if you cancel your trip, regardless of the reason. Default insurance covers you if your tour operator, airline, or cruise line goes out of business—the chances of which have been increasing. Trip-delay covers expenses that arise because of bad weather or mechanical delays. Study the fine print when comparing policies.

If you're traveling internationally, a key component of travel insurance is coverage for medical bills incurred if you get sick on the road. Such expenses aren't generally covered by Medicare or private policies. U.K. residents can buy a travel-insurance policy valid for most vacations taken during the year in which it's purchased (but check preexisting-condition coverage). British and Australian citizens need extra medical coverage when traveling overseas.

Always **buy travel policies directly from the insurance company**; if you buy them from a cruise line, airline, or tour operator that goes out of business you probably won't be covered for the agency or operator's default, a major risk. Before making any purchase, review your existing health and home-owner's policies to find out what they cover away from home.

? Travel Insurers In the U.S.: **Access America** ✉ 2805 N. Parham Rd., Richmond, VA 23294 ☎ 800/284-8300 🖷 804/673-1491 or 800/346-9265 ⊕ www.accessamerica.com. **Travel Guard International** ✉ 1145 Clark St., Stevens Point, WI 54481 ☎ 715/345-0505 or 800/826-1300 🖷 800/955-8785 ⊕ www.travelguard.com.

? In the U.K.: **Association of British Insurers** ✉ 51 Gresham St., London EC2V 7HQ ☎ 020/7600-3333 🖷 020/7696-8999 ⊕ www.abi.org.uk. In Canada: **RBC Insurance** ✉ 6880 Financial Dr., Mississauga, Ontario L5N 7Y5 ☎ 800/668-4342 or 905/816-2400 🖷 905/813-4704 ⊕ www.rbcinsurance.com. In Australia: **Insurance Council of Australia** ✉ Insurance Enquiries and Complaints, Level 12, Box 561, Collins St. W, Melbourne, VIC 8007 ☎ 1300/780808 or 03/9629-4109 🖷 03/9621-2060 ⊕ www.iecltd.com.au. In New Zealand: **Insurance Council of New Zealand** ✉ Level 7, 111-115 Customhouse Quay, Box 474, Wellington ☎ 04/472-5230 🖷 04/473-3011 ⊕ www.icnz.org.nz.

LANGUAGE

The national language of China is Mandarin, known in China as Putonghua (*pǔtōnghuà*), the "common language." Nearly everyone speaks Mandarin, but many also speak local dialects, some of which use the same characters as Mandarin with a very different pronunciation. In Hong Kong the main spoken language is Cantonese, although most people speak English

All of the Chinese languages are tonal; there are four possible tones for every syllable, in addition to the basic sound of the syllable, and they make up part of a word's pronunciation. Each syllable has a different meaning depending on the pitch or musical inflection the speaker gives it. For example, in Mandarin the syllable *ma* can mean mother, horse, curse, or hemp plant—or, it can be a particle denoting a question—depending on the tone used. Thus, the sentence "Ma ma ma ma" translates as "does mother curse the horse?," a classic example of the complexity of the tonal Chinese language. Additionally, many Chinese characters are homonyms, which makes it difficult if not impossible for the foreign ear to understand what is being said. Since 1949 the government has revamped the teaching of Mandarin, introducing a simplified phonetic system known as pinyin, which uses the roman alphabet to denote the pronunciations of the myriad Chinese characters (pinyin is taught alongside ideograms).

Although Chinese grammar is simple, it is still difficult for foreigners to speak Chinese and even harder to be understood. However, the Chinese will appreciate your making the effort to speak a few phrases understood almost everywhere. Try "Hello"—"*Ní hǎo*" (nee how); "Thank you"—"*Xiè xiè*" (shee-yeh, shee-yeh); and "Good-bye"—"*Zai jian*" (dzigh djyan). When pronouncing words written in pinyin, remember that "q" and "x" are pronounced like "ch" and "sh," respectively; "zh" is pronounced like the "j" in "just"; "c" is pronounced like "ts."

You can usually find someone who speaks English in Beijing and Shanghai. If you're lost and need help, look first to someone under 30, who will likely have studied some English in school. In most hotels and upscale dining establishments, the staff will speak English. But in shops, calculators do most of the talking. English signs are rare, though they are used on the subways in both cities. Street signs are often written in pinyin.

LODGING
There are hotels for every need and budget in Beijing and Shanghai, from simple hostels to luxury high-rises owned by international chains. Three-star hotels are common and offer a good value, with air-conditioning, color TV, and private Western-style bathrooms. Many also have Western and Chinese restaurants. Four- and five-star hotels also have swimming pools, business services, and other amenities. One-star hotels always have rooms with private bathrooms, but the toilets are generally just a hole in the floor.

The lodgings we list are the cream of the crop in each price category. We always list the facilities that are available, but we don't specify whether they cost extra; when pricing accommodations, always ask what's included and what costs extra. Properties are assigned price categories based on rack rates at high season (excluding holidays). A few minutes on the Internet can easily net you discounts up to 50% (*see* Discounts & Deals).

Assume that hotels operate on the European Plan (EP, with no meals) unless we

specify that they use the Continental Plan (CP, with a Continental breakfast), Modified American Plan (MAP, with breakfast and dinner), or the Full American Plan (FAP, with all meals).

APARTMENT & VILLA RENTALS
If you want a home base that's roomy enough for a family and comes with cooking facilities, consider a furnished rental. These can save you money, especially if you're traveling with a group. Home-exchange directories sometimes list rentals as well as exchanges.

Maple Place, owned by King Kok Investment Limited, a consortium of three of Asia's best-known property companies, has well-equipped apartments, villas, and luxury townhouses in northeast Beijing on the Wenyun River, aptly named the Beijing Riviera. Maple Place is convenient to Beijing International Airport and guests have access to the Beijing Riviera Country Club. Rentals cost about $500 a week.

Pacific Properties/Pacific Relocations can help you find short-term rental properties in Beijing and Shanghai.

International Agents Hideaways International ⊠ 767 Islington St., Portsmouth, NH 03801 ☎ 603/430-4433 or 800/843-4433 ☐ 603/430-4444 ⊕ www.hideaways.com; annual membership $145. **Local Agents** Maple Place ⊠ 1 Xiang Jiang Bei Lu, Chaoyang District 100103 ☎ 010/6517-1275 ☐ 010/6510-1368. **Pacific Properties/Pacific Relocations** ⊠ Chun Shen Jiang Mansion, Suite 910, 400 Zhe Jiang Zhong Road, Suite 910, Shanghai 200001 ☎ 021/6351-1503 ☐ 021/6351-8213 ✎ shanghai@worthenpacific.com ⊕ www.worthenpacific.com.

HOMESTAYS
Staying with a host family is a unique, inexpensive, and culturally rich experience. Generally your Chinese host family will speak enough English for basic communication, and you'll have the opportunity to experience life off the beaten tourist path.

Organizations American International Homestays, Inc. ☐ Box 1754, Nederland, CO 80466 ☎ 303/642-3088 or 800/876-2048 ☐ 303/642-3365 ⊕ www.commerce.com/homestays. **ULink Travel Center** ☐ Box 938, He Ping Men, Beijing 100051 ☎ 010/6775-8655 ☐ 010/6774-1523.

HOSTELS

No matter what your age, you can save on lodging costs by staying at hostels. In some 4,500 locations in more than 70 countries around the world, Hostelling International (HI), the umbrella group for a number of national youth-hostel associations, offers single-sex, dorm-style beds and, at many hostels, rooms for couples and family accommodations. Membership in any HI national hostel association, open to travelers of all ages, allows you to stay in HI-affiliated hostels at member rates; one-year membership is about $28 for adults (C$35 for a two-year minimum membership in Canada, £14 in the United Kingdom, A$52 in Australia, and NZ$40 in New Zealand); hostels charge about $10–$30 per night. Members have priority if the hostel is full; they're also eligible for discounts around the world, even on rail and bus travel in some countries.

🛈 Organizations **Hostelling International–USA** ✉ 8401 Colesville Rd., Suite 600, Silver Spring, MD 20910 ☎ 301/495-1240 🖶 301/495-6697 ⊕ www.hiusa.org. **Hostelling International–Canada** ✉ 205 Catherine St., Suite 400, Ottawa, Ontario K2P 1C3 ☎ 613/237-7884 or 800/663-5777 🖶 613/237-7868 ⊕ www.hihostels.ca. **YHA England and Wales** ✉ Trevelyan House, Dimple Rd., Matlock, Derbyshire DE4 3YH, U.K. ☎ 0870/870-8808, 0870/770-8868, 0162/959-2600 🖶 0870/770-6127 ⊕ www.yha.org.uk. **YHA Australia** ✉ 422 Kent St., Sydney, NSW 2001 ☎ 02/9261-1111 🖶 02/9261-1969 ⊕ www.yha.com.au. **YHA New Zealand** ✉ Level 1, Moorhouse City, 166 Moorhouse Ave., Box 436, Christchurch ☎ 03/379-9970 or 0800/278-299 🖶 03/365-4476 ⊕ www.yha.org.nz.

HOTELS

You'll have to show your passport when checking into a hotel. The reception desk clerk will record the number before giving you a room. Sometimes unmarried couples are not allowed to stay together in the same room, but simply wearing a band on your left finger is one way to avoid this complication. Friends of the same sex, especially women, shouldn't have a problem getting a room together. There may, however, be regulations about who is allowed in your room, and it's also normal for hotels to post "visitor hours" inside the room.

Major hotels generally have English speakers on staff, business centers, laundry service, foreign-currency exchange, and a concierge who can arrange tours and transportation. Many also have exercise facilities, hairdressers, and restaurants.

All hotels listed have private bath unless otherwise noted. Remember that water is a precious resource in China and use accordingly.

🛈 Toll-Free Numbers **Best Western** ☎ 800/528-1234 ⊕ www.bestwestern.com. **Choice** ☎ 800/424-6423 ⊕ www.choicehotels.com. **Clarion** ☎ 800/424-6423 ⊕ www.choicehotels.com. **Comfort Inn** ☎ 800/424-6423 ⊕ www.choicehotels.com. **Days Inn** ☎ 800/325-2525 ⊕ www.daysinn.com. **Four Seasons** ☎ 800/332-3442 ⊕ www.fourseasons.com. **Hilton** ☎ 800/445-8667 ⊕ www.hilton.com. **Holiday Inn** ☎ 800/465-4329 ⊕ www.ichotelsgroup.com. **Howard Johnson** ☎ 800/446-4656 ⊕ www.hojo.com. **Hyatt Hotels & Resorts** ☎ 800/233-1234 ⊕ www.hyatt.com. **Inter-Continental** ☎ 800/327-0200 ⊕ www.ichotelsgroup.com. **Marriott** ☎ 800/228-9290 ⊕ www.marriott.com. **Nikko Hotels International** ☎ 800/645-5687 ⊕ www.nikkohotels.com. **Radisson** ☎ 800/333-3333 ⊕ www.radisson.com. **Ramada** ☎ 800/228-2828, 800/854-7854 international reservations ⊕ www.ramada.com or www.ramadahotels.com. **Renaissance Hotels & Resorts** ☎ 800/468-3571 ⊕ www.renaissancehotels.com. **Ritz-Carlton** ☎ 800/241-3333 ⊕ www.ritzcarlton.com. **Sheraton** ☎ 800/325-3535 ⊕ www.starwood.com/sheraton.

MAIL & SHIPPING

Sending international mail from China is extremely reliable. Letters mailed from China to overseas destinations require 5 to 14 days for delivery. Within China, mail is subject to search so **do not send sensitive materials,** such as religious or political literature, that may cause you or the recipient trouble. Mail your letters from post offices rather than mailboxes. Post offices, which are often crowded, are open 8–6 Monday through Saturday. Large hotels generally have postal services open all day Monday through Saturday and Sunday 8–noon.

You can use the roman alphabet to write an address. It is customary to organize the address the way the Chinese do, the reverse of the order used in the West, beginning with the country (rather than the individual) and progressing to the province, city or town followed by the zip code, street and dwelling number, and finally the individual's name. It's best if you write or ask a local to write the destination country in Chinese characters. Do not use red ink, which has a negative connotation.

Chinese zip codes, which are mandatory for all mailing addresses, have six digits. The Beijing municipality is assigned the zip code 100000, and each neighboring county starts with 10. For example, Fangshan, to the immediate southwest of Beijing proper, is assigned 102400. The Shanghai municipality's zip code is 200000, and each of the city's districts differs in the third and fourth digits; for example, Shanghai County is 201100 and Songjiang is 201600.

OVERNIGHT SERVICES

🔢 Major Services in Beijing **DHL** ☎ 010/ 6466-5566. **FedEx** ☎ 010/6462-3183. **UPS** ☎ 010/ 6505-5005 🖷 010/6505-5115.

POSTAL RATES

Overseas postal rates are as follows: postcards Y4.20; letters less than 10 grams Y5.40; letters between 10 and 20 grams Y6.50; air-mail parcels up to 1 kilogram, Y95–Y159 to the United States, Y77–Y162 to the United Kingdom, Y70–Y144 to Australia; express parcels less than 500 grams, Y180–Y240 to the United States, Y220–Y280 to Europe, Y160–Y210 to Australia. Letters and parcels can be registered for a small extra charge. Registration forms and customs-declaration forms are generally available in Chinese and French.

RECEIVING MAIL

Long-term guests can receive mail at their hotels. Otherwise, the best place to receive mail is at an American Express office. Be sure to bring your American Express card, as the staff will not give you the mail without seeing it.

SHIPPING PARCELS

You can ship parcels of purchases made in China at the post office, but the price is very high. Most large stores offer shipping services that include insurance guaranteed in writing. Be prepared for a long negotiation, however. Large antiques stores often offer reliable shipping services that take care of customs in China.

MONEY MATTERS

Museum entrance fees range from Y20 to Y50 and vary according to whether you're a local or a foreigner. A soft drink costs about Y10. A dumpling costs about Y10; a slice of pizza costs about Y50. Newspapers are about Y20.

Prices throughout this guide are given for adults. Substantially reduced fees are almost always available for children, students, and senior citizens. For information on taxes, see Taxes.

While in China it's best to **carry currency in several forms** (and in several different places), such as cash, traveler's checks, and an ATM and/or credit card.

ATMS

ATMs using the Cirrus and Plus networks are becoming increasingly common throughout China; at last count there were more than 100 ATMs in Beijing and more than 50 in Shanghai that accept MasterCard/Cirrus cards.

Before leaving home, **make sure your credit cards have been programmed for ATM use in China.** Local bank cards often do not work overseas or may access only your checking account; ask your bank about a MasterCard/Cirrus or Visa debit card, which works like a bank card but can be used at any ATM displaying a MasterCard/Cirrus or Visa logo. These cards, too, may tap only your checking account; check with your bank about their policy.

CREDIT CARDS

American Express, JCB, MasterCard, and Visa are accepted at most hotels and a growing number of stores and restaurants. Diners Club is accepted at many hotels and some restaurants. Contact your credit card company before you go to inform them of your trip. Credit card companies have been known to put a hold on an account and send a report to their fraud division upon registering a purchase or cash advance in China. Be sure to copy your credit card numbers on a separate piece of paper, which you should carry in a place separate from your credit cards in case of theft.

Throughout this guide, the following abbreviations are used: **AE**, American Express; **DC**, Diners Club; **MC**, MasterCard; and **V**, Visa.

🖪 Reporting Lost Cards **American Express** ☎ 010/6606-2227 in China. **Diners Club** ☎ 303/799-1504 in the U.S. (call collect). **MasterCard** ☎ 010/800-110-7309 in China. **Visa** ☎ 010/800-110-2911 in China.

CURRENCY

The Chinese currency is officially called the renminbi (RMB), or "People's Money." The Bank of China issues RMB bills in denominations of 1, 2, and 5 *mao* (a *mao* equals 10 cents); 1, 2, 5, 10, 20, 50, 100, 500, and 1,000 yuan, also commonly referred to as *kuai* (koowhy). Bills worth less than 1 yuan come in denominations of 1, 2, and 5 *jiao* (jeeow), with 10 jiao making one yuan. Coins are in denominations of 1, 2, and 5 *fen*, and 100 fen make a yuan. The abbreviation for yuan is Y. The exchange rate at this writing is Y8.28 per U.S. dollar, Y6.06 per Canadian dollar, Y5.77 per Australian dollar, Y4.72 per British pound, Y5.03 per New Zealand dollar.

CURRENCY EXCHANGE

Certain branches of the Bank of China and other banks can cash traveler's checks and change money at a rate fixed by a government agency. Hotel desks can also often change money, usually on a 24-hour basis, at rates as good as or better than those at the banks. A passport is required. Hold on to your exchange receipt, which you'll need if, at trip's end, you want to convert your extra yuan back into your home currency. No private offices or kiosks offer currency-exchange services. Be sure to purchase a small amount of renminbi prior to your trip.

🖪 Exchange Services **International Currency Express** ⌧ 427 N. Camden Dr., Suite F, Beverly Hills, CA 90210 ☎ 888/278-6628 orders 🖷 310/278-6410 ⊕ www.foreignmoney.com. **Travel Ex Currency**

Services ☎ 800/287-7362 orders and retail locations ⊕ www.travelex.com.

TRAVELER'S CHECKS

You get a slightly better exchange rate for traveler's checks than for cash. Lost or stolen checks can usually be replaced within 24 hours. To ensure a speedy refund, buy your own traveler's checks—don't let someone else pay for them: irregularities like this can cause delays. The person who bought the checks should make the call to request a refund.

PACKING

Informal attire is appropriate for most occasions. Sturdy, comfortable walking shoes are a must. A raincoat, especially a light Goretex one or a fold-up poncho, is useful for an onset of rainy weather. Summers are very hot and winters very cold, so pack accordingly. Clothes are also inexpensive in China, so you can always buy what you need. Most hotels have reliable overnight laundry, mending, and pressing services, so you can have your clothes washed frequently.

If you're planning a longer trip or will be using local tour guides, bring a few inexpensive items from your home country as gifts. Popular gifts are candy, T-shirts, and small cosmetic items such as lipstick and nail polish. **Do not give American magazines and books as gifts,** as these can be considered propaganda and get your Chinese friends into trouble.

In your carry-on luggage, pack an extra pair of eyeglasses or contact lenses and enough of any medication you take to last a few days longer than the entire trip. You may also ask your doctor to write a spare prescription using the drug's generic name, as brand names may vary from country to country. In luggage to be checked, **never pack prescription drugs, valuables, or undeveloped film.** And don't forget to carry with you the addresses of offices that handle refunds of lost traveler's checks.

To avoid customs and security delays, carry medications in their original packaging. Don't pack any sharp objects in your carry-on luggage, including knives of any size or material, scissors, nail clippers, corkscrews, or anything else that might arouse suspicion.

CHECKING LUGGAGE

You're allowed to carry aboard one bag and one personal article, such as a purse or a laptop computer. Your carry-on must fit under your seat or in the overhead bin. Get to the gate early, so you can board as soon as possible, before the overhead bins fill up. If you're flying within China on a local carrier, carry on as little as possible; flights can be very crowded and overhead bin space hard to get.

Baggage allowances vary by carrier, destination, and ticket class. On international flights, you're usually allowed to check two bags weighing up to 70 pounds (32 kilograms) each, although a few airlines allow checked bags of up to 88 pounds (40 kilograms) in first class. Some international carriers don't allow more than 66 pounds (30 kilograms) per bag in business class and 44 pounds (20 kilograms) in economy for domestic flights within China, you're officially allowed one checked piece that weighs no more than 44 pounds (20 kilograms). On domestic flights in the United States, the limit is usually 50 to 70 pounds (23 to 32 kilograms) per bag. For domestic flights within China, be sure to lock your bags—for safety reasons and because some local carriers require that all checked bags be locked.

In general, carry-on bags shouldn't exceed 40 pounds (18 kilograms). Most airlines won't accept bags that weigh more than 100 pounds (45 kilograms) on domestic or international flights. Expect to pay a fee for baggage that exceeds weight limits. Check baggage restrictions with your carrier before you pack.

Airline liability for baggage is limited to $2,500 per person on flights within the United States. On international flights it amounts to $9.07 per pound or $20 per kilogram for checked baggage (roughly $640 per 70-pound bag), with a maximum of $634.90 per piece, and $400 per passenger for unchecked baggage. You can buy additional coverage at check-in for about $10 per $1,000 of coverage, but it often excludes a rather extensive list of items, shown on your airline ticket.

Before departure, itemize your bags' contents and their worth, and label the bags with your name, address, and phone number. (If you use your home address, cover it so potential thieves can't see it readily.) Include a label inside each bag and **pack a copy of your itinerary.** At check-in, make sure each bag is correctly tagged with the destination airport's three-letter code. Because some checked bags will be opened for hand inspection, the U.S. Transportation Security Administration recommends that you leave luggage unlocked or use the plastic locks offered at check-in. TSA screeners place an inspection notice inside searched bags, which are re-sealed with a special lock.

If your bag has been searched and contents are missing or damaged, file a claim with the TSA Consumer Response Center as soon as possible. If your bags arrive damaged or fail to arrive at all, file a written report with the airline before leaving the airport.

🚩 Complaints **U.S. Transportation Security Administration Contact Center** ☎ 866/289-9673 ⊕ www.tsa.gov.

PASSPORTS & VISAS

When traveling internationally, carry your passport even if you don't need one (it's always the best form of ID) and **make two photocopies of the data page** (one for someone at home and another for you, carried separately from your passport). If you lose your passport, promptly call the nearest embassy or consulate and the local police.

U.S. passport applications for children under age 14 require consent from both parents or legal guardians; both parents must appear together to sign the application. If only one parent appears, he or she must submit a written statement from the other parent authorizing passport issuance for the child. A parent with sole authority must present evidence of it when applying; acceptable documentation includes the child's certified birth certificate listing only the applying parent, a court order specifically permitting this parent's travel with the child, or a death certificate for the nonapplying parent. Application forms and instructions are available on the Web site of the U.S. State Department's Bureau of Consular Affairs (⊕ travel.state.gov).

ENTERING CHINA

All U.S. citizens, even infants, need a valid passport with a tourist visa stamped in it to enter China (except for Hong Kong, where you only need a valid passport) for stays of up to 90 days.

It takes about a week to get a visa in the United States. Travel agents in Hong Kong can also issue visas for visits to the rest of China. Costs range from about $35 for a visa issued within two working days to $50 for a visa issued overnight. The visa application will ask for your occupation. The Chinese government is not fond of journalists or anyone who works in publishing or the media. Americans and Canadians in these professions routinely list "teacher" as their occupation. U.K. passports state the bearer's occupation, which can be problematic for anyone in the "wrong" line of work. Before you go, contact the consulate or embassy of the People's Republic of China to see how strict the current mood is. The Web site www.visatoasia.com/china.html provides up-to-date information on visa application to China.

⌨ In Australia **Chinese Embassy** ☎ 02/6273-4780 Ext. 218 or Ext. 258 🖷 02/6273-9615 ⊕ www. chinaembassy.org.au.
⌨ In Canada **Chinese Embassy** ☎ 613/789-3434 🖷 613/789-1911 ⊕ www.chinaembassycanada.org.
⌨ In New Zealand **Chinese Embassy** ☎ 04/472-1382 🖷 04/499-0419 ⊕ www.chinaembassy.org.nz.
⌨ In the U.K. **Chinese Embassy** ☎ 0171/636-2580 🖷 0171/636-2981 ⊕ www.chinese-embassy.org.uk.
⌨ In the U.S. **Chinese Consulate** ✉ Visa Office, 520 12th Ave., New York, NY 10036 ☎ 212/736-9301 automatic answering machine with 24-hour service, 212/502-0271 information desk open weekdays 2-4 🖷 212/502-0245 ⊕ www.nyconsulate.prchina.org. **Chinese Embassy** ✉ Room 110, 2201 Wisconsin Ave. NW, Washington, DC 20007 ☎ 202/338-6688 🖷 202/588-9760 ⊕ www.china-embassy.org.

PASSPORT OFFICES

Before any trip, check your passport's expiration date, and, if necessary, renew it as soon as possible.

⌨ Australian Citizens **Passports Australia** Australian Department of Foreign Affairs and Trade ☎ 131-232 ⊕ www.passports.gov.au.
⌨ Canadian Citizens **Passport Office** ✉ to mail in applications: 200 Promenade du Portage, Hull, Québec J8X 4B7 ☎ 819/994-3500 or 800/567-6868 ⊕ www.ppt.gc.ca.
⌨ New Zealand Citizens **New Zealand Passports Office** ☎ 0800/22-5050 or 04/474-8100 ⊕ www. passports.govt.nz.
⌨ U.K. Citizens **U.K. Passport Service** ☎ 0870/ 521-0410 ⊕ www.passport.gov.uk.
⌨ U.S. Citizens **National Passport Information Center** ☎ 877/487-2778, 888/874-7793 TDD/TTY ⊕ travel.state.gov.

RESTROOMS

You'll find public restrooms in the streets, parks, restaurants, department stores, and major tourist attractions in Beijing and Shanghai, but these are not very clean and seldom provide toilet paper or soap. The restrooms in the newest shopping plazas, fast-food outlets, and deluxe restaurants catering to foreigners are much cleaner and often meet international standards. The public restrooms charge a small fee (usually less than Y1), but seldom provide Western-style facilities or private booths, relying instead on squat toilets, open troughs, and rusty spigots; WC signs at intersections point the way to these facilities. It's a good idea to **carry toilet paper or tissues and antibacterial hand sanitizer or wipes** with you at all times.

SAFETY

There is little violent crime against tourists in China, partly because the penalties are severe for those who are caught—execution is the most common. Use the lockbox in your hotel room to store any valuables, but always carry your passport with you for identification purposes. Be aware that a money belt or a waist pack pegs you as a tourist, and a backpack makes an easy target for thieves in crowded conditions. Be sure to keep your bags in front of you, so that thieves cannot cut them open without your noticing. Distribute your cash and any valuables (including your credit cards and passport) between a deep front pocket, an inside jacket or vest pocket, and a hidden money pouch.

The traffic in Chinese cities is usually heavy and just as out of control as it looks. Be very careful when crossing streets. Drivers do not give pedestrians the right-of-way; note in particular that drivers seldom stop or look for pedestrians before making a right turn on a red light. Be wary of the countless bicyclists as well as drivers.

Respiratory problems may be aggravated by the severely polluted air in China's cities. Some residents as well as visitors find that wearing a surgical mask, or a scarf or bandana, helps.

WOMEN IN CHINA

The Chinese do not approve of women wearing revealing clothing so it's best to wear tops that cover most of your torso and shorts that reach your knees in summer. Foreign women rarely face unwanted attention from men, as Chinese custom frowns upon lewd behavior.

If you carry a purse, choose one with a zipper and a thick strap that you can drape across your body; adjust the length so that the purse sits in front of you at or above hip level. Store only enough money in the purse to cover casual spending; distribute the rest of your cash in deep front pockets, inside jacket or vest pockets, and a concealed money pouch.

SENIOR-CITIZEN TRAVEL

To qualify for age-related discounts, mention your senior-citizen status up front when booking hotel reservations (not when checking out) and before you're seated in restaurants (not when paying the bill). Be sure to have identification on hand. When renting a car, ask about promotional car-rental discounts, which can be cheaper than senior-citizen rates.

🎓 Educational Programs **Elderhostel** ✉ 11 Ave. de Lafayette, Boston, MA 02111-1746 ☎ 877/426–8056, 978/323–4141 international callers, 877/426–2167 TTY 🖷 877/426–2166 ⊕ www.elderhostel.org. **Interhostel** ✉ University of New Hampshire, 6 Garrison Ave., Durham, NH 03824 ☎ 603/862–1147 or 800/733–9753 🖷 603/862–1113 ⊕ www.learn.unh.

edu. **Folkways Institute** ✉ 14600 S.E. Aldridge Rd., Portland, OR 97236-6518 ☎ 503/658–6600 🖷 503/658–8672.

SHOPPING

Good souvenirs include Chinese medicines, silk, and tea. There are shops specializing in jade, old Chinese porcelain, and antique furniture, but **be alert for forgery when shopping.** Stick to Friendship Stores (formerly emporiums selling luxury goods for foreigners only, now more like an upscale department store chain) and shops attached to international hotels for some assurance of getting what you pay for. When you buy goods in established shops, you first pay the cashier and then present the receipt of sale to the store attendant, who will wrap your purchase.

With antiques, an item more than 100 years old will have an official red wax seal attached—but not all items with seals attached are more than 100 years old. The Chinese government has cleared only certain antiques for sale to foreigners. Save the bill of sale to show customs when you leave the country, or the antique will be confiscated. For exports, antiques must have been made after 1797.

China's antiques market exists in state-run tourist sites such as courtyards or gardens. Often, items in these places range from panels ripped off of old house facades to carved headboards. Antiques bought in these places are not old enough to warrant an official seal for customs.

Post offices in hotels usually have interesting Chinese stamps for sale. Ask about designs that were issued during the Cultural Revolution.

WATCH OUT

In Shanghai, the open-air markets that line the entrances to major tourist attractions generally charge extravagant prices for poor-quality, mass-produced kitsch and outright fakes. The pearls and jade sold here and throughout China are often fake. It's particularly difficult to evaluate jade, but you can trust government-owned factories. Many of these factory showrooms offer free bus services and a glimpse of the production process.

Beware of "student artists" who seek out foreign tourists and persuade them to visit their studios. The artworks in the studios are mass-produced and are marked up way beyond their market value.

Note that expensive fashion items such as silk, batik, and cotton clothes may shrink when dry-cleaned. If you still wish to buy these items, be prepared to hand-wash them in cold water with mild soap. Also keep in mind that some countries, including the United States, prohibit the import of ivory.

Goods are usually not returnable, even with a receipt. Never put down a deposit for a purchase you are still considering; if you decide against the purchase you may not be able to get your deposit back.

STUDENTS IN CHINA

Nonresidents studying at Chinese schools are entitled to discounts on museum and park fees, as well as 40% discounts on intracontinental air tickets. To obtain these discounts you must present an official Chinese student card issued by your school.

🔗 IDs & Services **STA Travel** ✉ 10 Downing St., New York, NY 10014 ☎ 212/627-3111, 800/777-0112 24-hr service center 🖨 212/627-3387 ⊕ www.sta. com. **Travel Cuts** ✉ 187 College St., Toronto, Ontario M5T 1P7, Canada ☎ 800/592-2887 in the U.S., 416/979-2406 or 866/246-9762 in Canada 🖨 416/979-8167 ⊕ www.travelcuts.com.

TAXES

There is no sales tax in China. Hotels charge a 5% tax and sometimes a 10%–15% service fee. Some restaurants charge a 10% service fee.

A departure tax of Y50 (about $6) for domestic flights and Y90 (about $11) for international flights (including flights to Hong Kong and Macau) must be paid in cash in dollars or yuan at the airport. People holding diplomatic passports, passengers in transit who stop over for less than 24 hours, and children under 12 are exempt from the departure tax. There are also taxes for international ferry departures at some ports.

TELEPHONES

AREA & COUNTRY CODES

The country code for China is 86; the city code for Beijing is 10, and the city code for Shanghai is 21. To call China from the United States or Canada, dial the international access code (011), followed by the country code (86), the area or city code, and the eight-digit phone number. When dialing from within China to another city, dial 0 before the city code. To make an international call from within China, dial 00 (the international access code within China) and then the country code, area code, and phone number. The country code is 1 for the United States and Canada, 61 for Australia, 64 for New Zealand, and 44 for the United Kingdom.

Numbers beginning with 800 within China are toll-free. Note that a call from China to a toll-free number in the United States or Hong Kong is a full-tariff international call.

CELL PHONES

Consider renting a cell phone with a SIM card for travel in China, as this allows you to take advantage of low rates. The SIM card, which slips into the cell phone, is prepaid and rechargeable, so you will never receive a phone bill. Try to avoid cell rentals that charge you per-minute rates.

🔗 Cell-Phone Rental **Cellular Abroad** ✉ 3019 Pico Blvd., Santa Monica, CA 90405 ☎ 800/287-3020 ⊕ www.cellularabroad.com/chinasg.html.

DIRECTORY & OPERATOR ASSISTANCE

For directory assistance, dial 114. If you want information for other cities, dial the city code followed by 114 (note that this is considered a long-distance call). For example, if you're in Beijing and need directory assistance for a Shanghai number, dial 021–114. The operators do not speak English, so if you don't speak Chinese you're best off asking your hotel for help.

INTERNATIONAL CALLS

IDD (international direct dialing) service is available at all hotels, post offices, major shopping centers, and airports. In hotels, an operator will dial the number and place the call for you. Note that it is much cheaper, however, to use a calling card or a rental cell phone.

LOCAL CALLS

You can make local calls from your hotel or any public phone on the street; most public phones use calling cards, which you can purchase at convenience stores and newsstands. For local calls within the same city, omit the city code.

LONG-DISTANCE CALLS

Long-distance rates in China are very low, and hotels are only allowed to add a service charge of up to 15%. To make long-distance calls from a public phone you need an IC card ($\Rightarrow$ Phone Cards). To place a long-distance call, dial 0, the city code, and the eight-digit phone number.

LONG-DISTANCE SERVICES

AT&T, MCI, and Sprint access codes make calling long-distance relatively convenient, but you may find the local access number blocked in many hotel rooms. First ask the hotel operator to connect you. If the hotel operator balks, ask for an international operator, or dial the international operator yourself. One way to improve your odds of getting connected to your long-distance carrier is to travel with more than one company's calling card (a hotel may block Sprint, for example, but not MCI). If all else fails, call from a pay phone.

The local access code in China is 11 for AT&T, 12 for MCI, and 13 for Sprint—dial these numbers after dialing the local operator (108), who will speak English.

∆ Access Codes AT&T Direct ☎ 800/874-4000. **MCI WorldPhone** ☎ 800/444-4444. **Sprint International Access** ☎ 800/793-1153.

PHONE CARDS

There are two main kinds of calling cards in China: the IP card (Internet protocol; *aipi ka*) and the IC card (integrated circuit; *àicei ka*), both of which are available from post offices, convenience stores, and street vendors. The IC card is used for domestic local and long distance calls on any public phone that has an IC card slot. To make an international long distance call, you

will need to use the IC card to activate a public phone for a dial tone, and then provide the access codes on the IP card to make your call. Both cards' minutes are deducted at the same time, one for local access (IC card) and one for the long distance call you placed (IP card). You should bargain to pay less than the face value of the card—as little as Y70 for a Y100 card. Instructions are on the back of the cards, but you simply dial the access number, choose English from the menu, and follow the prompts to dial in the number behind a scratch-off panel. Using an IC card for a domestic call, Y50 can give you as much as an hour of talking time. Using the IP card, you can call internationally for a fraction of the cost of a hotel-assisted call.

PUBLIC PHONES

Most hotels have phone booths where you can place domestic and international calls. You pay a deposit of about Y200 and receive a card with the number of the booth. A computer times the call and processes a bill, which you pay at the end. Post offices have telecommunications centers where you can buy IC and IP cards in denominations of Y20, Y50, and Y100 to make long-distance calls. Standard pay phones accept these cards and coins. The cards tend to be less expensive but only work in the province in which they're purchased.

TIME

Beijing and Shanghai are 8 hours ahead of London, 13 hours ahead of New York, 14 hours ahead of Chicago, and 16 hours ahead of Los Angeles. There's no daylight saving time, so subtract an hour in summer.

TIPPING

Although tipping is officially forbidden by the government, it's still expected in many cases. Bell hops routinely receive Y5–Y10 per bag, and hairdressers receive 10%. For taxi drivers, you can simply round up the fare. Most restaurants charge a 10% service fee, so there's no need to tip. If this fee has not been added to your bill, leave 10%. Tour guides often expect Y10 from each person for the day.

CTS tour guides are not allowed to accept tips, but you can give them candy, T-shirts, and other small gifts. If you hire a driver and guide independently, the tipping norm is Y80 per day for the guide and Y40 for the driver.

TOURS & PACKAGES

Because everything is prearranged on a prepackaged tour or independent vacation, you spend less time planning—and often get it all at a good price.

BOOKING WITH AN AGENT

Travel agents are excellent resources. But it's a good idea to collect brochures from several agencies, as some agents' suggestions may be influenced by relationships with tour and package firms that reward them for volume sales. If you have a special interest, find an agent with expertise in that area; the American Society of Travel Agents (ASTA; ⇨ Travel Agencies) has a database of specialists worldwide. You can log on to the group's Web site to find an ASTA travel agent in your neighborhood.

Make sure your travel agent knows the accommodations and other services of the place being recommended. Ask about the hotel's location, room size, beds, and whether it has a pool, room service, or programs for children, if you care about these. Has your agent been there in person or sent others whom you can contact?

Do some homework on your own, too: local tourism boards can provide information about lesser-known and small-niche operators, some of which may sell only direct.

BUYER BEWARE

Each year consumers are stranded or lose their money when tour operators—even large ones with excellent reputations—go out of business. So check out the operator. Ask several travel agents about its reputation, and try to **book with a company that has a consumer-protection program.** (Look for information in the company's brochure.) In the United States, members of the United States Tour Operators Association are required to set aside funds ($1 million) to help eligible customers cover payments and travel arrangements in the event that the company defaults. It's also a good idea to choose a company that participates in the American Society of Travel Agents' Tour Operator Program; ASTA will act as mediator in any disputes between you and your tour operator.

Remember that the more your package or tour includes, the better you can predict the ultimate cost of your vacation. Make sure you know exactly what is covered, and beware of hidden costs. Are taxes, tips, and transfers included? Entertainment and excursions? These can add up.

🛈 Tour-Operator Recommendations **American Society of Travel Agents** (⇨ Travel Agencies). **National Tour Association (NTA)** ✉ 546 E. Main St., Lexington, KY 40508 ☎ 859/226–4444 or 800/682–8886 🖷 859/226–4404 ⊕ www.ntaonline.com. **United States Tour Operators Association (USTOA)** ✉ 275 Madison Ave., Suite 2014, New York, NY 10016 ☎ 212/599–6599 🖷 212/599–6744 ⊕ www. ustoa.com.

TRAIN TRAVEL

There's train service between Beijing and Shanghai, including an overnight train. Train tickets must be purchased in the city of origin. If you do not speak Mandarin, it may be difficult to negotiate the ticket windows at the train station, even though there is a special ticket counter just for foreigners. It's best to buy tickets from the local CTS office or ask your hotel concierge to make the arrangements. Fares are more expensive for foreigners than for the Chinese. Make train reservations at least a day or two in advance, if you can. Try to **avoid traveling during the three national holidays**—Chinese New Year (two days in mid-January–February), Labor Day (May 1), and National Day (October 1)—when tickets are sold out weeks in advance and the stations are insanely crowded.

Boiled water and hot meals are available onboard. Trains are always crowded, but you are guaranteed your designated seat, though not always the overhead luggage rack.

Note that theft on trains is increasing; on overnight trains, sleep with your valuables or else keep them on the inside of the bunk.

CLASSES

The train system offers a glimpse of old-fashioned socialist euphemisms. Instead of first-class and second-class accommodations, you choose hard seat or soft seat, and for overnight journeys, hard sleeper or soft sleeper. The soft sleeper has four compartments with soft beds and is recommended if you're taking a long journey (though it is much more expensive than the hard sleeper).

FARES & SCHEDULES

The tour operator Travel China Guide has an English-language Web site (⊕ www.travelchinaguide.com/china-trains/index.htm) that can help you figure out train schedules and fares.

TRAVEL AGENCIES

A good travel agent puts your needs first. Look for an agency that has been in business at least five years, emphasizes customer service, and has someone on staff who specializes in your destination. In addition, **make sure the agency belongs to a professional trade organization.** The American Society of Travel Agents (ASTA)—the largest and most influential in the field with more than 20,000 members in some 140 countries—maintains and enforces a strict code of ethics and will step in to help mediate any agent-client disputes involving ASTA members if necessary. ASTA (whose motto is "Without a travel agent, you're on your own") also maintains a Web site that includes a directory of agents. (If a travel agency is also acting as your tour operator, *see* Buyer Beware *in* Tours & Packages.)

🛂 Local Agent Referrals **American Society of Travel Agents (ASTA)** ✉ 1101 King St., Suite 200, Alexandria, VA 22314 ☎ 703/739–2782 or 800/965–2782 24-hr hot line 🖷 703/684–8319 ⊕ www.astanet.com. **Association of British Travel Agents** ✉ 68–71 Newman St., London W1T 3AH ☎ 020/7637–2444 🖷 020/7637–0713 ⊕ www.abta.com. **Association of Canadian Travel Agencies** ✉ 130 Albert St., Suite 1705, Ottawa, Ontario K1P 5G4 ☎ 613/237–3657 🖷 613/237–7052 ⊕ www.acta.ca. **Australian Federation of Travel Agents** ✉ Level 3, 309 Pitt St., Sydney, NSW 2000 ☎ 02/9264–3299 or 1300/363–416 🖷 02/9264–1085 ⊕ www.afta.com.

au. **Travel Agents' Association of New Zealand** ✉ Level 5, Tourism and Travel House, 79 Boulcott St., Box 1888, Wellington 6001 ☎ 04/499–0104 🖷 04/499–0786 ⊕ www.taanz.org.nz.

VISITOR INFORMATION

Learn more about foreign destinations by checking government-issued travel advisories and country information. For a broader picture, consider information from more than one country.

For general information before you go, including information about tours, insurance, and safety, call or visit the China National Tourist Office in New York City, Los Angeles, London, or Sydney.

Within China, China International Travel Service (CITS) and China Travel Service (CTS) are under the same government ministry. Local offices, catering to sightseeing around the area (and to visitors from other mainland cities), are called CTS. CITS offices can book international flights.

🛂 China National Tourist Offices **Australia** ✉ 44 Market St., 19th floor, Sydney, NSW 2000 ☎ 02/9299–4057 🖷 02/9290–1958 ⊕ www.cnto.org.au. **Canada** ✉ 556 W. Broadway, Vancouver, BC V5Z 1E9 ☎ 604/872–8787 🖷 604/873–2823 ⊕ www.citscanada.com. **United Kingdom** ✉ 4 Glentworth St., London NW1 ☎ 0171/935–9427 🖷 0171/487–5842. **United States** ✉ 350 5th Ave., Suite 6413, New York, NY 10118 ☎ 212/760–8218 🖷 212/760–8809 ✉ 333 W. Broadway, Suite 201, Glendale, CA 91204 ☎ 818/545–7504 🖷 818/545–7506 ⊕ www.cnto.org.

🛂 China International Travel Service (CITS) **United States** ✉ 2 Mott St., New York, NY 10002 ☎ 212/608–1212 or 800/899–8618.

🛂 U.S. Government Advisories **U.S. Department of State** ✉ Overseas Citizens Services Office, 2100 Pennsylvania Ave. NW, 4th floor, Washington, DC 20520 ☎ 202/647–5225 interactive hot line, 888/407–4747 ⊕ www.travel.state.gov. **Consular Affairs Bureau of Canada** ☎ 613/944–6788 or 800/267–6788 ⊕ www.voyage.gc.ca. **U.K. Foreign and Commonwealth Office** ✉ Travel Advice Unit, Consular Division, Old Admiralty Building, London SW1A 2PA ☎ 0870/606–0290 or 020/7008–1500 ⊕ www.fco.gov.uk/travel. **Australian Department of Foreign Affairs and Trade** ☎ 300/139–281 travel advice, 02/6261–1299 Consular Travel Advice Faxback Service

⊕ www.dfat.gov.au. **New Zealand Ministry of Foreign Affairs and Trade** ☎ 04/439-8000 ⊕ www.mft.govt.nz.

WEB SITES

Do check out the World Wide Web when planning your trip. You'll find everything from weather forecasts to virtual tours of famous cities. Be sure to visit Fodors.com (⊕ www.fodors.com), a complete travel-planning site. You can research prices and book plane tickets, hotel rooms, rental cars, vacation packages, and more. In addition, you can post your pressing questions in the Travel Talk section. Other planning tools include a currency converter and weather reports, and there are loads of links to travel resources.

Government and regional tourist agencies in China sponsor a number of helpful Web sites for travelers to China. Try www.chinatips.net, www.travelchinaguide.com, www.china.com, and www.chinavista.com. The China National Tourism Office is at www.cnto.org. You can also visit CITS at www.chinatravelservice.com or www.citsusa.com.

BEIJING
THE HEART OF THE DRAGON

1

Revised by
Guy Rubin and
Caroline Liou

WIDE-EYED CHINESE TOURISTS converge on Tiananmen Square each day at dawn to watch a military honor guard raise China's flag. As soldiers march forth from the vast Forbidden City, these visitors, who usually number in the hundreds, begin to take pictures. They jockey for spots beneath the fluttering banner. They pose before the vermilion Gate of Heavenly Peace, its huge Chairman Mao portrait gazing benignly from atop the imperial doorway. This same shot, snapped by countless pilgrims, adorns family albums across the Middle Kingdom.

The daily photographic ritual and the giddy throng illustrate Beijing's position—unrivaled to this day—at the center of the Chinese universe. In spite of widespread urban renewal, parts of old Beijing continue to convey an imperial grandeur. But the city is more than a relic or a feudal ghost. Modern temples to communism—the Great Hall of the People, Chairman Mao's mausoleum—hint at the monumental power that still resides within the city's secret courtyards. If China is a dragon, Beijing is its beating heart.

Beijing's 13 million official residents—plus another 2 million migrant workers—are a fascinating mix of old and new. Early morning *taiqi* (tai chi) enthusiasts, bearded old men with caged songbirds, and amateur Peking opera crooners still frequent the city's many charming parks. Cyclists, most pedaling cumbersome, jet black Flying Pigeons, clog the roadways. But few wear padded blue Mao jackets these days, and they all must share the city's broad thoroughfares with China's steadily increasing number of car owners. Beijing traffic has gone from nonexistent to nightmarish in less than a decade, adding auto emissions to the city's winter coal smoke and sparking the newest threat to social order—road rage.

As the seat of China's immense national bureaucracy, Beijing still carries a political charge. The Communist Party, whose self-described goal is "a dictatorship of the proletariat," has yet to relinquish its political monopoly. In 1989 student protesters in Tiananmen Square dared to challenge the party. The government's brutal response, carried live on TV, remains etched in global memory. More than 10 years later, secret police still mingle with tourists and kite fliers on the square, ready to haul away all those so brave or foolish as to distribute a leaflet or unfurl a banner. Mao-style propaganda persists. Slogans that preach unity among China's national minorities, patriotism, and love for the People's Liberation Army (the military arm of the Communist Party) still festoon the city on occasion. Yet as Beijing's already robust economy is boosted even farther by the massive influx of investment prompted by the 2008 Olympics, such campaigns appear increasingly out of touch with the cellphone-primed generation. The result in the streets is an incongruous mixture of new prosperity and throwback politics: socialist slogans adorn shopping centers selling Gucci and Big Macs. Beijing is truly a land of opposites where the ancient and the sparkling new collide.

EXPLORING BEIJING

Be curious. Beijing rewards the explorer. Most temples and palaces have gardens and lesser courtyards that are seldom visited. Even at the height of the summer tourist rush, the Forbidden City's peripheral

Numbers in the text correspond to numbers in the margin and on the Beijing and Forbidden City maps.

If you have
1 day

Begin your day in **Tiananmen Square** ❶ ➤—you may want to catch the flag-raising ceremony at dawn—to admire the communist icons of modern China. Then, heading north, walk back through time into the **Forbidden City** ❽– ⓲. Keep in mind that in 1421, when the imperial palace was built, its structures were the tallest in Asia. You can spend the morning leisurely examining the many palaces, exhibitions, and gardens of the Forbidden City. If this has not exhausted you, head north into **Jingshan Park** ㉓ and climb Coal Hill to get a panoramic view over the entire Forbidden City. Then, jump in a cab and head to Lotus Lane where you can eat lunch overlooking **Qianhai Lake** ㉕.

In the afternoon, take a trip outside the city (*see* Chapter 2, Side Trips from Beijing). Hire a car and driver to take you on the one-hour journey to the Badaling section of the **Great Wall,** which is the closest to Beijing. On your way back, consider a stop at either the **Ming Tombs** or the **Summer Palace.** The Ming Tombs are en route; the Summer Palace will add an additional half hour to your journey. For both sights, the tickets are sold until one hour before closing time.

If you have
3 days

On your first day, visit **Tiananmen Square** ❶ ➤ and the **Forbidden City** ❽– ⓲. Depart through the Gate of Obedience and Purity (the north gate) and walk west to **Beihai Park** ㉔ for lunch at the food stalls. Arrive at the north gate before 1:30 for a half-day hutong tour, a guided pedicab ride through a maze-like neighborhood to the **Drum Tower** ㉚. Have dinner at the ✕ **Quanjude Peking Duck Restaurant,** south of Tiananmen Square.

On Day 2 visit the **Temple of Heaven** ㊲, the **Lama Temple** ㉝, and nearby the **Temple of Confucius** ㉞. Allow time for shopping at **Beijing Curio City, Silk Alley,** and the **Yihong Carpet Factory.** For dinner, eat Sichuanese in the Sanlitun area.

Set aside Day 3 for a trip to the **Ming Tombs** and the **Great Wall** at Mutianyu, where a Japanese gondola offers a dramatic ride to the summit. Bring a brown-bag lunch.

---

courtyards offer ample breathing room, even seclusion. The Temple of Heaven's vast grounds are a pleasure year-round—and enchanting during a snowstorm.

Although the Forbidden City and Tiananmen Square represent the heart of Beijing from imperial and tourist perspectives, the capital lacks a definitive downtown area in terms of shopping (with the exception, perhaps, of Wangfujing) or business, as commercial and entertainment districts have arisen all over.

When planning your day, keep in mind that Beijing is sprawling. City blocks are very large. To avoid arriving exhausted at sites that appeared deceptively close on the map, ride the subway, rent a bicycle, or hire a taxi to get between sites, saving your legs to walk around once you get there. Ration your foot time for Beijing's intriguing back alleys.

Tiananmen Square to Liulichang Antiques Market

The fame and symbolism of China's heart, Tiananmen, the Gate of Heavenly Peace, have been potent for generations of Chinese, but the events of June 1989 have left it forever etched into world consciousness. South of the square, a district of antiques shops and bookstores shows another side of Chinese culture.

A Good Walk

Start at the Renmin Yingxiong Jinianbei (Monument to the People's Heroes) in **Tiananmen Square ❶ ▶**. Look to either side of the square for the monuments to the new dynasty—the individual is meant to be dwarfed by their scale. To the west lies the **Great Hall of the People ❷**, home to China's legislative body, the National People's Congress. The equally solid building opposite is host to the important **China National Museum ❸**, which is due to be under renovation until 2007.

Southward, straight ahead, between two banks of heroic sculptures, is the **Mao Zedong Memorial Hall ❹**, housing Chairman Mao's tomb. Beyond it stands **Qianmen** (Front Gate), the colloquial name for the **Facing the Sun Gate ❺**, which affords great views of the city from the top. At street level, the Qianmen area remains as bustling as ever.

Head down Qianmen Dajie, the large road leading south, for about 90 feet before turning right (west) and sharply left (south) down a parallel north–south avenue, Zhu Bao Shi Jie (Jewelry Market Street). The old Beijing Silk Shop, at No. 5, will confirm you are on the right track. Here, in the **Dazhalan Market Area ❻**, amid the silk and fur bargains of the present, continue traditions of commerce and entertainment stretching back to the Ming era.

To escape the bustle into the calm of residential Beijing, take the second alley to your right, Langfang Ertiao; 65 feet in on the left is a three-story house with carved decorative panels. You'll see a number of such former inns and shops as you proceed west past a small alleyway on your left to the Meishijie (Coal Market Street) crossing, where you should head diagonally over to the Qudeng (Fetch Light) Hutong.

Follow Qudeng Hutong past traditional courtyard houses marked by wooden doorways, auspicious couplets, lintel beams, and stone door gods. At its end, veer left, then right and onto Tan'er (Charcoal) Hutong. At its close, turn left again down Yanshou Jie (Long Life Street), and the eastern end of **Liulichang Jie ❼** (Glazed-Tile Factory Street) will soon be apparent (look for the traditional post office).

TIMING   Allow three hours for the walk, longer if the museums arrest you and if serious antique/curio browsing is anticipated in Liulichang.

Peking Opera

Pop music has taken root in every Chinese city, but in Beijing it is still possible to see authentic Peking opera. Tragedy, warfare, palace intrigue—this is the stuff of the capital's traditional stage. Operas range from slothful to acrobatic; voices soar to near-shrill heights for female roles and sink to throaty baritones for generals and emperors. Costumes and makeup are without exception extravagant. Shortened performances catering to tourists are held at the Liyuan Juchang Theater. Full operas, and Beijing's enthusiastic opera crowd, can be seen several times each week at a number of theaters, including Chang'an Grand Theater.

Shopping

Numerous "old goods markets" peddle everything from Chairman Mao souvenirs to antique porcelain, jewelry, and furniture—plus a full selection of fakes. The Sunday flea market at Panjiayuan is the first stop for many portable antiques (wood carvings, statues, jade, old tile, and so on) entering Beijing from the countryside. Vendors, especially in the market's open-air rear section, are usually peasants who've journeyed to Beijing to sell items collected in their village. Antique rugs and furniture are perhaps Beijing's best bargain. A few dealers will arrange to ship larger items overseas.

Walking

Never bypass an intriguing alleyway. Strolls into a *hutong* frequently reveal ancient neighborhoods: mud-and-timber homes; courtyards full of children, *laobaixing* (ordinary folk), and, in winter, mountains of cabbage and coal; and alleys so narrow that pedestrians can't pass two abreast. This is Old Peking. See it before it vanishes. Make sure you have a Chinese/English map with you so you can be directed somewhere—Tiananmen Square, for example—to regain your bearings.

What to See

★ ❸ **China National Museum** (Zhongguo Guojia Bowuguan). On the east side of Tiananmen Square stands a grandiose structure: the forthcoming China National Museum. Until 2003 this iconic building housed both the massive China History Museum and the rather tired Museum of the Chinese Revolution. In honor of the 2008 Beijing Olympics, city authorities have embarked on a renovation and expansion program to create an art institution befitting one of the world's major capitals. The building is scheduled to be closed between April 2005 and December 2007. Prior to that time, visitors may enjoy a reduced but still exquisite collection of bronze, ceramic, and jade pieces, as well as a new waxworks exhibition—a 35-model who's who of Chinese ancient and modern cultural history. Bags must be checked (Y1) before you enter. ⊠ *Central entrance on building on east side of Tiananmen Sq., Chongwen District* ☎ *010/6512–8967* ✉ *Y30; bag check, Y1* ⊙ *Mar.–June and Sept.–Oct., Mon.–Sun. 8:30–4:30; July–Aug. and Nov.–Feb., Mon.–Sun. 8:30–4; ticket office closes one hour before museum.*

❻ **Dazhalan Market Area** (Large Wicker Gate Market Area). In the Ming era, the Dazhalan gate was lowered each night to enforce a curfew. The area

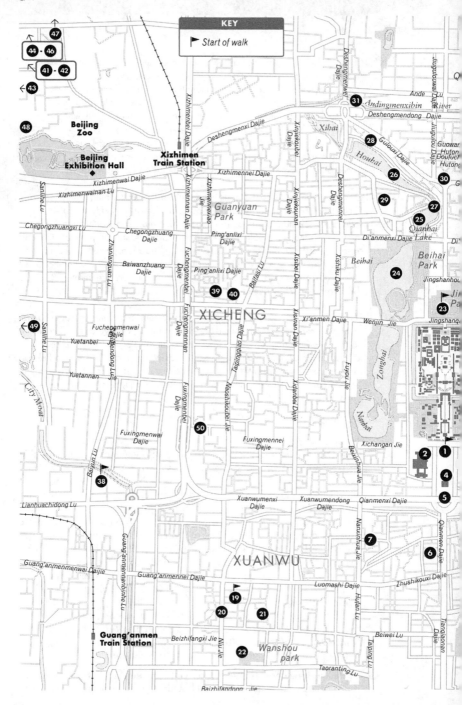

around the gate, known by the same name, is a neighborhood of close-packed lanes crowded with flags and sideboards. It was once filled with a cacophony of merchants, eateries, teahouses, wine shops, theaters, and brothels. Palace officials (and the occasional emperor in disguise) would escape here for a few hours' respite from the suffocating imperial maze. Traditional shops and crowded alleys still make Dazhalan one of Beijing's most interesting commercial areas, especially now that most shopping in the capital is conducted behind the glass screens of glitzy malls. Dazhalan's specialties include clothing, fabric, shoes, Chinese medicine, and Peking opera costumes. ⊠ *Zhubaoshi Jie, near Qianmen.*

❺ **Facing the Sun Gate** (Zhengyangmen). From its top looking south, you can see that Zhengyangmen actually comprised two gates: the **Arrow Tower** (Tian Lou) in front was, until 1915, connected to Zhengyangmen by a defensive half-moon wall. The central gates of both structures opened only for the emperor's biannual ceremonial trips to the Temple of Heaven to the south. Don't miss the evocative photo exhibition of Old Peking. Have some tea atop Zhengyangmen before heading up the Arrow Tower for views of the old Qianmen railway station, now the Railway Workers Cultural Palace. ⊠ *Xuanwumen Jie.*

❷ **Great Hall of the People** (Renmin Dahuitang). This solid edifice owes its Stalinist weight to the last years of the Sino-Soviet pact. Its gargantuan dimensions (205,712 square yards of floor space) exceed that of the Forbidden City. It was built by 14,000 laborers who worked around the clock for eight months. China's legislature meets in the aptly named Ten Thousand People Assembly Hall, beneath a panoply of 500 star lights revolving around a giant red star. Thirty-one reception rooms are distinguished by the arts and crafts of the provinces they represent. Call a day ahead to confirm that it's open. ⊠ *West side of Tiananmen Sq., Xuanwu District* ☎ *010/6309–6156* 🎫 *Y30* ⊙ *Daily 9 AM–1 PM.*

❼ **Liulichang Jie** (Glazed-Tile Factory Street). The Ming factory that gave the street its name and the Forbidden City its yellow top was destroyed by the Qing, but renovation has restored the many book, arts, and antiques shops that crowded here in early Qing times. Be sure to visit the **China Bookstore** (Zhongguo Shu Dian; ⊠ Opposite No. 115) and the most famous shop on the street, **Rongbaozhai** (⊠ 19 Liulichang Xi Jie), which sells paintings, woodblock prints, antiques, and calligraphy materials.

need a break? Old shops line the sides of Liulichang, where high-rises and fancy restaurants are juxtaposed with ancient courtyards and teahouses. You can get a bowl of noodles and a cup of tea upstairs at the **Jiguge teahouse** (⊠ 136 Liulichang Dong Jie), next to the stone pedestrian bridge. Employees lunch at the cafeteria in the **Great Hall of the People.** You won't find many English-speakers (or forks) here, but you can order good and inexpensive food (by picture) and get friendly with the locals, with whom you'll share a long table.

❹ **Mao Zedong Memorial Hall** (Maozhuxi Jiniantang). Sentries here will assure that your communion with the Great Helmsman is brief. You'll be guided into a spacious lobby dominated by a marble Mao statue and

Beijing
Subway

Subway Line 5

Subway Line 13

Fuxingmen-Bawangfen
Subway Line 2

Pingguoyuan
Subway Line 1

TO
TUQIAO →

then to the Hall of Reverence, where his embalmed body lies in state, wrapped in the red flag of the Communist Party of China inside a crystal coffin that is lowered each night into a subterranean freezer. In a bid to limit Mao's deification, a second-story museum, dedicated to the former Premier Zhou Enlai, former general Zhu De, and China's Vice Chairman before the Cultural Revolution Liu Shaoqi (whom Mao persecuted to death during the Cultural Revolution), was added in 1983. The hall's builders willfully ignored Tiananmen square's geomancy: the mausoleum faces north, boldly contradicting centuries of imperial ritual. Out back, where reverence turns to tack, hawkers still push "Maomorabilia." For Cultural Revolution souvenirs, wait until Liulichang. ⊠ *Tiananmen Sq., Chongwen District* ☎ *010/6513–2277* ☒ *Free* ☉ *Tues. and Thurs. 8:30–11:30 AM and 2–4 PM; Wed. and Fri.–Sun. 8:30 AM–11:30 AM.*

► **①** **Tiananmen Square** (Tiananmen Guangchang). The world's largest pub-
Fodor'sChoice lic square, and the heart of modern China, it owes little to the grand
★ imperial designs of the Yuan, Ming, and Qing—and everything to the successor dynasty of Mao Zedong. Turn your back on the entrance to the Forbidden City, the Gate of Heavenly Peace, and the wonders of feudalism. Looking south, across the proletarian panorama, is the Great Helmsman's tomb. The old Imperial Way once stretched south from the Forbidden City. Where photographers now hustle for customers once

A SHORT HISTORY OF BEIJING

DIFFERENT TOWNS OF VARYING SIZE and import have existed at or near the site where Beijing is now since the birth of Chinese civilization. For example, the delicious local beer, Yanjing, refers to a city–kingdom based here 3,000 years ago. With this in mind, it is not unreasonable to describe Beijing's modern history as beginning with the Jin Dynasty, approximately 800 years ago. Led by nine generations of the Jurchen tribe, the Jin Dynasty eventually fell in a war against the Mongol horde expanding their control from the north.

Under the command of the legendary warrior Genghis Khan, few armies between the Mediterranean and the East China Sea had been able to withstand the wild onslaught of the armed Mongol cavalry, the front for largest land-based empire in the history of humankind. The Jurchen tribe proved no exception, and the magnificent city of the Jin was almost completely destroyed. A few decades later in 1260, when Kublai Khan, the grandson of Genghis Khan, returned to use the city as an operational base for his conquest of southern China, reconstruction was the order of the day. By 1271, Kublai Khan had achieved his goal, declaring himself Emperor of China under the Yuan Dynasty (1271–1368), with Beijing (or Dadu, as it was then known) as its capital.

The new capital was built on a scale befitting the world's then superpower. Its palaces were founded around Zhonghai and Beihai lakes. (Actually, Beijing's Imperial Fangshan Restaurant is located on the site of the former kitchens built for Kublai Khan's palace 700 years ago.) Beijing's current layout still reflects the Mongolian design. The imperial city was protected on four sides by a fortified wall, surrounded by a moat. Within the walls, broad streets connected the main gates and city sections were by alleyways or hutong.

Like today, a limiting factor on Beijing's growth seven centuries ago was its remoteness from water. To ensure an adequate water supply, the famous hydraulic engineer, Guo Shoujing (1231–1316), designed a canal that brought water to the city from the mountains in the west. Then, to improve communications and increase trade, he designed another canal that extended east to the connect with eastern China's Great Canal.

Barely more than 100 years after the Mongolians settled Beijing, they suffered a devastating attack by rebels from the south. Originally nomadic, the Mongolians had softened with the ease of Chinese city life and were easily overwhelmed by the rebel coalition, which drove out the emperor and wrecked Beijing. Thus ended the Yuan Dynasty. The southern roots of the quickly unified Ming Dynasty (1368–1644) deprived Beijing of its capital status for a half century. But in 1405, the third Ming emperor, Yongle, began construction on a magnificent new palace in Beijing, and 16 years later, he relocated his court there. In the interim, the emperor had mobilized 200,000 corvée laborers to build his new palace, an enormous maze of interlinking halls, gates, and courtyard homes, known as the Forbidden City. To the north of the palace, the city was further embellished with the stately Bell and Drum towers. And to the south in 1553, walls were added to encompass an oblong-shape residential suburb.

The Ming also contributed mightily to China's grandest public works project: the Great Wall. The Ming Great Wall linked or reinforced several existing walls, especially near the capital, and traversed seemingly impassable mountains. Most of the most spectacular stretches of the wall that can be visited near Beijing were built by the Ming. But wall-building drained Ming coffers and in the end failed to prevent Manchu horsemen from taking the capital—and China—in 1644.

This foreign dynasty, the Qing, inherited the Ming palaces, built their own retreats (most notably, the Old and New Summer palaces), and perpetuated feudalism in China for another 267 years. In its decline, the Qing proved impotent to stop humiliating foreign encroachment. It lost the first Opium War to Great Britain in 1842 and was forced to cede Hong Kong "in perpetuity" as a result. In 1860 a combined British and French force stormed Beijing and razed the Old Summer Palace, carting away priceless antiquities.

After the Qing crumbled in 1911, its successor, Sun Yat-sen's Nationalist Party, struggled to consolidate power. Beijing became a cauldron of social activism. On May 4, 1919, students marched on Tiananmen Square to protest humiliations in Versailles, where Allied commanders negotiating an end to World War I gave Germany's extraterritorial holdings in China to Japan, not Sun's infant republic. Patriotism intensified. In 1937 Japanese imperial armies stormed across Beijing's Marco Polo Bridge to launch a brutal eight-year occupation. Civil war followed close on the heels of Tokyo's 1945 surrender and raged until the Communist victory. Chairman Mao himself declared the founding of a new nation, the People's Republic of China, from the rostrum atop the Gate of Heavenly Peace on October 1, 1949.

Like Emperor Yongle, Mao built a capital that conformed to his own vision. Soviet-inspired institutions rose up around—and in—Tiananmen Square. Beijing's city wall, the grandest rampart of its kind in China, was demolished to make way for a ring road. Temples were looted, torn down, closed, or turned into factories during the 1966–76 Cultural Revolution. In more recent years old Peking has suffered most, ironically, from prosperity. Many ancient neighborhoods, replete with traditional courtyard homes, have been bulldozed to make room for a new city of fancy apartment blocks and glitzy commercial developments. Preservationism has slowly begun to take hold, but CHAI (to pull down) and QIAN (to move elsewhere) remain common threats to denizens of Beijing's historic neighborhoods.

— Guy Rubin, George Wehrfritz, and Diana Garrett

stood quarters for the Imperial Guard and rice and wood stores for the imperial kitchen. Fires and demolition resulted in the beginnings of the square during the Republican era. The young protesters who assembled here in the 1919 May Fourth Movement established an honorable tradition of patriotic dissent.

At the square's center stands the tallest monument in China, the **Monument to the People's Heroes** (Renmin Yingxiong Jinianbei), 125 feet of granite obelisk remembering those who died for the revolutionary cause of the Chinese people. Exhortations from Chairman Mao and Premier Zhou Enlai decorate it; eight marble reliefs line the base with scenes of revolution from 1840 to 1949. Constructed from 1952 to 1958, the monument marks the formal passing of Old Peking; once, the outer palace gate of the imperial city stood here.

As you leave the terrace southward, imagine mass Soviet-style parades with 600,000 marchers. At the height of the Cultural Revolution in 1967, hundreds of thousands of Red Guards crowded the square, chanting Mao's name and waving his Little Red Book. In June 1989 the square was the scene of tragedy when hundreds of student demonstrators and bystanders were killed by troops breaking up the pro-democracy protest. Known as "six-four" or "June 4th," the movement became a weight about the Chinese government's neck in regards to human rights and freedom of speech, a traditional point of contention in modern Sino-American relations. Aside from the grand and tragic events here over the last 50 years, Tiananmen is truly a people's square, alive with local kite fliers and wide-eyed tourists from out of town. ⊠ *Bounded by Changan Jie on north and Xuanwumen Jie on south, Chongmen District.*

The Forbidden City

Fodor's Choice ★ It was from these nearly 200 acres at the heart of the Northern Capital that 24 emperors and two dynasties ruled the Middle Kingdom for more than 500 years. When it was first built, the imperial palace was named the Purple Forbidden City (Zi Jin Cheng), in reference to the North Star, which was also called the purple palace and thought to be at the center of the cosmos. Putting "purple" into the name of the imperial residence strengthened the belief that the emperor, by association with the North Star, was a divine instrument of universal power. Officially and colloquially in China the site is called the Gugong Bowuguan (the Ancient Palace Museum) or just Gugong.

In imperial times, no buildings were allowed to exceed the height of the palace walls, so the palace towered above old Peking and humbled everything in view. Moats and gigantic timber doors protected the emperor or "son of heaven." Shiny double-eaved roofs, glazed imperial yellow, marked the vast complex as the royal court's exclusive dominion. Ornate interiors displayed China's most exquisite artisanship—ceilings covered with turquoise and blue dragons, walls draped with scrolls holding priceless calligraphy or lined with intricate cloisonné screens, sandalwood thrones padded in delicate silks, floors of ceramic-fired, golden-color bricks. Miraculously, the palace survived fire, war, and imperial China's final collapse.

Equally miraculous is how quickly the Forbidden City rose. The third Ming emperor, Yongle, oversaw 200,000 laborers build the complex in just 14 years, finishing in 1420. Yongle relocated the Ming capital to Beijing to strengthen China's vulnerable northern frontier, and Ming and Qing emperors ruled from inside the palace walls until the dynastic system crumbled in 1911.

The Forbidden City embodies architectural principles first devised three millennia ago in the Shang dynasty. Each main hall faces south, and looks upon a courtyard flanked by lesser buildings. This symmetry of *taoyuan,* a series of courtyards leading to the main and final courtyard, repeats itself along a north–south axis that bisects the imperial palace. This line is visible in the form of a broad walkway paved in marble and reserved for the emperor's sedan chair. All but the sovereign—even court ministers, the empress, and favored concubines—trod on pathways and passed through doors set to either side of this Imperial Way. ☏ *010/ 6513–2215 or 010/8511–7311* ✉ *Apr.–Oct. Y60; Nov.–Mar. Y40* ⊙ *Apr.–Oct., daily 8:30–5; Nov.–Mar., daily 8:30–4:30.*

A Good Walk

Enter the Forbidden City through the **Gate of Heavenly Peace (Tiananmen)** ❽ ►, easily identified by its massive Chairman Mao portrait overlooking Tiananmen Square. Northward beyond the **Meridian Gate** ❾, where military victories were celebrated, stands the outer palace, consisting of three halls used for high public functions. You'll first reach the **Hall of Supreme Harmony** ❿, once the tallest building in China, then the **Hall of Complete Harmony** ⓫, and after this the **Hall of Preserving Harmony** ⓬. For a change from the Forbidden City's grand central halls, turn right beyond the Hall of Preserving Harmony to visit smaller peripheral palaces—once home to imperial relatives, attendants, and eunuchs, and the scene of much palace intrigue. Next comes the **Hall of Treasures** ⓭. Continue northward to Qianlong's Garden and the Pearl Concubine Well. Return via a narrow north–south passage that runs to the west of these courtyards. On the way is the **Hall of Clocks and Watches** ⓮. Walk northward from the nine-dragon carving and through the **Gate of Heavenly Purity** ⓯ to enter the **Inner Palace** ⓰, where you'll find the private rooms of some imperial families. West of the palace you'll find the entrance to the **Hall of Mental Cultivation** ⓱, where later Qing emperors lived. Heading north, you'll find the rocks, pebbles, and greenery of the **Imperial Gardens** ⓲ just beyond the Inner Palace. Past the gardens is the Forbidden City's northern gate and exit.

TIMING   The walk through main halls, best done by audio tour, takes about two hours. Allow two more hours to explore side halls and gardens.

What to See

► ❽ **Gate of Heavenly Peace** (Tiananmen). This imposing structure was the traditional rostrum for the reading of imperial edicts. The Great Helmsman himself used it to establish the People's Republic of China on October 1, 1949, and again to review millions of Red Guards during the Cultural Revolution. Ascend the gate for a dramatic vantage on Tiananmen Square. Bags must be checked prior to entry, and visitors are re-

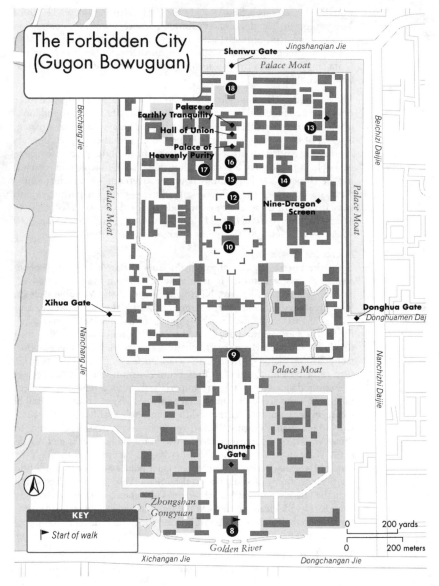

The Forbidden City (Gugon Bowuguan)

Jingshanqian Jie

Shenwu Gate

Palace Moat

Beichang Jie

Palace Moat

Palace of Earthly Tranquility

Hall of Union

Palace of Heavenly Purity

Beichizi Dajie

Palace Moat

Nine-Dragon Screen

Xihua Gate

Nanchang Jie

Donghua Gate

Donghuamen Daj

Palace Moat

Nanchizhi Dajie

Duanmen Gate

Zhongshan Gongyuan

KEY

Start of walk

Golden River

Xichangan Jie

Dongchangan Jie

0 — 200 yards
0 — 200 meters

Gate of Heavenly Peace
(Tiananmen) **8**

Gate of Heavenly
Purity (Qianqingmen) .. **15**

Hall of Clocks and
Watches
(Zhongbiaoguan) **14**

Hall of
Complete Harmony
(Zhonghedian) **11**

Hall of
Mental Cultivation
(Yangxindian) **17**

Hall of Preserving
Harmony (Baohedian) .. **12**

Hall of Supreme
Harmony (Taihedian) ... **10**

Hall of Treasures
(Zhenbaoguan) **13**

Imperial Gardens
(Yuhuayuan) **18**

Inner Palace (Nei Ting) . **16**

Meridian Gate
(Wumen) **9**

quired to pass through a metal detector. ⊠ *Changan Jie at Tiananmen Guangchang, Forbidden City* ☎ *010/6513–2255* 🎟 *Y30* ⊘ *Daily 8–4:30.*

⓯ Gate of Heavenly Purity (Qianqingmen). Even the emperor's most trusted ministers never passed beyond this gate; by tradition, they gathered outside at dawn, ready to report to their sovereign. ⊠ *Forbidden City.*

need a break? Believe it or not, there's a **Starbucks** (⊠ East of the Gate of Heavenly Purity, Forbidden City) close by! As you descend the marble stairs on the north side of the Hall of Preserving Harmony, look diagonally across the courtyard to your right. Starbucks is in the first pavilion.

⓮ Hall of Clocks and Watches (Zhongbiaoguan). Here you'll find a collection of water clocks and early mechanical timepieces from Europe and China. Clocks astride elephants, implanted in ceramic trees, borne by a herd of goats, and mounted in a pagoda are among this collection's many rewards. Don't miss the temple clock, with its robed monks. ⊠ *Forbidden City* 🎟 *Y5.*

⓫ Hall of Complete Harmony (Zhonghedian). In this more modest building emperors greeted audiences and held banquets. It housed the royal plow, with which the emperor himself would turn a furrow to commence spring planting. ⊠ *Forbidden City.*

⓱ Hall of Mental Cultivation (Yangxindian). West of the Inner Palace, running on a north–south axis, is a group of six courtyard palaces that were reserved for emperors and concubines. The Hall of Mental Cultivation is the most important of these; starting with Emperor Yongzheng, all Qing Dynasty emperors lived and attended to daily state business in this hall. It was here that the last young emperor, Puyi, declared his abdication and formally recognized the Republic of China on February 12, 1912. Those who have prepared for their trip to China by watching Bertolucci's monumental movie, *The Last Emperor,* may recognize the north–south passage outside Yangxindian where the young Puyi is portrayed riding his bicycle in the film. ⊠ *Forbidden City.*

⓬ Hall of Preserving Harmony (Baohedian). The highest civil service examinations, which were personally conducted by the emperor (who possessed superior knowledge of Chinese literature, rhetoric, and politics), were once administered in this hall. Candidates from across China were selected according to merit and, of course, family connections, and those who were successful were assured lives of wealth and power at the imperial court. Behind the hall, a 200-ton marble relief of nine dragons, the palace's most treasured stone carving, adorns the descending staircase. ⊠ *Forbidden City.*

⓾ Hall of Supreme Harmony (Taihedian). The building—used for coronations, royal birthdays, weddings, and Lunar New Year ceremonies—is fronted by a broad flagstone courtyard, the largest open area in the complex. Bronze vats, once kept brimming with water to fight fires, ring this vast expanse. The hall sits atop three stone tiers with an elaborate drainage system that channels rainwater through 1,142 carved dragons. On the top tier outside the hall, bronze cranes symbolize longevity, and an imperial sundial and grain measures invite bumper harvests. Inside, cloisonné cranes flank a massive throne beneath grand timber pillars decorated with golden dragons. Above the imperial chair hangs a heavy bronze ball—put there to crush any pretender to the throne. ☒ *Forbidden City.*

⓭ Hall of Treasures (Zhenbaoguan). Actually a series of halls, it has breathtaking examples of imperial ornamentation. The first room displays imperial candleholders, wine vessels, tea-serving sets, and—in the center—a 5-foot-tall golden pagoda commissioned by Qing emperor Qian Long in honor of his mother. A cabinet on one wall contains the 25 imperial seals, China's equivalent of the crown jewels in their embodiment of royal authority. Jade bracelets and rings, golden hair pins, and ornamental coral fill the second hall; and carved jade landscapes a third. ☒ *Forbidden City* ▭ Y5.

⓲ Imperial Gardens (Yuhuayuan). Beyond the private palaces at the Forbidden City's northern perimeter stand ancient cypress trees, stone mosaic pathways, and a rock garden. You can exit the palace at the north through the park's **Gate of Obedience and Purity** (Shenwumen). ☒ *Forbidden City.*

⓰ Inner Palace (Nei Ting). Several emperors chose to live in the Inner Palace along with their families. The **Hall of Heavenly Purity** (Qianqinggong) holds another imperial throne; the **Hall of Union** (Jiaotaidian) was the venue for the empress's annual birthday party; and the **Palace of Earthly Peace** (Kunninggong) was the empress's residence and also where royal couples consummated their marriages. ☒ *Forbidden City.*

❾ Meridian Gate (Wumen). Also known as Five Phoenix Tower (Wufenglou) because of the five towers along its unique U-shape crown, Wumen is the main, southern gate to the Imperial Palace. (Tiananmen is the gate to the Imperial City as opposed to the Palace.) Here, the emperor reviewed his armies and announced yearly planting schedules according to the lunar calendar for the coming year. Before entering, you can buy tickets to the Forbidden City and rent the accompanying Acoustiguide audio tour at the ticket office in the outer courtyard. ☒ *Forbidden City* ▭ *Y55; audio tour, Y30* ☽ *Daily 8:30–4:30.*

> **need a break?**
>
> A small snack bar, **Fast Food,** on the north end of vendors' row between the Gate of Heavenly Peace and the Meridian Gate, has instant noodles, tea, and soft drinks.

The Muslim Quarter (Xuanwu District)

Southeast of Liulichang is the lively Niu Jie (Ox Street) and its important mosque. Ethnic Hui—Han Chinese whose ancestors converted to Islam—make up most of the area's faithful. Their enclave, which occupies one of Beijing's oldest neighborhoods, has kept its traditional flavor despite ongoing urban renewal. Nearby is the extensive Buddhist Temple of the Source of Law, buried deep in a quiet hutong that houses a mixture of ancient and modern buildings.

A Good Walk

Begin at the **Ox Street Mosque** ⑲ ▶. From the mosque walk south 500 yards along Niu Jie (Ox Street) until you reach a crossroad. Turn left into **Nanheng Xi Jie** ⑳, the center of commerce in the enclave. Continue eastward for 500 yards past a derelict temple on your left and turn left into Jiaozi Hutong just before you reach the massive, five-domed, lime-green building on your left. This is the headquarters of the Chinese Islamic Association (you should spot a red flag fluttering in front of the dome). Turn right immediately into the narrow Fayuan Si Qian Jie, passing new apartments on your left and traditional courtyard houses on your right.

On the left you'll see the ancient **Source of Law Temple** ㉑, which has an outstanding collection of bronze Buddha images. Continue eastward on Fayuan Si Qian Jie until it ends at Qijing Hutong (Seven Well Alley). Turn right, cross Nanheng Xi Lu, and continue southward on Meng'er Hutong. Past a typical stretch of new high-rise apartments, you'll find **Wanshou Park** ㉒ on your right. Exit through the south gate and turn right on Baizhifang Dong Jie (White Paper Lane East). Continue westward and turn right at Youannei Dajie, which becomes Niu Jie one block north.

TIMING This walk takes about three hours, allowing for time in the mosque and the temple. Exploring alleys in this neighborhood, especially those running west from Niu Jie, is always rewarding.

What to See

⑳ **Nanheng Xi Jie** (Southern Cross Street West). Nanheng Xi Jie is filled with restaurants and shops catering to both the local Hui Muslims and newcomers from China's distant Xinjiang province. Restaurants serve Muslim dishes, including steamed meat buns, beef noodles, and a variety of baked breads; shops offer tea from across China; and street vendors sell flatbreads, fruit, and snacks. ⊠ *Nanheng Xi Jie, Xuanwu District.*

▶ ⑲ **Ox Street Mosque** (Niu Jie Qingzhen Si). Built during the Northern Song dynasty in 996, Beijing's oldest and largest mosque sits at the center of the Muslim quarter. Its exterior looks decidedly Chinese, with a traditional tile roof adorning its front gate. The freestanding wall opposite the mosque's main entrance is similarly Chinese rather than Muslim in origin. It is called a spirit wall, and was erected to prevent ghosts, who are believed not to navigate tight corners, from passing into the mosque. Today the main gate to the mosque is kept closed. Enter the mosque from the alley just to the south. Inside, arches and posts are inscribed with Koranic verse, and a Tower for Viewing the Moon allows imams to measure the beginning and end of Ramadan, Islam's month of fasting and prayer. Male visitors must wash themselves in designated bathrooms and remove their shoes before entering the main prayer hall. Women are confined to a rear prayer hall. At the rear of the complex is a minaret from which a muezzin calls the faithful to prayer. All visitors must wear long trousers or skirts and keep their shoulders covered. Women are not permitted to enter some areas. ⊠ *88 Niu Jie, Xuanwu District* ⊡ *Y10* ⊙ *Daily 8–sunset.*

㉑ Source of Law Temple (Fayuan Si). The Chinese Buddhist Theoretical Institute houses and trains monks at this temple. Theoretical institutes in China are centers for the study of Buddhist teachings; they generally function within the boundaries of current regime policy. You can observe both elderly practitioners chanting mantras in the main prayer halls at Fayuan Si, as well as robed students kicking soccer balls in a side courtyard. Before lunch the smells of vegetarian stir-fry tease the nose. The dining hall has simple wooden tables set with cloth-wrapped bowls and chopsticks. Dating from the 7th century but last rebuilt in 1442, the temple holds a fine collection of Ming and Qing statues, including a sleeping Buddha and an unusual grouping of copper-cast Buddhas seated on a thousand-petal lotus. ✉ *7 Fayuan Si Qianjie, Xuanwu District* ☎ *010/ 6303–4171 or 010/6353–4171* 🎟 *Y5* ⊙ *Thurs.–Tues. 8:30–4.*

㉒ Wanshou Park. Though smaller and more modern than Beijing's more famous parks, this one offers an attractive lawn and inviting shaded benches. Enter through the east gate and wander among the groups of old men with caged songbirds, mah-jongg (a chess-like game), and cards; roller-skating kids; croquet players; and qi gong practitioners. ✉ *Between Meng'er Hutong and Baizhifang Dong Jie, Xuanwu District* 🎟 *Y2* ⊙ *Daily 6 AM–8:30 PM.*

North & East of the Forbidden City

Historic temples, parks, and houses that once lay within the walls of imperial Beijing now provide islands of tranquillity among the busy streets of this modern downtown area, most of which lies in the Dongcheng (East City) District.

A Good Tour

Start just north of the Forbidden City at the first in a series of parks, **Jingshan Park** ㉓ ►. For a panoramic view of the Forbidden City, climb to the five pavilions on the crest of this park's artificial hill. From here you can walk through **Beihai Park** ㉔ around its lake, particularly beautiful during August's lotus season, exiting at the north gate. After crossing the road, and walking a few hundred meters west you will arrive at **Qianhai Lake** ㉕.

Continue north to **Houhai Lake** ㉖, passing the famous Ming Dynasty **Silver Ingot Bridge** ㉗. Following the lake's northern shore, you will arrive at the traditional courtyard of **Soong Ching-ling's Former Residence** ㉘, once the home of Sun Yat-sen's wife. Next, take a cab to **Prince Gong's Palace** ㉙ to see how imperial relatives lived. Walk or take a cab to the **Drum Tower** ㉚ and the nearby bell tower. Take a cab again to get to the **Museum of Antique Currency** ㉛ to see rare Chinese coins, and to the **Ditan Park** ㉜. Walk on to the **Lama Temple** ㉝, Beijing's main Tibetan Buddhist temple; then to the **Temple of Confucius** ㉞; and the neighboring **Imperial Academy** ㉟, where Confucian scholars sat imperial examinations.

TIMING If you want to do this all at once, it will take you a full day. The neighborhood is ideal for bike exploration.

A Good Bike Ride

A great way to explore Old Peking is by bicycle. The ride between Ditan Park and Coal Hill includes some of the city's most famous sights and finest hutong. Begin at **Ditan Park** ㉜, just north of the Second Ring Road on Yonghegong Jie. Park your bike in the lot outside the south gate and take a quick walk. Next, ride south along Yonghegong Jie until you come to the main entrance of **Lama Temple** ㉝. Running west, across the street from the temple's main gate, is Guozijian Jie (Imperial Academy Street). Shops near the intersection sell Buddhist statues, incense, texts (in Chinese), and tapes of traditional Chinese Buddhist music. Browse them before riding west to **Temple of Confucius** ㉞ and the neighboring **Imperial Academy** ㉟. The arches spanning Guozijian Jie are the only ones of their kind remaining in Beijing.

Follow Guozijian Jie west until it empties onto Andingmennei Dajie. Enter this busy road with care (there's no traffic signal) and ride south to Guloudong Dajie, another major thoroughfare. Turn right (west) and ride to the **Drum Tower** ㉚. From here detour through the alleys just north to the Zhonglou. A market of tiny noodle stalls and restaurants links the two landmarks. Retrace your route south to Di'anmenwai Dajie (the road running south from the Drum Tower), turning onto Yandai Jie, the first lane on the right. Makers of long-stem pipes once lined the lane's narrow way (one small pipe shop still does). Sadly, much of the area is slated for redevelopment.

Wind northwest on Yandai Jie past guest houses, bicycle repair shops, tiny restaurants, and crumbling traditional courtyard houses toward Houhai Park. Turn left onto Xiaoqiaoli Hutong and pass the arched **Silver Ingot Bridge** ㉗, which separates **Houhai** ㉖ and **Qianhai** ㉕ lakes. Before the bridge, follow the trail along Houhai's north shore, traveling west toward **Soong Ching-ling's Former Residence** ㉘. Circle the lake until you arrive at Deshengmennei Dajie. Follow it south to the second alley, turning east (left) onto Yangfang Hutong, which leads back to the arched bridge. Park your bike in the first alley off Yangfang Hutong, Dongming Hutong, and walk toward the lake. At the footpath and market that hugs its banks, turn left and walk about 100 yards to find a tiny lane lined with antiques and curio shops.

After bargain hunting, ride along Yangfang Hutong past the stone bridge and follow Qianhai Lake's west bank. Sip a soda, beer, or tea at the teahouse pavilion on the lake. Continue along the lane to Qianhai Xi Jie, then fork right (northwest) just after a restaurant sign bearing a large heart. Nearby, but difficult to find, is **Prince Gong's Palace** ㉙, 300 yards north of the China Conservatory of Music. Look for the brass plaque.

TIMING   Allow a half day for this ride, longer if you expect to linger at the sights or explore the parks on foot.

What to See

★ ㉔ **Beihai Park** (North Lake Park). Immediately north of Zhongnanhai, the tightly guarded residential compound of China's senior leaders, the park is easily recognized by the white Tibetan pagoda perched on a nearby hill. Near the south gate is the **Round City** (Tuan Cheng). It contains a white-jade Buddha, said to have been sent from Burma to Qing emperor Qian Long, and an enormous jade bowl given to Kublai Khan. Nearby, the well-restored **Temple of Eternal Peace** (Yongan Si) contains a variety of Buddhas and other sacred images. Climb to the pagoda from Yongan Temple. Once there, you can pay an extra Y1 to ascend the Buddha-bedecked **Shangyin Hall** for a view into forbidden Zhongnanhai.

The lake is Beijing's largest and most beautiful public waterway. Amusement park rides line its east edge, and kiosks stock assorted snacks. On summer weekends the lake teems with paddle boats. The **Five Dragon Pavilion** (Wu Long Ting), on Beihai's northwest shore, was built in 1602 by a Ming dynasty emperor who liked to fish and view the moon. The halls north of it were added later. Among the restaurants in the park is **Fangshan,** an elegant establishment open since the Qing dynasty. ⊠ *South Gate, Weijin Lu, Xicheng District* ☎ *010/6404–0610* ⬟ *Y10; extra fees for some sights* ☉ *Daily 9–dusk.*

㉜ Ditan Park (Temple of Earth Park). In the 16th-century park are the square altar where emperors once made sacrifices to the earth god and the Hall of Deities. ⊠ *Yonghegong Jie, just north of Second Ring Rd., Dongcheng District* ☎ *010/6421–4657* ⬟ *Y2* ☉ *Daily 6–6:30.*

★ ㉚ Drum Tower (Gulou). Until the late 1920s the 24 drums once housed in this tower were Beijing's timepiece. Sadly, all but one of these huge drums have been destroyed, and the survivor is in serious need of renovation. Kublai Khan built the first drum tower on this site in 1272. You can climb to the top of the present tower, which dates from the Ming dynasty. Old photos of Beijing's hutong line the walls beyond the drum; there's also a scale model of a traditional courtyard house. The nearby **Bell Tower** (Zhonglou), renovated after a fire in 1747, offers worthwhile views from the top of a long, narrow staircase. The huge 63-ton bronze bell, supported by lacquered wood stanchions, is also worth seeing. ☎ *010/ 6404–1710* ⊠ *North end of Dianmen Dajie, Dongcheng District* ⬟ *Y20* ☉ *Daily 9–4:30.*

㉟ Imperial Academy (Guozijian). Once the highest educational institution in China, this academy was established in 1306 as a rigorous training ground for high-level government officials. It was notorious, especially during the early Ming Dynasty era, for the harsh discipline imposed on scholars perfecting their knowledge of the Confucian classics. ⊠ *Guozijian Lu next to Temple of Confucius, Dongcheng District* ☎ *010/ 6406–2418* ⬟ *Y6* ☉ *Daily 9–5.*

▶ ㉓ Jingshan Park (Prospect Hill Park). This park was built around Coal Hill (Meishan), a small peak formed from earth excavated for the Forbidden City's moats. The hill was named for an imperial coal supply supposedly buried beneath it. Climb a winding stone staircase past peach and apple trees to Wanchun Pavilion, the park's highest point. It overlooks the Forbidden City to the south and the Bell and Drum towers to the north. Chongzhen, the last Ming emperor, is said to have hanged himself on Coal Hill as his dynasty collapsed in 1644. ⊠ *Jingshanqian Dajie at Forbidden City, Dongcheng District* ☎ *010/6404–4071 or 010/6403–2244* ⬟ *Y2* ☉ *Daily 6:30 AM–8 PM.*

③③ Lama Temple (Yonghegong). This Tibetan Buddhist temple is Beijing's most
Fodor'sChoice visited religious site. Its five main halls and numerous galleries are hung
★ with finely detailed *thangkhas* (painted cloth scrolls) and decorated with
carved or cast Buddha images—all guarded by young lamas (monks). Originally a palace for Prince Yongzheng, it was transformed into a temple
after he became the Qing's third emperor in 1723. The temple flourished
under Yongzheng's successor, Emperor Qianlong, housing some 500 resident monks. Unlike most "feudal" sites in Beijing, the Lama Temple survived the 1966–76 Cultural Revolution unscathed.

You'll walk past trinket stands with clattering wind chimes to reach the
temple's five main halls. The Hall of Heavenly Kings has statues of
Maitreya, the future Buddha, and Weitou, China's guardian of Buddhism.
In the courtyard beyond, a pond with a bronze mandala represents a
Buddhist paradise. In the Hall of Harmony sit Buddhas of the Past, Present,
and Future. Note the exquisite silk thangkha of White Tara—the embodiment of compassion—hanging from the west wall. The Hall of Eternal Blessing contains images of the Medicine and Longevity Buddhas.
Beyond, courtyard galleries display numerous statues depicting Tibetan
deities and dharma guardians, some passionately entwined.

A large statue of Tsong Khapa (1357–1419), founder of the Gelug order,
sits in the Hall of the Wheel of Law. Resident monks practice here on
low benches and cushions. A rare sand mandala is preserved under
glass on the west side of the building. The temple's tallest building,
the **Pavilion of Ten Thousand Fortunes** (Wanfuge), houses a breathtaking 85-foot Maitreya Buddha carved from a single sandalwood block.
White-and-gold blessing scarves drape the statue, which wears a massive string of prayer beads. English-speaking guides are available at
the temple entrance. ⊠ *12 Yonghegong Dajie, Beixingqiao, Dongcheng
District* ☎ *010/6404–3769 or 010/6404–4499* ⊠ *Y25* ☉ *Daily 9–4
or 4:30.*

③① Museum of Antique Currency (Gudai Qianbi Zhanlanguan). This museum in a tiny courtyard house showcases a small but impressive selection of rare Chinese coins. Explanations are in Chinese only. Also
in the courtyard are coin and curio dealers. ⊠ *Deshengmen Tower south
bldgs., Bei'erhuan Jie, Xicheng District* ☎ *010/6201–8073* ⊠ *Y10*
☉ *Tues.–Sun. 9–4.*

②⑨ Prince Gong's Palace (Gongwangfu). This grand compound sits in a
neighborhood once reserved for imperial relatives. Built during the
Ming dynasty, it fell to Prince Gong, brother of Qing emperor Xianfeng
and later an adviser to Empress Dowager Cixi. With nine courtyards
joined by covered walkways, it was once one of Beijing's most lavish
residences. The largest hall, now a banquet room, offers summer Peking
opera and afternoon tea to guests on guided hutong tours. Some literary scholars believe this was the setting of the *Dream of the Red Chamber,* China's best-known classic novel. ⊠ *Xicheng District* ☎ *010/
6618–0573* ⊠ *Y20* ☉ *Daily 8:30–4:30.*

★ **②⑤–②⑥ Qianhai and Houhai Lakes.** These lakes, along with Xihai Lake in the
northwest, were together known as *Shichahai,* the Scattered Temples

Lake, in reference to the many temples scattered around this historic quarter. Most people come here to stroll casually around the lakes and enjoy the bars and restaurants that perch on their shores. In summer you can boat, swim, fish, and even, on occasion, windsurf on the lakes. In winter sections of the frozen surfaces are fenced off for ice hockey and casual skating. ⊠ *North side of Dianmen Xi Lu, north of Beihai Lake, Xicheng District.*

need a break?

Along **Lotus Lane,** which lines the west side of Qianhai Lake, you'll find several traditional pavilions housing trendy coffeehouses, including **Starbucks,** and juice bars, like **Kosmo.** A few doors down, the restaurant **South Silk Road** is a great place to rest your wearied legs and get a bite to eat.

㉗ Silver Ingot Bridge (Yin Ding Qiao). This Ming Dynasty bridge was named for its shape, which is said to resemble a silver ingot turned upside down. Along with the Old Wanning Bridge and the Gold Ingot Bridge, it divides the three rear lakes north of Beihai Park known as Qianhai (Front Lake), Houhai (Rear Lake), and Xihai (Western Lake). These three lakes together are called Shichahai, which means "Lake of the Ten Temples," after the nine monasteries and a nunnery that once graced the lakes' banks. ⊠ *Xicheng District.*

㉘ Soong Ching-ling's Former Residence (Song Qing Ling Guju). Soong Ching-ling (1893–1981) was the youngest daughter of the wealthy, American-educated bible publisher, Charles Soong. At the age of eighteen, disregarding her family's strong opposition to the union, she eloped to marry the much older Sun Yat-sen, a then friend of the family. When her husband founded the Republic of China in 1911, Soong Ching-ling became a nationally significant political figure. As early as 1924 she headed the Women's Department of the Nationalist Party. Then in 1949 she became the Vice-President of the People's Republic of China as well as Honorary President of the All-China Women's Federation. Throughout her career she campaigned tirelessly for the emancipation of women. Indeed, the rights of modern-day Chinese women owe a great deal to her participation in the Communist revolution. Though she was hailed a key supporter of the revolution, Soong Ching-ling never actually joined the Communist Party. This former palace was her residence and work place. Even after her death, the Soong Ching-ling Foundation continues to work for her causes. A small museum documents her eventful life and work. Exhibits are labeled in English as well as Chinese. ⊠ *46 Houhai Beiyan, Xicheng District* ☎ *010/6403–5997 or 010/6404–4205* ☞ *Y20* ☺ *Tues.–Sun. 9–4:30.*

★ ㉞ Temple of Confucius (Kong Miao). This austere temple to China's great sage has endured close to eight centuries of additions and restorations. Stelae and ancient musical instruments are the temple's main attractions. The Great Accomplishment Hall houses Confucius's funeral tablet and shrine, flanked by copper-color statues depicting China's wisest Confucian scholars. A selection of unique musical instruments are played only on the sage's birthday. A forest of stone stelae, carved in the mid-

1700s to record the *Thirteen Classics,* philosophical works attributed to Confucius, lines the west side of the grounds. ✉ *Guozijian Lu at Yunghegong Lu near Lama Temple, Dongcheng District* ☎ *010/ 8401–1977* 💲 *Y10* 🕐 *Daily 8:30–5.*

The Observatory & the Temple of Heaven

Once among the city's largest structures, these ancient sites, now dwarfed by overpasses and skyscrapers, illustrate the importance of astronomy and astrology to the imperial household. The Temple of Heaven, which rivals the Great Wall as the best-known symbol of Beijing, and the busy park surrounding the temple should not be missed. (The temple and the observatory are actually in different districts, though quite close to one another.)

A Good Tour

Start at the **Ancient Observatory** ㊱ ▶, where the wide central avenue—called Jiangguonen Dajie here—meets the eastern leg of the Second Ring Road. From the observatory take a taxi, following the Second Ring Road south and then west to Chongwenmenwai Dajie and turning south to Tiantandong Lu and west on Yongdingmen Dajie to the south gate of the **Temple of Heaven** ㊲, one of the most important historic sites in Beijing.

TIMING   Allow three hours for this tour. Weekends or early mornings are better if you want to see Tiantan Park at its best (consider reversing the tour). This is when you will see people enjoying ballroom dancing, qi gong, martial arts, chess, Peking opera, calligraphy, badminton, traditional Yang Ge dancing, and many other activities.

What to See

▶ ㊱   **Ancient Observatory** (Guguanxiangtai). To China's imperial rulers, interpreting the heavens was the better part of keeping power. Celestial phenomena like eclipses and comets were believed to portend change; if left unheeded they might cost an emperor his legitimacy—or Mandate of Heaven. The observatory dates back to the time of Genghis Khan, who believed that his fortunes could be read in the stars. This belief was not new to the Chinese: from laypeople to the emperor, celestial changes played a big part in everyday and political life. In feudal China, the emperor was revered as someone sent from heaven who received order from the supreme ruler there. Heavenly beings were not to be offended; paying attention to celestial changes was one way of safeguarding one's position and power.

The instruments in this ancient observatory, established in 1442 atop the city wall's **Jianguo Gate,** were among an emperor's most valuable possessions. Many of the bronze devices on display were gifts from Jesuit missionaries who arrived in Beijing in 1601 and shortly thereafter ensconced themselves as the Ming court's resident stargazers. Rare documents and a replica of a Ming dynasty star map are on display inside. ✉ *2 Dongbiaobei Hutong, Jianguomenwai Dajie, Chaoyang District* ☎ *010/6524–2202* 💲 *Y10* 🕐 *Mon.–Sun. 9–4.*

CloseUp

IMPERIAL SACRIFICES

TO UNDERSTAND THE SIGNIFICANCE of the harvest sacrifice at the Temple of Heaven, it is important to keep in mind that the legitimacy of a Chinese emperor's rule depended on what is known as the *tian ming*, or mandate of heaven, essentially the emperor's relationship with the Gods. A succession of bad harvests, for example, could be interpreted as the emperor losing the favor of Heaven and could be used to justify a change in emperor or even in dynasty.

Hence, when the emperor came to the Temple of Heaven to pray for good harvests and to pay homage to his ancestors, there may have been a good measure of self-interest to his fervor. The sacrifices consisted mainly of animals and fruit placed on altars surrounded by lighted candles. Many Chinese still make sacrifices on special occasions, such as births, deaths, and weddings.

— Guy Rubin

---

③⑦
Fodor'sChoice
★

Temple of Heaven (Tiantan). Ming emperor Yongle built the Temple of Heaven, one of Beijing's grand attractions, as a site for imperial sacrifices, which were conducted twice a year, on the 15th day of the first lunar month (in either January or February) and on the winter solstice.

The temple grounds, double the size of the Forbidden City, were designed in strict accordance with numerology and feng shui. The four gates mark the four points on the compass. The park is semicircular on the north end and square on the south—the curve corresponding to heaven's supposed shape, the square to earth's. Audio guides can be rented just inside the south gate for a small fee.

Beyond the south gate rests the **Round Altar** (Huanqiutan), a three-tiered prayer platform. Nearby, the **Imperial Vault of Heaven** (Huangqiong Yu), a round temple that housed tablets commemorating the ancestors of the emperors, is surrounded by the **Echo Wall** (Huiyinbi), where a whisper supposedly can be heard across the courtyard's 213-foot expanse. On the courtyard's step are three echo stones able to rebound hand claps. Extreme quiet is needed to hear the effect.

A raised walkway, the **Red Stairway Bridge** (Danbi Qiao), leads northward to the **Hall of Prayer for Good Harvests** (Qiniandian), the temple's hallmark structure. This magnificent blue-roofed wooden tower, originally built in 1420, burned to the ground in 1889 and was immediately rebuilt using Ming architectural methods (and timber imported from Oregon). The building's design is based on the calendar: four center pillars represent the seasons, the next 12 pillars represent months, and 12 outer pillars signify the parts of a day. Together these 28 poles, which correspond to the 28 constellations of Heaven, support the structure without nails. A carved dragon swirling down from the ceiling represents the emperor, or "son of heaven."

The **Hall of Abstinence** (Zhaigong), on the western edge of the grounds, is not of particular interest. But for Y1 you can climb the bell tower and ring the bell for good luck. Its chimes once served notice that the emperor approached to worship or had completed the rites and would depart. ✉ *Yongdingmen Dajie (South Gate), Chongwen District* ☎ *010/ 6702–2617 or 010/6702–8866* ✉ *Y10; extra Y20 for individual halls; Y30 for audio guide* ☉ *Daily 8–4:30.*

Western Beijing

Western Beijing, a vast industrial suburb, was once the domain of monks, nuns, and imperial hunting parties. Beijing's oldest temples dot the forested hills just west of the city. The Qing-era summer palace is the city's grandest park.

Two Good Tours

DAY 1 This full-day tour takes you to some of Beijing's finest temples and gardens, ending with the majesty of the summer palaces. Hire a car plus driver for a full day, starting from **White Clouds Taoist Temple** ㊳ ▶, noted for its tranquil courtyards and rare statuary. Next, head north to the **Lu Xun House and Museum** ㊴, where exhibits document the life and work of one of China's most famous 20th-century writers. Close to the museum is the restored **Temple of the White Pagoda** ㊵, named after its 700-year-old Tibetan-style white stupa.

Head northwest out of the city as far as **Summer Palace** ㊶, set amid one of China's finest man-made landscapes, complete with lakes, bridges, hills, pavilions, gardens, temples, courtyards, and a Qing shopping street. Nearby the **Old Summer Palace** ㊷, which once outshone its newer rival, offers quieter walks among splendid ruins. Don't miss the two summer palaces even if you have to skip other sights.

DAY 2 If you have another day, there are several more places of interest on this side of town. Start at the 16th-century **Temple of Longevity** ㊸ on Xisanhuan Bei Lu, slightly north of Zizhuyuan Lu. Continuing through the northwest suburbs, you reach the open spaces of **Xiangshan Park** ㊹ (Fragrant Hills Park). Here, at the base of Xiangshan peak, you can admire the famous sculptures of arhats inside the **Temple of Azure Clouds** ㊺. Across the road from the park, within the Beijing Botanical Garden, lies another: the **Temple of the Sleeping Buddha** ㊻, home to a giant reclining Buddha. A short drive east brings you to the **Big Bell Temple** ㊼. Head back south to visit the Indian-style **Five-Pagoda Temple** ㊽. The Big Bell and Five Pagoda temples are two of the capital's ancient seats of Buddhism. The latter abuts a park, on the other side of which you'll find the **Beijing Exhibition Hall** planetarium.

Heading south on Xisanhuan Bei Lu you pass the **Central Radio and Television Tower** ㊾, and then cutting back west you reach the **Treasure House Museum** ㊿.

TIMING There are so many sights in Western Beijing, that you really need two days to take it all in. If you have only one, make the two summer palaces a priority. Both suggested tours will take the better part of a day, so it's best to get an early start. Make arrangements with your hotel to hire the car and driver in advance.

What to See

> **off the beaten path**

BEIJING EXHIBITION HALL (Beijing Zhanlan Guan) – During the past four decades, hundreds of foreign and Chinese commercial exhibitions have been held here. The impressive if slightly grubby planetarium is a favored field-trip destination for Beijing area students. Programs change frequently. Call in advance to check schedules and reserve seats. ⊠ *138 Xizhimenwai Dajie, at Beijing Zoo, Xicheng District* ☎ *010/6831–2517* ☎ *Y12 per show* ⊙ *Daily 9–5.*

47 **Big Bell Temple** (Dazhong Si). The two-story bell here is cast with the texts of more than 100 Buddhist scriptures. Believed to date from Emperor Yongle's reign, the 46-ton relic is considered a national treasure. The temple also houses the **Ancient Bell Museum** (Guzhong Bowuguan), a collection of bells from various dynasties and styles. ⊠ *1A Beisanhuanxi Lu, Haidian District* ☎ *010/6255–0843* ☎ *Y10* ⊙ *Daily 8:30–4:30.*

49 **Central Radio and Television Tower** (Zhongyang Dianshita). On a clear day this needlelike tower offers an awe-inspiring perspective on eastern Beijing and beyond. An outdoor viewing platform hangs 1,325 feet above the ground. Elevators take visitors there first, then down a few floors to an indoor deck where drinks and snacks are served. Another two levels down is a Chinese restaurant with simple set meals. This tower rests on the foundation of the **Altar of the Moon,** a Ming dynasty sacrificial temple. ⊠ *11 Xisanhuanzhong Lu, Haidian District* ☎ *010/6845–0715* ☎ *Y50* ⊙ *Daily 8:30 AM–10 PM.*

48 **Five-Pagoda Temple** (Wuta Si). Hidden behind trees and set amid carved stones, the temple's five pagodas reveal obvious Indian influences. Indeed, the Five-Pagoda Temple was built during the Yongle Years of the Ming Dynasty (1403–1424), in honor of an Indian Buddhist who came to China and presented a temple blueprint to the emperor. Elaborate carvings of curvaceous female figures, floral patterns, birds, and hundreds of Buddhas decorate the pagodas. Also on the grounds is the **Beijing Art Museum of Stone Carvings** (Beijing Shike Yishu Bowuguan), with its collection of some 1,000 stelae and stone carvings. ⊠ *24 Wuta Si, Baishiqiao, Haidian District* ☎ *010/6217–3836* ☎ *Y2.5 includes admission to museum and pagodas* ⊙ *Daily 8:30–4:30.*

39 **Lu Xun House and Museum** (Lu Xun Bowuguan). Lu Xun, one of China's most celebrated modern writers, lived here in the 1920s. His best-known works are *Diary of a Madman* and *The True Story of Ah Q.* In the small courtyard garden, he wrote novels and short stories that typically depict the plight of poor, uneducated people in prerevolutionary China. The rooms around the courtyard display documents and artifacts relating to Lu Xun's life and literature. ⊠ *Fuchenmennei Dajie, next to Baita Si, Xicheng District* ☎ *010/6615–6549* ☎ *Y5* ⊙ *Tues.–Sun. 9–4.*

★ ㊷ **Old Summer Palace** (Yuanmingyuan). Once a grand collection of palaces, this complex was the emperor's summer retreat from the 15th century to 1860, when it was looted and systematically blown up by British and French soldiers. The Western-style buildings—patterned after Versailles in France—were added during the Qing dynasty and designed by Jesuits. Catholic missionaries carried the gospel into China in 1583 and settled in Guangdong Province (it was on their map that Chinese intellectuals saw their country's position in the world for the first time). In 1597 the missionary Matteo Ricci was appointed director of Jesuit activities in China, and in 1601 he finally achieved his goal of being admitted to Beijing, the capital.

Beijing has chosen to preserve the vast ruin as a "monument to China's national humiliation." Beijing students take frequent field trips to the site and (encouraged by their teachers, no doubt) scrawl patriotic slogans on the rubble. A large lake, ideal for summer boating or winter ice-skating, is in the center of the grounds. ✉ *Qinghuan Xi Lu, Haidian District* ☎ *010/6255–1488 or 010/6254–3673* 🖃 *Park, Y10; extra 15Y fee for sites* ☉ *Daily 7–7.*

㊶ **Summer Palace** (Yiheyuan). This expansive, parklike imperial retreat
Fodor'sChoice dates from 1153, midway through the Jin Dynasty. Shortly thereafter,
★ under the Yuan Dynasty, engineers channeled in spring water to create a series of man-made lakes. It was not until the Qing that the Summer Palace took on its present form. In 1750 Emperor Qianlong commissioned the retreat for his mother's 60th birthday. Construction of palaces, pavilions, bridges, and numerous covered pathways on the shores of Kunming Lake continued for 15 years. The resort suffered heavy damage when Anglo-French forces plundered, then burned, many of the palaces in 1860. Renovation commenced in 1888 using funds diverted from China's naval budget. Empress Dowager Cixi retired to the Summer Palace in 1889, and nine years later, after the failure of his reform movement, imprisoned her nephew, Emperor Guangxu, on the palace grounds, reclaiming control of the government. Four years later, in 1903, she moved the seat of government from the Forbidden City to Yiheyuan from which she controlled China until her death in 1908.

Enter the palace grounds through the **East Palace Gate** (Donggongmen). Inside, a grand courtyard leads to the **Hall of Benevolent Longevity** (Renshoudian), where Cixi held court. Just beyond, next to the lake, the **Hall of Jade Ripples** (Yulantang) was where Cixi kept the hapless Guangxu under guard while she ran China in his name. Cixi's own residence, the **Hall of Joyful Longevity** (Leshoutang), sits just to the north and affords a fine view of Kunming Lake. The residence is furnished and decorated as Cixi left it. Cixi's private **theater,** just east of the hall, was constructed for her 60th birthday at a cost of 700,000 taels of silver. The **Long Corridor** skirts Kunming Lake's northern shoreline for 2,388 feet until it reaches the **marble boat,** an elaborate two-deck pavilion built of finely carved stone and stained glass. Above the Long Corridor on **Longevity Hill** (Wanshou Shan), intersecting pathways lead to numerous pavilions and several Buddhist prayer halls. Below, Kunming Lake extends southward for 3 km (2 mi), ringed by tree-lined dikes, arched stone bridges, and numerous gazebos. In summer you can explore the lake by paddleboat (inexpensive rentals are available at several spots along the shore). In winter, walk—or skate—on the ice. Although the palace area along Kunming Lake's north shore is usually crowded, the less-traveled southern shore near Humpbacked Bridge is an ideal picnic spot. ⊠ *Yiheyuan Lu and Kunminghu Lu, Haidian District, 12 km (7½ mi) northwest of downtown Beijing* ☎ *010/6288–1144* ✆ *Y30 additional fees at some exhibits* ⊙ *Apr.–Oct., daily 6:30* AM*–6* PM, *Nov.–Mar., daily 7* AM*–5* PM.

㊺ Temple of Azure Clouds (Biyun Si). Once the home of a Yuan dynasty official, the site was converted into a Buddhist temple in 1366 and enlarged during the 16th and 17th centuries by imperial eunuchs who hoped to be buried here. The temple's five main courtyards ascend a slope in ⇨ **Xiangshan Gongyuan** (Fragrant Hills Park). Although severely damaged during the Cultural Revolution, the complex has been attentively restored.

The main attraction is the Indian-influenced Vajra Throne Pagoda. Lining its walls and five pagodas are gracefully carved stone-relief Buddhas and bodhisattvas. The pagoda once housed the remains of Nationalist China's founding father, Dr. Sun Yat-sen, who lay in state here between March and May 1925, while his mausoleum was being constructed in Nanjing. A hall in one of the temple's western courtyards houses about 500 life-size wood and gilt arhats—each sitting or standing in a glass case. ⊠ *Xiangshan Park, Haidian District* ☎ *010/6259–1155* ✆ *Park Y5; temple Y10* ⊙ *Mar.–June and Sept.–Oct., daily 6:30* AM*–7* PM; *Nov.–Feb and July–Aug, daily 6:30* AM*–6:30* PM.

㊸ Temple of Longevity (Wanshou Si). A Ming empress built this temple to honor her son in 1578. Qing emperor Qianlong later restored it as a birthday present to his mother. From then until the fall of the Qing, it served as a rest stop for imperial processions traveling by boat to the Summer Palace and Western Hills. Today Wanshou Temple is managed by the Beijing Art Museum and houses a small but exquisite collection of Buddha images. The Buddhas in the main halls include Sakyamuni sitting on a thousand-petal, thousand-Buddha bronze throne and dusty Ming-period Buddhas. ⊠ *Xisanhuan Lu, on the north side of Zizhuqiao Bridge, Haidian District* ☎ *010/6841–3380 or 010/6841–9391* ✆ *Y20* ⊙ *Tues.–Sun. 9–4.*

㊻ Temple of the Sleeping Buddha (Wofo Si). Although the temple was damaged during the Cultural Revolution and poorly renovated afterward, the Sleeping Buddha remains. Built in 627–629, during the Tang Dynasty, the temple was later named after the reclining Buddha that was brought in during the Yuan Dynasty (1271–1368). An English-language description explains that the casting of the beautiful bronze, in 1321, enslaved 7,000 people. The temple is inside the **Beijing Botanical Gardens**; stroll north from the entrance through the neatly manicured grounds. ⊠ *Xiangshan Lu, 2 km (1 mi) northeast of Xiangshan Park, Haidian District* ✆ *Temple Y5; gardens Y5* ⊙ *Daily 8:30–4.*

40 Temple of the White Pagoda (Baita Si). This 13th-century Tibetan stupa, the largest of its kind in China, dates from Kublai Khan's reign and owes its beauty to a Nepalese architect (name lost to history) who built it to honor Sakyamuni Buddha. Once hidden within the structure were Buddha statues, sacred texts, and other holy relics. Many of the statues are now on display in glass cases in the **Miaoying** temple, at the foot of the stupa. English-language captions on the displays, and explanations of the temples' history and renovations, add to the pleasure of visiting this site. A local qi gong association also runs a traditional clinic on the premises. ⊠ *Fuchenmennei Dajie near Zhaodengyu Lu; turn right at first alley east of stupa, Xicheng District* ☎ *010/6616–6099* 🚇 *Y10* ⊙ *Daily 9–4:30.*

50 Treasure House Museum (Zhenbaoguan). Ceramics, stone carvings, lacquerware, and other traditional craft items are on display in this small museum run by the China National Art and Craft Museum. The museum is on the fifth floor of the Parkson department store. A shopping area outside the exhibition hall sells quality reproductions of priceless antiques. ⊠ *101 Fuxingmennei Dajie, Xuanwu District* ☎ *010/ 6607–3677* 🚇 *Y8* ⊙ *Daily 9:30–4.*

▶ **38 White Clouds Taoist Temple** (Baiyunguan). This Taoist temple serves as a center for China's only indigenous religion. Monks wearing blue-cotton coats and black-satin hats roam the grounds in silence. Thirty of them now live at the monastery, which also houses the official All-China Taoist Association. Visitors bow and burn incense to their favorite deities, wander the back gardens in search of a qi gong master, or rub the bellies of the temple's three monkey statues for good fortune.

In the first courtyard, under the span of an arched bridge, hang two large brass bells. Ringing them with a well-tossed coin is said to bring wealth. In the main courtyards, the **Shrine Hall for Seven Perfect Beings** (Laolu Tang) is lined with meditation cushions and low desks. Nearby is a museum of Taoist history (explanations in Chinese). In the western courtyard, the temple's oldest structure is a shrine housing the **60-Year Protector** (Liushi Huajiazi). Here the faithful locate the deity that corresponds to their birth year, bow to it, and light incense, then scribble their names, or even a poem, on the wooden statue's red cloth cloak as a reminder of their dedication. A trinket stall in the front courtyard sells pictures of each protector deity. Also in the west courtyard is a shrine to Taoist sage Wen Ceng, depicted in a 10-foot-tall bronze statue just outside the shrine's main entrance. Students flock here to rub Wen Ceng's belly for good fortune on their college entrance exams. ⊠ *Lianhuachidong Lu near Xibianmen Bridge, Xuanwu District* 🚇 *Y5* ⊙ *Daily 9–4:30.*

44 Xiangshan Park (Fragrant Hills Park). This hillside park west of Beijing was once an imperial retreat and hunting ground. From the eastern gate you can hike to the summit on a trail dotted with shady pavilions and small temples. If you're short on time, ride a cable car to the top. Avoid weekends to avoid the crowds. ⊠ *Haidian District, northwestern Beijing suburbs near Sanjiadian* ☎ *010/6259–1155* 🚇 *Y5; cable car, Y50* ⊙ *Daily 6–6.*

WHERE TO EAT

China's economic boom has revolutionized dining in Beijing. Gone are shabby state-run restaurants, driven out of business (or into the care of new management) by private establishments that cater to China's emerging middle class. You can now enjoy a hearty Cantonese or Sichuan meal for under $5 per person—or spend $100 or more on a lavish imperial-style banquet. One popular restaurant has commandeered a former palace, while dumpling shops offer dining under the stars in restored courtyard homes. Hamburgers (or sushi, lasagna, and burritos) are available at numerous new eateries that target tourists, expatriates, and Chinese yuppies. While beer is available everywhere in Beijing, wine is usually only available in Western-style restaurants. It is not customary to tip in restaurants (or anywhere else for that matter) in Beijing, and casual attire is acceptable in most restaurants.

WHAT IT COSTS In Yuan				
	$$$$	$$$	$$	$	¢
AT DINNER	over Y180	Y121–Y180	Y81–Y120	Y40–Y80	under Y40

Prices are for a main course.

Dongcheng (East City)

The Dongcheng District flanks the Forbidden City to the east.

Chinese

$$$$ ✕ **Huang Ting.** The courtyards of Beijing's traditional noble houses, which are fast facing extinction as entire neighborhoods are demolished to make way for new high-rises, are the theme of Huang Ting. The beautifully decorated walls are constructed from original *hutong* (alleyway) bricks taken from centuries-old courtyard-houses that were destroyed. The pine floorboards and beams are from a large mansion in Suzhou. Huang Ting is also arguably Beijing's best Cantonese restaurant, serving southern favorites like braised shark fin with crab meat; steamed abalone and chicken diced with egg-white cake; and pan-fried cod flavored with yellow tea leaves. Other specialities include sautéed prawns in Sichuan chili sauce, and delicious Peking Duck brought out on a trolley and sliced by a chef. ✉ *Palace Hotel, 8 Jinyu Hutong, Wangfujing, Dongcheng District* ☎ *010/6512–8899 Ext. 6707* 🚍 *AE, MC, V.*

$$$–$$$$ ✕ **Red Capital Club.** Occupying a meticulously restored courtyard home
Fodor$Choice in one of Beijing's few remaining traditional Chinese neighborhoods,
★ the Red Capital Club oozes nostalgia. Cultural Revolution memorabilia and books dating from the Great Leap Forward era (1958–60) adorn every nook. The fancifully written menu reads like an imperial fairy tale, with the names of dishes to match—the South of Clouds is a Yunnan dish of fish baked over a bamboo basket, and Dream of the Red Chamber is a fantastic vegetarian dish cooked according to a recipe in the classic novel by the same name. ✉ *66 Dongsi Jiutiao,*

Dongcheng District ☎ *010/6402–7150* ♨ *Reservations essential* ▤ *AE, DC, MC, V* ⊘ *No lunch.*

$$–$$$ ✕ **Afunti.** Beijing's largest and best-known Xinjiang Muslim restaurant has become a popular and boisterous dinner-show venue. Uzbek musicians and belly dancers entertain you, and later encourage you to dance on your table! Afunti offers a variety of Xinjiang kebabs, hotpot, baked flat bread, and handmade noodles. ✉ *166 Chaonei Dajie, Dongcheng District* ☎ *010/6525–1071* ♨ *Reservations essential* ▤ *AE, V* ⊘ *No lunch.*

★ **$$** ✕ **Li Qun Roast Duck Restaurant.** If you prefer to stay away from the crowds and commercialism of Quanjude (Beijing's most famous Peking duck restaurant), try this small, casual, family-run restaurant near Qianmen. Juicy, delicious whole ducks roasting in a traditional oven greet you as you enter the simple courtyard house. Li Qun is a good option for the more adventurous at heart, as the restaurant is hidden deep in a hutong neighborhood. It should take you about 10 minutes to walk there, though you may have to stop to ask for directions. The restrooms and dining room are a bit shabby, but the restaurant on the whole is cozy and charming. A menu in English is available. ✉ *11 Beixiangfeng, Zhengyi Lu, Dongcheng District, northeast of Qianmen* ☎ *010/6705–5578* ♨ *Reservations essential* ▤ *No credit cards.*

$ ✕ **Lao Hanzi.** If you're in the mood for something other than the ubiquitous home-style Beijing or Sichuan fare, try Hakka cuisine. Specialties like *sanbei* (smoked) duck, *yanju* (salt-coated) shrimp, and *zhao* fish (baked in aluminum foil) are served at this casual restaurant, which stands in good company among the many watering holes around Houhai Lake. If you're coming in a group, be sure to book one of the private rooms on the second floor with beautiful views over the lake. ✉ *Shichahai Dongan, Houhai, Dongcheng District, across the street from the north gate of Beihai Park* ☎ *010/6404–2259* ▤ *No credit cards.*

¢–$ ✕ **Si He Xuan.** For homestyle snacks such as dumplings, congee, noodles, and steamed buns, try this cheerful, informal restaurant in the Jinglun Hotel. Wooden gateways separating the dining rooms, and bird cages hanging above the doorways, give it an old Beijing feel. Open until 2 AM, it's also a great place to satisfy the late-night munchies. ✉ *Jinglun Hotel, 4th floor, 3 Jianguomenwai Dajie, Dongcheng District* ☎ *010/6500–2266 Ext 8116* ♨ *Reservations not accepted* ▤ *AE, MC, V.*

¢ ✕ **Goubuli Baozi Pu.** Juicy *baozi* (steamed dumplings) are the specialty of this traditional eatery in a very busy district of Beijing directly north of Tiananmen and Jingshan Park. No trip to China is complete without trying the *goubuli baozi*—dog-doesn't-even-want-to-bother dumpling—filled with meat and scallions and a unique sauce. ✉ *155 Di'anmenwai Dajie, Dongcheng District, north of Jingshan Park* ☎ *010/6404–3097* ♨ *Reservations not accepted* ▤ *No credit cards.*

Contemporary

$$$–$$$$ ✕ **The Courtyard.** Beijing's most elegant and upscale restaurant, the Courtyard has its own celebrity chef and an amazing view of the east gate of the Forbidden City. The cuisine showcases a creative fusion of Chinese and Continental styles. You might find steamed sea bass with

Fodor'sChoice
★

Fodor'sChoice
★

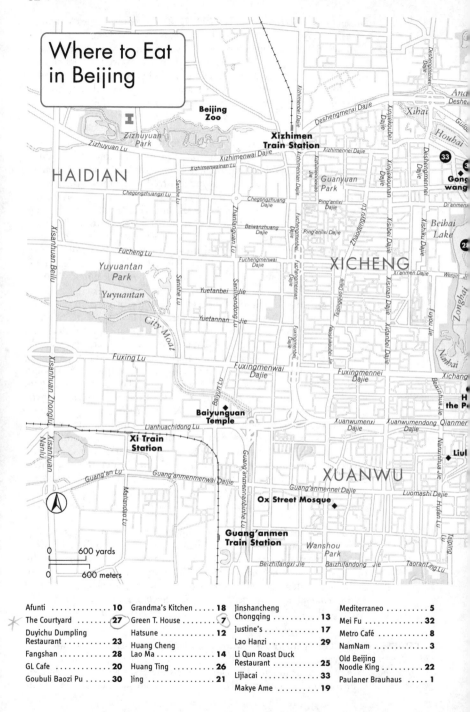

Where to Eat in Beijing

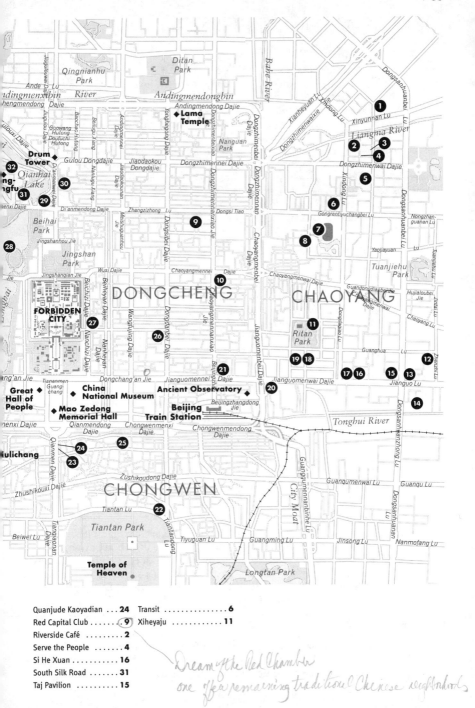

Dream of the Red Chamber
one of a few remaining traditional Chinese neighborhoods

ON THE MENU IN BEIJING

Peking duck is the most famous dish of the capital, though it is normally available only in specialist or larger restaurants. Imperial-style banquets offer a contrast to staples like noodles and jiaozi (meat- and vegetable-filled dumplings). New eateries offer regional delights like spicy Sichuan tofu, Cantonese dim sum, Shanghainese steamed fish, Xinjiang kebab—even Tibetan yak penis soup. A slew of fast-food outlets—both Chinese versions and the global franchises—have also taken root.

Against all this competition from inside and outside China, traditional-style Beijing dining is making a comeback. Waiters whisk dishes through crowded, lively restaurants furnished with wooden menu boards and lacquered square tables, while doormen, dressed (like the waiters) in traditional cotton jackets, loudly announce each arrival and departure.

pickled bell pepper; jumbo shrimp with lemongrass-caramel glacé; and grilled lamb tenderloin with ratatouille. Come here to get away from Beijing's crowded streets, treat yourself to a nice bottle of wine, and perhaps sample a cigar from the cigar den on the second floor. Don't miss the tiny but cutting-edge art gallery in the basement. ⊠ *95 Donghuamen Dajie, Dongcheng District* ☎ *010/6526–8883* ⌖ *Reservations essential* ⊟ *AE, DC, MC, V* ⊘ *No lunch.*

$$$–$$$$ ✕ **Jing.** Rated one of the 75 Hottest Tables in the World by *Condé Nast Traveler* in 2003, Jing offers up east-west fusion cuisine in a sleek and ultramodern atmosphere. Signature dishes include the scrumptious duck rolls, the tiger prawns, and the fragrant coconut soup as appetizers; and the fillet of barramundi, and risotto with seared langoustines, as main courses. For dessert, do not miss the mouth-watering warm chocolate cake with almond ice cream. Jing also offers an excellent selection of fine wines from around the world by the glass—a rarity in Beijing. ⊠ *Palace Hotel, 8 Jinyu Hutong, Wangfujing, Dongcheng District* ☎ *010/6523–0175 Ext 6714* ⊟ *AE, DC, MC, V.*

French

$$$–$$$$ ✕ **Justine's.** Classic French cuisine and wine, including foie gras, snails, and Chateau Haut-Brion, are served with the utmost attention at Beijing's best and oldest French restaurant. Justine's also has delicious desserts and tip-top service. Treat yourself to a satisfying brunch here on Sunday. ⊠ *Jianguo Hotel, 5 Jianguomenwai Dajie, Dongcheng District* ☎ *010/6500–2233 Ext 8039* ⊟ *AE, MC, V.*

Chaoyang

The Chaoyang District stretches east from Dongcheng and encompasses Beijing's diplomatic neighborhood, the Sanlitun bar area, and several outdoor markets and upscale shopping malls.

American

$–$$ ✕ **Grandma's Kitchen.** Run by a real American grandma, this is definitely the most authentic American restaurant in Beijing. The country-style checked tablecloths and pastel-colored walls, along with a friendly English-speaking waitstaff, attracts homesick American expats, who indulge in blueberry pancakes, Philly cheesesteak sandwiches, hamburgers with fries, and the best cheesecake in Beijing. ⊠ *11A Xiushui Nan Jie, Jianguomenwai, Chaoyang District* ☎ *010/6503–2893* ▭ *No credit cards.*

Chinese

$$$–$$$$ ✕ **Green T. House.** Owned by Beijing's "Queen of Style," Jin R., this cutFodor'sChoice ting-edge restaurant rivals any you'd find in New York, Paris, or Lon-
  ★ don. Minimalist and industrial, yet oh-so-elegant, the Green T. is frequented by Beijing's growing population of young nouveaux riches. Dishes are painstakingly prepared and presented, but portions are dainty, so don't come here too hungry or be prepared to order a lot. The restaurant calls its cuisine neo-classical Chinese, and it's anything but standard Chinese fare—you might have caviar with rose petals, green-tea dumplings, and thin slices of beef or veal covered with black sesame seeds. Tea drinkers should sample one (or more) of the tantalizing teas. ⊠ *6 Gongti Xi Lu, Sanlitun, Chaoyang District* ☎ *010/6552–8310* ⌢ *Reservations essential* ▭ *AE, MC, V.*

$–$$$ ✕ **Huang Cheng Lao Ma.** If you are visiting Beijing in winter, eating hotpot is a must. Of Beijing's many hotpot restaurants, Huang Cheng Lao Ma serves the freshest of these popular stews with the widest variety of ingredients, and it has a large, clean, bright, and cheery dining room to boot. Hotpot entails cooking your own raw food in boiling (and spicy!) broths in the center of the table, then dipping them in your choice of sauce before finally putting the tasty morsels in your mouth. ⊠ *39 Nanqingfengzha Houjie Dabeiyao, Chaoyang District (south of China World)* ☎ *010/6779–8801* ▭ *No credit cards.*

¢–$ ✕ **GL Cafe.** Open 24 hours, this popular Hong Kong–style restaurant is fast-paced, slick, and bright. It's a good choice for a quick meal or snack anytime of the day. Stick with the Chinese menu—you might try the soy chicken, roast duck, fried noodles, or congee with fish—and steer clear of the Western menu unless you enjoy the generally bland Hong Kong interpretations of Western food. ⊠ *21 Jianguomenwai Dajie, Chaoyang District* ☎ *010/6532–8282* ⌢ *Reservations not accepted* ▭ *No credit cards.*

Continental

$–$$$ ✕ **Riverside Café.** The owners of Riverside, a friendly Australian couple, have successfully combined a formal restaurant upstairs and a deli, café, and wine shop downstairs. The café offers the best and freshest selection of bread in Beijing, not to mention some of the city's best desserts—try the cheesecake or lemon tart. In summer, the outdoor verandah is a nice place to have a leisurely lunch. ⊠ *10 Sanlitun Beixiaojie, Chaoyang District* ☎ *010/6466–1241* ▭ *AE, MC, V.*

German

$$ ✕ **Paulaner Brauhaus.** Traditional German food is served up in heaping portions at this spacious and bright restaurant in the Kempinski Hotel. Wash it all down with delicious Bavarian beer made right in the restaurant—try the Maibock served up in genuine German steins. In summer, you can enjoy your meal outdoors in the beer garden. ⊠ *Kempinski Hotel, 50 Liangmaqiao Lu, Chaoyang District* ☎ *010/ 6465–3388* ▤ *AE, MC, V.*

Italian

$$$ ✕ **Mediterraneo.** Summer or winter, this restaurant manages to pack in a full house most nights of the week. Fresh Italian-Mediterranean food served in large portions, a decent wine list, good service, and a convenient location on the north end of the Bar Street undoubtedly make up its winning combination. This is also one of the few places in Beijing where you can get a good salad. To start, try the baby-spinach salad with bacon or the warm tomato tart, followed by the slightly sweet pumpkin ravioli or the fresh red snapper pan-fried with rosemary. In summer there is a large outdoor seating area. ⊠ *1A Sanlitun Bei Jie, Building 8, Chaoyang District* ☎ *010/6415–3691* ▤ *AE, MC, V.*

$$$ ✕ **Metro Café.** This informal restaurant offers a good assortment of fresh Italian pastas. You can start with soup and bruschetta, and meat eaters can choose from chicken or beef entrées. Although service is inconsistent, the food is usually very good, and the outdoor tables are wonderful (if you can get one) on mild evenings. ⊠ *6 Gongrentiyuguan Xi Lu, Chaoyang District* ☎ *010/6501–3377 Ext. 7706* ▤ *AE, V* ⊘ *Closed Mon.*

Indian

$–$$$ ✕ **Taj Pavilion.** Beijing's best Indian restaurant, Taj Pavilion serves up all the classics, including chicken tikka masala, *palak panir* (creamy spinach with cheese), and *rogan josht* (tender lamb in curry sauce). Consistently good service and an informal but slightly upscale atmosphere add to the pleasant dining experience. ⊠ *China World Trade Center, L-1 28 West Wing, 1 Jianguomenwai Dajie, Chaoyang District* ☎ *010/6505–5866* ▤ *AE, MC, V.*

Japanese

$$–$$$$ ✕ **Hatsune.** Owned by a Chinese-American with impeccable taste, this is hands down the best Japanese restaurant in Beijing. The food is delicious and authentic, the interior design is ultra-modern and interesting, and the service is friendly. Try the fresh sashimi, tempura, grilled fish, or one of the many innovative sushi rolls. There's also an extensive sake menu. Hatsune is usually packed for lunch and dinner, so be sure to make a reservation. ⊠ *8 Guanghua Dong Lu, Heqiao Dasha, Building C, second floor, Chaoyang District* ☎ *010/6581–3939* ▤ *AE, MC, V.*

Sichuan

$–$$$ ✕ **Jinshancheng Chongqing.** As Beijing's largest and most popular Sichuan restaurant, this place is always crowded so come prepared to wait in line unless you arrive by 6 PM. When you do finally get seated, you might order the *laziji* (chicken buried under a mound of hot peppers), *ganbian sijidou* (green beans), and *mapou doufu* (spicy tofu). All three are delicious, and even people unaccustomed to spicy food claim to love these dishes. The food is definitely the focus here—don't expect much by way of decor. ⊠ *Zhongfu Mansion, second floor, 99 Jianguo Lu, Chaoyang District, across from the China World Trade Center* ☎ *010/6581–1598* ⚑ *Reservations not accepted* ▭ *No credit cards.*

$–$$$ ✕ **Xiheyaju.** In Beijing's embassy neighborhood, this restaurant is a favorite of diplomats and journalists, many of whom live and work in the surrounding area. The pleasant outdoor courtyard is a perfect choice on a sunny spring day. The standard Sichuan fare includes *ganbian sijidou* (stir-fried green beans), *mapou doufu* (hot bean curd), and *kungpao jiding* (chicken with peanuts). ⊠ *Northeast corner of Ritan Park, Chaoyang District* ☎ *010/8561–7643* ▭ *AE, MC, V.*

$ ✕ **Transit.** This little hideaway is a lovely retreat, both quiet and intimate. Come with a date, or book the private room for a small group of friends. The kitchen serves refined versions of fiery Sichuan classics. Traditional-style wooden furniture is complemented by bright, modern murals. This is a good place to unwind and have a long, leisurely dinner followed by a round (or two) of drinks. To get here, go down the alley across the street from the north gate of Worker's Stadium, turn right at the first intersection, and continue about 10 yards. The restaurant is on your left. ⊠ *1 Xingfu Yicun, Sanlitun, Chaoyang District* ☎ *010/ 6417–6765* ▭ *No credit cards.*

Thai

$–$$ ✕ **Serve the People.** Though it's the favorite of Thais living in Beijing, don't come to this restaurant expecting the kind of light, fresh Thai you'd find in Thailand. The food served here is definitely more of the Chinese–Thai variation. Still, almost everything is tasty. Try the duck salad, pomelo salad, green curry, or one of the many hot-and-spicy soups. ⊠ *1 Xiwujie, Sanlitun, Chaoyang District, across the street from the Spanish embassy* ☎ *010/8454–4580* ▭ *AE, MC, V.*

Tibetan

$ ✕ **Makye Ame.** Tibetan arts and handicrafts decorate this colorful restaurant, and the kitchen serves a range of hearty dishes well beyond the Tibetan staples of yak-butter tea and *tsampa* (barley flour mixed with water and sometimes yak butter to form a dough which is then eaten raw). Try the vegetable *pakoda* (a deep-fried dough pocket filled with vegetables) or the braised beef topped with yak cheese. Heavy wooden tables, dim lighting, and Tibetan textiles make this an especially cozy choice on a chilly winter evening. ⊠ *11 Xiushui Nan Jie, 2nd floor, Chaoyang District* ☎ *010/6506–9616* ▭ *No credit cards.*

Vietnamese

$–$$ ✕ **NamNam.** A sweeping staircase to the second floor, a tiny indoor fish pond, wooden floors, and posters from old Vietnam set the scene in this atmospheric restaurant. The light and delicious cuisine is matched by the speedy service. Try the chicken salad, beef noodle soup, or the raw or deep-fried vegetable or meat spring rolls. The portions are on the small side though, so order plenty. Finish off your meal with a real Vietnamese coffee prepared with a slow-dripping filter and accompanied by sweetened condensed milk. ⊠ *7 Sanlitun Jie, Sanlitun, Chaoyang District* ☎ *010/6468–6053* ⊟ *AE, MC, V.*

Xicheng

The Xicheng District extends west and north of the Forbidden City, and includes Beihai Lake.

Chinese

$$$$ ✕ **Lijiacai** (Li Family Restaurant). The restaurant's imperial dishes are prepared and served by members of the Li family in a cozy, informal atmosphere. Li Li established the restaurant in 1985 (after flunking her college entrance exams), using recipes handed down from her great-grandfather, once a steward for the Qing court. The tiny eatery was once in such demand that you had to book a table weeks in advance. Since Beijing's restaurant scene blossomed, however, offering diners many other tantalizing choices, it's been much easier to get into. ⊠ *11 Yangfang Hutong, Denei Dajie, Xicheng District* ☎*010/6618–0107* ⚑*Reservations essential* ⊟ *No credit cards.*

$$$$
Fodor'sChoice
★
✕ **Mei Fu.** In a lavish, restored courtyard on the south bank of Houhai Lake, Mei Fu offers an intimate and elegant dining experience. The interior is decorated with antique wooden furniture and velvet curtains, set off by pebbled hallways and little waterfalls. On the walls hang black-and-white photos of Mei Fang, China's most famous Peking opera star. Diners choose from set menus, starting from Y200 per person, that feature dishes typical of Shanghainese cuisine, such as fried shrimp, pineapple salad, and tender leafy green vegetables. ⊠ *24 Daxiangfeng Hutong, south bank of Houhai Lake, Xicheng District* ☎ *010/6612–6845* ⚑ *Reservations essential* ⊟ *MC, V.*

$$$–$$$$ ✕ **Fangshan.** In a traditional courtyard villa on the shore of Beihai Lake you can sample China's imperial cuisine. Established in 1925 by three royal chefs, Fangshan serves dishes once prepared for Qing emperors based on recipes garnered from across China. Fangshan is best known for its filled pastries and steamed breads—traditional snack foods developed to satisfy Empress Dowager Cixi's sweet tooth. To experience Fangshan's exquisite imperial fare, order one of the banquet-style set meals. Be sure to make reservations two or three days in advance. ⊠ *Beihai Park, north of the Forbidden City, Xicheng District, (enter through east gate, cross stone bridge, and bear right)* ☎ *010/6401–1879* ⚑ *Reservations essential* ⊟ *AE, DC, MC, V.*

$–$$$ ✕ **South Silk Road.** China is an immense country populated with literally hundreds of ethnic minorities that have little in common with the Han majority. If you're curious about the cuisine from a minority group, consider a meal at this trendy restaurant, which serves food from Yunnan province, China's southernmost province bordering Thailand and Laos. Yunnan is home to many of China's minorities as well as a distinctive type of cuisine that you'd be hard pressed to find outside of China. Typical (and delicious) Yunnan specialties include smoked ham, wild mushrooms, and goat cheese. A tasty homemade rice wine is the perfect accompaniment. The two-story glass restaurant, owned by artist Fang

Lijun, has plenty of outdoor seating and excellent views over the lake. ✉ *19A Lotus La., Shichahai, Xicheng District* ☎ *010/6615–5515* ▤ *No credit cards.*

Chongwen

The Chongwen District lies to the southeast of the Forbidden City, south of Dongcheng.

Chinese

$$$ ✕ **Quanjude Kaoyadian.** This establishment has served succulent Peking duck since 1852 and is far and away China's most famous Peking duck restaurant. Nationalized after the 1949 Communist Revolution, it since has opened several branches across Beijing, each more glitzy and commercial than the last. Every branch serves the same traditional feast: cold duck tongue, sautéed webs, sliced livers, and gizzards to start; a main course of roast duck, to be dipped in plum sauce and wrapped with spring onion in a thin pancake; and duck soup to finish. There are several Quanjude branches around the city, with the palatial seven-story Da Ya (Big Duck) the largest with 40 dining rooms seating up to 2,000 people. *Big Duck* ✉ *14 Qianmen Xi Dajie, Chongwen District* ☎ *010/6301–8833* ▤ *AE, DC, MC, V.*

¢   ✕ **Duyichu Dumpling Restaurant.** History has it that this Shandong-style dumpling house won fame when Qing emperor Qianlong stopped in on his way back to the Forbidden City after a rural inspection tour. A plaque hanging on the wall, supposedly in Qianlong's own hand, attests to the restaurant's flavorful fare. Today the Duyichu's large, raucous dining hall is decidedly proletarian. But the dumplings and assorted Shandong dishes still command applause. Expect to wait for a seat during the dinner rush. Customers share large round tables. ✉ *36 Qianmen Dajie, Chongwen District* ☎ *010/6511–2093 or 010/6511–2094* ⌨ *Reservations not accepted* ▤ *No credit cards.*

¢   ✕ **Old Beijing Noodle King.** Close to the Temple of Heaven and Hongqiao Pearl market, this restaurant serves traditional-style fast food in a lively Old Peking atmosphere. Waiters shout across the room to announce customers arriving or leaving. Try the tasty noodles, usually eaten with a thick sesame- and soy-based sauce. Look for the decorative rickshaws parked outside. ✉ *29 Chongwenmen Dajie, Chongwen District, west side of Chongwenmen, north of Temple of Heaven east gate* ☎ *010/ 6705–6705* ⌨ *Reservations not accepted* ▤ *No credit cards.*

WHERE TO STAY

China's 1949 Communist victory closed the doors on the opulent accommodations once available to visiting foreigners in Beijing and elsewhere. Functional concrete boxes served the needs of the few "fellow travelers" admitted into the People's Republic of China in the 1950s and '60s. By the late '70s China's lack of high-quality hotels had become a distinct embarrassment, and opening the market to foreign investment was the only answer.

Two decades later a multitude of polished marble palaces awaits your dollars with attentive service, improved amenities—such as conference centers, health clubs, and nightclubs—and rising prices. Glitz and Western comfort, rather than history and character, are the main selling points for Beijing's hotels. Some traditional courtyard houses have been converted into small hotels—a quiet alternative to the Western-style establishments. Courtyard hotels usually have a more distinct Chinese character, but those in older buildings may be lacking in the range and standard of facilities. They are often managed by entrepreneurs who bought the courtyard houses from people who once lived there. Given that fewer and fewer old courtyards exist in China, courtyard hotels are often favored by savvy travelers who go to China for its history. Because of the smaller number of rooms in courtyard hotels, reservations are important.

If you're looking for Chinese-style accommodations with gardens and rockeries, consider the Lusongyuan, Haoyuan, Bamboo Garden, and Red Capital Residence guest houses.

As traffic conditions worsen, more business travelers are choosing hotels closer to their interests. However, the more distant hotels, such as the Lido, Friendship, Shangri-La, and Fragrant Hills, do offer shuttle-bus service into the city center. Most hotels will also book restaurants, day tours, taxis, cars with drivers, and travel tickets. Booking rooms in advance is always recommended, but the current glut of accommodations means room availability is rarely a problem, whatever the season.

WHAT IT COSTS In Yuan				
$$$$	**$$$**	**$$**	**$**	**¢**
FOR 2 PEOPLE	over Y1800	Y1401–Y1800	Y1101–Y1400	Y700–Y1100	under Y700

Prices are for two people in a standard double room in high season, excluding 10%–15% service charge.

Dongcheng (East City)

The Dongcheng District lies east and north of the Forbidden City and incorporates the city's most important historical sites and temples. The hotels off Dongchang'an Jie and Wangfujing Dajie are within walking distance of Tiananmen Square.

Contemporary Hotels

★ $$$–$$$$ 📺 **Grand Hotel.** Standing on the north side of Chang'an Avenue is this luxury hotel whose roof terrace overlooks Beijing's Forbidden City. A former imperial palace, the Grand blends the traditions of China's past with modern comforts and technology. The Red Wall Café, Ming Yuan dining room, Rong Yuan Restaurant, and Old Peking Grill provide a range of cuisines, from Chinese to European. The third floor has a spectacular atrium decorated in marble with Chinese art and antiques. There's a shopping arcade and a fully equipped spa. Even if you don't stay here, try to make it to the rooftop terrace for sunset drinks overlooking the yellow roofs of the Forbidden City. ✉ *35 Dongchang'an Jie, Dongcheng District, 100006* ☎ *010/6513–7788* 🖷 *010/6513–0048*

⊕ *www.grandhotelbeijing.com* ↩ *217 rooms, 40 suites* ♿ *6 restaurants, in-room data ports, in-room fax, in-room safes, cable TV, pool, health club, sauna, spa, bicycles, shops, Internet, business services, meeting rooms, car rental* ▭ *AE, DC, MC, V.*

$$$ ▣ **Grand Hyatt Beijing.** The impressive Grand Hyatt Beijing, open since
Fodor'sChoice 2001, is the centerpiece of Oriental Plaza, a mammoth mall and office
★ complex that dominates Chang'an Avenue. Rooms and suites are dec-
orated in muted tones: beige carpets and curtains, cherry-color wood
furnishings, and brown upholstery. The hotel has an Olympic-size swim-
ming pool—the largest in Beijing—surrounded by lush, jungle-like veg-
etation, waterfalls, statues, and comfortable teak chairs and tables.
Over the pool, a "virtual sky" ceiling imitates different weather patterns.
The chic Redmoon lounge and restaurant includes a wine bar, a sushi
bar, and a cigar bar. The Hyatt is within walking distance of Tianan-
men Square and the Forbidden City. ✉ *1 Dongchang'an Jie, Dongcheng
District, 100738, corner of Wangfujing* ☎ *010/8518–1234* 🖷 *010/
8518–0000* ⊕ *www.beijing.grand.hyatt.com* ↩ *480 rooms, 102 suites*
♿ *7 restaurants, in-room data ports, cable TV, indoor pool, health
club, sauna, spa, steam room, bar, shops, Internet, business services, con-
ference center, airport shuttle, no-smoking floors* ▭ *AE, DC, MC, V.*

$$$ ▣ **Peninsula Palace.** The Peninsula Palace Hotel (Beijing Wangfu Fan-
Fodor'sChoice dian) is a beautiful combination of ultramodern facilities and traditional
★ Asian luxury. A waterfall cascades down through the spacious lobby,
which is decorated with Chinese antiques. The hotel is in the center of
Beijing's business and commercial districts about 10 minutes' walk
from the Forbidden City. Rooms have hardwood floors and area rugs,
high-quality wood and upholstered furnishings, and 42-inch, flat-screen
TVs. A custom bedside control panel lets you adjust the lights, temperature,
television, and radio. In the Peninsula arcade you'll find designer stores,
including Chanel, Jean Paul Gaultier, and Tiffany & Co. ✉ *8 Dong-
danbeidajie, Jinyu Hutong, Dongcheng District, 100006* ☎ *010/
6559–2888* 🖷 *010/6512–9050* ⊕ *www.beijing.peninsula.com* ↩ *420
rooms, 41 suites* ♿ *2 restaurants, room service, snack bar, in-room
data ports, some in-room fax machines, in-room safes, minibars, cable
TV, tennis court, indoor pool, hair salon, health club, massage, sauna,
steam room, bar, lobby lounge, shops, laundry service, business services,
conference center, travel services* ▭ *AE, DC, MC, V* ⦿ *BP.*

$$ ▣ **Beijing Hotel.** The forerunner of them all, the Beijing Hotel is the cap-
ital's oldest, born in 1900 as the Hotel de Pekin. Within sight of Tianan-
men Square, it has housed countless foreign delegations, missions, and
friends of China, such as Field Marshal Montgomery from Britain and
the American writer Edgar Snow. Room 1735 still bears a sign indicating
where China's longtime premier Zhou Enlai stayed and worked. The
central section retains its old-fashioned splendor. The west wing—now
the Grand Hotel—was added in 1955 and the east wing in 1974. ✉ *33
Dongchang'an Jie, off Wangfujing Dajie, Dongcheng District, 100004*
☎ *010/6513–7766* 🖷 *010/6513–7307* ⊕ *www.cbw.com/hotel/beijing*
↩ *800 rooms, 100 suites* ♿ *5 restaurants, room service, in-room data
ports, minibars, cable TV, indoor pool, gym, sauna, bar, Internet, busi-
ness services, meeting rooms* ▭ *AE, DC, MC, V.*

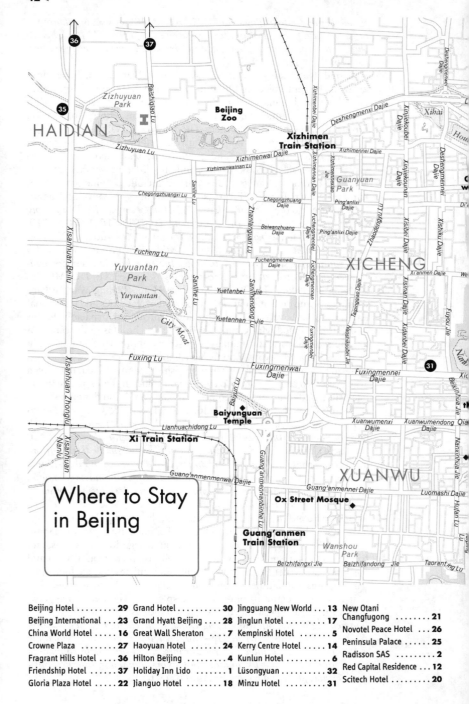

Where to Stay in Beijing

$ ⊞ **Beijing International.** This white monolith, built in the mid-1980s, symbolized the takeoff of China's tourist industry. The modern hotel rooms and good service attract a lot of tour groups. Opposite the old train station, it's only a few minutes' ride from Tiananmen Square. ⊠ 9 *Jianguomennei Dajie, off Wangfujing Dajie, Dongcheng District, 100005* ☎ *010/6512–6688* 🖶 *010/6512–9961* ⌨ *1,008 rooms, 42 suites* ⑤ *2 restaurants, cable TV, pool, gym, massage, sauna, steam room, bowling, bar, shops, business center, Internet, shops, snack bar* ▤ *AE, DC, MC, V.*

$ ⊞ **Crowne Plaza.** A big, contemporary cube, the Crowne Plaza offers some of the best amenities of any downtown hotel. The second floor has an art gallery and a salon, from which Western classical and traditional Chinese music pours forth every evening into the nine-story atrium. The rooms are not large, but they're equipped with the latest facilities, including coffeemakers, hair dryers, and irons; plus they're stocked with two bottles of water daily. The location, near the Wangfujing shopping area, 10 minutes' walk from the Forbidden City, and 15 minutes' walk from Tiananmen Square, is unbeatable. ⊠ *48 Wangfujing Dajie, Dongfeng District, 100006* ☎ *010/6513–3388* 🖶 *010/6513–2513* ⊕ *www.ichotelsgroup.com* ⌨ *332 rooms, 27 suites* ⑤ *2 restaurants, room service, in-room data ports, minibars, cable TV, indoor pool, gym, hair salon, gym, sauna, bicycles, bar, shops, baby-sitting, laundry service, business services, free parking, travel services, no-smoking rooms* ▤ *AE, DC, MC, V.*

$ ⊞ **Novotel Peace Hotel.** Twenty-two stories of tinted-glass windows tower over everything surrounding this hotel. Naturally, rooms have floor-to-ceiling windows with views of the city. The hotel is in downtown Wangfujing, opposite the Palace Hotel, and within walking distance of plenty of shops and restaurants, as well as Tiananmen Square. Although service is fairly basic, the hotel offers good value for the location. For dinner, you might try one of the three Chinese restaurants, or Le Cabernet, a French-style brasserie. ⊠ *3 Jinyu Hutong, Wangfujing Dajie, Dongcheng District, 100004* ☎ *010/6512–8833* 🖶 *010/6512–6863* ⊕ *www.accorhotels-asia.com* ⌨ *304 rooms, 33 suites* ⑤ *2 restaurants, room service, minibars, cable TV, indoor pool, gym, hair salon, sauna, bicycles, 2 bars, dance club, laundry service, concierge, Internet, business services, car rental, parking (fee), no-smoking rooms* ▤ *AE, DC, MC, V.*

Traditional Hotels

$$–$$$
Fodor'sChoice
★
⊞ **Red Capital Residence.** Beijing's first luxury boutique hotel is in a carefully restored, traditional Chinese courtyard in Dongsi, a historic preservation district. Five small rooms are differently decorated with original period antiques. The Residence also has a cigar lounge where you can sit on original furnishings used by China's early revolutionary leaders, as well as a wine bar in a Cultural Revolution–era bomb shelter. Special arrangements can also be made for guests to tour Beijing at night in Madame Mao's Red Flag limousine. A second hotel, the Red Capital Ranch, which bills itself as an eco-resort and includes a spa, opened near the Great Wall in the summer of 2004. ⊠ *9 Dongsi Liutiao, Dongcheng District 100007* ☎ *010/ 6402–7150* 🖶 *010/6402–7153*

⊕ *www.redcapitalclub.com.cn* ↪ *5 rooms* ♢ *Cable TV, bar, laundry service* ⊟ *AE, DC, MC, V* ⊙| *CP.*

¢ 🖭 **Haoyuan Hotel.** Tucked away in a hutong near Wangfujing and the Palace Hotel, the tiny Haoyuan has rooms surrounding two courtyards. Try to book one of the larger, more expensive rooms in the tranquil and very pleasant back courtyard, where you can sit under the date trees and listen to the evening chorus of cicadas in the summer. The hotel's small restaurant serves good traditional dishes. ⊠ *53 Shijia Hutong, Dongsinan Dajie, Dongcheng District, 100010* ☎ *010/6512–5557* 🖷 *010/6525–3179* ↪ *17 rooms* ♢ *Restaurant* ⊟ *No credit cards.*

¢ 🖭 **Lüsongyuan.** In 1980 China Youth Travel Service set up this delight-
Fodor'sChoice ful courtyard hotel on the site of an old Qing Mandarin's residence, a
★ few lanes south of the Youhao Guesthouse. The traditional wooden entrance is guarded by two *menshi* (stone lions). Inside are five courtyards, decorated with pavilions, rockeries, and plants. Rooms are elegant, with large window panels. Though it calls itself an International Youth Hostel, the hotel has no self-service cooking facilities; but it is cheap and has a great Chinese restaurant. ⊠ *22 Banchang Hutong, Kuanjie, Dongcheng District, 100009* ☎ *010/6401–1116* 🖷 *010/6403–0418* ↪ *38 rooms* ♢ *Restaurant, bar* ⊟ *No credit cards.*

¢ 🖭 **Youhao Guesthouse.** Behind a high gray wall with a wrought-iron gate, deep in hutong land near the Drum Tower, the Youhao (Friendly) Guesthouse forms a small part of the large traditional compound where Nationalist leader Chiang Kai-shek once stayed. Rooms are basic in the two-story guest house, but have a view of either the spacious front courtyard or the back garden where there are trees, flowers, and Chinese-style corridors. The main building is used for karaoke, but other pleasures remain, such as a Roman-style folly and rockery gates. Beijing's first Japanese restaurant is located here. Though dozens of Japanese restaurants can now be found in Beijing, this is still a good choice for a quiet meal. ⊠ *7 Houyuanensi, Jiaodaokou, Dongcheng District, 100009* ☎ *010/6403–1114* 🖷 *010/6401–4603* ↪ *30 rooms* ♢ *2 restaurants* ⊟ *No credit cards.*

★ ¢ 🖭 **Zhuyuan Hotel** (Bamboo Garden Hotel). This charming small hotel was converted from the residence of Sheng Xuanhuai, a high-ranking Qing official, and later, of Mao's henchman Kang Sheng, who lived here after the 1949 Revolution. A powerful and sinister character, responsible for "public security" during the Cultural Revolution, Kang nevertheless had fine taste in art and antiques. The Bamboo Garden cannot compete on comfort and facilities with the high-rise crowd, but its lovely courtyards and gardens bursting with bamboo make it a genuine treasure. ⊠ *24 Xiaoshiqiao Hutong, Jiugulou Dajie, Dongcheng District, 100009* ☎ *010/6403–2229* 🖷 *010/6401–2633* ↪ *40 rooms, 1 suite* ♢ *Restaurant, hair salon, sauna, bicycles, bar* ⊟ *AE, DC, MC, V.*

Chaoyang

The Chaoyang District extends east of Dongcheng and includes Sanlitun, Beijing's main nightlife area, plus some of the city's best shopping malls and markets. The hotels in this urban district are nearly all modern high-rises and mid-rises.

$$$$ Fodor'sChoice ★ **China World Hotel.** One of the finest hotels in Beijing, the China World, managed by Shangri-La Hotels & Resorts, is part of the prestigious China World Trade Center, home to offices, luxury apartments, and premium retail outlets. The lobby, conference center, ballroom, and all the guest rooms, were completely renovated in 2003 to the tune of $30 million. Marble floors and gold accents in the lobby lead to comfortable, contemporary rooms with marble baths. Scene a Cafe is a casual eatery where eight different cuisines are featured, along with chef-entertainers. ✉ *1 Jianguomenwai Dajie, Chaoyang District, 100004* ☎ *010/6505–2266 or 010/6505–0828* 📠 *010/6505–3167* 🌐 *www.shangri-la.com* *700 rooms, 56 suites* *6 restaurants, snack bar, in-room data ports, in-room safes, minibars, cable TV, health club, hair salon, massage, 2 bars, dance club, shops, laundry service, Internet, business services, conference center, airport shuttle, travel services, car rental, parking (fee), no-smoking rooms* 💳 *AE, DC, MC, V.*

$$$$ **New Otani Changfugong.** Managed by the New Otani Group from Japan, this hotel combines that country's signature hospitality and attentive service with a premium location in downtown Beijing (near the Friendship Store and the old observatory). The hotel offers authentic Chinese meals that are unforgettable, and the main restaurant serves delicious (and expensive) Japanese food. The hotel is popular with businesspeople and large groups from Japan. It's accessible for people with disabilities. ✉ *26 Jianguomenwai Dajie, Chaoyang District, 100022* ☎ *010/6512–5555* 📠 *010/6513–9810* 🌐 *www.cfgbj.com* *480 rooms, 20 suites* *2 restaurants, in-room safes, cable TV, tennis court, pool, gym, hair salon, massage, sauna, bicycles, bar, shop, laundry service, concierge, Internet, car rental* 💳 *AE, DC, MC, V* 🍽 *BP.*

$$$$ Fodor'sChoice ★ **St. Regis.** Generally considered to be the best hotel in Beijing, the St. Regis is a favorite of the foreign business community and visiting dignitaries. This is where President Bush stayed during his visit to China, and where Uma Thurman and crew stayed during the filming of Quentin Tarantino's *Kill Bill.* The luxurious interiors combine classical Chinese elegance and fine, modern furnishings—you won't be disappointed. The Press Club Bar, with its grand piano, dark wood, and bookcases, feels like a private club. And the on-site Japanese restaurant has good, moderately priced lunch specials. ✉ *21 Jianguomenwai Dajie, Chaoyang District, 100020* ☎ *010/6460–6688* 📠 *010/6460–3299* 🌐 *www.stregis.com* *137 rooms, 135 suites* *5 restaurants, in-room data ports, in-room safes, some kitchenettes, cable TV, tennis court, golf privileges, 2 indoor pools, hair salon, health club, hot tub, massage, sauna, spa, steam room, bicycles, badminton, billiards, racquetball, squash, 4 bars, 3 lounges, recreation room, shops, baby-sitting, playground, laundry service, Internet, business services, convention center, airport shuttle, car rental, travel services, parking (fee), no-smoking rooms* 💳 *AE, DC, MC, V.*

$$$ **Kempinski Hotel.** This fashionable hotel forms part of the Lufthansa Center, together with a luxury department store, offices, and apartments. It's within walking distance of the Sanlitun embassy area and dozens of bars and restaurants. There is an excellent German restaurant with its own micro-brewery, as well as a deli that is frequented by many Beijing

expats. The gym and swimming pool are on the 18th floor. ⊠ *50 Liang-maqiao Lu, Chaoyang District, 100016* ☎ *010/6465–3388* ⊕ *www.kempinski-beijing.com* 🖷 *010/6465–3366* ⬐ *500 rooms, 114 suites* ⬧ *11 restaurants, room service, in-room data ports, in-room safes, cable TV, some minibars, indoor pool, gym, bicycles, 2 bars, shops, laundry service, concierge, business services, conference center, car rental, travel services* ⊟ *AE, DC, MC, V.*

$$$ 🏨 **Kunlun Hotel.** At this 28-story property topped by a revolving restaurant, impressive presentation and a full range of facilities make up for occasional lapses in service. The hotel was built in the 1980s and named for the Kunlun Mountains, a range between northwestern China and northern Tibet that features prominently in Chinese mythology. A magnificent Chinese landscape painting greets you in the spacious lobby. All the rooms are spacious, with armchairs and entertainment cabinets, but some have not been updated since the mid-1990s. The business and superior suites, with hardwood floors, marble baths, and new furnishings, are the most attractive. ⊠ *2 Xinyuan Nan Lu, Sanlitun, Chaoyang District, 100004* ☎ *010/6590–3388* 🖷 *010/6590–3214* ⊕ *www.hotelkunlun.com* ⬐ *767 rooms, 14 suites* ⬧ *4 restaurants, tea shop, cable TV, some kitchens, indoor pool, hair salon, health club, hot tub, massage, sauna, steam room, bicycles, billiards, bar, lounge, Internet, business services, meeting rooms* ⊟ *AE, DC, MC, V* ⧖ *BP.*

$$–$$$ 🏨 **Zhaolong Hotel.** This hotel was a gift to the nation as a sign of friendship from Hong Kong shipping magnate Y. K. Pao, who named it for his father. It's in an excellent location near the Sanlitun embassies and nightlife area, but the interiors are starting to show some wear and tear around the edges. The back of the hotel now houses a youth hostel (*see* Zhaolong Youth Hostel, *below*). ⊠ *2 Gongren Tiyuchang Bei Lu, Sanlitun, Chaoyang District, 100027* ☎ *010/6597–2299* 🖷 *010/6597–2288* ⊕ *www.greatdragonhotel.com.cn* ⬐ *260 rooms, 20 suites* ⬧ *Restaurant, in-room data ports, cable TV, pool, hair salon, gym, massage, sauna, bicycles, bar, business services, Internet* ⊟ *AE, DC, MC, V* ⧖ *BP.*

$$ 🏨 **Hilton Beijing.** The comfortable and elegant Hilton lies at the northeast corner of Beijing's imperial grid pattern. Its rooms are simply furnished, and most have two large picture windows and balconies. Among its restaurants is the Louisiana, which serves Cajun cuisine. ⊠ *1 Dongfang Lu, Dongsanhuan Bei Lu, Chaoyang District, 100027* ☎ *010/6466–2288* 🖷 *010/6465–3052* ⊕ *www.beijing.hilton.com* ⬐ *316 rooms, 24 suites* ⬧ *5 restaurants, in-room safes, minibars, refrigerators, cable TV, indoor pool, hot tub, sauna, bicycles, bar, baby-sitting, business services, meeting rooms, car rental, no-smoking rooms* ⊟ *AE, DC, MC, V.*

$$ 🏨 **Holiday Inn Lido.** This enormous Holiday Inn—the largest in the world—is part of Lido Place, a commercial and residential complex northeast of the city center and close to the airport. With a high concentration of international businesses, including retail stores, a deli, and a Starbucks, Lido Place is home to a number of expats, and the Holiday Inn, too, is a haven for foreigners. The hotel has an Italian restaurant called Pinocchio, a steak restaurant called the Texan Bar & Grill, and a British-style pub called the Pig and Thistle. Key cards let you into your hotel room, and you also need them to turn on the room lights. ✉ *Jichang Lu at Jiangtai Lu, Chaoyang District, 100004* ☎ *010/6437–6688 or 800/810–0019 in China* 🖷 *010/6437–6237* ⊕ *www.beijing-lido.holiday-inn.com* ⇝ *374 rooms, 66 suites* 🍴 *4 restaurants, ice cream parlor, room service, cable TV, indoor pool, hair salon, health club, hot tub, massage, sauna, steam room, bar, lounge, shops, baby-sitting, laundry service, concierge, Internet, business services, meeting rooms, airport shuttle, car rental, travel services, free parking, no-smoking rooms* 🚫 *AE, DC, MC, V.*

$$ 🏨 **Jianguo Hotel.** Despite its 1950s-style name ("build the country"), this is actually a U.S.–China joint venture. Wonderfully central, it is close to the diplomatic compounds and southern embassy area, as well as the Silk Alley Market. Nearly half the rooms have balconies overlooking busy Jianwai Dajie. The Jianguo has maintained its friendly and cozy feel, and Western classical music, including opera, is performed Sunday morning in the lobby. Justine's is the best French restaurant in Beijing. ✉ *5 Jianguomenwai Dajie, Chaoyang District, 100020* ☎ *010/6500–2233* 🖷 *010/6501–0539* ⊕ *www.jianguohotels.com* ⇝ *400 rooms, 68 suites* 🍴 *4 restaurants, in-room safes, cable TV, indoor pool, hair salon, massage, bar, shop, laundry services, concierge, Internet, business services, conference center, no-smoking rooms* 🚫 *AE, DC, MC, V.*

★ $$ 🏨 **Kerry Centre Hotel.** The Shangri-La hotel chain opened this palatial, upscale hotel to much fanfare in 1999. Its ultra-modern interiors and convenient location close to Beijing's embassy and business district make it an excellent choice for business travelers and anyone who wants to be near shopping. The Forbidden City is a 10- to 15-minute drive away. What really distinguishes it from other five-star hotels in Beijing is the amazing health club. With a full-service fitness center and spa, a jogging track, squash and tennis courts, and, of course, a pool, it's *the* health club of choice for expats living in Beijing. ✉ *1 Guang Hua Lu, Chaoyang District 100020* ☎ *010/6561–8833* 🖷 *010/6561–2626* ⊕ *www.shangri-la.com* ⇝ *445 rooms, 42 suites* 🍴 *3 restaurants, in-room data ports, in-room safes, cable TV, minibars, pool, 2 tennis courts, health club, hot tub, massage, sauna, spa, steam room, basketball, billiards, Ping-Pong, squash, bar, shops, playground, Internet* 🚫 *AE, DC, MC, V.*

$$ 🏨 **Swissôtel.** This hotel is a joint venture between Switzerland and the Hong Kong and Macau Affairs Office of the State Council (hence the hotel's Chinese name—Gang'ao Zhongxin—the Hong Kong Macau Center). The Hong Kong connection means Hong Kong Jockey Club members can place bets here. In the large and impressive marble lobby you can enjoy excellent jazz every Friday and Saturday evening. Rooms have high-quality, European-style furnishings in cream and light grey, plus temperature controls and coffeemakers. ✉ *Dongsishiqiao Flyover Junction (2nd Ring Road), Chaoyang District, 100027* ☎ *010/6553–2288* 🖷 *010/6501–2501* ⊕ *www.swissotel-beijing.com* ⇝ *362 rooms, 30 suites, 62 apartments* 🍴 *5 restaurants, room service, in-room data ports, some in-room fax machines, in-room safes, minibars, cable TV, indoor pool, gym, hair salon, sauna, bar, baby-sitting, shops, laundry service, concierge, Internet, business services, conference center, car rental, travel services, no-smoking rooms* 🚫 *AE, DC, MC, V.*

$$ ⛪ **Traders Hotel.** Inside the China World Trade center complex, this hotel is connected to its sister property, the China World Hotel, and a shopping mall. The hotel is a favorite of international business travelers, who appreciate its central location, good service, top-notch amenities, and excellent value. Rooms are done in muted colors, such as beige and light green, with queen- or king-size beds. Guests have access to the state-of-the-art health club at the China World Hotel. ✉ *1 Jianguomenwai Dajie, Chaoyang District, 100004* ☎ *010/6505–2277* 🖷 *010/6505–0828* ⊕ *www.shangri-la.com* 🖧 *544 rooms, 26 suites* ⚿ *2 restaurants, in-room data ports, in-room safes, minibars, cable TV, massage, bar, shop, baby-sitting, business services, conference center, airport shuttle, car rental, travel services, no-smoking rooms* ▭ *AE, DC, MC, V.*

$–$$ ⛪ **Scitech Hotel.** This is part of the Scitech complex, which consists of an office tower, a hotel, and a luxury shopping center. The hotel enjoys a good location on busy Jianguomenwai Dajie opposite the Friendship Store. You are greeted by a small fountain in the lobby, which also has a small teahouse off to one side. The rooms are pleasant, if somewhat nondescript, and the service is quite good. ✉ *22 Jianguomenwai Dajie, Chaoyang District, 100004* ☎ *010/6512–3388* 🖷 *010/6512–3542* ⊕ *www.scitechgroup.com* 🖧 *262 rooms, 32 suites* ⚿ *4 restaurants, room service, in-room safes, minibars, cable TV, tennis court, indoor pool, gym, hair salon, hot tub, sauna, bar, dance club, shops, baby-sitting, laundry service, business services, conference center, car rental, parking (fee), no-smoking rooms* ▭ *AE, DC, MC, V* ⛾ *BP.*

$ ⛪ **Gloria Plaza Hotel.** This hotel, built in the late 1990s, is in a commercial area near the Beijing embassy, the New Otani Changfugong, and Scitech. Rooms have good views of the city. The Sports City Cafe broadcasts sports events from around the world and serves up American food along with beer, wine, and cocktails. There's a dance floor and nightly entertainment, such as a DJ or band. ✉ *2 Jiangguomen Nan Dajie, Chaoyang District, 100022* ☎ *010/6515–8855* 🖷 *010/6515–5273* ⊕ *www.gphbeijing.com* 🖧 *377 rooms, 46 suites* ⚿ *3 restaurants, room service, in-room data ports, cable TV, indoor pool, health club, hot tub, massage, sauna, bar, lobby lounge, laundry service, business services, conference center, airport shuttle, travel services, parking (fee)* ▭ *AE, DC, MC, V.*

$ ⛪ **Great Wall Sheraton.** The oldest luxury hotel in Beijing, the Great Wall is still going strong as a favorite of tour groups. Rooms are comfortable though no different from rooms in any other Sheraton. An elegant Sichuan restaurant on the top floor has nice views of the city, and another restaurant serves French cuisine. While the Sheraton is an old standby, the service is uneven and many of the staff surprisingly don't speak English. ✉ *10 Dongsanhuan Bei Lu, Chaoyang District, 100026* ☎ *010/6590–5566* 🖷 *010/6590–5504* ⊕ *www.sheratonbeijing.com* 🖧 *800 rooms, 207 suites* ⚿ *4 restaurants, in-room data ports, in-room safes, minibars, cable TV, indoor pool, health club, sauna, bar, lounge, Internet, business services, conference center, no-smoking floors* ▭ *AE, DC, MC, V.*

$ ⛪ **Jinglun Hotel.** Just 10 minutes' drive from Tiananmen Square, the Jinglun is a well-appointed business and leisure hotel with competitive prices.

It's known for its good, fourth-floor, Chinese restaurant, Si He Xuan, and its outdoor café, which serves drinks and barbecue beside a fountain from spring through autumn. Rooms are spacious with standard chain-hotel furnishings in bright blue, pink, and orange. ⊠ *3 Jianguomenwai Dajie, Chaoyang District, 100020* ☎ *010/6500–2266* 🖷 *010/6500–2022* ⊕ *www.jinglunhotel.com* 🛏 *512 rooms, 126 suites* ⚒ *4 restaurants, in-room safes, minibars, refrigerators, cable TV, indoor pool, gym, hair salon, hot tub, massage, sauna, bicycles, bar, shops, babysitting, Internet, business services, car rental, travel services* ▤ *AE, DC, MC, V.*

$ 🏨 **Radisson SAS.** A boxy mid-rise near the international exhibition center in northeast Beijing, this high-end hotel receives business and leisure travelers from around the world. The good rates reflect the slightly out-of-the-way location. You can choose between rooms decorated Chinese style, in navy and beige with gold accents, or Italian style, in bright green and yellow. The restaurants—one open-air—offer good food, including a Western-style Sunday brunch with music. ⊠ *6A Beisanhuan Dong Lu, Chaoyang District, 100028* ☎ *010/6466–3388* 🖷 *010/6465–3181* ⊕ *www.radisson.com* 🛏 *362 rooms, 16 suites* ⚒ *3 restaurants, in-room safes, minibars, cable TV, tennis court, indoor pool, gym, massage, sauna, bicycles, squash, bar, dance club, shop, baby-sitting, Internet, business services, conference center, car rental, airport shuttle* ▤ *AE, DC, MC, V.*

¢ 🏨 **Jingguang New World.** Modern China's obsession with blue glass finds its most monstrous expression in this 53-story building. The Jingguang Center houses the hotel plus offices, shops, and luxury apartments. It's hard to miss on the eastern Third Ring Road, not far from Jianguomenwai Dajie. The restaurants serve Cantonese, Korean, and Western food. ⊠ *Jingguang center, Hujialou, Chaoyang District, 100020* ☎ *010/6597–8888* 🖷 *010/6597–3333* ⊕ *www.newworldhotels.com* 🛏 *426 rooms, 20 suites* ⚒ *3 restaurants, cable TV, pool, hair salon, gym, sauna, massage, 2 bars, shops, Internet, business center, conference center* ▤ *AE, DC, MC, V.*

¢ 🏨 **You Yi Youth Hostel.** Backpackers who don't mind that this youth hostel is attached to one of Beijing's most popular bars (Poachers) should stay here. Rooms sleep two to four people and are well-kept, with clean white walls and dark-wood trim. Best of all, the hostel is located smack in the middle of Beijing's bar street area. ⊠ *43 Beisanlitun Nan, Sanlitun, Chaoyang District, 100027* ☎ *010/6417–2632* 🖷 *010/6415–6866* ⊕ *www.poachers.com.cn* 🛏 *35 rooms with shared bath* ⚒ *Restaurant, bar, laundry service; no TV in some rooms* ▤ *No credit cards* ⛾ *BP.*

¢ 🏨 **Zhaolong Youth Hostel.** If partaking in Beijing's lively nightlife scene is on your itinerary, consider this clean and comfortable youth hostel in Sanlitun. The hostel offers clean rooms with two to six beds each, a reading room, a kitchen, and bicycle rentals. The organized hiking trips to the Great Wall (Y90) every other day make this a popular choice for many backpackers. ⊠ *2 Gongti Bei Lu, Sanlitun, Chaoyang District, 100027* ☎ *010/6597–2299 Ext. 6111* 🖷 *010/6597–2288* ⊕ *www. greatdragonhotel.com.cn* 🛏 *20 rooms* ⚒ *Bar, laundry facilities; no room phones, no room TVs* ▤ *AE, MC, V* ⛾ *CP.*

Haidian

The Haidian District is in the far northwestern corner of Beijing, where you'll find the Summer Palace, the city zoo, and numerous parks.

$$ 🏨 **Shangri-La Hotel.** Set in delightful landscaped gardens in the western part of the city, 30 minutes from downtown, this Shangri-La is a wonderful retreat. The lobby and restaurants underwent a major renovation in early 2004, and a new wing, the Horizon Tower, is scheduled for completion in 2006. ⊠ *29 Zizhuyuan Lu, Haidian District, 100084* 🕿 *010/6841–2211* 🖷 *010/6841–8002* ⊕ *www.shangri-la.com* 🛏 *616 rooms, 19 suites, 15 1- to 3-bedroom apartments* 🍴 *3 restaurants, room service, in-room data ports, in-room safes, some kitchenettes, minibars, cable TV, indoor pool, gym, hair salon, health club, massage, sauna, bar, lobby lounge, shops, baby-sitting, laundry service, Internet, business services, conference center, car rental, travel services, parking (fee)* 🖃 *AE, DC, MC, V* ⦿ *BP.*

¢–$ 🏨 **Friendship Hotel.** The Friendship's name is telling: it was built in 1954 to house foreign experts, mostly Soviet, who had come to help build New China. Beijing Friendship Hotel is one of the largest "garden-style" hotels in Asia. The architecture is Chinese traditional and the public spaces are classic and elegant. Rooms are large with modern, if somewhat outdated, furnishings. With 14 restaurants, an Olympic-size pool, and a driving range, the hotel aims to be a one-stop destination. ⊠ *3 Baishiqiao Lu, Haidian District, 100873* 🕿 *010/6849–8888* 🖷 *010/6849–8866* ⊕ *www.cbw.com/hotel/friendship* 🛏 *800 rooms, 32 suites* 🍴 *14 restaurants, minibars, cable TV, driving range, tennis courts, 2 pools (1 indoor), gym, massage, sauna, billiards, bowling, bar, dance club, theater, business services, conference center, car rental* 🖃 *AE, DC, MC, V.*

¢ 🏨 **Fragrant Hills Hotel.** This unusual hotel surrounded by gardens—there's a large lake and a miniature stone forest nearby—takes its name from the beautiful park on which it is set. In the western suburbs of Beijing, Fragrant Hills was a favored retreat of emperors through the centuries. The hotel was designed by the Chinese-American architect I. M. Pei and opened in 1983. The lobby forms a traditional courtyard, and rooms extend along a hillside. Each has a balcony overlooking the park. The outdoor swimming pool is covered for year-round use. Despite its lovely surroundings, the hotel is somewhat run-down, and it is a 1½-hour drive from downtown. ⊠ *Fragrant Hills Park, Haidian District, 100093* 🕿 *010/6259–1166* 🖷 *010/6259–1762* ⊕ 🛏 *200 rooms, 27 suites* 🍴 *3 restaurants, pool, hair salon, massage, sauna, bar, shop, laundry service, business services, parking (fee)* 🖃 *AE, DC, MC, V* ⦿ *BP.*

Xicheng

The Xicheng District is on the west side of the Forbidden City, opposite Dongcheng. This is where to get lost among Beijing's old hutong alleyways and to take long walks by Qianhai and Houhai lakes.

¢ 🏨 **Minzu Hotel.** At its birth in 1959, the Minzu (Nationalities) Hotel was labeled one of the Ten Great Buildings in Beijing. This paean to the unity of China's different peoples has welcomed many prominent foreign visitors over the years. It's been renovated into yet another shiny pleasuredome but maintains its original appeal. The hotel lies on western Changan Dajie, 10 minutes' ride from Tiananmen Square and next to the Nationalities' Cultural Palace. ⊠ *51 Fuxingmennei Dajie, Xicheng District, 100031* ☎ *010/6601–4466* ᐈ *010/6601–4849* ⬚ *600 rooms, 52 suites* ⚿ *4 restaurants, cable TV, hair salon, massage, sauna, bar, shops, business services, conference center, car rental* ⊟ *AE, DC, MC, V.*

Beijing Airport

★ **\$\$** ⊞ **Sino-Swiss Hotel.** This nine-story contemporary hotel near the airport overlooks a gorgeous, enormous outdoor pool surrounded by trees, shrubs, and colorful umbrellas. All the rooms and public areas are completely up-to-date. You'll find large standard rooms with deep-blue carpeting and white bedcovers. The restaurant Mongolian Gher offers barbecue and live entertainment inside a traditional-style felt yurt, while Swiss Chalet serves familiar Continental food to tables on the outdoor terrace. The hotel caters to business travelers with a full-service conference center and duplex business suites. ⊠ *Xiao Tianzhu Nan Lu (Box 6913), Beijing Capital Airport, Shunyi County, 100621* ☎ *010/6456–5588* ᐈ *010/ 6456–1588* ⊕ *www.sino-swisshotel.com* ⬚ *408 rooms, 35 suites* ⚿ *5 restaurants, in-room safes, minibars, cable TV, 2 tennis courts, 2 pools (1 indoor), gym, hot tub, massage, sauna, bicycles, billiards, Ping-Pong, squash, 2 bars, shop, laundry service, business services, meeting rooms* ⊟ *AE, DC, MC, V* ⦿ *BP.*

NIGHTLIFE & THE ARTS

Until the late 1970s the best night out most Beijingers could hope for was dinner at a friend's apartment followed by a sing-along. Since China's more liberal economic policies came into effect, however, countless bars and clubs have opened, many of them hip enough to attract internationally renowned DJs. Just a few years ago much of Beijing's nightlife scene was dominated by Beijing's expat population. Today, the emerging middle-class (not to mention the growing ranks of nouveaux-riche) have breathed real life into the city's entertainment venues. Peking opera, strangled almost to death in the Cultural Revolution (1966–76), has revived just enough to generate some interest among the older generations.

The free magazines *That's Beijing, City Weekend, Beijing Talk,* and *Beijing This Month* (the city's official tourist publication) have useful guides to entertainment, the arts, and expat events in Beijing. The most useful and entertaining of the bunch is *That's Beijing* (⊕ www. thatsbeijing.com), which appears the first week of every month. Pick them up at your hotel or one of the expat bars. Useful maps giving names in both Chinese and English can be bought at many hotels. Chinese name cards for hotels and other destinations are handy for showing taxi drivers.

The Arts

The arts in China took a long time to recover from the Cultural Revolution (1966–76), and political works are still generally avoided. Film and theater reflect an interesting mix of modern and avant-garde Chinese and Western influences. For example, on any given night in Beijing, you might see a drama by the famous Chinese playwright Lao She, a satire by a contemporary Taiwanese playwright, or a Chinese stage version of *Animal Farm*.

Your concierge can make recommendations about performances, and the free monthly English-language magazine *That's Beijing,* which you can find in hotels, restaurants, and bars around the city, also lists performances and special events.

Acrobatics

Chaoyang Theater (Chaoyang Juchang). Spectacular individual and team acrobatic displays involving bicycles, seesaws, catapults, swings, and barrels are performed here nightly. Same-day tickets cost between Y50 and Y300. ✉ *36 Dongsanhuan Bei Lu, Hujialou, Chaoyang District* ☎ *010/6507–2421.*

Universal Theater (Tiandi Juchang). The China Acrobatics Troupe puts on a nightly repertoire of breathtaking, usually flawless stunts. ✉ *Dongsishi Tiao, Chaoyang District* ☎ *010/6502–3984.*

Music & Variety

Beijing Concert Hall (Beijing Yinyueting). Beijing's main venue for Chinese and Western classical music concerts also hosts folk dancing and singing, and many celebratory events throughout the year. ✉ *1 Beixinhua Jie, Xicheng District* ☎ *010/6605–5812.*

Forbidden City Concert Hall (Zhongshan Yinyutang). With a seating capacity of 1400, this is one of Beijing's largest concert halls. It is also one of the most well-appointed, with plush seating and first-class acoustics. Recent performances include classical pieces by the Beijing Symphony Orchestra and the China Philharmonic. ✉ *In Zhongshan Park, Xichang'an Jie, Xicheng District, on the west side of Tiananmen Square* ☎ *010/6559–8285.*

Tianqiao Happy Teahouse (Tianqiao Le Chaguan). In an old, traditional theater, the teahouse hosts Chinese variety shows like those that were so popular before 1949, including Peking opera, acrobatics, cross talk, jugglers, illusionists, and contortionists. ✉ *113 Tianqiao Shichang, Xuanwu District* ☎ *010/6303–9013.*

Peking Opera

Although language can be a major barrier for foreigners watching plays, it's much less of a problem for viewers of Peking opera, which involves elaborate costumes and make-up, vocal and instrumental music, and stylized acting. Peking opera was introduced to Qing Emperor Qianlong in 1790 and quickly developed into China's favorite and most sophisticated performing art. Performances were banned during the Cultural Revolution, but they have since resurfaced, albeit with a less significant following.

In fact, Chinese people under 60, who grew up in Communist China, are as likely to listen to Western opera as Peking opera; they'll watch performances of the latter only at the Chinese New Year temple fairs.

Chang'an Grand Theater (Chang'an Da Xiyuan). At this contemporary theater, like at a cabaret, the audience sits at tables and can eat and drink while watching lively performances of Peking opera. English subtitles appear above the stage. ⊠ *7 Jianguomennei Dajie, Dongcheng District* ☎ *010/6510–1155.*

FodorsChoice **Huguang Guildhall** (Huguang Huiguan). Beijng's oldest Peking opera the-
★ ater, the Guildhall has staged performances since 1807. The hall has been restored to display its original architecture and appearance, and it's certainly the most atmospheric place to take in Peking Opera. ⊠ *3 Hu-fangqiao, Xuanwu District* ☎ *010/6351–8284.*

Lao She Teahouse (Lao She Chaguan). Performances vary, but usually include Peking opera and a variety of other folk arts, such as acrobatics, magic, or comedy. ⊠ *3 Qianmenxi Dajie, 3rd floor, Chongwen District* ☎ *010/6303–6830* 🖷 *010/6301–7529.*

Liyuan Theater (Liyuan Juchang). Popular with tourists, the Liyuan hosts Peking opera with English subtitles as well as acrobatics performances. ⊠ *Qianmen Hotel, 175 Yongan Lu, Chongwen District* ☎ *010/ 6301–6688 Ext. 8860* 🖷 *010/6303–2301.*

Theater

Beijing Exhibition Center Theater (Beijing Zhanlanguan Juchang). Chinese and Western plays, operas, and ballet performances are staged at this theater, in a Soviet-style building that's part of the Exhibition Center complex. ⊠*135 Xizhimenwai Dajie, Xicheng District* ☎*010/6835–4455.*

Capital Theater (Shoudu Juchang). This is Beijing's most respected theater, where big-name international and Chinese shows play when in town. ⊠ *22 Wangfujing Dajie, Dongcheng District* ☎ *010/6524–9847.*

China Experimental Drama Theater (Zhongyang Shiyan Huajuyuan Xiao Juchang). Here lesser-known directors and actors put on avant-garde theater and Chinese dramatizations of such works as *Romeo and Juliet, Death of a Salesman,* and *A Streetcar Named Desire.* ⊠ *45 Maoer Hu-tong, Dianmen, Dongcheng District* ☎ *010/6403–1099 or 010/ 6403–1109.*

☾ **China Puppet Theater** (Zhongguo Mu'ou Juyuan). Shadow and hand-puppet shows about traditional stories provide lively entertainment for children and adults alike. ⊠ *1 Anhuaxili, Chaoyang District* ☎ *010/ 6425–4849.*

Nightlife

A few years ago, nightlife was mainly contained in hotel bars and karaoke lounges, but now you can find everything from dance clubs with internationally known DJs to gay bars to sophisticated jazz lounges. Packed almost every night of the week by Chinese yuppies and expats, Beijing's nightlife scene is sure to satisfy even the most discerning of nightowls.

Beijing has two main nightlife neighborhoods: Sanlitun and Houhai. A third, Dashanzi, an artsy warehouse area, is slowly gaining popularity, but for now it attracts people mainly for special events. Sanlitun's Jiuba Jie, or "Bar Street," has expanded into the surrounding alleyways. Houhai, once a quiet lakeside neighborhood home to Beijing's *laobaixing* (ordinary folk), has in recent years been the site of a flourishing of bars, restaurants, boutiques, and coffee shops—even a Starbucks.

Bars

SANLITUN AREA **Poacher's.** A predominantly young expat crowd with a thirst for cheap drinks frequents this bar. ⊠ *43 Bei Sanlitun Lu, Chaoyang District* ☎ *010/ 6617–2632 Ext. 8505.*

The Tree (Yinbideshu). Just behind Poacher's is one of Beijing's oldest bars and a favorite with working expats. Pizza, salads, and other light meals are served along with beer, wine, and cocktails. ⊠ *43 Bei Sanlitun Lu, Chaoyang District* ☎ *010/6509–3642.*

Suzy Wong (Suxihuang Julebu). This place just west of Chaoyang Park packs in a mixed crowd of expats and locals, especially *xiaojies* (young ladies). Although it's elegant and stylishly decorated in a 1930s Shanghai theme, it has nevertheless earned a reputation as a pick-up bar. Women should expect advances. ⊠ *1A Nongzhaguan Lu, Chaoyang District* ☎ *010/6593–6049.*

HOUHAI AREA **Lotus** (Lianhua). Tiny Lotus, in one of Houhai's more atmospheric back alleyways, is a place to see and be seen in Beijing. ⊠ *24 Yandai Xiejie, Xicheng District* ☎ *010/6407–7857.*

No Name Bar (Bai Feng's). The first bar to open in Houhai is still the best— the so-called No Name Bar (because it technically has no name, though locals refer to it by the owner's name: Bai Feng) is decorated with plants and wicker furniture, and has a perfect view of the lake. ⊠ *3 Qianhai East Bank, Xicheng District* ☎ *010/6401–8541.*

Sanwei Bookstore (Sanwei Shuwu). Here you'll find the traditional Chinese arrangement of a bookstore with an adjacent café. In the past these bookstore–cafés attracted writers who sipped tea while listening to live Peking opera and talking about their work. At Sanwei, there's a popular bar upstairs. Friday is jazz night, and Saturday brings in Chinese classical musicians playing such traditional instruments such as the *pipa* and the *guzheng*. ⊠ *60 Fuxingmennei Dajie, Xicheng District* ☎ *010/ 6601–3204.*

Dance Clubs

SANLITUN AREA **Public Space** One of the Bar Street's old standbys, this small bar is a good place to start off the evening with a beer or two. There's also decent, though basic, food and coffee. ⊠ *50 Sanlitun Lu, Chaoyang District,* ☎ *010/6416–0759.*

DASHANZI AREA **Vibes** (Weibishi). DJs who know their music spin a mix of house, hip-hop, and rock at this cool, little lounge. ⊠ *4 Jiuxianqiao Lu, Chaoyang District* ☎ *010/6437–8082.*

CloseUp
PREPARING FOR THE 2008 OLYMPIC GAMES

ACCORDING TO NEWSPAPER REPORTS, $22 billion are being invested to host the Olympic games. Whether this figure is accurate or not, there is no doubt that the face and infrastructure of Beijing is undergoing dramatic change as a result of the nation's commitment to hosting the Olympics.

Large-scale city planning projects are the most expensive and ambitious undertakings, yet some of these have already been completed. Two new beltways, the city's fifth and sixth, were built in 2004, and a new, seventh, 270-mile ring road is on the way. Of the city's four new rail lines, one was completed in 2003 and two more are scheduled to begin operating in late 2004. At Beijing Airport, a new, $2 billion, Norman Foster–designed terminal has been proposed, and another terminal has been completely renovated.

Within the city, a massive refurbishment of the China National Museum is underway and scheduled to be completed in 2007. Additionally, tickets will soon be available for shows at the new National Theatre, popularly referred to as the "duck egg" for its shape, a few hundred yards west of the Great Hall of the People. Meanwhile, ground has been broken at the site reserved for the Olympic Green between the north sections of the fourth and fifth beltways. Apart from the Olympic Village, the Green will contain an 80,000-seat National Stadium and a 17,000-seat National Swimming Center. At the same time but at different locations, construction has begun on the Beijing Shooting Range and the Laoshan Velodrome.

In step with these major developments, many Chinese and international hotel chains have secured locations for new hotels, some of which are scheduled to open in late 2005 and 2006. While we must wait until 2008 to witness the achievements of the world's athletes, the Olympics fascinating pre-show is unfolding now, as the sterling efforts of the Beijing Olympics Committee are realized.

— Guy Rubin

SPORTS & THE OUTDOORS

A few years ago, exercise in the capital was mainly limited to bicycling—a major form of transportation—and a few older people doing tai chi in the morning. As personal-car sales have skyrocketed, however, there are fewer and fewer cyclists and more and more (you guessed it) health clubs. Since the late 1990s, dozens of Chinese and foreign health-club companies have opened branches in Beijing, but most of them are only open to members (or hotel guests, if the club is in a hotel).

As in the West, yoga is also hitting it big, and you'll find yoga classes in health clubs and independent studios. Golf has a loyal following in *daquan* (entrepreneurs), and weekend golf outings are often as much for business deal-making as for pleasure.

Biking

Many of Beijing's pleasures are best sampled off the subway and out of taxis. In other words, walk or pedal. Rent bikes (available at many hotels) and take an impromptu sightseeing tour. Beijing is flat, and bike lanes exist on most main roads. Pedaling among the city's cyclists isn't as challenging as it looks: copy the locals—keep it slow and ring your bell often. Punctured tire? Not to worry: curb-side repairmen line most streets. Remember to park your bike (and lock it to something stationary as bike theft is common) only in designated areas. Most bike parking lots have attendants and cost Y20.

CycleChina. This tour company offers guided bike rides around Beijing on weekends. ☎ 1391/188–6524 ⊕ *www.cyclechina.com.*

Golf

Beijing International Golf Club. Nestled on a hillside above the Ming Tombs, this spectacular 18-hole course is Beijing's finest. Long (par 72), challenging, and meticulously groomed, it has hosted professional tournaments. Facilities include a restaurant, pro shop, and driving range. ⊹ *46 km (29 mi) north of Beijing near Changping* ☎ *010/6076–2288* ☒ *Greens fees: Y650 weekdays, Y1,100 weekends. Caddies (required): Y150. Rental clubs available* ☉ *Mar.–Nov., daily 7–5.*

Huang Tang International Golf Club. Another excellent golf course in the Beijing area, Huang Tang is loved by expat golfers. You'll find a pro shop, putting green, and driving range. ⊹ *Yanjiao Development Zone; shuttle bus from the Jingguang Center on weekends* ☎ *010/6159–3832* ☒ *Greens fees: Y770 weekdays, Y1,500 weekends.* ☉ *Mar.–Nov., daily 7–5.*

Hiking

Beijing Hikers. This outfitter offers guided hiking trips squarely aimed at expat hikers and tourists. The trips are rated from 1 to 5 in terms of difficulty, and they take you into the hills around Beijing. You might visit a rural village, historic temple, or the Great Wall. Groups depart from the Starbucks in the Lido Hotel. ☎ *1391/002–5516* ⊕ *www. bjhikers.com* ☒ *Y150, including round-trip transportation* ☉ *Weekends from 8:30 or 9–4:30 or 5.*

Ice Skating

If you are visiting in winter, a nice way to spend an afternoon is skating on Qianhai Lake. A vendor on the lake rents skates on a first-come, first-served basis.

Skiing

Nanshan Ski Resort. Though small with limited runs, Nanshan is Beijing's best resort. The 10 trails are well groomed, and there are two lifts (a two-seater and a four-seater). Beginners and intermediate skiers will find nothing lacking, but experts may be disappointed. ✉ *Shunyi County, 25 mi (40 km) north of Beijing Airport* ☎ *010/6445–0990* ⊕ *www. nanshanski.com* ✉ *Ski rental and lift ticket: Y220 weekdays, Y360 weekends* ⊙ *Dec.–Mar., daily 7–dusk.*

Tai Chi

Chinese Culture Club. Interested in practicing the exercise of choice of traditional Beijingers? This club host regular classes in an opera theater. ✉ *29 Liangmaqiao Lu, Chaoyang District, east of the Kempinski Hotel* ☎ *010/6432–9341* ⊕ *www.chinesecultureclub.org.*

Yoga

Yoga Yard. Owned and operated by two American yoga teachers, this wonderful studio is the perfect place to keep up your yoga practice while in Beijing. ✉ *Yong He Jia Yuan, Building 4, Room 108, Chaoyang District* ☎ *1360/110–3497 or 1361/126–6962* ⊕ *www.yogayard.com* ✉ *Y80 per class.*

SHOPPING

Rapid economic growth and an explosion of commercialism have transformed Beijing into a consumer's paradise. Modern shopping malls, department stores, and boutiques can now be found alongside Beijing's traditional markets. The trend for moving outdoor street markets indoors (such as Yaxiu Market) so far has left the famous Silk Alley Market unscathed, though rumors abound that its days are numbered. For a more traditional flavor—and bargain reproduction antiques—don't miss the marvelous Sunday market at Panjiayuan. The city's main shopping area, along Wangfujing Dajie and its offshoots, remains as popular (and crowded) as ever.

Major Shopping Districts

Dazhalan

Dazhalan is one of Beijing's oldest shopping streets. Many of the shops here are centuries old and sell traditional Chinese goods such as silk, tea, and Chinese medicines. China's most famous traditional Chinese medicine shop, Tongrentang, is on this street and is staffed by specialists who can examine you and make a prescription for you. If you don't speak Chinese, be sure to bring a translator along, as the doctors here don't speak English.

Jianguomenwai Dajie

One of Beijing's most important tourist shopping areas is along this major avenue in Chaoyang District. Jianguomenwai Dajie is lined with big hotels as well as numerous shops, including the Beijing Friendship Store. You'll also find the outdoor Silk Alley Market and the modern China World shopping mall.

Liulichang Jie

The classical architecture on this narrow street, which has been carefully restored to its Ming-era grandeur, is as much an attraction as the art and antiques shops lining it. Artists come here for the selection of brushes, paper, and ink sold in many stores.

Wangfujing Dajie

Beijing's premier shopping street underwent major restoration in the period leading up to Communist China's 50th anniversary in 1999. Joining, and to some extent replacing, the street's tiny shops are shiny, new malls and department stores. If you want to experience how the locals shop, Wangfujing is well worth a browse.

Department Stores

Beijing Department Store. Wangfujing's grand dame continues to attract large crowds with stores selling everything from jewelry to clothing to sports equipment, despite the allure of Sun Dongan and the even bigger Oriental Plaza complex. ⊠ *255 Wangfujing Dajie, Dongcheng District* ☎ *010/6512–6677.*

Beijing Friendship Store. A longtime tourist favorite, the Friendship Store sells the widest range of traditional Chinese goods and handicrafts under one roof, including hand-drawn tablecloths, silk and cashmere goods and clothing, porcelain, watercolor paintings, traditional Chinese medicine, teas, jade and gold jewelry, rugs (both silk and wool), and groceries. ⊠ *17 Jianguomenwai Dajie, Chaoyang District* ☎ *010/6500–3311.*

Lufthansa Center. This top Beijing department store stocks cosmetics, consumer electronics, wool and cashmere clothing, and new rugs; a Western grocery store occupies the basement. ⊠ *52 Liangmaoqiao, Chaoyang District* ☎ *010/6465–1188.*

Oriental Plaza. This shopping complex begins at the southern end of Wangfujing, where it meets Changan Jie, and stretches a block east to Dongan Dajie. You'll find upscale shops including Kookai, TSE, MaxMara, and Sisley. ⊠ *1 Dongchang'an Jie, Dongcheng District* ☎ *010/8518–6363.*

Pacific Century Place. Managed by a Japanese company, this department store has three Japanese restaurants as well as an organic-grocery store in the basement. ⊠ *2A Gongti Bei Lu, Sanlitun, Chaoyang District* ☎ *010/6539–3888.*

Malls & Shopping Centers

Malls are gradually replacing markets as the main places to shop and socialize in Beijing. Most malls here have been built since the late 1990s, so they are generally new and shiny, with international chains and independent boutiques, as well as food courts, restrooms, and ATMs.

★ **China World Shopping Mall.** You'll find designer boutiques such as Prada and Ferragamo at this upscale shopping mall. For quality souvenirs, check out **Tian Fu,** a branch of the famous Chinese tea sellers. The teas are of high quality and come in very attractive packaging. **Emperor** sells bedding, tablecloths, and napkins made from Chinese silk. **Zhang's Textiles** is a Chinese crafts store and antique shop; and **Liuligongfang** sells Chinese-style crystal creations and jewelry. ⊠ *1 Jianguomenwai Dajie, Chaoyang District* ☎ *010/6505–2288.*

Malls at Oriental Plaza. This enormous mall is in Beijing's downtown area just east of the Forbidden City. Similar to China World, there are branches of Emperor, Liuligongfang, and Tian Art here. ⊠ *1 Dongchang'an Jie, Dongcheng District* ☎ *010/8518–6363.*

Sun Dongan Plaza. This massive shopping center has dozens of designer shops but makes a concession to Old Peking with a traditional-style shopping street on the second floor. On the fourth floor, **Mu Zhen Liao Chinese Fashion Boutique** sells high-quality, ready-made *qipaos* (Chinese-style dresses) as well as tailor-made ones. The store is especially popular with brides-to-be. ⊠ *138 Wangfujing Dajie, Dongcheng District* ☎ *010/6527–6688.*

Tongli Studio. A tiny but welcome addition to Beijing's growing collection of malls, Tongli Studio has several one-of-a-kind artsy and upscale shops by local designers. This is a good place to spend some time browsing for jewelry, ceramics, and home decor shops if you are in the Sanlitun area. ⊠ *Sanlitun Lu, Chaoyang District* ☎ *010/6417–6668.*

Markets

Shopping in the city's lively, colorful markets is one of the distinctive pleasures of a trip to Beijing. Bargaining is acceptable at all markets. The best way to get what you want at a fair price without becoming overwhelmed by the negotiation process is to decide what you would be willing to pay for an item in advance and pay no more than that. Vendors will sometimes quote a price 10 times what they are willing to sell for, especially if a potential buyer looks wealthy or indecisive, but usually the first quote is two or three times the amount of the final sale.

Beijing Curio City (Beijing Gu'an Chang). This complex has four stories of kitsch and curio shops and a few furniture vendors, some selling authentic antiques. Prices are high (driven by tour groups), so don't be afraid to low-ball. If you are looking for antique furniture, try **Dong Fang Yuan** (⊠ 4th floor, no. 11 ☎ 1352/047–5513). ⊠ *Dongsanhuan Nan Lu, Chaoyang District, exit 3rd Ring Rd. at Panjiayuan Bridge* ☎ *010/ 6774–7711 or 010/6773–6021 Ext. 63.*

Hongqiao Market. Everything from porcelain to toilet paper is sold at this indoor market, but the main attraction is the good selection of freshwater pearls on the third floor. ⊠ *Tiantan Lu, between Chongemenwai Lu and Tiyuguan Dajie, Chongwen District* ☎ *010/6711–7630.*

Fodor's Choice **Panjiayuan Market.** The Panjiayuan Sunday market is Beijing's liveliest
★ and should not be missed. Vendors, many from faraway provinces, fill
hundreds of open-air stalls with a dizzying array of collectibles, as well
as lots of junk. Old clocks, new porcelain, jade, bronzes, tomb art, wood
carvings, Tibetan rugs, "Maomorabilia"—it's all here. The market is
grubby, so dress down. Arrive at sunrise to beat the crowds. The market is open Saturdays and Sundays from sunrise to about 3 PM. Be sure
to bargain, as many vendors set their first price up to 10 times higher
than what they are willing to sell for. ✉ *Huaweiqiaoxinan Jie, Dongsanhuan, Chaoyang District.*

Ritan Office Building Market. Over 40 indoor stalls on two floors sell fashionable women's clothing, some of it real name brands such as Ann Tay-
lor, BCBG, DKNY, and Eileen Fisher. A stall on the first floor sells
reasonably priced cashmere scarves and sweaters. ✉ *15A Guanghua Lu,
southeast corner of Ritan Park, Chaoyang District* ☎ *010/6502–1528.*

Fodor's Choice **Silk Alley Market.** Beijing's most famous market moved indoors in 2005.
★ You can roam among dozens of clothing and accessory stalls selling made-
for-export apparel, such as North Face jackets, Esprit sportswear, designer suites, and cashmere shawls. Just be aware that much of the
brand-name clothing, and even the cashmere, is fake. Start at the south
end of Silk Alley as the north end, which is near to the American embassy, is closed for security reasons. ✉ *Xiushui Nan Jie and Xiushui Dong
Jie, Chaoyang District.*

Yaxiu Market. Yaxiu is an indoor market just west of Sanlitun Bar Street
known for knock-off brand-name clothing bargains. The first two floors
carry women's clothing, while the third has children's clothing. ✉ *Gongti
Bei Lu, Chaoyang District.*

Zhaojia Chaowai Market. Beijing's best-known venue for affordable antique and reproduction furniture houses scores of independent vendors
who sell everything from authentic Qing chests to traditional baskets,
ceramics, carpets, and curios. Be sure to bargain; vendors routinely sell
items for less than half their starting price. ✉ *43 Huawei Bei Li,
Chaoyang District, two exits south of China World on Dongsanhuan
Lu* ☎ *010/6770–6402.*

Specialty Stores

Antiques & Furnishings

Antiques began pouring out of China more than a decade ago despite
strict rules banning the export of precious "cultural relics." According
to Chinese law, nothing that predates the death of Qing emperor Qianlong (1795) can be legally exported. Also, certain post-1795 imperial
porcelains, and any item deemed important to China's Communist Revolution, cannot be taken out of the country. Many antiques—from Tang
Dynasty tomb art to priceless Zhou Dynasty bronzes—are smuggled out
of China every year, and vendors may try to sell you an antique piece
illegally. Buy antiques only from licensed shops (they should have a special customs sticker carrying a Temple of Heaven symbol). Also note
that fakes abound in China, so buyer beware. **Tongli Studio** (*see* Malls

& Shopping Centers) and **Zhaojia Chaowai Market** (*see* Markets) are good places to shop for home decor items.

Century Arts. This store carries an amazing collection of genuine antique Tibetan cabinets. On display in the shop are only a small fraction of what is available; many more cabinets are at the shop's warehouse. ⊠ *Gongrentiyuchang Dong Lu A-6, Chaoyang District* ☎ *010/6595–0998.*

Chengguzhai Antique Store. You'll find more handicrafts—ceramics, jewelry, and knickknacks—than antiques here. ⊠ *194 Wangfujing Dajie* ☎ *010/6522–0673.*

Cottage. This charming little boutique sells Chinese giftware and home decor, such as cushion covers, antique-style furniture, table runners, and placemats at reasonable prices. ⊠ *Northeast corner of Ritan Park, Chaoyang District.*

Art Galleries

The international success of contemporary Chinese artists, such as Zhu Wei and Xu Bing, have helped fuel the Beijing art scene. For a real change of pace, spend a day away from the Old Beijing sites to explore the city's contemporary art galleries. The art you'll see offers a glimpse into China's modern culture.

Artists' Village Gallery. If you'd like to see artists in action in their studio spaces (and homes), head out to one of the artists' villages in the suburbs of Beijing. Make an appointment first, and arrange for car service to the village. Most of the art—contemporary watercolors, oil paintings, and sculptures—is for sale. ⊠ *1 Chunbei, Ren Zhuang, Tongxian Songzhuang* ☎ *010/6438–1784.*

The Courtyard Gallery. Although the space here is minuscule—it's in the basement of the Courtyard restaurant—this gallery still manages to attract some of the most sought-after names in contemporary Chinese art, such as Wang Qingsong, Zhang Dali, and the Gao Brothers. ⊠ *95 Donghuamen Dajie, Dongcheng District* ☎ *010/6526–8882* ⊕ *www.courtyard-gallery.com.*

China Art & Archives Warehouse. One of the forerunners in the up-and-coming Dashanzi art district, this gallery showcases cutting-edge art in a variety of mediums, including painting and sculpture. Be sure to call ahead to make sure there's an exhibit, as the space doesn't have regular shows. ⊠ *Caochangdi Cun, Jichang Fulu, Chaoyang District, east of Tiedao Bridge, opposite the Nangao Police Station* ☎ *010/8456–5152.*

Creation Gallery. You'll find more conservative art here than at the Red Gate and the Courtyard. The collection is large and the prices vary considerably. Some pieces are surprisingly affordable. ⊠ *Southeast corner of Ritan Park, Chaoyang District* ☎ *010/8561–7570* ⊕ *www.creationgallery.com.cn.*

Red Gate Gallery at the Watch Tower. This gallery, one of the first to open in Beijing, displays and sells modern Chinese paintings and sculpture in

DVDS IN BEIJING

DIGITAL VIDEO DISCS *of current movies often hit the streets of Beijing the same week as they open in U.S. theaters—and sometimes even before. While the sales of these pirated DVDs are illegal (they blatantly disregard international copyright laws), DVD sales take place so openly in Beijing that it doesn't give the impression of being wrong. Unlike in countries where pirated DVDs are sold down back alleys and behind closed doors, in China they are sold in permanent shops that will even exchange your DVD if the quality isn't good. Prices range from Y7 on the street to Y10 in the shops. The shops claim to have better-quality copies than the street vendors. Most countries, however, including the United States, forbid the importation of pirated DVDs. Those caught carrying DVDs out of China or into another country will likely be fined and the discs will most certainly be confiscated. For more information about U.S. Customs rules, visit www.customs.gov.*

a centuries-old Beijing landmark building. ⊠ *Dongbianmen Watchtower, 2nd Ring Road at Jianguomen, Chongwen District* ☎ *010/ 6525–1005* ⊕ *www.redgategallery.com.*

Yan Club Art Centre. Among the best known galleries in Dashanzi is the Yan Club, which has hosted some excellent contemporary art exhibits. ⊠ *4 Jiuxianqiao Lu, Chaoyang District, behind Hongyuan Apartments* ☎ *010/8457–3506.*

Books

In general China has a very poor selection of English-language books and magazines, thanks to strict censorship authorities. Some hotel kiosks, such as the Kempinski and China World, sell a limited selection of international newspapers and magazines, but rarely do they stock novels. You're best off bringing enough reading material to last your entire trip.

Beijing Friendship Store. The famous department store geared toward tourists has a small bookstore with a good selection of titles on Chinese history and culture. You'll also find foreign news magazines, imported fiction, and a few children's books. ⊠ *17 Jianguomenwai Dajie, Chaoyang District* ☎ *010/6500–3311.*

Foreign Languages Bookstore. For the most variety, try this four-story shop, which stocks textbooks, tapes, maps, art books, dictionaries, and some foreign-language novels (mainly classics à la Dickens and Austen). ⊠ *235 Wangfujing Dajie, Dongcheng District* ☎ *010/6512–6922.*

Clothing & Fabric

Beijing's outdoor and indoor markets are some of the best places to find cheap brand-name clothes, though much of the stock is made up of copies of the real designer goods. Among the best markets for clothing are the **Silk Alley Market, Ritan Office Building Market,** and **Yaxiu Market** (*see*

Markets). You can also check out the designer boutiques and Chinese and international chain stores in Beijing's malls (see Department Stores and Malls & Shopping Centers).

Authentic cashmere from Inner Mongolia is one of Beijing's best buys, selling for less than half of what you'd pay at home. As with most things in China, however, look out for unscrupulous dealers trying to pass off synthetic materials as cashmere, as well as poor-quality cashmere. That said, there are some good places to buy real cashmere at bargain prices.

Chinese silk, the best of which comes from Suzhou and Hangzhou in Jiangsu and Zhejiang provinces, can also be purchased for a fraction of what it costs in the United States. The range of colors, designs, and styles available in China are unequalled anywhere in the world. Some of the most popular buys are robes and traditional Chinese dresses and tunics.

Beijing Friendship Store. The city's most popular tourist shop sells a large selection of all things cashmere, from scarves and shawls to sweaters and long underwear. The Friendship Store guarantees authenticity, so rest assured that cashmere items you buy here are the real thing. ⊠ *17 Jianguomenwai Dajie, Chaoyang District* ☎ *010/6500–3311.*

Beijing Friendship Supermarket. This grocery and fabric store, conveniently located north of the Sanlitun Bar Street, carries a good selection of silk, cotton, and linen, as well as tailors who speak some English and make Chinese-style clothing (and can copy just about anything else). ⊠ *7 Sanlitun Lu, Chaoyang District* ☎ *010/6532–1871.*

China Star Silk Store. This is the place to order a qipao, a traditional Chinese silk dress. ⊠ *133 Wangfujing Dajie, Dongcheng District* ☎ *010/6525–7945.*

Huan Huan Cashmere Shop. You can find plenty of synthetic "pashminas" in Silk Alley, but the real thing is harder to find. Huan Huan is one of the few stalls that does sell authentic, high-quality men's and women's cashmere sweaters and shawls starting at Y250. There's another Huan Huan stall at **Hongqiao Market** (⊠ Tiantan Lu, between Chongemenwai Lu and Tiyuguan Dajie, 2nd floor ☎ 010/6711–7630). ⊠ *Silk Alley, Chongwen District* ☎ *010/6773–2866.*

Mystery Garments. Modern ethnic clothing made from natural fibers, such as linen and silk, and encompassing Chinese embroidery from Guizhou, are sold at this store in the Kerry Center. There's another branch in the Holiday Inn Lido. ⊠ *Kerry Center, 1 Guang Hua Lu, Chaoyang District* ☎ *010/8529–9403.*

Yuanlong Embroidery and Silk Store. Beijing's best yardage shop, Yuanlong has sold silks and yard goods for more than a century. It also offers custom tailoring and shipping. ⊠ *55 Tiantan Lu, Chongwen District, across from north gate of Temple of Heaven Park* ☎ *010/6701–2859.*

Jewelry

Check out **Hongqiao Market** (*see* Markets) for moderately priced fresh-water pearls sold from stalls on the third floor.

Liuligongfang. Taiwanese designer Liuligongfang offers exquisite crystal necklaces drawing on traditional Chinese motifs and symbols. ✉ *Lufthansa Center, 50 Liangmaoqiao, Sanlitun, Chaoyang District* ☎ *010/6465–1188* ✉ *Oriental Plaza, 1 Dongchang'an Jie, Dongcheng District* ☎ *010/8518–6363.*

Luwu Jewelry and Craft Store. This store on the main shopping street in Dongcheng carries silk, jade, and wood Chinese crafts and jewelry. ✉ *268 Wangfujing Dajie, Dongcheng District.*

Shard Box Store (Shendege Gongyipin Shangdian). Many of the silver, jade, coral, and turquoise pieces sold here are one-of-a-kind items from Tibet or Yunnan. The store takes its name from traditional jewelry boxes, which were often made from pottery shards. ✉ *1 Ritan Bei Lu, Chaoyang District* ☎ *010/8561–3712.*

Things of the Jing. For modern designs inspired by traditional Chinese motifs, try this shop, which carries a beautiful selection of silver earrings, rings, and necklaces at reasonable prices. ✉ *221 Tongli Studio, Sanlitun, Chaoyang District* ☎ *010/417–2271.*

Rugs

Antique Chinese, Mongolian, Tibetan, and Central Asian rugs are sold in many of Beijing's antiques shops. Many offer shipping services.

Beijing Yihong Carpet Factory (Women's Carpet Cooperative). This back-alley showroom is managed by women from a state-owned carpet factory. You'll find stacks of dusty rugs from Mongolia, Xinjiang, and Tibet. Although it's primarily an outlet for old rugs, new items are on sale as well, and copies of old designs can be made to order, usually within weeks. Cleaning and repairs are free. ✉ *35 Juzhang Hutong, Chongwen District* ☎ *010/6712–2195.*

Gangchen Carpet of Tibet. This shop in the Kempinski Hotel is the best place to buy new, high-quality, hand-made Tibetan rugs in Beijing. You'll find traditional and modern designs, and the rugs are made according to traditional Tibetan techniques with highland wool, handspun yarn, and hand-dyeing. ✉ *Kempinski Hotel, 50 Liang Ma Qiao Lu, Chaoyang District* ☎ *010/6465–3388 Ext. 5542.*

Stamps & Coins

Museum of Antique Currency (Gudai Qianbi Zhanlanguan). Collectors buy, sell, and trade old coins and paper currency outside this museum every day. ✉ *Bei'erhuan Jie, Xicheng District.*

Wangfujing Post Office. For new Chinese stamp sets, visit this busy post office in the Wangfujing shopping area. ✉ *2 Xuanwumendong Dajie, at Wangfujing Dajie, Dongcheng District.*

Yuetan Schichang. For old stamps, try the stamp traders' stalls along the west side of Yuetan Park. Coins are sold at many antiques and curio shops in the same area. ✉ *Yuetan Park, Haidian District.*

BEIJING A TO Z

To research prices, get advice from other travelers, and book travel arrangements, visit www.fodors.com.

AIR TRAVEL

Air China, China Eastern, and China Southern fly from the United States to Beijing and also provide domestic service. Northwest and United have service between Beijing and the United States. Air France, Austrian Airlines, British Airways, and KLM fly to Beijing from Paris, Vienna, London, and Amsterdam, respectively. Japan Airlines has service to Beijing via Tokyo, and Korean Air via Seoul.

🛂 Carriers **Air China** ☎ 010/6601-7755 ⊕ www.airchina.com. **Air France** ☎ 010/6588-1388 ⊕ www.airfrance.com. **Austrian Airlines** ☎ 010/6462-2161 ⊕ www.austrianair.com. **British Airways** ☎ 010/6512-4070 ⊕ www.ba.com. **China Eastern** ☎ 010/6468-1166 ⊕ www.ce-air.com. **China Southern** ☎ 010/6459-0539 or 010/6459-6490 ⊕ www.cs-air.com/en. **Japan Airlines** ☎ 010/6513-0888 ⊕ www.jal.com. **KLM** ☎ 010/6505-3505 ⊕ www.klm.com. **Korean Air** ☎ 010/6505-0088 ⊕ www.koreanair.com. **Northwest** ☎ 010/6505-3505 ⊕ www.nwa.com. **United** ☎ 010/6463-1111 or 800/810-8282 in China ⊕ www.ual.com.

AIRPORTS

The efficient Beijing Capital International Airport is 27 km (17 mi) northeast of the city center. Departing international passengers must pay a Y90 airport tax before check-in. Passengers on domestic flights must pay Y50. Coupons are sold at booths inside the terminal and collected at the entrance to the main departure hall. After checking in, plan on long lines at immigration if you're flying in from another country, especially in the morning.

🛂 Airport Information **Beijing Capital International Airport (BJS or PEK)** ☎ 010/6456-3604 ⊕ www.bcia.com.cn/en/index.html.

TRANSFERS   The easiest way to get from the airport to Beijing is by taxi. In addition, most major hotels have representatives at the airport able to arrange a car or minivan. When departing from Beijing by plane it's best to pre-book transportation through your hotel.

The taxi line is just outside the terminal beyond a small covered parking area. The (usually long) line moves quickly. Do not accept rides from drivers who try to coax you away from the line. These privateers simply want more cash. At the head of the line, a dispatcher will give you your taxi's number, useful in case of complaints or forgotten luggage. Insist that drivers use their meters, and do not negotiate a fare. If the driver is unwilling to comply, feel free to change taxis. Most of the taxis serving the airport are large-model cars. Flag fall is Y12 (good for 3½ km) plus Y2 per additional kilometer. Passengers are expected to pay the Y10 toll for the airport expressway. If you're caught in rush-hour traffic, expect standing surcharges. A taxi to the eastern district of Beijing (including the toll) costs about Y75; the trip to the center of town costs about Y90. In light traffic it takes about 30 minutes to reach Beijing's eastern district; during rush hour, allow at least 45 minutes. For the city center expect a one-hour cab ride. After 11 PM, taxis impose a 20% late-night surcharge.

The airport bus (Y12) terminal is outside the arrivals area. Buy tickets from the booth, which is easy to spot, before you exit, then cross the road to the buses. There are two routes (A and B), clearly marked in English and Chinese. On board, stops are often announced in English and Chinese (if not, the drivers on these routes speak basic English). Route A runs between the airport and the Beijing railway station, stopping at the airport expressway/Third Ring Road intersection, Lufthansa Center, Kunlun Hotel, Great Wall Sheraton Hotel, Dongzhimen subway station/Second Ring Road, Hong Kong Macau Center (Swissôtel), Chaoyangmen subway station, and one block north of the Beijing train station/Beijing International Hotel. Route B runs from the airport to the CAAC ticket office on Changan Dajie. It travels west along the Third Ring Road, following it south to Changan Jie. Stops include the SAS Hotel, Asian Games Village, Friendship Hotel, and Shangri-La Hotel.

BIKE TRAVEL

Although in many ways Beijing is made for pedaling, the proliferation of cars has made biking less pleasant and more dangerous. Fortunately, all of the city's main boulevards and many secondary streets have wide, well-defined bike lanes often separated from other traffic by an island with hedges or trees. If a flat tire or sudden brake failure strikes, seek out the nearest street-side mechanic (they're everywhere), easily identified by their bike parts and pumps.

Bikes can be rented just about everywhere in Beijing, although your hotel and CITS (the government tourism office) are the best places from which to rent.

BUS TRAVEL

TO BEIJING Beijing is served by several long-distance bus stations. The main ones are: Beijiao, also called Deshengmen (North); Dongzhimen (Northeast); Haihutun (South); Majuan (East); and Xizhimen (West). Long-distance buses are usually quite basic—much like an old-fashioned school bus—although some overnight buses now have two cramped decks with reclining seating or bunks.

🚩 **Beijiao** ✉ Deshengmenwai Dajie, Xicheng District ☎ 010/6204-7096. **Dongzhimen** ✉ Dongzhimenwaixie Jie, Chaoyang District ☎ 010/6467-4995 or 010/6460-8131. **Haihutun** ✉ Yongwai Chezan Lu, Fengtai District ☎ 010/6726-7149 or 010/6722-4641. **Majuan** ✉ Guangqumenwai Dajie, Chaoyang District ☎ 010/6771-7620 or 010/6771-7622. **Xizhimen** ✉ 2 Haidian Tou Duicun ☎ 010/6217-6075.

WITHIN BEIJING Getting on or off a Beijing city bus is often, quite literally, a fight. Buses are hot and crowded in summer and cold and crowded in winter. If you choose the bus—and you shouldn't—watch your belongings very carefully. The Beijing Public Transportation Corporation is the city's largest bus service provider. Fares are Y1 during the day and Y2 at night.

🚩 **Beijing Public Transportation Corporation** ⊕ www.bptc.com.

CAR TRAVEL

It is easy and inexpensive to hire a car and driver for travel and sight-seeing tours in and around Beijing. Most hotels can make arrangements for you, or you can even flag down a taxi and hire the driver for the day at a similar rate, between Y350 and Y600, depending on the type of car. Most drivers do not speak English, however, so be sure to have your destination and hotel names written down in Chinese.

Renting a car and driving yourself is not a good idea—the traffic is terrible and it's easy to get lost. American car-rental agencies include mandatory chauffeurs as part of all rental packages. *See* Car Rental in Smart Travel Tips.

EMBASSIES

🔼 Australia ✉ 21 Dongzhimenwai Dajie, Chaoyang District ☎ 010/6532-2331 🖷 010/6532-6718.

🔼 Canada ✉ 19 Dongzhimenwai Dajie, Chaoyang District ☎ 010/6532-3536 🖷 010/6532-4972.

🔼 New Zealand ✉ 1 Donger Jie, Ritanlu, Chaoyang District ☎ 010/6532-2732 or 010/6532-2733 🖷 010/6532-4317.

🔼 Republic of Ireland ✉ 3 Ritan Dong Lu, Chaoyang District ☎ 010/6532-2691 🖷 010/6532-6857.

🔼 South Africa ✉ Suite C801, Lufthansa Center, 50 Liangmaqiao Lu, Chaoyang District ☎ 010/6532-0172 🖷 010/6465-1965.

🔼 United Kingdom ✉ 11 Guanghua Lu, Jianguomenwai, Chaoyang District ☎ 010/6532-1961 🖷 010/6532-1937.

🔼 United States ✉ 3 Xiushui Bei Jie, Chaoyang District ☎ 010/6532-3431 Ext. 229 or 010/6532-3831 Ext. 264 🖷 010/6532-2483.

EMERGENCIES

In case of an emergency, call your embassy first; embassy staff members are available 24 hours a day to help handle emergencies and facilitate communication with local agencies. Often the police, and fire and medical emergency staff, do not speak much English. Asia Emergency Assistance Center (AEA) has 24-hour emergency and pharmacy assistance. Probably the best place for treatment in Beijing, the Beijing United Family Health Center has 24-hour emergency services. International Medical Clinic (IMC) has 24-hour emergency and pharmacy services, as well as a dental clinic.

🔼 Doctors & Dentists **Asia Emergency Assistance Center** ✉ 2-1-1 Tayuan Diplomatic Office Bldg., 14 Liangmahe Nan Lu, Chaoyang District ☎ 010/6462-9112 during office hrs, 010/6462-9100 after hrs. **Beijing United Family Health Center** ✉ 2 Jiangtai Lu, near Lido Hotel, Chaoyang District ☎ 010/6433-3960, 010/6433-2345 for emergencies. **International Medical Clinic** ✉ Beijing Lufthansa Center, Regis Office Bldg., Room S110, 50 Liagmaoqiao Lu, Chaoyang District ☎ 010/6465-1561 or 010/6465-1562.

🔼 Emergency Services **Fire** ☎ 119. **Police** ☎ 110. **Medical Emergency** ☎ 120. **Traffic Accident** ☎ 122.

ENGLISH-LANGUAGE MEDIA

There are several monthly English-language magazines and newspapers produced for travelers and expatriates, including *Beijing This*

Month, Metrozine, Beijing Journal, and *City Weekend.* They're available at hotels and restaurants around town. The Foreign Languages Bookstore and the Friendship Store carry English-language books. Most major hotels sell international newspapers and magazines, plus books about China.

▣ Bookstores **Foreign Languages Bookstore** ✉ 235 Wangfujing Dajie, Dongcheng District ☎ 010/6512-6922. **Friendship Store** ✉ 17 Jianguomenwai Dajie, Chaoyang District ☎ 010/6500-3311.

PEDICAB TRAVEL

Pedicabs were once the vehicle of choice for Beijingers laden with a week's worth of groceries or tourists eager for a street's-eye city tour. Today many residents are wealthy enough to bundle their purchases into taxis, and the tourist trade has moved on to the tight schedules of air-conditioned buses. But pedicabs still can be hired outside the Friendship Store on Jianguomenwai Dajie and near major tourist sites such as Liulichang and Beihai Park. Be sure to negotiate the fare in advance, clarifying which currency will be used (yuan or dollars), whether the fare is considered a one-way or round-trip (some drivers will demand payment for a round-trip whether or not you use the pedicab for the return journey), and whether it is for one person or two. Fares start at Y10.

SIGHTSEEING TOURS

Every major hotel can arrange guided tours to sights outside Beijing. Among the hotel-based travel agencies are Beijing Panda Tour and China Swan International Tours. China International Travel Service (CITS), the official government agency, can arrange tours. New travel agencies are springing up all the time in Beijing; ask at your hotel about alternatives to CITS.

▣ Fees & Schedules **Beijing Panda Tour** ✉ Holiday Inn Crowne Plaza, 48 Wangfujing Dajie, Dongcheng District ☎ 010/6513-3388 Ext. 1212 ⊕ www.pandatourchina.com. **China International Travel Service** ✉ 28 Jianguomenwai Dajie, Chaoyang District ☎ 010/6515-8565 🖨 010/6515-8603 ⊕ www.citsusa.com. **China Swan International Tours** ✉ Rm. 718, Beijing Capital Times Square, 88 Changan Jie, Xicheng District ☎ 010/8391-3058 ⊕ www.china-swan.com/english.htm.

BIKE TOURS   CycleChina leads guided one-day bicycling tours around Beijing and the Great Wall on weekends.

▣ Fees & Schedules **CycleChina** ☎ 1391/188-6524 ⊕ www.cyclechina.com.

PEDICAB TOURS   The Beijing Hutong Tourist Agency offers the only guided pedicab tour of Beijing's back alleys, with glimpses of buildings usually closed to the public. This half-day trip winds its way through what was once Beijing's most prestigious neighborhood (Houhai), stops at the Drum and Bell towers, and finishes with tea at Prince Gong's Palace. Advance reservations are recommended. Tours, which begin on Di'anmen Xidajie near the back entrance of Beihai Park, start at 9 and 2 daily, and cost about Y180 per person.

▣ Fees & Schedules **Beijing Hutong Tourist Agency** ✉ 26 Di'anmen Xidajie, Dongcheng District ☎ 010/6612-3236 🖨 010/6400-2787.

SUBWAY TRAVEL

The subway is a good way to travel if you want to avoid Beijing's increasingly frequent traffic jams. However, with only two lines, Beijing's subway service is limited. One line circles Beijing beneath the Second Ring Road and the other runs east–west from the city center to the western and eastern suburbs. The lines meet at Fuxingmen. The subway runs from 5 AM to midnight daily. Fares are Y3 per ride for any distance. Stations are marked in both Chinese and English.

TAXIS

There are three classes of taxis in Beijing. The cheapest grade of taxi is the *xiali,* a domestically produced car reminiscent of the first Honda hatchbacks. Tall people find xialis cramped. Flag fall for these taxis is Y10 for the first 4 km (2½ mi) and Y1.2 per kilometer thereafter. The next grade of taxi is similar to the xiali but is generally cleaner and more comfortable; it's often a Citroën or Volkswagen. Flag fall for these taxis is Y10 for the first 4 km (2½ mi) and Y1.6 per kilometer thereafter. At the top end are the sedans found waiting at the airport, major hotels, and large tourist sights. They're clean, comfortable, and still cheap compared with Western cabs. Flag fall is Y12 for the first 3½ km (2 mi) and Y2 per kilometer thereafter, depending on the vehicle. For all taxis, a 20% nighttime surcharge kicks in at 11 PM. Be sure to check that the meter has been engaged to avoid fare negotiations at your destination.

🚩 **Taxi Complaints** ☎ 010/6835-1150 🖷 010/6831-5960.

TRAIN TRAVEL

Beijing is served by four stations: the Beijing Zhan (Main) and Beijing Xi Zhan (West) stations (both of which have International Passenger Booking offices for foreigners), and the Beijing Bei Zhan (North) and Beijing Nan Zhan (South) stations. Most domestic routes depart from the massive Beijing Xi Zhan, Beijing's most modern station. Some major-city routes depart from the Beijing Zhan, as do international routes to Hong Kong or Siberia. Trains are directed to different stations depending on the intricate rail system and not on their travel destinations.

Tickets, which are sold up to five days in advance, can be purchased at all stations for trips that leave from that station, and you can also buy tickets at FESCO Travel Service in the China World Trade Center. Book early to ensure a seat. Ticket office hours are 5:30 AM–7:30 AM, 8 AM–5:30 PM, and 7 PM–12:30 AM.

🚩 **Train Information Beijing Bei Zhan** North Station ✉ 1 Xizhimenwai Beibinhelu,, Xicheng District ☎ 010/6223-1003. **Beijing Nan Zhan** South Station ✉ Yongdingmen, Chongwen District ☎ 010/6303-0031. **Beijing Xi Zhan** West Station ✉ Lianhuachi Dong Lu, Haidian District ☎ 010/5182-6253. **Beijing Zhan** Main Station ✉ Beijing Zhan Jie, Dongcheng District ☎ 010/6563-3262. **FESCO Travel Service** ✉ Level 1, China World Trade Center, Jianguimenwai Dajie, Chaoyang District ☎ 010/6461-4441.

VISITOR INFORMATION

China International Travel Service (CITS), an official government agency, maintains offices in many hotels and at some tourist venues. The Beijing Tourism Administration maintains a 24-hour hot line for tourist inquiries and complaints, with operators fluent in English.

Tourist Information **Beijing Tourism Administration hot line** ☎ 010/6513–0828. **China International Travel Service** ⊠ 28 Jianguomenwai Dajie, Chaoyang District ☎ 010/6515–8565 🖶 010/6515–8603.

SIDE TRIPS FROM BEIJING

THE GREAT WALL, THIRTEEN MING TOMBS, AND EASTERN QING TOMBS

2

Revised by
Guy Rubin

A VISIT TO BEIJING IS INCOMPLETE without a side trip to the Great Wall, one of China's most important sights. Within a few hours' drive of the city limits you can visit the wall at three different points, plus a cornucopia of other historical and natural wonders. Beyond the wall is a valley beautiful enough to serve as the burial ground for 13 Ming emperors. Also in the valley you can find one of the world's premier paleontological sites, Beijing's oldest bridge, and several important temples.

Adventurers will find excellent hiking opportunities at the Great Wall at Simatai, Thirteen Ming Tombs, and Eastern Qing Tombs. You can explore the ruins on foot and bring a picnic (a tradition among Beijing's expatriate community since the 1920s). Most hotels can arrange for car service to sites outside the city as well as elegant boxed lunches.

THE GREAT WALL

60–120 km (37–74 mi) north and west of Beijing.

Close to Beijing, 9 km (5½ mi) above the giant Juyongguan garrison and
❶ an hour by car from downtown, the **Great Wall at Badaling** (Badaling Changcheng) is where visiting dignitaries go for a quick photo-op. Its large sections of restored wall rise steeply to either side of the fort in a rugged landscape. Convenient to the Thirteen Ming Tombs, Badaling is popular with tour groups and is often crowded. People with disabilities find access to the wall at Badaling better than elsewhere in the Beijing area. You can either take the cable car to the top of the wall, or you can walk. ⊠ *Yanqing County, 70 km (43 mi) northwest of Beijing* ☎ *010/6912–1235 or 010/6912–1338* ✆ *Y45; cable car, Y40 one-way, Y60 round-trip* ⊙ *Daily 6:30 AM–sunset.*

★ ❷ A bit farther from downtown Beijing, the **Great Wall at Mutianyu** (Mutianyu Changcheng) is more spectacular and usually less crowded than Badaling. Here, a long section of restored wall is perched on a high ridge above serene wooded canyons. Views from the top of the surrounding landscape are memorable. The lowest point on the wall is a strenuous one-hour climb above the parking lot. As an alternative, you can take a cable car on a breathtaking ride to the highest restored section, from which several hiking trails descend. If you don't plan to hike, phone ahead to make sure the cable car is running. The Mutianyu section is also famed for its toboggan run, which starts three beacon towers east of the cable-car stop and runs all the way down the slope to the site entrance. Look for its reflective steel track snaking down the mountain side. Thrill-seeking teens and adults may want to take a toboggan down (one person at a time), but children under 1.2 meters (4 feet) are not allowed. ⊠ *Huairou County, 90 km (56 mi) northeast of Beijing* ☎ *010/6162–6873 or 010/6162–6506* ✆ *Y35; cable car, Y35 one-way, Y50 round-trip, Y55 with toboggan descent* ⊙ *Daily 7 AM–5 PM.*

❸ Remote and largely unrestored, the **Great Wall at Simatai** (Simatai
Fodor's Choice Changcheng) is ideal if you're seeking adventure. Near the frontier gar-
★ rison at Gubeikou, this section of wall traverses towering peaks and

hangs precariously above cliffs. In some places stairways are crumbling and the trail is so steep that the journey is more a crawl than a hike. Be prepared for no-handrails hiking, tough climbs, and unparalleled vistas. Several trails lead to the wall from the parking lot. The hike takes about two hours. A cable car serves a drop-off point about 40 minutes on foot from the wall. If you want a quieter, easier hike, head west from the small lake below the wall, toward the restored Jinshanling section. If you head east, you're in for a good but difficult walk. Eventually you will reach an ascent called the Ladder to Heaven that requires basic rock-climbing skills to scale. After this, the wall narrows to a foot wide with steep vertical drops on either side, sometimes hundreds of yards down. ⊠ *Near Miyun, Miyun County* ☎ *010/6903–5025 or 010/6903–1051* ☜ *Y20; cable car, Y40 one-way, Y60 round-trip* ☉ *Daily 8–5.*

THIRTEEN MING TOMBS

★ ❹ *48 km (30 mi) north of Beijing.*

A narrow valley just north of Changping is the final resting place for 13 of the Ming Dynasty's 16 emperors (the first Ming emperor was buried in Nanjing, the burial site of the second one is unknown, and the seventh Ming emperor was dethroned and buried in an ordinary tomb in west Beijing). Ming monarchs would journey here each year to kowtow before their clan forefathers and make offerings to their memory. The area's vast scale and imperial grandeur convey the importance attached to ancestor worship in ancient China.

The road to the Thirteen Ming Tombs (Ming Shisanling) begins beneath an imposing stone portico that stands at the valley entrance. Beyond the entrance, a **shendao** (☜ Y16 ☉ Daily 9–5:30), or spirit way, once reserved for imperial travel, passes through an outer pavilion and between rows of stone sculptures—imperial advisers and huge, serene elephants, lions, horses, and other creatures—on its 7-km (4½-mi) journey to the burial sites.

The spirit way leads to **Changling** (☎ 010/6076–1886 ☜ Y30), the head tomb built for Emperor Yongle in 1427. Architecturally, it matches the design of Yongle's great masterpiece, the Forbidden City, which he built after moving the Ming's imperial capital north to Beijing. The tomb is open daily from 8:30 to 4:30.

Changling and a second tomb, **Dingling** (☎ 010/6076–1424 ☜ Y60 Mar.–June and Sept.–Nov.; Y40 July–Aug. and Dec.–Feb.), were rebuilt in the 1980s and opened to the public. Both complexes suffer from over-restoration and overcrowding, but they're worth visiting if only for the tomb relics on display in the small museums at each site. Dingling is particularly worth seeing because this tomb of Emperor Wanli is the only Ming Dynasty tomb which has been excavated. Unfortunately, this was done in 1956 when China's archaeological skills were sadly lacking, resulting in irrecoverable losses. Nonetheless, it is interesting to compare this underground vault with the tomb of Emperor Qianlong

Numbers in the text correspond to numbers in the margin and on the Side Trips from Beijing map.

If you have
2 days

On the first day hire a car and visit the **Great Wall at Simatai** ❸ ⌐,
one of the most impressive sections of the Great Wall of China. Here,
long, unrestored strands ascend steep crags. Be prepared for tough
climbs, which will be rewarded by fantastic views. On the second
day, head west to **Fahai Temple** ❺ about an hour from the center
of Beijing. See **Jietai Temple** ❻ in the afternoon before returning
to the city.

If you have
3 days

On your third day head to the **Eastern Qing Tombs** ❿, where a "spirit
way" lined with carved stone animals leads to templelike tombs in a beautiful rural setting. Wear walking shoes and bring a lunch. The drive from Beijing takes about five hours round-trip, so depart early.

at Qingdongling. Dingling is open daily from 8:30 to 5:30. Allow
ample time for a hike or drive northwest from Changling to the six fenced-
off **unrestored tombs,** a short distance farther up the valley. Here,
crumbling walls conceal vast courtyards shaded by venerable pine
trees. At each tomb, a stone altar rests beneath a stela tower and burial
mound. In some cases the wall that circles the burial chamber is accessible on steep stone stairways that ascend from either side of the altar.
At the valley's terminus (about 5 km [3 mi] northwest of Changling),
the **Zhaoling tomb** rests beside a traditional walled village. This thriving hamlet is well worth exploring.

Picnics amid the Ming ruins have been a favorite weekend activity
among Beijing-based diplomats for nearly a century. The signs pro-
hibiting this activity are largely ignored; if you do choose to picnic
here, though, be sure to carry out all trash. ⊠ *Near Changping, Changping County.*

FAHAI TEMPLE

❺ *20 km (12 mi) west of Beijing.*

The stunning works of Buddhist mural art at Fahai Temple (Fahaisi) are
among the most underappreciated sights in Beijing. Li Tong, a favored
eunuch in the court of Emperor Zhengtong (1436–1449), donated funds
to construct Fahai Temple in 1443. The project was highly ambitious:
Li Tong invited only celebrated imperial and court painters to decorate
the temple. As a result, the murals in the only surviving chamber of that
period, Daxiongbaodian (the Mahavira Hall), are considered the finest
examples of Buddhist mural art from the Ming Dynasty. Sadly, statues
of various Buddhas and one of Li Tong himself were destroyed during
China's Cultural Revolution.

Side Trips from Beijing

HEBEI

Guanting Reservoir

Yanqing

JUNDU SHAN

Great Wall at Mutianyu ❷

Great Wall at Badaling ❶

Thirteen Ming Tombs ❹

Changling

Changping

BEIJING SHI

Capital Airport

Old Summer Palace

Summer Palace

Xiangshan Park (Fragrant Hills Park)

Qingshui He

Yongding He

XI SHAN

Mentougou

❺ **Fahai Temple**

CENTRAL BEIJING

Tanzhe Temple

Jetai Temple ❻

❼

Marco Polo Bridge (Lougouqiao)

Yongding He

Lian

Daxing

Fangshan

Zhoukoudian Peking Man Site ❽

❾ **Yunju Temple**

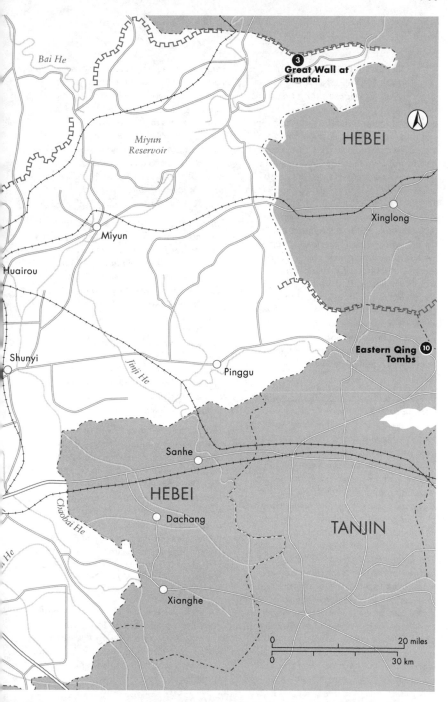

Bai He

3
Great Wall at Simatai

Miyun Reservoir

HEBEI

Xinglong

Miyun

Huairou

Eastern Qing Tombs **10**

Shunyi

Jinji He

Pinggu

Sanhe

HEBEI

Chaobai He

Dachang

TANJIN

Xianghe

| 0 | | 20 miles |
| 0 | | 30 km |

CloseUp

HOW THE WALL WAS BUILT

BUILT BY SUCCESSIVE DYNASTIES OVER TWO MILLENNIA, the Great Wall (Changcheng) isn't actually one structure built at one time, but a series of layered defensive installations that grew and shrank with the empire. This protective cordon extends 4,000 km (2,480 mi) from the East China Sea west to central Asia; estimates for the combined length of the varying structures range from 10,000 km (6,200 mi) to 20,000 km (12,400 mi). The construction techniques and materials used on the Great Wall varied by location. In the Taklimakan Desert, for example, you can still find sections of the Great Wall dating to the second century BC that were made by combining twigs, straw, rice, and sand. Other sections of the wall from this period were made of rammed earth. The more substantial brick-and-earth ruins that snake across the mountains north of Beijing date from the Ming Dynasty (14th–17th centuries).

The first wall built along China's northern frontier dates to the seventh century BC, but is no longer standing. The oldest surviving section of wall dates to the fifth century BC and is in modern-day Shandong province. These and other sections were built to protect China's northern kingdoms from marauding nomadic tribes, such as the Xiongnu. Over subsequent centuries, more portions of wall were built, creating a motley collection of northern borders. It was the first emperor of a unified China, Qin Shihuang (circa 259–210 BC), founder of the Qin Dynasty in 221 BC, who linked together these various fortifications into a single defense network that would protect the entire northern frontier of his massive empire. By some accounts, Qin mustered nearly a million people, or about a fifth of China's total workforce, a mobilization that claimed countless lives and gave rise to many tragic folktales. (The most famous concerns Lady Meng, a woman whose husband was kidnapped on their wedding night to build the Great Wall. She traveled to the work site to wait for his return, believing her determination would eventually bring him back. In the end, she was turned into a rock, which to this day stands at the head of the Great Wall in the beautiful seaside town of Qinhuangdao, some 480 km [300 mi] east of Beijing.)

Later dynasties repaired existing walls or built new ones. The Ming Dynasty, which took power in 1368, committed vast resources to wall building as a defense against increasingly restive northern tribes. The Ming wall, which is about 26 feet tall and 30 feet wide at its base, could accommodate five horsemen riding abreast on its top. It incorporated small wall-top garrisons linked by beacon towers used for sending smoke signals or setting off fireworks to warn of enemy attack. In the end, however, the wall failed to prevent the Manchu invasion that toppled the Ming in 1644.

That historical failure hasn't tarnished the Great Wall's image. Although China's official line once cast it as a model of feudal oppression—focusing on the brutality suffered by work crews and the vast treasures squandered on the useless fortification—the Great Wall is now touted as a national patriotic symbol. "Love China, Restore the Great Wall," declared Deng Xiaoping in a 1984 campaign that kicked off the official revisionism. Since then large sections of the Great Wall have been repaired and opened to visitors.

If you've hired a car to the Great Wall, consider venturing a bit farther into the countryside where farming villages await. Don't be surprised if local farmers invite you into their homes for a rest and some tea.

The most famous of the nine murals in Mahavira Hall is a large-scale triptych featuring Guanyin (the Bodhisattva of Compassion) and Wenshu (the Bodhisattva of Marvelous Virtue and Gentle Majesty) in the center, and Poxian (the Buddha of Universal Virtue) on either side. The depiction of Guanyin follows the theme of "moon in water," which compares the Buddhist belief in the illusoriness of the material world to the reflection of the moon in the water. Typically painted with Guanyin are her legendary mount Jin Sun and her assistant Shancai Tongzi. Wenshu is often presented with a lion, symbolic of the bodhissatva's wisdom and strength of will, while Poxian is shown near a six-tusked elephant, each tusk representing one of the qualities that leads to enlightenment. On the opposite wall is the *Sovereign Sakra and Brahma* mural, with a panoply of characters from the Buddhist canon.

The murals were painted during the time of the European Renaissance, and though the subject matter is traditional, there are comparable experiments in perspective taking place in the depiction of the figures, as compared with examples from earlier dynasties. Also of note is a highly unusual decorative technique; many contours in the hall's murals, particularly on jewelry, armor, and weapons, have been set in bold relief by the application of fine gold threads.

The temple grounds are also beautiful, but of overriding interest are the murals themselves. Plans are in the works to limit access to the poorly lit, original murals by one day creating a visitor center with well-illuminated reproductions. For now, visitors stumble through the dark temple with rented flashlights. Fahai Temple is only a short taxi ride from Beijing's Pinguoyuan subway station. ⊠ *Moshikou Lu, Shijingshan District, Beijing* ☎ *010/8871–5776* ☒ *Y20* ☉ *Daily 9–4:30.*

Eunuchs have played an important role throughout Chinese history, often holding great influence over affairs of state, yet surprisingly little is known about them. The **Beijing Eunuch Culture Exhibition Hall** (Beijing Huangguan Wenhua Chenlie Guan), near the magnificent **Tian Yi Mu** (Tomb of Tian Yi), begins to redress this lack of information. Tian Yi (1534–1605) was only nine when he was castrated and sent into the service of the Ming emperor Jiajing. He spent the next 63 years of his life serving three emperors and rose to one of the highest ranks in the land, the Director of Ceremonies. His tomb, though not as magnificent as the Thirteen Ming Tombs, nonetheless befits a man of such high social status. Particularly noteworthy in the tomb complex are the stone carvings around the base of the central mound depicting ancient anecdotes. The four smaller tombs on either side belong to other eunuchs who wished to pay tribute to Tian Yi by being buried in the same compound with him.

The small exhibition hall at the front of the tomb complex contains limited background information, most of it in Chinese, about famous eunuchs. Keep an eye out for the ancient Chinese character meaning " to castrate," which resembles two knives, one inverted, side by side. Also here is a list of all the temples in Beijing that were founded by eunuchs. The hall and tomb are a five-minute walk from Fahai Temple; just ask people the way to Tian Yi Mu. ✉ *80 Moshikou Lu, Shijingshan District, Beijing* ☎ *010/8872–4148* 🎫 *Y8* ⏲ *Daily 9–5.*

JIETAI TEMPLE

❻ *35 km (22 mi) west of Beijing.*

On a wooded hill west of Beijing, Jietai Temple (Jietaisi) is one of China's most famous ancient Buddhist sites. Its four main halls occupy terraces on a gentle slope up to Ma'an Shan (Saddle Hill). Originally built in AD 622, the temple complex expanded over the centuries and grew to its current scale in a major renovation conducted by devotees during the Qing Dynasty (1644–1912). The temple buildings, plus three magnificent bronze Buddhas in the Mahavira Hall, date from this period. To the right of this hall, just above twin pagodas, is the Ordination Terrace, a platform built of white marble and topped with a massive bronze Sakyamuni (Buddha) seated on a lotus flower. Tranquil courtyards, where ornate stelae and well-kept gardens bask beneath the Scholar Tree and other ancient pines, augment the temple's beauty. Many modern devotees from Beijing visit the temple on weekends. ✉ *Mentougou County* ☎ *010/6980–6611* 🎫 *Y35* ⏲ *Daily 8–5.*

en route

Farther along the road past Jietai Temple, **Tanzhe Temple** (Tanzhe Si) is a Buddhist complex nestled in a grove of *zhe* (cudrania) trees. Established around AD 400 and once home to more than 500 monks, Tanzhe was heavily damaged during the Cultural Revolution; it has since been restored. The complex makes an ideal side trip from Jietai Temple or Lugouqiao. ✉ *Mentougou County* ☎ *010/6086–2500* ✣ *10 km (6 mi) northeast of Jietai Temple, 45 km (28 mi) west of Beijing* 🎫 *Y35* ⏲ *Daily 8–5.*

MARCO POLO BRIDGE

❼ *16 km (10 mi) southwest of Beijing's Guanganmen Gate.*

Built in 1192 and reconstructed after severe flooding during the Qing Dynasty, this impressive span—known as Marco Polo Bridge (Lugouqiao) because it was praised by the Italian wayfarer—is Beijing's oldest bridge. Its 11 segmented stone arches cross the Yongding River on what was once the imperial highway that linked Beijing with central China. The bridge's marble balustrades support nearly 485 carved stone lions that decorate elaborate handrails. Note the giant stone slabs that comprise the bridge's original roadbed. Carved imperial stelae at either end of the span commemorate the bridge and surrounding scenery.

The Marco Polo Bridge is best remembered in modern times as the spot where invading Japanese armies clashed with Chinese soldiers on June 7, 1937. The assault began Japan's brutal eight-year occupation of eastern China, which ended with Tokyo's surrender at the end of World War II. The bridge has become a popular field-trip destination for Beijing students. On the Beijing side of the span is the **Memorial Hall of the**

War of Resistance Against Japan (Kangri Zhanzheng Jinianguan). Below the bridge on the opposite shore, local entrepreneurs rent horses (the asking price is Y120 per hour, but you should bargain) and lead tours of the often-dry riverbed. ⊠ *Near Xidaokou, Fengtai District* ☎ *010/ 8389–3919* 🎟 *Y10* ⊙ *Daily 8:30–6.*

ZHOUKOUDIAN PEKING MAN SITE

8 *48 km (30 mi) southwest of Beijing.*

This area of lime mines and craggy foothills ranks among the world's great paleontological sites (and served as the setting for Amy Tan's *The Bonesetter's Daughter*). In 1929 anthropologists, drawn to Zhoukoudian by apparently human "dragon bones" found in a Beijing apothecary, unearthed a complete cranium and other fossils dubbed homo erectus pekinensis, or Peking Man. These early remains, believed to be nearly 700,000 years old, suggest (as do similar homo erectus discoveries in Indonesia) that humankind's most recent ancestor originated in Asia, not Europe (though today some scientists posit that humans evolved in Africa first and migrated to Asia). A large-scale excavation in the early 1930s further unearthed six skullcaps and other hominid remains, stone tools, evidence of fire, plus a multitude of animal bones, many at the bottom of a large sinkhole believed to be a trap for woolly rhinos and other large game. Sadly, the Peking Man fossils disappeared under mysterious circumstances during World War II, leaving researchers only plaster casts to contemplate. Subsequent digs at Zhoukoudian have yielded nothing equivalent to Peking Man, although archaeologists haven't yet abandoned the search. Trails lead to several hillside excavation sites. A small museum showcases a few (dusty) Peking Man statues, a collection of Paleolithic artifacts, two mummies, and some fine animal fossils, including a bear skeleton and a saber-toothed tiger skull. Because of the importance of Peking Man and the potential for other finds in the area, Zhoukoudian is a UNESCO World Heritage Site, but it may not be of much interest to those without a particular inclination for the subject. ⊠ *Zhoukoudian* ☎ *010/6930–1272* 🎟 *Y30* ⊙ *Daily 9:30–5.*

YUNJU TEMPLE

9 *75 km (47 mi) southwest of Beijing.*

Yunju Temple (Yunjusi) is best known for its mind-boggling collection of 14,278 minutely carved Buddhist tablets. To protect the Buddhist canon from destruction by Taoist emperors, the devout Tang-era monk Jing Wan carved Buddhist scriptures into stone slabs that he hid in sealed caves in the cliffs of a mountain. Jing Wan spent 30 years creating these tablets until his death in AD 637; his disciples continued his work for the next millennium into the 17th century, thereby compiling one of the most extensive Buddhist libraries in the world. A small pagoda at the center of the temple complex commemorates the remarkable monk. Although the tablets were originally stored inside Shijing Mountain behind the temple, they are now housed in rooms built along the temple's southern perimeter.

Four central prayer halls, arranged along the hillside above the main gate, contain impressive Ming-era bronze Buddhas. The last in this row, the Dabei Hall, displays the spectacular *Thousand-Arm Avalokiteshvara.* This 13-foot-tall bronze sculpture—which actually has 24 arms and five heads and stands in a giant lotus flower—is believed to embody boundless compassion. A group of pagodas, led by the 98-foot-tall Northern Pagoda, is all that remains of the original Tang complex. These pagodas are remarkable for their Buddhist reliefs and ornamental patterns. Heavily damaged during the Japanese occupation and again by Maoist radicals in the 1960s, the temple complex remains under renovation. ✉ *Off Fangshan Lu, Nanshangle Xiang, Fangshan County* ☎ *010/ 6138–9612* 💰 *Y30* ⊗ *Daily 8:30–5:30.*

EASTERN QING TOMBS

❿ *125 km (78 mi) east of Beijing.*

Fodor'sChoice
★

Modeled on the Thirteen Ming Tombs, the Eastern Qing Tombs (Qing Dongling) replicate the Ming spirit ways, walled tomb complexes, and subterranean burial chambers. But they're even more extravagant in their scale and grandeur. The ruins contain the remains of five emperors, 14 empresses, and 136 imperial concubines, all laid to rest in a broad valley chosen by Emperor Shunzhi (1638–61) while on a hunting expedition. By the Qing's collapse in 1911, the tomb complex covered some 18 square mi of farmland and forested hillside, making it the most expansive burial ground in all China.

The Eastern Qing Tombs are in much better repair than their older Ming counterparts. Although several of the tomb complexes have undergone extensive renovation, none is overdone. Peeling paint, grassy courtyards, and numerous stone bridges and pathways convey a sense of the area's original grandeur. Often, visitors are so few that you may feel as if you've stumbled upon an ancient ruin unknown beyond the valley's farming villages.

Of the nine tombs open to the public, two are not to be missed. The first, **Yuling,** is the resting place of the Qing Dynasty's most powerful sovereign, Emperor Qianlong (1711–99), who ruled China for 59 years. Beyond the outer courtyards, Qianlong's burial chamber is accessible from inside Stela Hall, where an entry tunnel descends some 65 feet into the ground and ends at the first of three elaborately carved marble gates. Beyond, exquisite carvings of Buddhist images and sutras rendered in Tibetan adorn the tomb's walls and ceiling. Qianlong was laid to rest, along with his empress and two concubines, in the third and final marble vault, amid priceless offerings looted by warlords early in the 20th century.

Dingdongling was built for the infamous Empress Dowager Cixi (1835–1911). Known for her failure to halt Western imperialist encroachment, Cixi once spent funds allotted to strengthen China's navy on a traditional stone boat for the lake at the Summer Palace. Her burial compound, reputed to have cost 72 tons of silver, is the most elaborate (if not the largest) at the Eastern Qing Tombs. Many of its stone carvings are considered significant because the phoenix, which symbolized the female, is level with, or even above, the imperial (and male) dragon—a feature, ordered, no doubt, by the empress herself. A peripheral hall paneled in gold leaf displays some of the luxuries amassed by Cixi and her entourage, including embroidered gowns, jewelry, a selection of imported cigarettes, and even a coat for one of her dogs. In a bow to tourist kitsch, the compound's main hall contains a wax statue of Cixi sitting Buddha-like on a lotus petal flanked by a chambermaid and a eunuch.

The Eastern Qing Tombs are a two- to three-hour drive from the capital. The rural scenery is dramatic, and the trip is arguably the best full-day excursion outside Beijing. ⊠ *Near Malanguan, HebeiIn, Zunhua County* ☎ *0315/694–5348* ⊠ *Y80* ☉ *Daily 8:30–5.*

SIDE TRIPS FROM BEIJING A TO Z

To research prices, get advice from other travelers, and book travel arrangements, visit www.fodors.com.

BUS TRAVEL

Although bus travel can provide an interesting insight into the life of local Beijingers, it is neither timely nor convenient for visitors with little time to spare. Taxis, which in Beijing are both plentiful and reasonably priced, are the best way to get to sights outside the city.

TAXI

The best way of getting to Fahai Temple is to take a taxi from Pinguoyuan subway station directly to the temple. The taxi ride should cost little more than Y10.

TOURS

Every major hotel can arrange guided tours to sights outside Beijing. Among the hotel-based travel agencies are Beijing Panda Tour and China Swan International Tours. China International Travel Service (CITS), the official government agency, can arrange tours. New travel agencies are springing up all the time in Beijing; ask at your hotel about alternatives to CITS.

On weekends, CycleChina leads guided one-day bicycling tours to the Great Wall.

🚩 **Fees & Schedules Beijing Panda Tour** ⊠ Holiday Inn Crowne Plaza, 48 Wangfujing Dajie, Dongfeng District ☎ 010/6513-3388 Ext. 1212. **China International Travel Service** ⊠ 28 Jianguomenwai Dajie, Chaoyang District ☎ 010/6515-8565 🖷 010/6515-8603. **China Swan International Tours** ⊠ Rm. 718, Beijing Capital Times Square, 88 Changan Jie, Xicheng District ☎ 010/8391-3058 ⊕ www.china-swan.com/english.htm. **CycleChina** ☎ 1391/188-6524 ⊕ www.cyclechina.com.

VISITOR INFORMATION

China International Travel Service (CITS), an official government agency, maintains offices in many hotels and at some tourist venues. The Beijing Tourism Administration maintains a 24-hour hot line for tourist inquiries and complaints, with operators fluent in English.

🚩 Tourist Information **Beijing Tourism Administration hot line** ☎ 010/6513-0828. **China International Travel Service** ✉ 28 Jianguomenwai Dajie, Chaoyang District ☎ 010/6515-8565 📠 010/6515-8603.

SHANGHAI
THE HEAD OF THE DRAGON

3

Revised by
Kristin Baird
Rattini

SHANGHAI, THE MOST NOTORIOUS OF CHINESE CITIES, once known as the Paris of the East, now calls itself the Pearl of the Orient. No other city can better capture the urgency and excitement of China's economic reform, understandably because Shanghai is at the center of it.

A port city, lying at the mouth of Asia's longest and most important river, Shanghai is famous as a place where internationalism has thrived. Opened to the world as a treaty port in 1842, Shanghai for decades was not one city but a divided territory. The British, French, and Americans each claimed their own concessions, neighborhoods where their laws and culture—rather than China's—were the rule.

By the 1920s and '30s, Shanghai was a place of sepia-lighted nightclubs, French villas, and opium dens. Here rich taipans walked the same streets as gamblers, prostitutes, and beggars, and Jews fleeing persecution in Russia lived alongside Chinese intellectuals and revolutionaries.

But now Shanghai draws more parallels to New York City than Paris. A true city, it is laid out on a grid (unlike sprawling Beijing), and with a population of 16 million, it is one of the world's most crowded urban areas. The Shanghainese have a reputation for being sharp, open-minded, glamorous, sophisticated, and business-oriented, and they're convinced they have the motivation and attitude to achieve their place as China's powerhouse. Far away from Beijing's watchful political eyes, yet supported by state officials who call Shanghai their hometown, the people have a freedom to grow that their counterparts in the capital don't enjoy. That ambition can be witnessed firsthand across Shanghai's Huangpu River, which joins the Yangzi at the northern outskirts of the city. Here lies Shanghai's most important building project—Pudong New Area, China's 21st-century financial, economic, and commercial center. Pudong, literally "the east side of the river," is home to Shanghai's stock market building, the tallest hotel in the world, the city's international airport, and the world's first commercial "mag lev" (magnetic levitation) train. Rising from land that just a few years ago was dominated by farm fields is the city's pride and joy, the Oriental Pearl Tower—a gaudy, flashing, spaceshiplike pillar, the tallest in Asia. As Shanghai prepares to host the 2010 World Expo, Pudong is again immersed in a decade-long round of construction.

Puxi, the west side of the river and the city center, has also gone through staggering change. Charming old houses are making way for shiny high-rises. The population is moving from alley housing in the city center to spanking-new apartments in the suburbs. Architecturally spectacular museums and theaters are catching the world's attention. Malls are popping up on every corner. In 1987 there were about 150 high-rise buildings in the city. Today there are more than 3,000, and the number continues to grow. Shanghai is reputed to be home to one-fifth of all the world's construction cranes.

Shanghai's open policy has also made the city a magnet for foreign investors. As millions of dollars pour in, especially to Pudong, Shanghai has again become home to tens of thousands of expatriates. Foreign influence has made today's Shanghai a consumer heaven. Domestic stores rub

Numbers in the text correspond to numbers in the margin and on the Shanghai map.

If you have

3 days

Start with a trip to **Yu Garden ❶ ▶**, sip some tea, and take a walk around the surrounding old Chinese city and its antiques markets. Afterward, work your way over to **the Bund ❻** for a leisurely stroll, take a quick look at the historic **Peace Hotel ⓫**, and walk down **Nanjing Lu** to experience Shanghai's busiest street. For dinner, the exceptional M on the Bund offers good views of the river and the Bund lit up at night.

The next day take a cab north to **Jade Buddha Temple ㉕**. Afterward, head back to Nanjing Lu if you didn't finish its sights the day before. Spend the afternoon people-watching at **People's Square ⓯**, taking in China's ancient treasures at **Shanghai Museum ⓱**, and swinging over to the nearby **Bird and Flower Market ⓳**.

Day 3 can be spent walking in the French Concession, particularly around Huaihai Lu, for a view of old Shanghai and the city's new chic stores. Here you can also tour **Sun Yat-sen's former residence ㉘** and the **First Chinese Communist Party Congress site ㉖ ▶**. The evenings of Days 2 and 3 can be spent catching a show of the Shanghai acrobats, relaxing on a night cruise of the Huangpu River, or experiencing Shanghai's happening nightlife.

If you have

5 days

Follow the three-day itinerary and on the fourth day make a trip to Pudong and go to the top of the **Oriental Pearl Tower ㊹** or the spectacular **Jinmao Tower ㊸**—or both—for a bird's-eye view of the city. On Day 5 go to the Hongkou District to stroll around the old houses and **Ohel Moshe Synagogue ㊶**, take a peek at **Lu Xun Park and Memorial ㊽**, and spend some time on **Duolun Lu ㊾**. Fill any spare time with visits to Shanghai's antiques markets, antique-furniture warehouses, and arts and crafts stores.

shoulders with the boutiques of Louis Vuitton, Christian Dior, and Ralph Lauren. Newly made businessmen battle rush-hour traffic in their Mercedes and Lexus cars. Young people keep the city up until the wee hours as they dance the night away in clubs blasting techno music. And everyone walks around with a cell phone. It's not surprising that the Shanghainese enjoy one of the highest living standards in China. Higher salaries and higher buildings, more business and more entertainment—they all define the fast-paced lives of China's most cosmopolitan and open people.

EXPLORING SHANGHAI

Shanghai as a whole encompasses a huge area. However, the city center is a relatively small district in Puxi (west of the river). On the east side lies what many think is Shanghai's future—Pudong (east of the river).

Shanghai's main east–west roads are named for Chinese cities, while some north–south streets are named for Chinese provinces.

The city was once delineated by its foreign concessions, and to some extent, the former borders still define the city. The old Chinese city is now surrounded by the Zhonghua Lu–Renmin Lu circle. North of the city, the International Settlement—run by the British, Americans, Europeans, and Japanese—was the area between the Huangpu River and Huashan Lu, and bordered by Suzhou Creek to the north and Yanan Lu to the south. The former French Concession lies south of Yanan Lu, north of Zhaojiabang Lu. The southwest corner of the Concession lies at Xujiahui, from which point it runs all the way east to the Bund, with the exception of the northern half of the old Chinese city.

Although technically most Shanghainese consider the city center to be whatever lies within the Ring Road, the heart of the city is found on its chief east–west streets—Nanjing Lu, Huaihai Lu, and Yanan Lu—cut off in the west approximately at Wulumuqi Lu and in the east by the Bund. At one time, the closer you got to the Bund, the stronger the heartbeat became, but with the city's constant construction, demographics are also changing, and the heart of Shanghai seems to beat ever outward.

To the east and west of city center lie Shanghai's new development areas. In Hongqiao, the area outside the Ring Road to the west, are office and commercial buildings for foreign and domestic business and the residential area of Gubei. Rising from countryside across the Huangpu River to the east is Pudong, the new concrete behemoth that Deng Xiaoping designated as China's future financial, economic, and commercial center. It's quickly fulfilling its destiny.

Shanghai is very much a walking city, so parts of it are easily explored on foot, and taxis are readily available. In compact central Shanghai, cab rides would be short if not for the outrageous traffic. Water towns outside Shanghai offer getaways from the city's urban chaos, and with ever-improving roads and public transportation, day trips to Suzhou, Zhouzhuang, and Hangzhou are possible.

The Old City & the Bund

When Shanghai was carved up by foreign powers, one part of the central city remained under Chinese law and administration. These old winding back alleys eventually became notorious as a gangster- and opium-filled slum. Today the narrow meandering lanes and a dwindling number of tiny pre-1949 houses are still standing (though the vices have disappeared for the most part). A walk through the Old City gives an idea of how most Shanghainese once lived and many still do. The city's most important sightseeing spot, the Bund, on Shanghai's waterfront, has outstanding foreign buildings from pre-1949 times.

A Good Walk

Start at **Yu Garden** ❶ ▶. Stroll through the garden, check out the bazaar surrounding it, and stop at the teahouse for a serene rest. Just outside

3

Architecture   Shanghai's history is eclectic, and so is its architecture. Although significant portions of the city are making way for skyscrapers, some of what has defined its original charm still exists. From the neoclassicism of the Bund to the art deco of the French Concession to the quaint Chinese alleys of the old city, a walk through town can evoke memories of romantic old Shanghai. But hurry: as you read this, old buildings are being torn down. The high points, literally, of new architecture are the skyscraping Jinmao Tower and Oriental Pearl Tower in Pudong, both of which have opened sky-high observatories.

Shopping   Because of Shanghai's commercial status as China's most open port city, it has the widest variety of goods to be found in the nation after Hong Kong. Ritzy chrome shopping malls stand alongside dingy state-run stores and around the corner from local markets, inundating the consumer with both foreign name brands and domestic goods. Take some time to browse the curio stands and stores around Yu Garden and to do some window-shopping on Nanjing Xi Lu, China's premier shopping street for designer and luxury goods.

---

the bazaar, meander through the **Cang Bao Antiques Building ②** on Fangbang Lu or, just one block north, stop in at the **Chen Xiang Ge Temple ③**. You can also wander the small alleys of the Old City, which lies inside the Renmin Lu–Zhonghua Lu circle. Within these alleys is a bustle of activity. Follow Dajing Lu west from Henan Lu and you can watch how locals shop for groceries at a wet market or see the last standing section of the **Old City Wall ④**. A bit farther, southwest of the intersection of Dajing Lu and Xizang Lu, lies **Dongtai Lu Antiques Market ⑤**, several blocks lined with antique vendors' stalls.

From the Old City, you can take a taxi or walk east along Jinling Lu to **the Bund ⑥**, which begins along the river. A raised concrete promenade borders the side of the street nearest the river. At the intersection of Zhongshan Dong Lu and Jinling Lu, marked by a pedestrian overpass, you'll see the observation tower that houses the **Bund Museum ⑦**. If you're feeling adventurous, you can jump on a ferry boat and start a tour of Pudong here. The Huangpu River Cruises dock is also nearby. Or walk north and mingle with the crowds of strolling families, lovers walking hand in hand, and camera-snapping tourists.

If you continue walking north, historic buildings begin appearing on the west side of the street facing the river. Just north of Yanan Dong Lu, in the former Union Assurance Company Building, is the high-profile **Three On the Bund ⑧**, a dining, shopping, and art complex. Farther along is the **Former Hongkong and Shanghai Bank Building ⑨** and the **Customs House ⑩**, which houses the Big Qing, or clock tower. At Shanghai's main thoroughfare, Nanjing Lu, you'll see one of the city's most famous monuments: the **Peace Hotel ⑪** consists of the two buildings on the cor-

Shanghai

ner of the Bund and Nanjing Lu. Just north of the Peace Hotel is the **Bank of China** ⑫, the main bank in the city.

Across the street on the river lies **Huangpu Park** ⑬, which has a statue of Chen Yi, Shanghai's first mayor after 1949. North of him is the obelisk-like Memorial of the Heroes of the People and, at its base, the **Bund History Museum** ⑭. At this point you've come to the junction of the Bund and Beijing Dong Lu. Across the old Waibaidu Bridge on Suzhou Creek there are more pre-1949 buildings: the art deco Shanghai Dasha (Shanghai Mansions, now called Broadway Mansions) is in front of you to the left, and the former Shanghai Stock Exchange and the Russian Consulate are to the right. All these old buildings face the modern skyline of Pudong, which lies on the other side of the river, with the **Oriental Pearl Tower** and the **Jinmao Tower** rising above the water. The Bund provides a good vantage point for viewing both prerevolutionary and postopening Shanghai.

TIMING   It can take about two hours to stroll casually without stopping at any sights. Allow another two hours to wander through the Yu Garden, bazaar, and teahouse, which are almost always crowded, and especially so on weekends. Plan on another hour if you go to Dajing Ge and the Dongtai Lu antique market. Access to many of the Bund's old buildings is not allowed, but if you go inside the ones that are open to visitors, you should allow 15 minutes per building. Note that the Bund gets crowded on weekends, but isn't too bad on weekdays. For a cruise on the Huangpu River, count on one to three hours.

On National Day (October 1) and Labor Day (May 1), the Bund is closed to bicycle and automobile traffic, and the roads are choked with people. On those days a fireworks show is usually put on over the water.

What to See

⑫ **Bank of China** (Zhongguo Yinhang). Here, old Shanghai's Western architecture (British art deco in this case) mixes with Chinese elements. In 1937 it was designed to be the highest building in the city and surpassed the neighboring Cathay Hotel (now the Peace Hotel) by a hair, except for the green tower on the Cathay's roof. ✉ *23 The Bund (Zhongshan Dong Yi Lu), Huangpu District* ☎ *021/6329–1979.*

⑥ **The Bund** (Waitan). Shanghai's waterfront boulevard best shows both
Fodor'sChoice   the city's pre-1949 past and its focus on the future. The district's name
★   is derived from the Anglo-Indian and literally means "muddy embankment." In the early 1920s the Bund became the city's foreign street: Americans, British, Japanese, French, Russians, Germans, and other Europeans built banks, trading houses, clubs, consulates, and hotels in styles from neoclassical to art deco. As Shanghai grew to be a bustling trading center in the Yangzi Delta, the Bund's warehouses and ports became the heart of the action. With the Communist victory, the foreigners left Shanghai, and the Chinese government moved its own banks and offices here.

Today the municipal government has renovated the old buildings of this most foreign face of the city, highlighting them as tourist attractions, and even tried for a while to sell them back to the very owners it forced out after 1949.

On the riverfront side of the Bund, Shanghai's street life is in full force. The city rebuilt the promenade, making it an ideal gathering place for both tourists and residents. In the mornings just after dawn, the Bund is full of people ballroom dancing, doing aerobics, and practicing kung fu, *qi gong,* and tai chi. The rest of the day people walk the embankment, snapping photos of the Oriental Pearl Tower, the Huangpu River, and each other. Be prepared for the aggressive souvenir hawkers; while you can't completely avoid them, try ignoring them or telling them *"bu yao,"* which means "Don't want." In the evenings lovers come out for romantic walks amid the floodlit buildings and tower. ⊠ *5 blocks of Zhongshan Dong Yi Lu between Jinling Lu and Suzhou Creek, Huangpu District.*

⑭ **Bund History Museum** (Waitan Chenlieshi). The photo gallery here chronicles the role of the Bund in Shanghai's history: as an architectural showcase, as a commercial hub, and as a stage for the political upheaval of the 1920s to the '40s. ⊠ *1 Zhongshan Dongyi Lu, Huangpu District* ☎ *021/6321–6542* 🖼 *Free* ☉ *Daily 10 AM–2 AM.*

❼ **Bund Museum** (Waitan Bowuguan). The white and red observation tower has held watch over the weather and the Huangpu River since 1884. The base, now home to this tiny museum, was built 19 years earlier. Photos along the walls present a round-up of the Bund's most famous buildings, both past and present. ⊠ *Unit A, 1 Zhongshan Erlu (The Bund), Huangpu District* ☎ *No phone* 🖼 *Free* ☉ *Daily 9–5.*

❷ **Cang Bao Antiques Building** (Cang Bao Lou). This market, formerly on Fuyou Lu, occupies the four-story Cang Bao Antiques Building, a warehouse just west of Yu Garden. During the week, you can browse permanent booths selling everything from Mao paraphernalia to crossbows to real and fake porcelain. (It's difficult to distinguish the two; real porcelain will appear transparent when held against a light.) On Sunday, the action begins before sunrise, a time when, according to a popular saying, only ghosts should be awake—hence the market's nickname of the Ghost Market. Hawkers from the provinces arrive early to display their goods on the sidewalk or inside on the fourth floor. Ivory, jade, and wood carvings are among the many goods sold here, at prices that are always negotiable. ⊠ *457 Fangbang Zhonglu, Huangpu District* ☉ *Weekdays 9–6, weekends 5 AM–6 PM.*

❸ **Chen Xiang Ge Temple.** If you find yourself passing by this tiny temple on your exploration of the Old City, you can make an offering to Buddha with the free incense sticks that accompany your admission. Built in 1600 by the same man who built Yu Garden, it was destroyed during the Cultural Revolution and rebuilt in the 1990s. The temple is now a monastery and nunnery, and you can often hear the women's chants rising from the halls beyond the main courtyard. ⊠ *29 Chenxiangge Lu, Huangpu District* ☎ *021/6320–0400* 🖼 *Y5* ☉ *Daily 7–4.*

❿ **Customs House** (Haiguan Lou). Built in 1927, the Customs House still serves as the customs headquarters, although now in the service of a different government. You can't go inside, but a relief plaque at the entryway commemorates the People's Peace Preservation Corps, which was once headquartered here. The old clock tower is now called "Big Qing" by the Shanghainese. During the Cultural Revolution, the bells were taken down and replaced by speakers blaring out Mao Zedong's theme, "The East Is Red." Today the bells are back in the tower, but they can't always be heard amid the cacophony of the city. ⊠ *13 The Bund (Zhongshan Dong Yi Lu), Huangpu District.*

⑤ **Dongtai Lu Antiques Market** (Dongtai Lu Gudai Chang). A few blocks
Fodor's Choice west of the Old City, antiques dealers' stalls line the street. You'll find
★ porcelain, Victrolas, jade, and anything else worth hawking or buying. The same bowls and vases pop up in multiple stalls, so if your first bargaining attempt isn't successful, you'll likely have another opportunity a few stores down. Prices have shot up over the years, and fakes abound, so be careful what you buy. ⊠ *Off Xizang Lu, Huangpu District* ⊙ *Daily 9–dusk.*

⑨ **Former Hongkong and Shanghai Bank Building** (Pudong Fazhan Yinhang). One of the Bund's most impressive buildings—some say it's the area's pièce de résistance—the domed structure was built by the British in 1921–23, when it was the second-largest bank building in the world. After 1949 the building was turned into Communist Party offices and City Hall; now it is used by the Pudong Development Bank. In 1997 the bank made the news when it uncovered a beautiful 1920s Italian-tile mosaic in the building's dome. In the 1950s the mosaic was deemed too extravagant for a Communist government office, so it was covered by white paint, which, ironically, protected it from being found by the Red Guards during the Cultural Revolution. It was then forgotten until the Pudong Development Bank renovated the building. If you walk into the bank, look up, and you'll see the circular mosaic in the dome—an outer circle painted with scenes of the cities where the Hongkong & Shanghai Bank had branches at the time: London, Paris, New York, Bangkok, Tokyo, Calcutta, Hong Kong, and Shanghai; a middle circle made up of the 12 signs of the zodiac; and the center painted with a large sun and Ceres, the Roman goddess of abundance. ⊠ *12 The Bund (Zhongshan Dong Yi Lu), Huangpu District* ☎ *021/6329–6188* ⊠ *Free* ⊙ *Daily 9–6.*

⑬ **Huangpu Park** (Huangpu Gonyuan). The local government paved over what once was a lovely green garden to create this mildly interesting park. During colonial times Chinese could not enter the park; a sign at the entrance said, NO DOGS OR CHINESE ALLOWED. From its location at the junction of Suzhou Creek and the Huangpu River, it offers views of both sides of the river. Beneath the park's **Memorial of the Heroes of the People** obelisk is a sweeping relief of China's liberation as well as the ⇨ **Bund History Museum,** in which photographs chronicle the role of the Bund in Shanghai's history. ⊠ *North end of Bund, beside the river, Huangpu District* ☎ *021/5308–2636* ⊠ *Free* ⊙ *May 1–Oct. 31, daily 6 AM–10 PM; Nov. 1–April 30, daily 6 AM–6 PM.*

4 Old City Wall (Dajing Ge). The Old City used to be completely surrounded by a wall, built in 1553 as a defense against Japanese pirates. Most of it was torn down in 1912, except for one 50-yard-long piece that still stands at Dajing Lu and Renmin Lu. You can walk through the remnant and check out the rather simple museum nearby, which is dedicated to the history of the old city (the captions are in Chinese). Stroll through the tiny neighboring alley of Dajing Lu for a lively panorama of crowded market life in the Old City. ⊠ *269 Dajing Lu, at Renmin Lu, Huangpu District* ☎ *021/6385–2443* ✆ *Y5* ☉ *Daily 9–4:30.*

★ 11 Peace Hotel (Heping Fandian). This hotel at the corner of the Bund and Nanjing Lu is among Shanghai's most treasured old buildings. If any establishment will give you a sense of Shanghai's past, it's this one. Its high ceilings, ornate woodwork, and art deco fixtures are still intact, and the ballroom evokes old Shanghai cabarets and gala parties.

The south building was formerly the Palace Hotel. Built in 1906, it is the oldest building on the Bund. The north building, formerly the Cathay Hotel, built in 1929, is more famous historically. It was known as the private playroom of its owner, Victor Sassoon, a wealthy landowner who invested in the opium trade. The Cathay was actually part of a complete office and hotel structure collectively called Sassoon House. Victor Sassoon himself lived and entertained his guests in the green penthouse. The hotel was rated on a par with the likes of Raffles in Singapore and The Peninsula in Hong Kong. It was *the* place to stay in old Shanghai; Noel Coward wrote *Private Lives* here. In the evenings, the famous Peace Hotel Old Jazz Band plays in the German-style pub on the first floor. ⊠ *20 Nanjing Dong Lu, Huangpu District* ☎ *021/6321–6888* ⊕ *www.shanghaipeacehotel.com.*

need a break?

The Peace Hotel's Shanghai Night Bar. For a memorable view, take the hotel's middle elevators to the top floor of the north building and then climb the last two flights of stairs to the roof. There's an outdoor bar and café, from which you can see Sassoon's former penthouse and the action on the streets and river below. There is a Y50 admission charge (not always imposed), but it includes a soft drink or tea.

8 Three On The Bund (Waitan San Hao). The renovation of this stunning, seven-story, post-Renaissance-style building has garnered more headlines than any other building project on the Bund. Built in 1916 as the Union Assurance Company Building, it was the first in China to use a structural steel frame. It was given a second life in the hands of famed architect Michael Graves, who, between 2002 and 2004, transformed the 140,000 square feet of space into Three On The Bund, an upscale dining, shopping, spa, and art complex. ⊠ *3 The Bund (Zhongshan Dong Yi Lu), Huangpu District* ☎ *021/6323–3355* ⊕ *www.threeonthebund.com.*

▶ **1 Yu Garden** (Yuyuan). Since the 18th century, this complex, with its traditional red walls and upturned tile roofs, has been a marketplace and social center where local residents gather, shop, and practice *qi gong* in the evenings. Although not as impressive as the ancient palace gardens

FodorsChoice
★

of Beijing and accused of being overly touristed, Yu Garden is a piece of Shanghai's past, one of the few old sights left in the city.

Surrounding the garden is a touristy bazaar of stores that sell traditional Chinese arts and crafts, medicine, and souvenirs. Over the past few years, the bazaar has become more of a mall, with chain stores replacing many mom-and-pop stalls, and Western fast food outlets—McDonald's, KFC, Subway—popping up alongside noodle shops. A basement antiques market with somewhat inflated prices is in the Huabao Building.

At the southeast end of the bazaar lies the **Chenghuang Miao** (Temple of the City God). The temple was built during the early part of the Ming Dynasty but was later destroyed. In 1926 the main hall was rebuilt and has been renovated many times over the years. Inside are gleaming gold figures, and atop the roof you'll see statues of crusading warriors, flags raised, arrows drawn.

To get to the garden itself, you must wind your way through the bazaar. The ticket booth is just north of the lake and the pleasant **Huxingting Chashi** (teahouse). The garden was commissioned by the Ming Dynasty official Pan Yunduan in 1559 and built by the renowned architect, Zhang Nanyang, over 19 years. When it was finally finished it won international praise as "the best garden in southeastern China," an accolade that would be hard to defend today, especially when compared with the beautiful gardens of Suzhou. In the mid-1800s the Society of Small Swords used the garden as a gathering place for meetings. It was here that they planned their uprising with the Taiping rebels against the French colonialists. The French destroyed the garden during the first Opium War, but the area was later rebuilt and renovated.

Winding walkways and corridors bring you over stone bridges and carp-filled ponds and through bamboo stands and rock gardens. Within the park are an **old opera stage,** a **museum** dedicated to the Society of Small Swords rebellion, and an **exhibition hall,** opened in 2003, of Chinese calligraphy and paintings. One caveat: the park is almost always thronged with Chinese tour groups, especially on weekends. As with most sights in Shanghai, don't expect a tranquil time alone. ⊠ *218 Anren Lu, Bordered by Fuyou Lu, Jiujiaochang Lu, Fangbang Lu, and Anren Lu, Huangpu District* ☎ *021/6326–0830 or 021/6328–3251* ⊠ *Garden, Y30; Temple, Y5* ☯ *Gardens, daily 8:30–5; Temple, 8:30–4:30.*

> **need a break?**
>
> The **Midlake Pavilion Teahouse** (Huxingting Chashi; ⊠ 257 Yuyuan Lu, Huangpu District ☎ 021/6373–6950 downstairs, 021/6355–8270 upstairs), Shanghai's oldest, opened in 1856 and stands on a small man-made lake in the middle of the Yu Garden and Bazaar, at the center of the Bridge of the Nine Turnings. Although tea is cheaper on the first floor, be sure to sit on the top floor by a window overlooking the lake. Upstairs, a bottomless cup of tea comes with Chinese snacks. Every night from 8:30 PM to 10 PM a traditional tea ceremony is performed. An ensemble with *erhu, pipa,* and other traditional instruments performs Monday from 2 to 5 PM and Friday through Sunday from 6:30 to 9 PM.

On the west side of the central man-made lake in Yu Garden is **Nanxiang Steamed Bun Restaurant** (⊠ 85 Yuyuan Lu, Huangpu District ☎ 021/6355–4206), a great dumpling house famed for its *xiao long bao* (steamed pork dumplings). You'll spot it by the long line of people outside, but you can shorten your wait by heading to the upstairs dining room.

Nanjing Lu & the City Center

The city's *zhongxin,* or center, is primarily in the Huangpu and Jingan districts. These two areas make up most of what was known in imperial and republican times as the International Settlement. Nanjing Lu, Shanghai's main thoroughfare, crosses east–west through these two districts. You can spot it at night by its neon extravaganza and in daytime by the sheer volume of business going on. Hordes of pedestrians compete with bicycles and one another, and cars move at a snail's pace in traffic jams.

A Good Walk (or Drive)

The following long walk can also become a series of cab rides. Go west on the shopping street Nanjing Lu from the Heping Fandian, meandering among the crowds and stores. The first blocks of Nanjing Dong Lu are shorter and still have some of Old Shanghai's architecture. On the blocks north and south of the street you can also sense the atmosphere of the place in the 1920s. The portion of Nanjing Lu between Henan Lu and Xizang Lu is a pedestrian walkway, so no need to worry about the road's infamous traffic here, just the throngs of Chinese tourists. For Y2, you can take a tram ride along the walkway. At the start of Nanjing Xi Lu, turn left (south) on Xizang Lu, and in a block you'll arrive at the city's huge social and cultural center, **People's Square** ⑮ ⌐. At this former dog track–turned–public square you'll find the **Shanghai Urban Planning Exhibition Center** ⑯, the wonderful **Shanghai Museum** ⑰, and the impressive **Grand Theater** ⑱.

On their western side, the Grand Theater and People's Square are bordered by Huangpi Bei Lu. Turn right (north) on Huangpi Bei Lu, past the **Bird and Flower Market** ⑲, and to your right will be the **Shanghai Art Museum** ⑳, at the corner of Nanjing Lu. Adjacent the museum is the west gate of **People's Park** ㉑, Shanghai's largest and most important, though not necessarily the nicest. Opposite the park, on the north side of Nanjing Xi Lu, is the historic **Park Hotel** ㉒.

Continue west on Nanjing Lu. Once you pass Chengdu Lu, the street of the overhead Ring Road, the Shanghai Television Station and Broadcasting Building is on the left, with a very large TV screen in front. About a mile down, after the intersection of Xikang Lu, you'll see the huge hall built by the Russians that is now the **Shanghai Exhibition Center** ㉓. It sits directly across from the convenient Shanghai Center. Two blocks farther west on Nanjing Lu, on the corner of Huashan Lu, is the **Jingan Temple** ㉔. From here or from the Shanghai Center, jump into a cab to the important **Jade Buddha Temple** ㉕, which lies several blocks north of Nanjing Lu.

TIMING   The above walk is fairly long and doesn't have to be done all at once. You can hop a cab between sights, which is especially recommended for the trip to Jade Buddha Temple. The distance from the Bund to Jingan Temple is about 4 km (2½ mi). The whole walk without stopping will probably take you 1½ to 2 hours. The Shanghai Museum is worth at least three hours of your time, and you may want to return another day. If you go to the Jingan Temple, the Bird and Flower Market, or Jade Buddha Temple, block off half an hour for each of these sights. The rest you can walk through or by very quickly.

Nanjing Lu and the People's Square are both most crowded and most exciting on weekends. You may have to fight the hordes, but you'll get a good idea of what life is like in Shanghai.

What to See

⑲ Bird and Flower Market (Hua Niao Shichang). Just a block off the tourist track of Nanjing Road, winding Jiangyin Lu gives you a good slice of Shanghai life. A fair number of vendors decamped to the Xizang Nan Lu market as the neighboring JW Marriott was built. But the street is still home to hawkers selling fish and birds, orchids, and bonsai trees. You can see women airing out their bed linens on sunny days and students racing out the iron gate of a school building with traditional up-turned eaves. ⊠ *Jiangyin Lu, off Huangpi Bei Lu between Nanjing Lu and Weihai Lu, Huangpu District* ☉ *Daily 9–dusk.*

⑱ Grand Theater (Da Ju Yuan). The spectacular front wall of glass shines as brightly as the star power within this magnificent theater. Its three stages host the best domestic and international performances, including the debut of *Les Miserables* in China in 2002 and *Cats* in 2003. The dramatic curved roof atop a square base is meant to invoke the Chinese traditional saying, "the earth is square and the sky is round." See it at night. ⊠ *190 Huangpi Bei Lu, Huangpu District* ☎ *021/ 6318–4478* ☺ *Tour, Y40* ☉ *Tours daily 9–11 and 1–4, depending on performance schedule.*

★ ㉕ Jade Buddha Temple (Yufo Si). Completed in 1918, this temple is fairly new by Chinese standards. During the Cultural Revolution, in order to save the temple when the Red Guards came to destroy it, the monks pasted portraits of Mao Zedong on the outside walls so the Guards couldn't tear them down without destroying Mao's face as well. The temple is built in the style of the Song Dynasty, with symmetrical halls and court-yards, upturned eaves, and bright yellow walls. The temple's great trea-sure is its 6½-foot-high, 455-pound seated Buddha made of white jade with a robe of precious gems, originally brought to Shanghai from Burma. Other Buddhas, statues, and frightening guardian gods of the temple populate the halls, as well as a collection of Buddhist scriptures and paintings. The 100 monks who live and work here can sometimes be seen worshiping. There's a vegetarian restaurant on the temple grounds. ⊠ *170 Anyuan Lu, Putuo District* ☎ *021/6266–3668* ☺ *Y10* ☉ *Daily 8–4:30.*

㉔ Jingan Temple (Jingan Si). Originally built about AD 300, the Jingan Temple has been rebuilt and renovated numerous times, including at present. The sound of power tools often drowns out the monks' chanting. The temple's Southern-style halls, which face a central courtyard, gleam with new wood carvings of elephants and lotus flowers, but the hall interiors have stark, new concrete walls and feel generally antiseptic. The temple's main draw is its copper Hongwu bell, cast in 1183 and weighing in at 3.5 tons. ✉ *1686 Nanjing Xi Lu, next to the Jingan Si subway entrance, Jingan District* ☎ *021/6256–6366* 🚇 *Y5* 🕗 *Daily 7:30–5.*

㉒ Park Hotel (Guoji Fandian). This art deco structure overlooking People's Park was originally the tallest hotel in Shanghai. Completed in 1934, it had luxury rooms, a nightclub, and chic restaurants. Today it's more subdued, with the lobby the most vivid reminder of its glorious past. ✉ *170 Nanjing Xi Lu, Huangpu District* ☎ *021/6327–5225.*

㉑ People's Park (Renmin Gongyuan). In colonial days, this park was the northern half of the city's racetrack. Today the 30 acres of flower beds, lotus ponds, and trees, plus a small amusement park (which is rarely open), are crisscrossed by a large number of paved paths. The park is widely known for its English corner, where locals gather to practice their language skills. ✉ *231 Nanjing Xi Lu, Huangpu District* ☎ *021/6327–1333* 🚇 *Y2* 🕗 *Daily 6–6.*

▶ **⑮ People's Square** (Renmin Guang Chang). Shanghai's main square, once

Fodor'sChoice   the southern half of the city's racetrack, has become a social and cul-

★   tural center. The Shanghai Museum, Municipal Offices, Grand Theater, and Urban Planning Exhibition Center surround it. During the day, visitors and residents stroll, fly kites, and take their children to feed the pigeons. In the evening, kids roller-skate, ballroom dancers hold group lessons, and families relax together. Weekends here are especially busy. ✛ *Bordered by Weihai Lu on south, Xizang Lu on east, Huangpi Bei Lu on west, and Fuzhou Lu on north.*

⑳ Shanghai Art Museum (Shanghai Meishu Guan). At the northwest corner of People's Park, the former site of the Shanghai Library was once a clubhouse for old Shanghai's sports groups, including the Shanghai Race Club. The building is now the home of the state-run Shanghai Art Museum. Its permanent collection includes paintings, calligraphy, and sculpture, but its rotating exhibitions have favored modern artwork. There's a museum store, café, and rooftop restaurant. ✉ *325 Nanjing Xi Lu (at Huangpi Bei Lu), Huangpu District* ☎ *021/6327–2829* 🖨 *021/6327–2425* 🚇 *Varies, depending on exhibition* 🕗 *Daily 9–5.*

㉓ Shanghai Exhibition Center (Shanghai Zhanlan Zhongxin). This mammoth piece of Russian architecture was built as a sign of Sino-Soviet friendship after 1949. Today, it hosts conventions and special touring exhibitions. The complex has a restaurant that caters largely to tour groups. ✉ *1000 Yanan Zhonglu, Jingan District* ☎ *021/6279–0279* 🕗 *Daily 9–4.*

⑰ Shanghai Museum (Shanghai Bowuguan). Truly one of Shanghai's trea-

Fodor'sChoice   sures, this museum has the country's premier collection of relics and ar-

★   tifacts. Eleven state-of-the-art galleries exhibit Chinese artistry in all its forms: paintings, bronzes, sculpture, ceramics, calligraphy, jade, Ming and Qing Dynasty furniture, coins, seals, and art by indigenous populations. Its bronze collection is among the best in the world, and its gallery of minority dress showcases intricate handiwork from several of China's 52 minority groups. If you opt not to rent the excellent acoustic guide, information is well presented in English. You can relax in the museum's pleasant tearoom or buy postcards, crafts, and reproductions of the artwork in the stellar bookshop. Students are admitted to the museum for free on Saturday from 5 to 7 PM. ⊠ *201 Renmin Da Dao, Huangpu District* ☎ *021/6372–3500* ⊕ *www.shanghaimuseum.net* ☒ *Y20, Y60 with acoustic guide* ☉ *Sun.–Fri. 9–5, Sat. 9–8, last ticket sold one hour before closing.*

⑯ Shanghai Urban Planning Exhibition Center (Shanghai Chengshi Guihua Zhanianguan). To understand the true scale of Shanghai and its ongoing building boom, visit the Master Plan Hall of this museum. Sprawled out on the third floor is a 6,400-square-foot planning model of Shanghai—the largest model of its kind in the world—showing the metropolis as city planners expect it to look in 2020. You'll find familiar existing landmarks like the Pearl Tower and Shanghai Center as well as future sites like the so-called Flower Bridge, an esplanade over the Huangpu River to be built for Expo 2010. ⊠ *100 Renmin Dadao, Huangpu District* ☎ *021/6372–2077* ☒ *Y25* ☉ *Mon.–Thurs. 9–5, Fri.–Sun. 9–6, last ticket sold 1 hr before closing.*

> **need a break?**
>
> A hip café below street level in CITIC Square, **Wagas** (⊠ 1168 Nanjing Xi Lu, Jingan District ☎ 021/5292–5228) has a menu for all your moods. Illy espresso, fruit juices, and smoothies, freshly made soups, sandwiches, salads, and quiches are all reasonably priced. Enjoy exhaust-fume-free alfresco dining or grab a table inside.

The Old French Concession

The former French Concession is in the Luwan and Xuhui districts. Once populated primarily by White Russians, the area is today a charming historic district known for its atmosphere and beautiful old architecture, as well as its shopping, and bars and cafés. Most of the action centers on the main east–west thoroughfare, the tree-lined Huaihai Lu, a relaxed, upscale, international shopping street. Many of the old consulates and French buildings still line it.

A Good Walk

You can start your walk at the **First Chinese Communist Party Congress Site ㉖ ▶**, on Xingye Lu and Huangpi Lu. Once you exit, you're already at **Xintiandi ㉗**, a restaurant and shopping complex that's given a second life to an area of traditional Shikumen houses. The **Wulixiang Shikumen Museum** shows you what the houses were like in days long before Starbucks became one of the tenants. From here take a cab or walk 15 to 20 minutes to **Sun Yat-sen's Former Residence ㉘**. If you walk, go south on Huangpi Lu until you reach Fuxing Lu, where you turn right. On the corner of Chongqing Nan Lu and Fuxing Lu is **Fuxing Park ㉙**. Across the way, on the southeast corner of the intersection, is a beautiful old arrowhead-shape apartment building that was once American journalist and Communist sympathizer Agnes Smedley's residence. If you continue west on Fuxing Lu, turn right at the first corner (Sinan Lu); Sun Yat-sen's Former Residence is just ahead on your right, at Xiangshan Lu. From here, head north on Sinan Lu. At Huaihai Lu, the main street of the old French Concession, take a left. This middle stretch of the shopping street Huaihai Zhonglu is the heart of the Concession. State-run and foreign shops, boutiques, and department stores dominate the area.

Continue down a couple of blocks on Huaihai and turn right on Maoming Lu at the old **Cathay Cinema** ㉚. At the intersection with Changle Lu stand the historic Jinjiang and Garden hotels. On the northeast corner is the old **Lyceum Theatre** ㉛. If you're really into looking at old architecture, you can walk one block west and one block north to the corner of Shaanxi Nan Lu and Julu Lu. Here, you can view and stroll around the grounds of the dollhouselike **Heng Shan Moller Villa** ㉜. Another out-of-the-way old villa complex lies farther south on Maoming Lu, at what is now the Ruijin Hotel.

Back at Huaihai Lu and Maoming Nan Lu, continue west. As you pass Shaanxi Nan Lu, you'll enter the fray surrounding **Xiangyang Market** ㉝ and be inundated with hawkers asking you "DVD? CD? Bag? Watch?" A block past the market, turn left on Fenyang Lu. The **Shanghai Arts and Crafts Research Institute** ㉞ is in an old French mansion on this street. If you return to Huaihai Lu and continue westward, the shopping district will give way to the consulate area. You can end your walk anywhere between Fenyang Lu and Wulumuqi Lu. If you decide to continue walking, eventually you'll pass the Shanghai Library, on your left (south) side past Wulumuqi Lu. Farther down the street at the corner of Xingguo Lu is **Soong Ching-ling's Former Residence** ㉟. You can take a cab here.

Besides walking down Huaihai Lu, an excellent way of seeing the French part of town is to hop on Bus No. 911, a double-decker bus that runs up and down the thoroughfare. If you sit on the upper level, you can sneak a good view of the old homes that are otherwise hidden by compound walls.

Farther away in Xuhui District is the **Xujiahui Cathedral** ㊱. From Huaihai Lu, go south on Hengshan Lu, which will end in Xujiahui. The church is on the west side of Caoxi Bei Lu. On the way you'll pass Shanghai's **International Cathedral** ㊲, on Hengshan Lu near Wulumuqi Lu. You'll need to take a taxi to **Longhua Temple** ㊳ and **Shanghai Botanical Garden** ㊴.

TIMING Huaihai Lu, like Shanghai's other main thoroughfares, is most crowded on the weekends, when hordes of shoppers enjoy their weekly outings. Allow yourself at least two hours just to walk the above itinerary without stopping at any shops or taking a look around at the old houses. Allow about a half hour to an hour for each of the more major sights, such as Sun Yat-sen's former residence, Soong Chingling's former residence, and the site of the First National Party Congress. You can walk through some of the historic buildings, while others involve only a short look from the outside.

What to See

30 Cathay Cinema. (Guotai Dianyingyuan) Once part of millionaire Victor Sassoon's holdings, the art deco Cathay Cinema was one of the first movie theaters in Shanghai. The building still serves as a theater, showing a mix of Chinese and Western films. ✉ *870 Huaihai Zhonglu, at Maoming Nan Lu, Luwan District* ☎ *021/5403–2908.*

> **need a break?**

As implied by the name **1931** (✉ 112 Maoming Nan Lu, Luwan District ☎ 021/6472–5264), this café near the Cathay Cinema exudes an Old Shanghai atmosphere, down to the cute little tables, working Victrola, and the waitstaff clad in *qipao* (traditional Chinese dresses). The café serves simple drinks, coffee, and tea, and excellent home-style Shanghai cooking, with some Japanese selections, too.

One of the premier estates of old Shanghai, the **Morriss Estate** (✉ 118 Ruijin Erlu, Luwan District), now the Ruijin Hotel, was built by a Western newspaper magnate. Today the estate's three huge houses, standing among green lawns and trees, have also become home to such exceptional foreign restaurants as Lan Na Thai and Hazara. They share the north mansion with **Face**, one of Shanghai's most popular bars. Stop in here for a drink or Thai appetizer, or sip a cup of tea in the **View Cafe Bar** overlooking the main mansion's south lawn. Stroll around the estate to view its ornate details, such as a stained-glass scene in Old House No. 3 that shows a tiger crouched beside a tropical stream.

▶ 26 First Chinese Communist Party Congress Site (Zhonggong Yidahuizhi; short for Zhongguo Gongchangdang Di Yi Ci Quanguo Daibiao Dahui Huizhi Jinian Guan). The secret meeting on July 31, 1921, that marked the first National Congress was held at the Bo Wen Girls' School, where 13 delegates from Marxist, communist, and socialist groups gathered from around the country. Today, ironically, the site is surrounded by Xintiandi, Shanghai's center of conspicuous consumption. The upstairs of this restored shikumen is a well-curated museum explaining the rise of communism in China. Downstairs lies the very room where the first delegates worked. It remains frozen in time, the table set with matches and tea cups. ✉ *374 Huangpi Nan Lu* ☎ *021/5382–2171* ▦ *Y3* ☉ *Daily 9–5, last ticket sold at 4.*

29 Fuxing Park (Fuxing Gongyuan). The grounds of this European-style park—known as French Park before 1949—provide a bit of greenery in crowded Shanghai. Here you'll find people practicing tai chi and lovers strolling hand in hand. ✉ *2 Gaolan Lu, Luwan District* ☎ *021/ 6372–0662* ▦ *Y2* ☉ *Daily 6–6.*

> **need a break?**

One example of Shanghai's cultural resurgence is the **Yandan Lu Pedestrian Street** (✢ Yandan Lu between Huaihai Zhonglu and Nanchang Lu). Luwan District heads repaved one block of Yandan Lu with tile, lined it with classic lampposts, threw out all the traffic and run-down stores, and replaced them with pedestrians and quaint cafés.

㉜ Heng Shan Moller Villa (Heng Shan Ma Le Bie Shu Fandian). With its colorful details, gingerbread–like brickwork, and pointy roof, this Shanghai mansion is part dollhouse, part castle. British businessman Eric Moller built the Norwegian–style house to resemble a castle his daughter once envisioned in a dream. Construction took 10 years and was completed in 1936. The family fled the invading Japanese in 1941, and after 1949 the house served as the Communist Youth League's headquarters. It's now a boutique hotel. Check out the lobby's ornately carved ceilings and stairwells and vast landscape painting, or rest in the Bonomi Café in the house's south garden. ✉ *30 Shaanxi Nan Lu, just north of Julu Lu, Xuhui District* ☎ *021/6247–8881* ⊕ *www.mollervilla.com.*

㊲ International Cathedral (Guoji Libaitang). This small ivy-covered cathedral dates to Shanghai's Concession days. Today it's called the Shanghai Community Church and holds weekly Protestant services. ✉ *53 Hengshan Lu, Xuhui District* ☎ *021/6437–6576.*

need a break? | **The Promenade** (✉ 4 Hengshan Lu) lies across from the International Cathedral and is part of the popular bar and restaurant stretch of Hengshan Road. There are several Western and Asian restaurants as well as a coffee house and, if you're in need of a trim, a hair salon favored by expats.

★ ㊳ Longhua Temple (Longhua Si). Shanghai's largest and most active temple has as its centerpiece a seven-story, eight-sided pagoda. While the temple is thought to have been built in the third century, the pagoda dates from the 10th century; it's not open to visitors. Near the front entrance of the temple stands a three-story bell tower, where a 3.3-ton bronze bell is rung at midnight every New Year's Eve. Along the side corridors of the temple you'll find the Longhua Hotel, a vegetarian restaurant, and a room filled seven rows deep with small golden statues. The third hall is the most impressive. Its three giant Buddhas sit beneath a swirled red and gold dome. The monks gather here each day from 8 to 11 AM and from 1 to 3 PM to pray for the souls of the deceased, whose photos top the altar. You can watch this moving ceremony from the sidelines. ✉ *2853 Longhua Lu, Xuhui District* ☎ *021/6456–6085 or 021/6457–6327* 🎫 *Y5* ☉ *Daily 7–4:30.*

㉛ Lyceum Theatre. (Lanxin Dajuyuan) In the days of old Shanghai, the Lyceum was the home of the British Amateur Drama Club. The old stage was given a face-lift in 2003 and is still in use as a concert hall. ✉ *57 Maoming Nan Lu, Luwan District* ☎ *021/6217–8530.*

㉞ Shanghai Arts and Crafts Research Institute (Shanghai Gongyi Meishu Yanjiusuo Jiugong Yipin Xiufu Bu). It's a little dusty, run down, and bare bones, but you can watch Shanghai's artisans as they create traditional Chinese arts and crafts. Works you can purchase include everything from paper cuts to snuff bottles, but prices can be a bit high compared to quality. Formerly, the old French mansion housed an official of the Concession's pre-1949 government. ✉ *79 Fenyang Lu, Xuhui District* ☎ *021/6437–0509* 🎫 *Y8* ☉ *Daily 9–5.*

39 Shanghai Botanical Garden (Shanghai Zhiwuyuan). Spread over 200 acres, the Shanghai Botanical Garden has separate areas for peonies and roses, azaleas and osmanthus, bamboo and orchids, and medicinal plants. Its Penjing Garden (Y7) is among the world's best. *Penjing* translates as "pot scenery," and describes the Chinese art of creating a miniature landscape in a container. More than 2,000 bonsai trees line the Penjing Garden's courtyards and corridors, whose cut-out windows perfectly frame these miniature masterpieces. The world-class Chinese Cymbidium Garden (Y7) has more than 300 varieties. Within the glass canopy of the Grand Conservatory (Y30) are towering palms and more than 3,500 varieties of tropical plants. Opened in 1978, the garden's buildings are showing their age, but the natural beauty of the gardens blooms anew each year. Admission to the garden is free on the 10th of each month. ⊠ *1111 Longwu Lu, Xuhui District* ☎ *021/6451–3369* 🚇 *Y15, with additional fees for specific gardens* ⊙ *Daily 8–5.*

35 Soong Ching-ling's Former Residence (Song Qingling Guju). While she first came to national attention as the wife of Dr. Sun Yat-sen, Soong Ching-ling became revered in her own right for her dedication to the Communist party. Indeed, many mainland Chinese regard her as the "Mother of China." (On the other hand, Soong's sister, Meiling, married Chiang Kai-shek, who was the head of the Nationalist government from 1927 to 1949, at which point the couple fled to Taiwan.) This three-story house, built in 1920 by a German ship owner, was Soong's primary residence from 1948 to 1963. It has been preserved as it was during her lifetime: her 4,000 books in the study, furniture in the bedroom that her parents gave as her dowry. The small museum next door has some nice displays from Soong Ching-ling and Sun Yat-sen's life, including wedding pictures from their 1915 wedding in Tokyo. ⊠ *1843 Huaihai Zhonglu, Xuhui District* ☎ *021/6431–4965* 🚇 *Y8* ⊙ *Daily 9–4:30.*

28 Sun Yat-sen's Former Residence (Sun Zhongshan Guju). Dr. Sun Yat-sen, the father of the Chinese republic, lived in this two-story house for six years, from 1919 to 1924. His wife, Soong Chingling, continued to live here after his death until 1937. Today it's been turned into a museum, and you can tour the grounds. ⊠ *7 Xiangshan Lu, Luwan District* ☎ *021/ 6437–2954* 🚇 *Y8* ⊙ *Daily 9–4:30.*

off the beaten path

OLD CHINA HAND READING ROOM – To learn more about all the beautiful architecture you're seeing in Shanghai, have a cup of coffee at the Old China Hand Reading Room. Part library, part bookstore, part café, it's the brainchild of Shanghainese photographer Erh Dongqiang (also known as Deke Erh), who has partnered with author Tess Johnston on a series of coffee-table books about Shanghai. ⊠ *27 Shaoxing Lu, off Ruijin Erlu, Luwan District* ☎ *021/6473–2526.*

33 Xiangyang Market (Xiangyang Shichang). The most infamous of Shanghai's markets, Xiangyang Market is where tourists go to buy knock-off Rolexes, Prada bags, North Face jackets, Mont Blanc pens, and anything else that's been copyright-infringed. While the official market is about four blocks square, just as much business goes on in the dilapidated apartment blocks bordering the market, where many vendors have their showrooms of illicit goods. ✉ *999 Huaihai Zhonglu, Xuhui District, Bordered by Xiangyang Lu, Huaihai Zhonglu, Fenyang Lu, Shaanxi Nan Lu, and Nanchang Lu* ☺ *Daily 9–9.*

㉗ Xintiandi. At one time, 70% of Shanghai's residents lived in *shikumens,* or "stone gate" houses. Most have been razed in the name of progress, but this 8-acre collection of stone houses was renovated into an upscale shopping and dining complex and renamed Xintiandi, or "New Heaven on Earth." The restaurants are busy from lunchtime until past midnight, especially those with patios for watching the passing parade of shoppers and camera-toting tourists. Just off the main thoroughfare is the visitor's center and the **Wulixiang Shikumen Museum** (✉ House 25, North Block, 181 Taicang Lu, Luwan District ☎ 021/3307–0337), a shikumen restored to 1920s style and filled with furniture and artifacts collected from nearby houses. Exhibits explain the European influence on shikumen design, the history of the Xintiandi renovation, as well as future plans for the entire 128-acre project. ✉ *181 Taicang Lu, Luwan District, Bordered by Taicang Lu, Madang Lu, Zizhong Lu, and Huangpi Nan Lu* ☎ *021/6311–2288* ⊕ *www.xintiandi.com* ✉ *Museum Y20* ☺ *Museum, daily 10–10.*

㊱ Xujiahui Cathedral (Xujiahui Dajiaotang). Built by the Jesuits in 1848, this Gothic-style cathedral still holds regular masses in Chinese. Stained-glass artist Wo Ye is in the midst of a five-year project to design and install new windows for the entire cathedral. ✉ *158 Puxi Lu, Xuhui District* ☎ *021/6469–0930.*

Pudong New Area

If you're traveling to Shanghai on business, you'll probably spend at least part of your time in Pudong. And even if you're in Shanghai for pleasure, the high-rises and energy in Pudong are sure to draw you to the other, eastern side of the Huangpu River. Here, where before 1990 you'd find farm fields, is an urban experiment that is swiftly becoming the financial, economic, and commercial center of Asia. Many of the big international companies with a presence in China have their factories or headquarters here. Although much of Pudong is still empty, and its sterility can't match the pockets of charm in Puxi, it does give you an idea of where Shanghai is heading. You'll find superlatives of all sorts in Pudong—the tallest tower in China, the highest hotel in the world, the first commercial magnetic levitation ("mag lev") train. Among the district's wonders are the Yangpu and Nanpu bridges (supposedly the second and third longest in the world) connecting Pudong to Puxi, the architecturally absurd International Exhibition Center, the Jinmao Tower, and, of course, the Oriental Pearl Tower.

A Good Walk

Start by crossing underneath the Huangpu River on the **Bund Tourist Tunnel** ㊵ ▶. As you exit on the Pudong side, you'll see the unmistakable crown of the Bund Center to the west. Walk toward the crown and the

A SHORT HISTORY OF SHANGHAI

S HANGHAI, *which literally means the "City Above the Sea," lies on the Yangzi River delta at the point where China's main waterway completes its 5,500-km (3,400-mi) journey to the Pacific. Until 1842 Shanghai's location made it merely a small fishing village. After the first Opium War, however, the British named Shanghai a treaty port, opening the city to foreign involvement.*

The village was soon turned into a city carved up into autonomous concessions administered concurrently by the British, French, and Americans, all independent of Chinese law. Each colonial presence brought with it its particular culture, architecture, and society. Although Shanghai had its own walled Chinese city, many native residents still chose to live in the foreign settlements. Thus began a mixing of cultures that shaped Shanghai's openness to Western influence. Shanghai became an important industrial center and trading port that attracted not only foreign businesspeople (60,000 by the 1930s) but also Chinese migrants from other parts of the country.

In its heyday, Shanghai was the place to be—it had the best art, the greatest architecture, and the strongest business in Asia. With dance halls, brothels, glitzy restaurants, international clubs, and even a foreign-run racetrack, Shanghai was a city that catered to every whim of the rich. But poverty ran alongside opulence, and many of the lower-class Chinese provided the cheap labor that kept the city running.

The Paris of the East became known as a place of vice and indulgence. Amid this glamour and degradation the Communist Party held its first meeting in 1921. In the 1930s and '40s, the city weathered raids, invasions, then outright occupation by the Japanese. The party was over. By 1943, at the height of World War II, most foreigners had fled and the concessions had been ceded to the Japanese, bringing Shanghai's 101 years as a treaty port to a close. Despite the war's end, fighting continued as Nationalists and Communists fought a three-year civil war for control of China. The Communists declared victory in 1949 and established the People's Republic of China, after which the few remaining foreigners left the country. Closed off from the outside world with which it had become so comfortable, Shanghai fell into a deep sleep. Fashion, music, and romance gave way to uniformity and the stark reality of Communism.

The decades from 1950 to 1980 passed by with one Five Year Plan after another, marked by periods of extreme famine and drought, reform and suppression. Shanghai's industries soldiered on during these years; the city remained the largest contributor of tax revenue to the central government. Its political contribution, however, had far greater ramifications: the city was the powder keg for the Cultural Revolution and the base of operations for the infamous Gang of Four, led by Mao Zedong's wife, Jiang Qing. The so-called January Storm of 1967 purged many of Shanghai's leaders, and Red Guards in Shanghai fervently carried out their destruction of the "Four Olds": old ways of idea, living, traditions, and thought.

Yet, in 1972, with the Cultural Revolution still raging, Shanghai hosted the historic meeting that would help lay the groundwork for the China of today. Premier Zhou Enlai and U.S. president Richard Nixon signed the Shanghai Communiqué, which enabled the two countries to normalize relations and encouraged China to open talks with the rest of the world. Twenty years later, the 14th Party Congress endorsed the concept of a socialist market economy, opening the door ever wider to foreign investment.

Today Shanghai has once again become one of China's most open cities ideologically, socially, culturally, and economically, striving to return to the internationalism that defined it before the Revolution. Shanghai's path to this renewed prominence began in 1990 when China's leader, Deng Xiaoping, chose it as the engine of the country's commercial renaissance, aiming to rival Hong Kong by 2010. If China is a dragon, he said, Shanghai is its head. Indeed the city is once again all about business. Having embraced competition and a market-driven economy in just a few years, it now hosts the nation's stock market, accounts for approximately one-fifth of the country's gross national product, and serves as the most important industrial base in the nation.

Today, beauty and charm coexist with kitsch and commercialism. From the colonial architecture of the former French Concession to the forest of cranes and the neon-lighted high-rises jutting above the city, Shanghai is a city of paradox and change.

—— Revised by Kristin Baird Rattini

Riverside Promenade ㊶. From here you can see the most beautiful views of the Bund. Standing above Riverside Promenade is the **Shangri-La Hotel**, where you can get a drink and a somewhat higher vantage point over the Bund.

From the Shangri-La's front entrance on Fucheng Lu, cross the street and head left one block to Century Boulevard (Shi Ji Da Dao). Keep to the right on Century Boulevard, heading southeast away from the water, and you'll be facing the skyscrapers of Lujiazui, the central financial area, or Wall Street, of Pudong. Continue walking toward the tallest high-rise in front of you, the beautiful industrial pagoda **Jinmao Tower** ㊷. Go up to the 88th-floor observation deck for a great view, or take a sky-high coffee break at the Grand Hyatt, which occupies the Jinmao's 53rd through 87th floors.

From the base of the Jinmao Tower, take a look directly east at the **Shanghai Securities Exchange Building** ㊸ (Securities Exchange Building)—the building with the square hole in the middle. Then head back northwest toward the water and the **Oriental Pearl Tower** ㊹. You'll see it towering in its gargantuan grandeur at the northwest end of Century Boulevard. You can take a ride to the top for yet another 360-degree view of Shanghai. The **Shanghai History Museum** ㊺ is in the bottom of the tower.

From the base of the Pearl Tower, you can follow Yincheng Lu northeast two blocks to the **Shanghai Ocean Aquarium** ㊻. If you'd like to call it day, take a cab or hop on the subway back to Puxi. (Board the train on the side that says ZHONGSHAN PARK.) If you'd like to continue exploring, take the metro east three stops to the exceptional **Shanghai Science and Technology Museum** ㊼.

TIMING The tourist tunnel ride takes just five minutes. You can take a leisurely stroll on the Bingjiang Dadao. Then allow about 15 minutes to walk to the Jinmao from the Shangri-La and another 15 to get to the Pearl Tower from the Jinmao, or take a short taxi ride. You can spend a half-hour to an hour at the observatory decks and at the Shanghai History Museum. If lines are long, you may have to wait a while to get to the top. Allow an hour at the Ocean Aquarium. It takes less than 10 minutes by subway to reach the Science and Technology Museum, where you'll need an hour or two to explore.

What to See

▶ ㊵ **Bund Tourist Tunnel** (Waitan Guanguan Shuidao). For a look at Shanghai kitsch at its worst, you can take a trip across—actually, under—the Huangpu in plastic, capsular cars. The accompanying light show is part Disney, part psychedelia, complete with flashing strobes, blowing tinsel, and swirling hallucinogenic images projected on the concrete walls. The tackiest futuristic film of the 1960s couldn't have topped this. The five-minute ride will have your head spinning and you wondering if the Chinese central government isn't giving Shanghai just a little too much money. ⊠ *Entrances are on the Bund at Nanjing Dong Lu and in Pudong near the Riverside Promenade* ☎ *021/5888–6000* 🚇 *Y30 one-way, Y40 round-trip* ☉ *May–Oct., daily 8 AM–10:30 PM; Nov.–Apr., daily 8 AM–10 PM.*

★ ㊷ **Jinmao Tower** (Jinmao Dasha). This gorgeous 88-floor (8 being the Chinese number implying wealth and prosperity) industrial art deco pagoda is among the five tallest buildings in the world and the tallest in China. In it is also the highest hotel in the world—the Grand Hyatt Shanghai takes up the 53rd to 87th floors. The lower floors are taken up by office space, an entertainment center, and a neighboring exhibition center. The 88th-floor observation deck, reached in 45 seconds by two high-speed elevators, offers a 360-degree view of the city. The Jinmao, designed by Chicago's Skidmore Owings & Merrill, is both ancient and modern, Eastern and Western—the tapering tower combines the classic 13-tier Buddhist pagoda design with postmodern steel and glass. Check out the Hyatt's dramatic 33-story atrium. ⊠ *88 Shiji Dadao, Pudong* ☎ *021/5047–5101* ☒ *Observation deck Y50* ⊙ *Daily 8:30 AM–9 PM.*

★ ㊹ **Oriental Pearl Tower** (Dongfang Mingzhu). The tallest tower in Asia (1,535 feet) has become the pride and joy of the city, a symbol of the brashness and glitz of today's Shanghai. This UFO-like structure is especially kitschy at night, against the classic beauty of the Bund. Its three spheres are supposed to represent pearls (as in "Shanghai, Pearl of the Orient"). An elevator takes you to observation decks in the tower's three spheres. Go to the top sphere for a 360-degree bird's-eye view of the city or grab a bite in the Tower's revolving restaurant. On the bottom floor is the ⇨ **Shanghai History Museum.** ⊠ *1 Shiji Da Dao, Pudong* ☎ *021/5879–1888* ☒ *Y100, all three spheres plus museum; Y50 second sphere* ⊙ *Daily 8 AM–9:30 PM.*

㊶ **Riverside Promenade** (Bingjiang Da Dao). Although the park that runs 2,750 yards along the Huangpu River is sugary-sterile in its experimental suburbia, it still offers the most beautiful views of the Bund. You can stroll the grass and concrete and view a perspective of Puxi unavailable from the west side. If you're here in the summer, you can "enjoy wading," as a sign indicates, in the chocolate-color Huangpu River from the park's wave platform. ⊠ *Bingjiang Dadao* ☒ *Free.*

> **need a break?** With its curving glass facade and large patio along the Riverside Promenade, **Red Dot** (⊠ Binjiang Dadao, Fu Du Duan, Pudong ☎ 021/5887–1818) serves up great views of the Bund with its fair Western fare.

★ ㊺ **Shanghai History Museum** (Shanghai Lishi Bowuguan). This impressive museum in the base of the Pearl Tower recalls Shanghai's pre-1949 history. Inside you can stroll down a re-created Shanghai street circa 1900 or check out a street car that used to operate in the concessions. Dioramas depict battle scenes from the Opium Wars, shops found in a typical turn-of-the-20th-century Shanghai neighborhood, and grand French Concession buildings of yesteryear. ⊠ *1 Shiji Dadao, Pudong* ☎ *021/5879–1888* ☒ *Y35* ⊙ *Daily 9–9:30.*

☺ ㊻ **Shanghai Ocean Aquarium** (Shanghai Haiyang Shuizuguan). As you stroll through the aquarium's 12,000-foot-long, clear, sightseeing tunnel, you may feel like you're walking your way through the seven seas—or at least five of them. The aquarium's 10,000 fish span 300 species, five oceans, and four continents. You'll also find penguins and species representing all 12 of the Chinese zodiac animals, such as the tiger barb, sea dragon, and seahorse. ⊠ *158 Yincheng Bei Lu, Pudong* ☏ *021/5877–9988* ⊕ *www.aquarium.sh.cn* ⊡ *Y110 adults, Y70 children* ⊙ *9–9.*

☝ ❹ **Shanghai Science and Technology Museum** (Shanghai Kexue Bowuguan). This museum, a favorite attraction for kids in Shanghai, has more than 100 hands-on exhibits in its six main galleries. Earth Exploration takes you through fossil layers to the earth's core for a lesson in plate tectonics. Spectrum of Life introduces you to the animal and plant kingdoms within its simulated rainforest. Light of Wisdom explains basic principles of light and sound through interactive exhibits, and simulators in AV Paradise put you in a plane cockpit and on television. Children's Technoland has a voice-activated fountain and miniature construction site. And in Cradle of Designers, you can record a CD or assemble a souvenir. Two IMAX theaters and an IWERKS 4D theater show larger-than-life movies. All signs are in English; the best times to visit are weekday afternoons. ⊠ *2000 Shiji Dadao, Pudong* ☏ *021/6854–2000* ⊡ *Y60 adults, Y20 children* ⊙ *Tues.–Sun. 9–5, last ticket sold at 3:30.*

❹ **Shanghai Securities Exchange Building** (Shanghai Gupiao Dasha). The Shanghai Stock Exchange shares its Lujiazui home with such foreign banks as the Bank of America, the Royal Bank of Canada, and the International Bank of Paris and Shanghai. Your hotel's concierge can contact the Stock Exchange Club on the 27th floor to arrange free tours of the trading floor. ⊠ *528 Pudong Nan Lu, Pudong* ☏ *021/6880–8888.*

Hongkou District

On the west side of the river north of Suzhou Creek are the northeastern districts of Hongkou and Yangpu. At the turn of the 20th century Shanghai was not only an international port but also an open one, where anyone could enter regardless of nationality. As the century wore on and the world became riddled with war, Jews, first fleeing the Russian Revolution and then escaping Hitler, arrived in Shanghai from Germany, Austria, Poland, and Russia. From 1937 to 1941 Shanghai became a haven for tens of thousands of Jewish refugees. In 1943 invading Japanese troops forced all the city's Jews into the "Designated Area for Stateless Refugees" in Hongkou District, where they lived until the end of the war. Today you can still see evidence of their lives in the buildings and narrow streets of the area.

A Good Walk

Start with a stroll through **Lu Xun Park** ❹ ⊳. From the main gate on Sichuan Bei Lu, follow the wandering paths to the revered writer's tomb as well as his museum. Return to the park's entrance and continue straight, walking south two blocks on Sichuan Bei Lu to the archway that marks the beginning of **Duolun Lu** ❹. Take your time along this pedestrian street to browse the antiques shops and art galleries, especially the **Shanghai**

Duolun Museum of Modern Art ⑤. Continue east one more block to where Duolun Lu rejoins Sichuan Bei Lu to hail a taxi for the short ride to **Ohel Moishe Synagogue and Huoshan Park ⑤**.

What to See

㊾ Duolun Lu. Designated Shanghai's "Cultural Street," Duolun Road takes you back in time to the 1930s, when the half-mile–long lane was a favorite haunt of writer Lu Xun and fellow social activists. Bronze statues of those literary luminaries dot the lawns between the well-preserved villas and row houses, whose first floors are now home to antiques shops, cafés, and art galleries. As the street takes a 90° turn, its architecture shifts 180° with the seven-story stark gray ⇨ **Shanghai Duolun Museum of Modern Art**. ⊠ *Off Sichuan Bei Lu, Hongkou District.*

> **need a break?**

Old Film Café (⊠ 123 Duolun Lu, Hongkou District ☎ 021/ 5696–4763) shares the 1920s feel of its Duolun Lu surroundings but eschews Chinese culture for Hollywood. Pictures of Marilyn Monroe and Humphrey Bogart preside over the subdued café. Stick to the drink menu, which includes teas, coffee, wine, and other spirits.

⟩ ㊸ Lu Xun Park and Memorial (Luxun Gongyuan). Lu Xun (1881–1936)— scholar, novelist, and essayist—is considered the founder of modern Chinese literature. He is best known for his work *The True Story of Ah Q.* The park holds his tomb and a statue of the writer, as well as a **museum** of manuscripts, books, and photos related to his life and career. ⊠ *2288 Sichuan Bei Lu, Hongkou District* ☎*021/5696–4208* 🎟*Park, Y5; memorial and museum, Y8* ⊙ *Park, daily 5:30 AM–6:30 PM; memorial and museum, daily 9–5, last admittance 4.*

㊶ Ohel Moishe Synagogue and Huoshan Park (Moxi Huitang and Huoshan Gongyuan). Currently called the Jewish Refugee Memorial Hall of Shanghai, the Ohel Moishe Synagogue served as the spiritual heart of Shanghai's Jewish ghetto in the 1930s and '40s. In this sanctuary-turned-museum, the lively 85-year-old narrator Wang Faliang provides colorful commentary for the black-and-white photo collection depicting daily life for the 30,000 Jews—academics, writers, doctors, musicians—who flooded into the Hongkou District from Europe.

An attic bedroom is frozen in time, with photos and a menorah left behind by residents who moved on after World War II. Around the corner, down a lane just as well preserved, Huoshan Park bears a memorial tablet in the immigrants' honor. The museum's art gallery best conveys the refugees' lasting gratitude to their Chinese hosts, a bond made most clear by a crystal Star of David, engraved with Chinese characters. ⊠ *62 Changyang Lu, Hongkou District* ☎ *021/6541–5008* 🖷 *021/6512–0229* ⊕ *www.moishe.sh.cn* 🎟 *Y50* ⊙ *Mon.–Sat. 9 AM–4 PM.*

㊵ Shanghai Duolun Museum of Modern Art (Shanghai Duolun Xiandai Meishu Guan). Opened in December 2003, this is Shanghai's first official venue for modern art. The six-story museum's 14,400 square feet of exhibition space include a café and a metal spiral staircase that's a work of art in itself. A video installation roars to life underfoot as you step off on the second floor. The exhibitions, which change frequently, are cutting edge for Shanghai. They've showcased electronic art from American artists, examined gender issues among Chinese and featured musical performances ranging from Chinese electronica to the *dombra,* a traditional Kazak stringed instrument. ✉ *27 Duolun Lu, Hongkou District* ☎ *021/6587-2530* 🖷 *021/6587-6902* ⊕ *www.duolunart.org* 💳 *Y20* ⊘ *Daily 9–5.*

WHERE TO EAT

You'll notice most Chinese restaurants in Shanghai have large, round tables. The reason will become clear the first time you eat a late dinner at a local restaurant and are surrounded by jovial, loud, laughing groups of people toasting and topping off from communal bottles of beer, sharing cigarettes, and spinning the lazy Susan loaded with food. Dining out with friends and family isn't just a favorite social activity; it's ritual. Whether feting guests or demonstrating their growing wealth, hosts will order massive spreads, for the more dishes, the more honor. While takeaway boxes for leftovers are starting to become popular, proud hosts wouldn't deign to use them.

Besides Chinese restaurants and food stands, Shanghai has hundreds of restaurants representing cuisines from around the globe, a diversity befitting an international center. Brazilian *churrascaria* joints, all-you-can-eat Japanese teppanyaki restaurants, and tapas bars have proliferated over the past few years. Popular restaurant chains like Indian Kitchen, South Beauty, and Simply Thai have opened additional branches to satisfy demand, while respected restaurateurs Steve Baker and Eduardo Vargas have expanded their empires with the sophisticated Mesa and Azul/Viva, respectively. The Xintiandi complex and the Hengshan Road area remain dining hotspots, but all eyes have been on the Bund as well, where the venerable M on the Bund faces competition from its new neighbor, the Three on the Bund complex and its four high-profile restaurants: Jean Georges, Laris, New Heights, and Whampoa Club.

Most restaurants in Shanghai offer set lunches, multi-course feasts at a fraction of the usual price. It's the best dining deal going, allowing you to eat at local Chinese restaurants for Y25 or less and at such places at M on the Bund without completely blowing your budget. Also, check out the "Restaurant Events" section of *That's Shanghai,* which lists dining discounts and promotions around town.

WHAT IT COSTS In Yuan				
$$$$	**$$$**	**$$**	**$**	**¢**
AT DINNER over Y180	Y121–Y180	Y81–Y120	Y40–Y80	under Y40

Prices are for a main course.

Nanjing Lu & the City Center

American

★ **$–$$** ✕ **Element Fresh.** Freshly made and generously portioned salads and sandwiches draw crowds of people to this bright lunch spot in the Shanghai Center. In addition to the usual chef's salads and club sandwiches, you'll find such inventive combinations as bacon with blue cheese, and duck breast with grilled apple. An equally creative drink menu has long lists of juices and smoothies. ⊠ *Shanghai Center, 1376 Nanjing Xi Lu, Jingan District* ☎ *021/6279–8682* ▤ *AE, DC, MC, V.*

$–$$ ✕ **Malone's American Café.** Larger-than-life caricatures of Wayne Gretzky, Shaq, and other sports legends watch over the proceedings at this popular bar and grill. Its substantial menu includes American favorites like buffalo wings, burgers, and pizza, as well as Asian dishes. The food isn't superb but it's satisfying as a casual meal in a cheerful bar setting. ⊠ *255 Tongren Lu, Jingan District* ☎ *021/6247–2400* ▤ *AE, DC, MC, V.*

Brazilian

$ ✕ **Brasil Steak House.** Shanghai has developed a taste for *churrascarias,* Brazilian-style barbecue restaurants. Brasil Steak House is perhaps the best, due in large part to the percentage of South Americans on staff. The all-you-can-eat lunches and dinners pair a salad bar with an unending rotation of waiters brandishing skewers of juicy chunks of meat for your consideration; just nod your approval and they'll slice off a piece for your plate. The large picture windows brighten up the room and let you observe the parade of people passing through Jingan Park. ⊠ *1649 Nanjing Xi Lu, Jingan District* ☎ *021/6255–9898* ▤ *AE, DC, MC, V.*

Cantonese

$$–$$$$ ✕ **Summer Pavilion.** Helmed by Ho Wing, the former chef of Hong Kong's famed Jockey Club, Summer Pavilion serves delicious Cantonese specialties ranging from simple dim sum to delicacies such as shark fin, bird's nest soup, and abalone. As befits the Portman Ritz-Carlton, the restaurant's dining room is elegant, with black and gold accents and a raised platform that makes you feel as though you're center stage—a sense heightened by the attentive servers, who stand close, but not too close, at hand, anticipating your needs. ⊠ *2F, The Portman Ritz-Carlton, 1376 Nanjing Xi Lu, Jingan District* ☎ *021/6279–8888* ⌂ *Reservations essential* ▤ *AE, DC, MC, V.*

Chinese

$–$$$ ✕ **Meilongzhen.** Probably Shanghai's most famous restaurant, Meilongzhen is one of the oldest dining establishments in town, dating from 1938. The building served as the Communist Party headquarters in the 1930s, and the traditional Chinese dining rooms still have their intricate woodwork, and mahogany and marble furniture. The exhaustive menu features more than 80 seafood options, including such traditional Shanghainese fare as Mandarin fish, as well as dishes with a Sichuan flair, like shredded spicy eel and prawns in chili sauce. Since this is a stop for most tour buses, expect a wait if you don't book ahead. ⊠ *No. 22, 1081 Nanjing Xi Lu, Jingan District* ☎ *021/6253–5353* ⌂ *Reservations essential* ▤ *AE, DC, MC, V.*

Fodor'sChoice ★

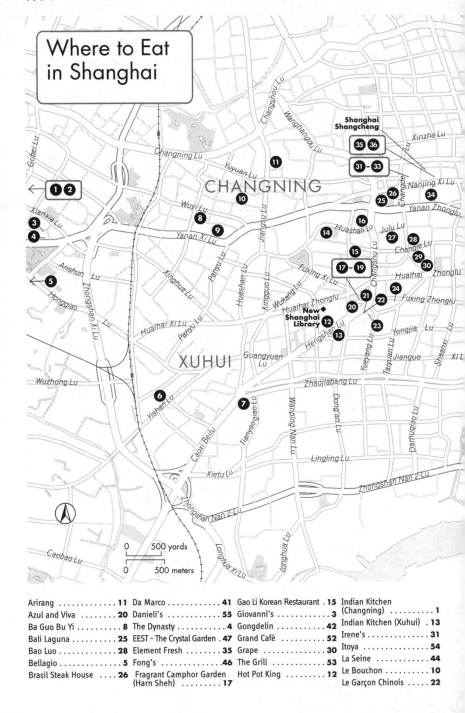

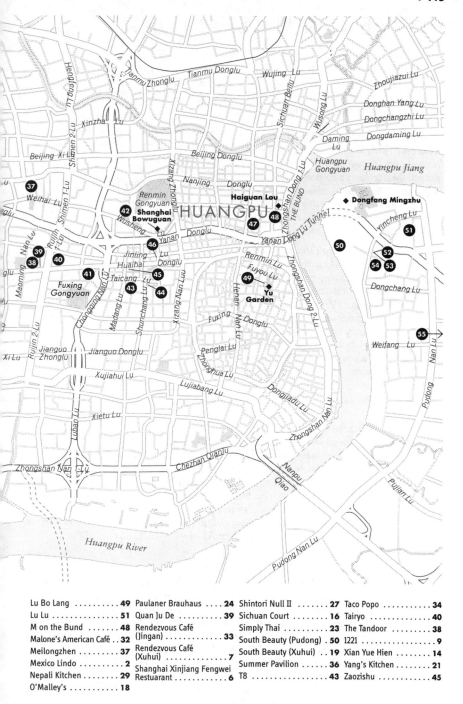

CloseUp
ON THE MENU IN SHANGHAI

SHANGHAI'S DINING SCENE *reflects the city's standing as China's most international city. You'll find restaurants representing not only every regional Chinese fare but also a world of other cuisines. Shanghainese food itself tends to be sweet and oily and is known for its own style of dim sum, especially xiao long bao (steamed pork dumplings). River fish is often the highlight (and most expensive part) of the meal, and hairy crab is a seasonal delicacy.*

The city's increasingly sophisticated dining scene means you can enjoy jiaotzi (Shanghai-style dumplings) for breakfast, foie gras for lunch, and Kobe beef teppanyaki for dinner. When eating out, it's traditional to order several dishes, plus rice, to share among your party. Tipping is not expected, but sophistication still comes at a price. While you can easily eat as the locals do at Chinese restaurants for less

than Y40, even the simplest Western meal will cost significantly more than it would in the United States.

Shanghai's street snacks are the city's main culinary claim to fame. You'll see countless sidewalk stands selling the famed xiao long bao, as well as shuijiao, (Chinese ravioli) and mantou (steamed dumplings without any filling).

Chinese Vegetarian

¢–$ ✕ **Gongdelin.** A two-story gold engraving of Buddha pays tribute to the origins of the inventive vegetarian dishes this restaurant has served for 80 years. Chefs transform tofu into such surprising and tasty creations as mock duck, eel, and pork. The interior is just as inspired, with Ming-style, wood-and-marble tables; metal latticework; and a soothing fountain. Tables fill up quickly after 6 PM, so either arrive early or buy some goodies to go at the take-out counter. ⊠ *445 Nanjing Xi Lu, Huangpu District* ☎ *021/6327–0218* 🖃 *AE, DC, MC, V.*

French

$$–$$$ ✕ **Le Bouchon.** This charming French wine bar and bistro serves up tasty traditional French fare in a cozy 12-table hideaway. The Y280 degustation menu is a greatest hits of French cuisine: escargot, foie gras, and duck breast. The baked Alaska (ice cream over a sponge cake topped with meringue), a rare treat in Shanghai, must be ordered separately, and it's worth it. The wine list includes two dozen reasonably priced French selections. ⊠ *1455 Wuding Xi Lu, Changning District* ☎ *021/6225–7088* 👌 *Reservations essential* 🖃 *AE, DC, MC, V* 🕙 *No lunch. Closed Sun.*

Indonesian

$–$$ ✗ **Bali Laguna.** Overlooking the lily pond in Jingan Park, with interior and alfresco dining, Bali Laguna is a popular choice for couples. Balinese music piped along the statue- and palm-lined walkway sets the mood even before the sarong-clad hostess welcomes you inside the traditional, three-story, Indonesian-style house or to a pond-side table. The menu is heavy on seafood, such as grilled fish cakes and chili crab, which captures the fire of Indonesian cuisine. Quench it with a Nusa Dua Sunset or other Bali-inspired cocktail. ✉ *Jingan Park, 189 Huashan Lu, Jingan District* ☎ *021/6248–6970* ⌦ *Reservations essential* ▭ *AE, DC, MC, V.*

Korean

$ ✗ **Arirang.** One of Shanghai's oldest Korean eateries, Arirang serves kimchi (pickled cabbage), noodles, unlimited cold appetizers, as well as meat and seafood that are barbecued on smoky coals right before your eyes. The meat dishes are the best choice here, although they fall a bit short of other Korean places in town. A specialty that is always delicious is the *congyoubing* (onion cake). ✉ *2F, 28 Jiangsu Bei Lu, Changning District* ☎ *021/6252–7146* ▭ *AE, DC, MC, V.*

Mexican

¢ ✗ **Taco Popo.** The menu is short but solid—tacos, burritos, enchiladas, and quesadillas. Throw in another Y5 to Y10 for extras like sour cream or tortilla chips. ✉ *78–80 Tongren Lu, 3/F, Jingan District* ☎ *021/6289–3602* ⌦ *Reservations not accepted* ▭ *No credit cards.*

Shanghainese

★ **¢–$$$** ✗ **1221.** This stylish but casual eatery is a favorite of hip Chinese and expatriate regulars. The dining room is streamlined chic, its crisp white tablecloths contrasting the warm golden walls. Shanghainese food is the mainstay, with a few Sichuan dishes as well. From the extensive 26-page menu (in English, pinyin, and Chinese), you can order dishes like sliced *you tiao* (fried bread sticks) with shredded beef, a whole chicken in a green-onion soy sauce, and *shaguo shizi tou,* or Lion's Head pork meatballs. ✉ *1221 Yanan Xi Lu, Changning District* ☎ *021/6213–6585 or 021/6213–2441* ⌦ *Reservations essential* ▭ *AE, DC, MC, V.*

Sichuan

¢–$$ ✗ **Ba Guo Bu Yi.** Its name translates as "Sichuan common people," which describes both the restaurant's style of food and the local clientele it attracts. The menu is a greatest hits of Sichuan cuisine, including *mapo tofu,* braised tofu with chili and brown pepper, and *lazi ji,* chicken smothered in chili peppers. The two-story dining room is arranged like a traditional Chinese house, around a central courtyard. The courtyard becomes a stage every evening for a traditional Sichuan opera performer, who amazes diners with his demonstration of *bian lian,* split-second changes of face masks. ✉ *1018 Dingxi Lu, Changning District* ☎ *021/5239–7779* ⌦ *Reservations essential* ▭ *No credit cards.*

Thai

$–$$$ ✕ **Irene's.** This traditional Thai teak house certainly stands out from its neighbors on Tongren Lu. The inside is just as distinctive, with pink and purple textiles, golden statues, and a platform with low tables and cushions on the floor. The food is good but not as inspired as the surroundings and somewhat overpriced. Spring rolls, pineapple rice, and papaya salad are among the best choices. Consider going on a Monday or Friday, when a Y150 all-you-can-eat special lets you sample across the menu. ✉ *263 Tongren Lu, Jingan District* ☎ *021/6247–3579* ⚑ *Reservations essential* ⊟ *AE, DC, MC, V.*

Old Town and the Bund

Chinese

$$–$$$ ✕ **Lu Bo Lang.** A popular stop for visiting dignitaries, Lu Bo Lang is a perfect photo op of a restaurant. This traditional three-story Chinese pavilion with upturned eaves sits next to the Bridge of Nine Turnings in the Yu Garden complex. The food is good but not great, with many expensive fish choices on the menu. Among the best dishes are the crab meat with bean curd, the braised eggplant with chili sauce, and the sweet osmanthus cake. ✉ *115 Yuyuan Lu, Huangpu District* ☎ *021/6328–0602* ⚑ *Reservations essential* ⊟ *AE, DC, MC, V.*

Contemporary

$$–$$$$
Fodor'sChoice
★

✕ **M on the Bund.** Espousing Shanghai's return to glamour, M does everything with flair. Its seasonal menus of Mediterranean- and Middle Eastern–influenced cuisine draw on the freshest of ingredients and the creative minds of owner Michelle Garnaut and executive chefs Julie and Michael Roper. Its rooftop location in the 1920s Nissin Shipping Building provides unparalleled views of the Bund, Huangpu River, and the Pudong skyline beyond. Consider lunch on the terrace; three course "simple lunches" run Y118, about half the typical dinner tab. Or stop for a drink in the adjoining **Glamour Bar,** a luxurious lounge with impeccable service that's popular among networking business types. ✉ *7F, 20 Guangdong Lu, Huangpu District* ☎ *021/6350–9988* ⚑ *Reservations essential* ⊟ *AE, DC, MC, V* ☯ *No lunch Mon.*

Japanese

$$–$$$$ ✕ **EEST–The Crystal Garden.** This impressive three-in-one venue has full Japanese, Cantonese, and Thai menus, all perfectly prepared. While the sushi bar and teppanyaki grill make it easy to zero in on the Japanese offerings, sampling across the menus is the best approach. Shark-fin dumpling, pomelo salad, and rice with green tea and crab meat are among the treasures buried in the pages of possibilities. This sunny glass-roofed garden of a restaurant has retracting overhead shades, which cool you during the day and allow you to stargaze at night. ✉ *The Westin Shanghai, 88 Henan Zhonglu, Huangpu District* ☎ *021/6335–1888* ⊟ *AE, DC, MC, V.*

WHERE TO REFUEL AROUND TOWN

F OR THOSE TIMES WHEN ALL YOU WANT IS A QUICK, *inexpensive bite, look for these local chains. They all have English menus and branches in Shanghai's tourist areas.*

Bi Feng Tang: *Dim sum is the sum of the menu, from chickens' feet to less exotic items such as shrimp wontons and barbecue pork pastries.*

Sumo Sushi: *Sit along the carousel and watch the chefs slice and dice fresh made-to-order sushi. You can order set lunches, à la carte, or all you can eat.*

Gino Café: *The inexpensive Italian fare at this café chain includes pizza, pasta, sandwiches, and good desserts.*

Manabe: *This Japanese coffee house chain serves Western fast food, such as club sandwiches and breakfast fare, as well as Japanese snacks and a long list of teas.*

The Old French Concession

American

¢–$ ✕ **Rendezvous Café.** With its inexpensive menu of juicy hamburgers and bacon-and-eggs breakfasts, Rendezvous Café offers satisfying and authentic American diner fare. Owner Richard Soo ran its predecessor in San Francisco before pulling up stakes for Taiwan, then Shanghai. The two locations are difficult to find—tucked behind Metro City shopping mall and down a small lane off Nanjing Xilu—but they're definitely worth seeking out. ✉ *#1-29, 1111 Zhaojiabang Lu, off of Tianyaoqiao Lu, Xuhui District* ☎ *021/6426–7152* ✉ *1486 Nanjing Xilu, Jingan District,* ☎ *021/6247–2307* ▭ *MC, V.*

Beijing

$–$$ ✕ **Quan Ju De.** The original Beijing branch of this restaurant has been *the* place to get Peking duck since 1864, though the Shanghai location only opened in 1998. The elevator doors open on a traditional Chinese restaurant: big and noisy, with red and gold columns, painted ceilings, and dangling lanterns whose tassels resemble the imperial-style headdresses worn by the hostesses. The roast duck is worthy of its hype, but be sure to order several other dishes—such as vegetables, crystal shrimp, or spicy peanuts—to offset its greasiness. ✉ *4F, 786 Huaihai Zhonglu, Luwan District* ☎ *021/5404–5799* ▭ *AE, DC, MC, V* ⚭ *Reservations essential.*

Cantonese

¢ ✕ **Xian Yue Hien.** Dim sum is the big draw at Xian Yue Hien. It's the featured fare at breakfast and lunch and has its own separate menu. The restaurant's Cantonese-Shanghainese dinner menu has a healthy slant, though the amount of grease often counteracts these efforts. The two-story restaurant is nestled in Dingxiang Garden, a verdant 35-acre playground the late Qing Dynasty mandarin Li Hongzhang gave to his concubine Ding Xiang. There's outdoor seating on a large terrace, and the second floor overlooks the garden. Book early if you want a table by the window. ⊠ *849 Huashan Lu, Xuhui District* ☎ *021/6251–1166* ⌕ *Reservations essential* ▤ *AE, DC, MC, V.*

Chinese

★ ¢–$ ✕ **Grape.** Entry-level Chinese food at inexpensive prices has been the Grape's calling card since the mid-1980s. This cheerful two-story restaurant remains a favorite among expatriates and travelers who've wandered north a few blocks from Xiangyang Market. The English and photo menu includes such recognizable fare as sweet and sour pork and lemon chicken as well as delicious dishes like garlic shrimp and *jiachang doufu* (home-style bean curd), all of which are served with a smile. ⊠ *55 Xinle Lu, Luwan District* ☎ *021/5404–0486* ▤ *No credit cards.*

¢–$ ✕ **Hot Pot King.** *Huo guo,* or hotpot, is a popular Chinese ritual of at-the-table cooking, in which you simmer fresh ingredients in a broth. Hot Pot King reigns over the hotpot scene in Shanghai because of its extensive menu as well as its refined setting. The most popular of the 17 broths is the *yinyang,* half spicy red, half basic white pork-bone broth. Add in a mixture of veggies, seafood, meat, and dumplings for a well-rounded pot, then dip each morsel in the sauces mixed tableside by your waiter. The minimalist white and gray interior has glass-enclosed booths and well-spaced tables, a nice change from the usual crowded, noisy, hotpot joints. ⊠ *2F, 10 Hengshan Lu, Xuhui District* ☎ *021/6474–6545* ▤ *AE, DC, MC, V.*

Contemporary

★ $$$–$$$$ ✕ **T8.** A favorite haunt for celebrities, T8 has garnered its share of headlines for its stunning interior and inspired contemporary cuisine. The restaurant occupies a traditional shikumen, or stone gate, house within Xintiandi and has modernized the space with raw stone floors, carved-wood screens, and imaginative lighting that transforms shelves full of glasses into a modern-art sculpture. The show kitchen turns out such Thai- and Chinese-inspired dishes as a slow-cooked, Sichuan-flavored lamb pie, and nori-wrapped sashimi-grade tuna. Like the clientele, the wine list is exclusive, with many labels unavailable elsewhere in Shanghai. ⊠ *House 8, North Block, Xintiandi, 181 Taicang Lu,, Luwan District* ☎ *021/6355–8999* ⌕ *Reservations essential* ▤ *AE, DC, MC, V* ☾ *No lunch Tues.*

★ $$–$$$ ✕ **Azul and Viva.** In creating his continent-hopping New World cuisine, owner Eduardo Vargas drew upon his globe-trotting childhood and seven years as a restaurant consultant in Asia. As a result, the menus in Azul, the tapas bar downstairs, and Viva, the restaurant upstairs, feature a delicious, delicate balance of flavors that should please any palate. Classics like beef carpaccio contrast cutting-edge dishes like coffee-glazed pork. Lunch and weekend brunch specials provide lower-priced options. The relaxed, romantic interior—dim lighting, plush pillows, splashes of color against muted backdrops—invites you to take your time on your culinary world tour. ⊠ *18 Dongping Lu, Xuhui District* ☏ *021/ 6433–1172* ▭ *AE, DC, MC, V.*

Continental

¢–$$ ✕ **Fragrant Camphor Garden** (Harn Sheh). Given Harn Sheh's desirable Hengshan Lu address, its budget prices come as a surprise. The 16-page menu, divided equally between Eastern and Western fare, ranges from curry to hotpot to pasta; drinks alone include 14 teas and 19 smoothies. Many dishes include salad, soup, and fruit. As Harn Sheh is considered a teahouse, you're welcome to linger, browse magazines from the towering rack, and gaze out the large windows at the hustle and bustle of Hengshan Road. ⊠ *2A Hengshan Lu, Xuhui District* ☏ *021/ 6433–4385* ▭ *MC, V.*

French

★ $–$$$ ✕ **La Seine.** Its stylish dining room and authentic contemporary fare make La Seine a perfect place to savor and contemplate the intricacies of French cuisine. Royal purple reigns, in the linens, flower arrangements, suede chairs, and the throw pillows on the generously sized booths. The artfully presented dishes range from the expected escargot and foie gras to delicate seafood like tilapia in mustard–cream sauce. The weekday lunch semi-buffet (pairing an entrée with salad and dessert bar), weekend brunch buffet, and dinner prix-fixe menus are the best deals. Be sure to stop in the patisserie, where the heavenly scent will inspire you to buy some truffles and croissants for the way home. ⊠ *8 Jinan Lu, Luwan District* ☏ *021/6384–3722* ⌨ *Reservations essential* ▭ *AE, DC, MC, V.*

German

$$–$$$$ ✕ **Paulaner Brauhaus.** There's a shortage of good German food in Shanghai. Paulaner Brauhaus does its best to fill the void with a menu of classic German dishes—Wiener schnitzel, bratwurst, apple strudel—accompanied by the house-brewed lager. The Fenyang Lu location is more laid-back, with a courtyard beer garden in the summer. The Xintiandi branch, open for lunch, is great for people-watching. ⊠ *150 Fenyang Lu, Xuhui District* ☏ *021/6474–5700* ☽ *No lunch* ⊠ *House 19-20, North Block Xintiandi, 181 Taicang Lu, Luwan District* ☏ *021/ 6320–3935* ▭ *AE, DC, MC, V.*

Indian

★ $–$$$ ✕ **The Tandoor.** Don't miss the unbelievable *murgh malei kebab* (tandoori chicken marinated in cheese and yogurt mixture) or try some vegetable curries—*palak aloo* (spinach with peas) or *dal makhani* (lentil). Decorated with mirrors, Indian artwork, and Chinese characters dangling from the ceiling, the restaurant is ingeniously designed to show the route of Buddhism from India to China. The management and staff, all from India, remain close at hand throughout the meal to answer questions and attend to your needs. ✉ *Jinjiang Hotel, South Building, 59 Maoming Nan Lu, Luwan District* ☎ *021/6472–5494* ⌆ *Reservations essential* ⊟ *AE, DC, MC, V.*

¢ ✕ **Indian Kitchen.** The Indian chefs working their magic in the show kitchen provide the entertainment while you wait for a table at this tremendously popular restaurant. Delicious butter chicken marsala and tandoor-cooked chicken tikka taste as good as they look in the picture menu, which is packed with classic Indian dishes. The 36 bread selections include melt-in-your-mouth spring onion *parotas* (fried flat bread). Two blocks from the Hengshan Lu metro station and bar district, Indian Kitchen is a convenient dining spot and the perfect start to an evening out on the town. ✉ *572 Yongjia Lu, Xuhui District* ☎ *021/6473–1517* ⌆ *Reservations essential* ⊟ *AE, DC, MC, V.*

Irish

$–$$$ ✕ **O'Malley's.** With a fire in the hearth, a super-friendly Irish staff, and a band playing traditional tunes from the balcony, O'Malley's feels every bit like an authentic Irish pub. The old French mansion has lots of dark, cozy corners, while the huge outdoor patio is packed to capacity during broadcasts of European football (soccer) and rugby matches. The requisite Guinness and Kilkenny are on tap and complement the meat-and-potatoes menu, but all come with rather steep price tags. ✉ *42 Taojiang Lu, Xuhui District* ☎ *021/6437–0667* ⊟ *AE, DC, MC, V.*

Italian

$–$$$ ✕ **Da Marco.** Its reasonably priced authentic Italian fare makes Da Marco a universal favorite in Shanghai. The original location on Dong Zhu An Bang Lu is a magnet for Italian expats in search of a late dinner, while the Yandang Lu location attracts a mix of locals, expats, and tourists. Lasagna, ravioli, Caprese salad, and pizza (11 types) are among the classic dishes on the menu. The wine list includes many selections under Y200. Three-course set lunches—with tiramisu for dessert—ring up at only Y68. You can choose alfresco dining under the bright orange awning or a comfy seat on the banquette in the sunshine-yellow dining room. ✉ *62 Yandang Lu, Luwan District* ☎ *021/6385–5998* ⌆ *Reservations essential* ⊟ *AE, DC, MC, V.*

Japanese

$$–$$$ ✕ **Shintori Null II.** The restaurant's plain gray wall facing Julu Lu belies the futuristic design masterpiece that lies behind it. With its magic sliding doors, etched glass, and concrete airplane hanger of a dining room, the restaurant is often compared to a set from *Blade Runner*. The French-influenced Japanese cuisine uses curry and foie gras to dress up the sushi, sashimi, tempura, and noodle dishes. ✉ *803 Julu Lu, Jingan District* ☎ *021/5404–5252* ⌆ *Reservations essential* ⊟ *AE, DC, MC, V* ☉ *No lunch Mon.–Fri.*

$–$$$ ✕ **Tairyo.** After indulging in the Y150 all-you-can-eat teppanyaki special at Tairyo, you might feel as big as the three sumo wrestlers in the restaurant's wall-sized mural. While locals seem to prefer the cheaper à la carte menu, Westerners come here for the endless delicious servings of sashimi, scallops, lemon prawns, and some of the best beef in town. Beer, sake, wine, and plum wine are included in the price, too. ☒ *139 Ruijin Yi Lu, Luwan District* ☎ *021/5382–8818* ♨ *Reservations essential* ☱ *AE, DC, MC, V.*

Korean

¢ ✕ **Gao Li Korean Restaurant.** Hidden on a small lane, Gao Li is a bit of a hole in the wall, but its eight tables are packed with patrons until 2 AM. It serves great, cheap food and specializes in tender and delicious grilled meats. You do the cooking, though, placing thin cuts of meat on a small gas grill and then wrapping them in a lettuce leaf and adding chili sauce. The noodle dishes are some of the best in town: try the cold Korean noodles for dessert. ☒ *No.1, 181 Wuyuan Lu, Xuhui District* ☎ *021/6431–5236* ☱ *AE, DC, MC, V.*

Middle Eastern/Xinjiang

¢–$ ✕ **Shanghai Xinjiang Fengwei Restaurant.** You'll probably hear this restaurant before you see its blue canopied entrance and streetside kabob stand; pounding Xinjiang music throbs from the second-story windows. The lively singing waitstaff frequently recruits diners as dance partners; service often falters as a result. The traditional Xinjiang menu is heavy on lamb but also includes a few chicken and fish dishes. A bottle of Xinjiang black beer is a must to wash it all down. ☒ *280 Yishan Lu, Xuhui District* ☎ *021/6468–9198* ☱ *No credit cards.*

Nepalese

¢ ✕ **Nepali Kitchen.** Whether you choose the plush cushions on the floor or the paper-lamp-lit tables, Nepali Kitchen is a cozy spot to sample the subtleties of Nepalese fare. In addition to the curries and naan found at most Indian restaurants, there are tasty starters like fried cheese balls and potato chili. ☒ *819 Julu Lu, Jingan District* ☎ *021/5404–6281* ♨ *Reservations essential* ☱ *No credit cards* ☉ *Closed Mon.*

Shanghainese

¢–$$$ ✕ **Yang's Kitchen.** Traditional Shanghainese food without the usual *renao* (hot and noisy atmosphere) draws customers down the narrow laneway to the restored villa that's now home to Yang's Kitchen. The 19-page menu includes familiar dishes like mandarin fish, the obligatory *xiao long bao* (steamed pork dumplings), as well as 22 soups. An apricot-and-white side dining room with small tables spaced widely for privacy is popular among couples and solo diners seeking a quiet and inexpensive meal. ☒ *No. 3, 9 Hengshan Lu, Xuhui District* ☎ *021/6445–8418* ☱ *AE, DC, MC, V.*

¢–$ × **Bao Luo.** While its English menu caters to tourists, Bao Luo is Chi-
Fodor'sChoice   nese dining as the Chinese enjoy it, a fact confirmed by the usual long
★   wait for a table. The freshness of the ingredients comes through in every
dish, from perfectly steamed broccoli to tender stewed crab and pork
meatballs. Tables are packed tightly in this small two-story restaurant,
and the light-wood interior merely serves as backdrop to the can't-miss
cuisine. However, look closely for the red scroll neon sign with a tiny
"BL," or you may miss the restaurant altogether. ⊠ *271 Fumin Lu, by
Changle Lu, Jingan District* ☎ *021/5403–7239* ⚑ *Reservations essential* ▤ *No credit cards.*

Sichuan

$$–$$$ × **Sichuan Court.** Get a sky-high view of the city at this upscale eatery
at the top of the Hilton. As a starter, the Sichuan treasure box combines
several delicacies: cold sliced garlic pork, sliced suckling pig, sliced
duck, some cold vegetables. The Chengdu tea-smoked duck, *mapo
doufu* (spicy tofu), and *dan dan* (noodles) are typical of the Sichuan dishes
served here. ⊠ *Shanghai Hilton, 250 Huashan Lu, Jingan District*
☎ *021/6248–0000* ⚑ *Reservations essential* ▤ *AE, DC, MC, V.*

★ $–$$$ × **South Beauty.** The elegant interior and spicy fare are both worth be-
holding at South Beauty. As the sliding glass front door opens—reveal-
ing a walkway between two cascading walls of water—it splits the
restaurant's trademark red Chinese opera mask in two. Likewise, the
menu is split down the middle between cooler Cantonese cuisine and
sizzling hot Sichuan fare. Don't be fooled: even dishes with a one-pep-
per rating, like sauteed baby lobster, will singe your sinuses. ⊠ *28 Tao-
jiang Lu, Xuhui District* ☎ *021/6445–2581* ⚑ *Reservations essential*
▤ *AE, DC, MC, V.*

Spanish

$$ × **Le Garçon Chinois.** This dimly lit restaurant in an old French villa is
a favorite spot for couples on a date. The walls are painted in warm
hues, the art deco fittings are tasteful, and large windows frame surrounding trees and old mansions. Run by a Japanese–European couple, the restaurant presents a predominantly Spanish menu, with several
tapas and paella selections. ⊠ *No. 3, Lane 9, Hengshan Lu, Xuhui District* ☎ *021/6445–7970* ⚑ *Reservations essential* ▤ *AE, DC, MC, V*
☉ *No lunch.*

Thai

¢–$$ × **Simply Thai.** Unpretentious Thai fare at moderate prices has earned
Fodor'sChoice   this restaurant a loyal expat clientele. Customers flock to the tree-
★   shaded patio to savor such favorites as green and red curries (on the spicy
side) and stir fried rice noodles with chicken (on the tame side). The ap-
petizers are all first-rate, especially the crispy spring rolls and samosas.
The wine list includes a half-dozen bottles under Y200 ($25), a rarity
in Shanghai. The branch in Xintiandi is a bit noisier but features the
same great food and prices. ⊠ *5C Dongping Road, Xuhui District*
☎ *021/6445–9551* ⚑ *Reservations essential* ▤ *AE, DC, MC, V.*

Vegetarian

¢ ✕ **Zaozishu.** Calling itself a "vegetarian lifestyle" restaurant, Zaozishu is perhaps the only place in Shanghai where you can get real vegetarian food, not just endless variations of tofu. You'll find hotpot and clay pot, dim sum, and desserts, plus 12 teas "for the health" formulated by a doctor from the Shanghai Xiangshan Chinese Medicine Hospital. ✉ 77 *Songshan Lu, Luwan District* ☎ *021/6384–8000* ▭ *No credit cards.*

Vietnamese

$–$$ ✕ **Fong's.** Don't be deterred by Fong's location in an office plaza. Inside, chirping birds, gauze curtains, bamboo furniture, and hostesses wearing *ao dai* (long Vietnamese dress with side slits worn over pants) set a romanticized scene for Fong's excellent French-style Vietnamese cuisine. The English and photo menu focuses on traditional dishes like spring rolls and a wonderfully smoky fried vermicelli with seafood, but it also includes bouillabaisse and other French specialties. Waiters are friendly but may not always hear you over the din in this busy and justifiably popular restaurant. ✉ *2F, Lippo Plaza 222 Huaihai Zhonglu, Luwan District* ☎ *021/6387–7228* ▭ *AE, DC, MC, V.*

Hongqiao Development Zone

Cantonese

$–$$$ ✕ **The Dynasty.** Although its cuisine is mostly Cantonese, Dynasty has expanded its reign to include other regional fare, such as first-rate Peking duck and Sichuan-influenced hot-and-sour soup. The Cantonese seafood dishes, especially the prawns and lobster, are particularly good, and the shrimp *jiaozi* (dumplings) are delicious. Keyhole cutouts in the subdued pewter walls showcase Chinese vases and artifacts. Thick carpets mute any hotel noise, but the prices quickly remind you this is indeed a hotel restaurant. ✉ *Renaissance Yangtze Hotel, 2099 Yanan Xi Lu, Changning District* ☎ *021/6275–0000* ⌦ *Reservations essential* ▭ *AE, DC, MC, V.*

Indian

¢ ✕ **Indian Kitchen.** The second outpost of Indian Kitchen features the same great food but in a more attractive setting: the cozy rooms of a renovated house. Delicious butter chicken marsala and tandoor-cooked chicken *tikka* taste as good as they look in the picture menu, which is packed with classic Indian dishes. The 36 bread selections include yummy spring onion parotas. ✉ *House 8, 3911 Hongmei Lu, Changning District* ☎ *021/ 6261–0377* ⌦ *Reservations essential* ▭ *AE, DC, MC, V.*

Italian

$$–$$$$ ✕ **Giovanni's.** Its Italian courtyard with a penthouse view provides a wonderful backdrop for Giovanni's traditional Italian fare. The antipasta and calamari are delicious, the pastas served perfectly al dente. Seasonal promotions add a taste of Tuscany and other regions to the menu. ✉ *Sheraton Grand Tai Ping Yang, 27th floor, 5 Zunyi Nan Lu, Changning District* ☎ *021/6275–8888* ⌦ *Reservations essential* ▭ *AE, DC, MC, V.*

Mexican

$$–$$$ ✗ **Mexico Lindo.** Fiery fare in a south-of-the-border setting has made Mexico Lindo Cantina & Grill the best entry on Shanghai's limited Mexican dining scene. This Spanish-style casa is hidden off Hongmei Lu, down a tiny alley that's evolved into a well-respected restaurant row. In addition to tacos, fajitas, and quesadillas, the menu includes spicy prawns— rated three peppers—and a tasty one-pepper carnita pork burrito. A stairway mural depicts farm workers as well as fiesta revelers, whose ranks you can join with the eight margaritas and eight tequilas on the drink menu. ⊠ *Villa 1, 3911 Hongmei Lu, Changning District* ☎ *021/ 6262–2797* ⌂ *Reservations essential* ▤ *AE, DC, MC, V.*

Taiwanese

¢–$ ✗ **Bellagio.** Taiwanese expatriates pack the bright, sunlit dining room of Bellagio for an authentic taste of home. Red fabric–covered chairs and black streamlined tables contrast the white walls and decorative moldings. Waiters, chic in black sweaters, move efficiently between the closely spaced tables. The menu includes such traditional entrées as three-cup chicken as well as 25 noodle dishes spanning all of Southeast Asia. Save room for dessert: shaved-ice snacks are obligatory Taiwanese fare and come in 14 varieties. ⊠ *778 Huangjin Cheng Dao, by Gubei Lu, Changning District* ☎ *021/6278–0722* ⌂ *No reservations accepted* ▤ *AE, DC, MC, V.*

Pudong New Area

Continental

$$$–$$$$ ✗ **Grand Café.** Two of the Grand Hyatt's restaurants (the other is the Grill) present Continental cuisine while offering absolutely spectacular views of Shanghai (unless the building is shrouded in fog). The sophisticated 24-hour restaurant Grand Café touts its "show kitchen"—a buffet that includes appetizers, daily specials, fresh seafood, and desserts. ⊠ *Grand Hyatt, 88 Shiji Dadao, Pudong* ☎ *021/5049–1234* ⌂ *Reservations essential* ▤ *AE, DC, MC, V.*

$$$–$$$$ ✗ **The Grill.** Part of the Hyatt's three-in-one, open-kitchen restaurant concept, the Grill shares the 56th floor with two other restaurants (serving Japanese and Italian cuisine). At the Grill you can feast on a great seafood platter or unbelievably tender steak. ⊠ *Grand Hyatt, 88 Shiji Dadao, Pudong* ☎ *021/5049–1234* ⌂ *Reservations essential* ▤ *AE, DC, MC, V.*

Italian

★ **$$–$$$$** ✗ **Danieli's.** The show kitchen in Danieli's reveals the magic of its prodigy of an executive chef, Luca Cesarini. His creations are, quite simply, the most inventive Italian fare in Shanghai. Seasonal menus include such dishes as tomato and onion soup, and pumpkin and amaretto ravioli. Pastry chef Brian Tan Beng Tai's desserts are equally divine and inspired: dark chocolate mousse is shaped like a coffee cup, with a delicate chocolate handle. On the 39th floor of the St. Regis, Danieli's lives up to the hotel's exacting standards of elegance and excellence. ⊠ *The St. Regis Shanghai, 889 Dongfang Lu, Pudong* ☎ *021/5050–4567* ⌂ *Reservations essential* ▤ *AE, DC, MC, V.*

Japanese

$–$$$ ✕ **Itoya.** The waitstaff's precision teamwork makes dining at Itoya a pleasure. Servers pause to greet all guests in unison. You're handed a hot towel upon sitting down and instantly after finishing your meal. The menu sticks to traditional Japanese fare: tempura, sushi, sashimi. In line with its location directly across from the Grand Hyatt's entrance, the restaurant also has several budget-busting items such as Kobe beef and lobster sashimi. Another location in the Kerry Center on Nanjing Xi Lu in Puxi is also a popular spot with businessmen in the city center. ⊠ *178 Huayuan Shiqiao Lu, Pudong* ☏ *021/5882–9679* ⊟ *AE, DC, MC, V.*

Shanghainese

$–$$$ ✕ **Lu Lu.** With its widely spaced round tables, black and gold color scheme, and tasteful paintings, Lu Lu resembles an executive dining room. Fitting, given its main clients are the businessmen from the surrounding Lujiazui office buildings. The menu focuses on traditional Shanghainese dishes such as sliced beef in black pepper sauce and sautéed bean curd with crab meat. Service is polite but not attentive, reacting to requests rather than anticipating them. ⊠ *2-3F, 161 Lujiazui Dong Lu, Pudong* ☏ *021/5882–6679* ⌂ *Reservations essential* ⊟ *AE, DC, MC, V.*

Sichuan

$–$$$ ✕ **South Beauty.** From its perch atop the top floor of the Super Brand Mall, the Pudong branch of South Beauty has a sweeping view of the beauty of the Bund. Although half of its menu is Cantonese, the restaurant is known for its sizzling hot Sichuan fare. Even dishes with a one-pepper rating will scorch your mouth. ⊠ *10F, Super Brand Mall 168 Lujiazui Lu, Pudong* ☏ *021/5047–1817* ⊟ *AE, DC, MC, V.*

WHERE TO STAY

Shanghai's hotels cater mostly to business travelers and can be divided into two categories: modern Western-style hotels that are elegant and nicely appointed, or hotels built in the city's glory days that became state-run after 1949. The latter may lack great service, modern fixings, and convenient facilities, but they often make up for it in charm, tradition, history, and value.

Hotels in China often have a "soft opening," a trial period to work out the kinks before the official ribbon-cutting ceremony. Judging by the number of five-star and Western chain hotels now in Shanghai, the city has surpassed the soft stage and proven just how grandly it has opened to the outside world. The Grand Hyatt, JW Marriott, Portman Ritz-Carlton, and St. Regis aren't merely hotels; they're landmarks on the Shanghai skyline and standard-bearers for all lodgings in town. Even the historic properties that make up the other half of Shanghai's hotel market feel the pressure to update their rooms and facilities. The increasing competition means there are bargains to be had, especially during the low season of November through March. Avoid traveling during the three national holidays—Chinese New Year (mid-January to mid-February), Labor Day (May 1), and National Day (October 1)—when rooms and prices will be at a premium.

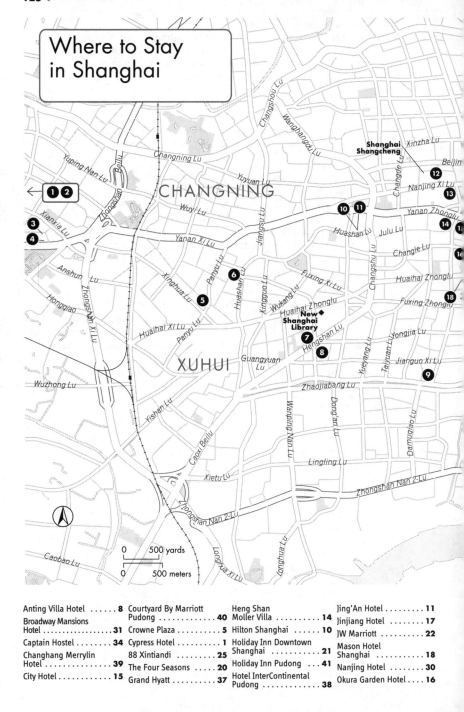

Where to Stay in Shanghai

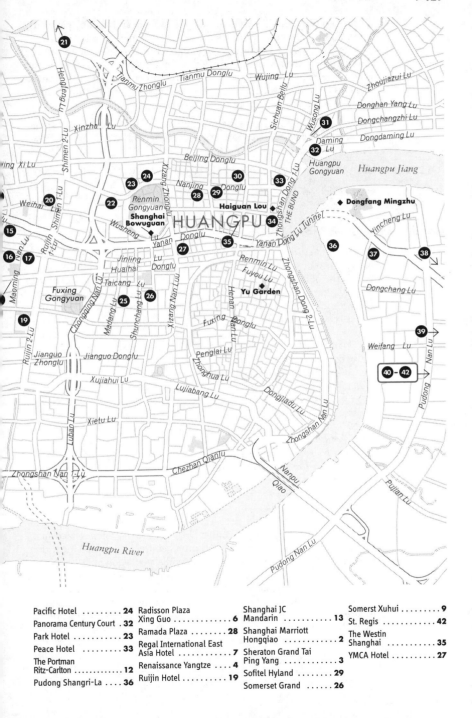

Thanks to Shanghai's excellent subway system and cheap, plentiful taxis, no one neighborhood has a distinct advantage as a base for exploring the city. As Pudong and Hongqiao have developed into business destinations in their own right, they've attracted some of the city's finest hotels. The Bund is home to the most budget properties. The Old French Concession and City Center have the broadest selection of hotels and many popular tourist sites within their districts.

WHAT IT COSTS In Yuan				
	$$$$	$$$	$$	$	¢
FOR 2 PEOPLE	over Y1800	Y1401–Y1800	Y1101–Y1400	Y700–Y1100	under Y700

Prices are for two people in a standard double room in high season, excluding 10%–15% service charge.

Nanjing Lu & the Bund

$$$$ ▣ **The Four Seasons.** With palm trees, fountains, and golden-hued marble as warm as sunshine, the lobby of the Four Seasons establishes the hotel's theme as an elegant oasis in bustling downtown Puxi. Opened in 2002, this 37-story luxury hotel caters to its largely business clientele with impeccable service and its 24-hour business center, gym, and butler service. The 439 spacious rooms—just 12 to 15 per floor—include a safe big enough for a laptop and a separate marble shower and tub. Nanjing Road and the Shanghai Museum are within a 10-minute walk, but the full-service spa, Jazz 37 club, and exceptional Si Ji Xuan Cantonese restaurant provide convincing reasons to stay in. ⊠ *500 Weihai Lu, Jingan District 200041* ☎ *021/6256–8888 or 800/819–5053* ▤ *021/6256–5678* ⊕ *www.fourseasons.com* ↷ *360 rooms, 79 suites* ♨ *4 restaurants, room service, some in-room fax, in-room data ports, in-room safes, minibars, cable TV, in-room VCRs, pool, gym, hair salon, hot tub, spa, steam room, bar, lounge, shop, baby-sitting, dry cleaning, laundry services, concierge, concierge floor, Internet, business services, convention center, travel services, some free parking, no-smoking floors* ▭ *AE, DC, MC, V.*

$$$$ ▣ **JW Marriott.** The JW Marriott's futuristic 60-story tower turns heads with its 90-degree twist, which divides the executive apartments below from the 22-story hotel above and creates 360-degree views of the Puxi skyline. The interior follows classic lines with subtle Chinese accents. Celadon vases, wedding boxes, and ornamental jades complement the soft green-and-yellow palette and warm fiddleback wood in the spacious rooms. The largely business clientele appreciates the one-touch "At Your Service" call button, while the hotel's Mandara Spa, excellent restaurants, and JW Lounge—which has 50-plus martinis—are big draws for leisure travelers. ⊠ *399 Nanjing Xi Lu, Huangpu District 200003* ☎ *021/5359–4969 or 888/236–2427* ▤ *021/6375–5988* ⊕ *www. marriotthotels.com/shajw* ↷ *305 rooms, 37 suites* ♨ *3 restaurants, coffee shop, room service, in-room data ports, in-room safes, some in-room fax, minibars, cable TV, indoor pool, outdoor pool, health club, hot tub, sauna, steam room, spa, lobby lounge, lounge, library, piano,*

shops, baby-sitting, dry cleaning, laundry service, concierge, concierge floor, Internet, business services, convention center, travel services, parking (fee), no-smoking rooms, no-smoking floor ☰ *AE, DC, MC, V.*

★ **$$$$** 🏨 **The Portman Ritz-Carlton.** Outstanding facilities, gold standard service, and a high-profile location in the Shanghai Center make the Portman Ritz-Carlton one of the city's top attractions. The 50-story hotel devotes three floors solely to its fitness center, another four to its executive club rooms. The two-story lobby—a popular networking spot—exudes cool refinement with its ebony, marble, and chrome touches, while the guest rooms are gradually adopting a warmer peach and salmon palette. In addition to the Shanghai Center's surrounding shops, banks, airline offices, and restaurants, the hotel has its own deli and four top-notch restaurants. Its consistent rankings as one of the best employers and hotels in Asia translates into content employees and even happier customers. ✉ *1376 Nanjing Xi Lu, Jingan District 200040* ☎ *021/6279–8888 or 800/241–3333* 🖷 *021/6279–8887* ⊕ *www.ritzcarlton.com* 🛏 *510 rooms, 68 suites* ♨ *4 restaurants, deli, room service, in-room data ports, in-room safes, minibars, cable TV, tennis court, indoor-outdoor pool, health club, hair salon, hot tub, massage, sauna, steam room, squash, racquetball, 2 bars, shops, baby-sitting, dry cleaning, laundry service, concierge, concierge floor, Internet, business services, convention center, helipad, parking (fee), no-smoking rooms* ☰ *AE, DC, MC, V.*

$$$$ 🏨 **Shanghai JC Mandarin.** At the base of the JC Mandarin's 30-story blue-glass towers lies the most memorable lobby in Shanghai. Its five-story hand-painted mural depicts the voyage of the Ming Dynasty admiral Zheng Ho. Opened in 1991, the hotel overhauled most public areas in 2003 and 2004. The Mandarin Club Lounge now occupies an inviting space on the second floor. The fitness center has added a spa. The Cuba cigar bar has carved a stylish lounge out of a former storeroom. The spacious rooms are due for an update, but are comfortable with earthy tones and natural wood. ✉ *1225 Nanjing Xi Lu, Jingan District 200040* ☎ *021/6279–1888 or 800/338–8355* 🖷 *021/6279–1822* ⊕ *www.jcmandarin.com* 🛏 *475 rooms, 35 suites* ♨ *4 restaurants, café, patisserie, room service, in-room data ports, in-room safes, minibars, cable TV, tennis court, indoor pool, gym, hair salon, hot tub, massage, sauna, spa, steam room, squash, 2 bars, piano, shops, baby-sitting, dry cleaning, laundry service, concierge, concierge floor, Internet, business services, conference center, parking (fee), no-smoking floors* ☰ *AE, DC, MC, V.*

★ **$$$$** 🏨 **The Westin Shanghai.** With its distinctive room layouts, glittering glass staircase, and 90-plus works of art on display, the Westin Shanghai is a masterpiece, fittingly located near the majestic Bund. Crowne Deluxe rooms are miniature suites; sliding doors divide the sitting area, bathroom, and bedroom. Luxurious amenities include rainforest showers, extra deep tubs, and Westin's trademark Heavenly Beds. Pampering continues at the Banyan Tree spa—China's first—and stellar EEST restaurant, a sunny three-in-one venue with full Thai, Japanese, and Cantonese menus. Sunday brunch at the Stage restaurant is considered Shanghai's best. Service is so attentive that extra staff stand in front of the check-in counter to assist. ✉ *Bund Center, 88 Henan Zhonglu,*

Huangpu District 200002 ☎ *021/6335–1888 or 888/625–5144* 🖷 *021/ 6335–2888* ⊕ *www.westin.com/shanghai* 🖙 *276 rooms, 25 suites* ♨ *3 restaurants, grocery, patisserie, juice bar, room service, in-room data ports, in-room fax, in-room safes, minibars, cable TV, indoor pool, health club, hair salon, hot tub, sauna, spa, steam room, bar, lobby lounge, piano, shops, baby-sitting, dry cleaning, laundry service, concierge, concierge floor, Internet, business services, convention center, travel services, some free parking, no-smoking floors* ⊟ *AE, DC, MC, V.*

$$$ ▦ **Sofitel Hyland.** Directly on the Nanjing Road pedestrian mall, the Sofitel Hyland is a convenient base for shopping and exploring the city center and the Bund. The rooms in this 30-story French-managed hotel are somewhat small and a bit tired, simply furnished, and decorated in light tones. The top-floor Sky Lounge serves Sunday brunch amid views of the Bund and downtown, and Le Pub 505 brews up its own beer. ⊠ *505 Nanjing Dong Lu, Huangpu District 200001* ☎ *021/6351–5888* 🖷 *021/ 6351–4088* ⊕ *www.accorhotels-asia.com* 🖙 *299 rooms, 73 suites* ♨ *4 restaurants, room service, in-room data ports, in-room safes, minibars, cable TV, pool, health club, hair salon, massage, sauna, spa, steam room, 2 bars, lobby lounge, pub, piano, shops, concierge floor, Internet, business services, convention center, airport shuttle, travel services, parking (fee), no-smoking floors* ⊟ *AE, DC, MC, V.*

★ **$$–$$$** ▦ **Peace Hotel.** With its art deco interior and unmistakable green pyramid roof, the Peace Hotel is among Shanghai's most treasured historic buildings. Opened in 1929 as the Cathay Hotel by millionaire Victor Sassoon, the 11-story north building was famous throughout Asia and a magnet for celebrities. Its high ceilings and ornate woodwork are intact, and the ballroom evokes old Shanghai cabarets and gala parties. However, save for the international suites, the rooms tend more toward small and stuffy than glamorous these days. The south building, opened in 1906 as the Palace Hotel, is the oldest structure on the Bund, but its rooms are the hotel's most modern, with larger bathrooms and nicer furniture. ⊠ *20 Nanjing Dong Lu, Huangpu District 200002* ☎ *021/ 6321–6888* 🖷 *021/6329–0300* ⊕ *www.shanghaipeacehotel.com* 🖙 *411 rooms, 9 suites* ♨ *2 restaurants, room service, in-room safes, minibars, small gym, hair salon, massage, sauna, steam room, billiards, Ping-Pong, 2 bars, lobby lounge, shops, baby-sitting, small playground, concierge, concierge floor, convention center, travel services, free parking, no-smoking rooms* ⊟ *AE, DC, MC, V.*

$$ ▦ **Holiday Inn Downtown Shanghai.** Adjacent to the Shanghai Railway Station and metro line 1, the Holiday Inn Downtown in the northern city center provides convenient—albeit not immediate—access to the rest of Shanghai and cities beyond. Formerly two separate Chinese hotels, the Great Wall and Plaza wings both have a full slate of restaurants and services, as well as separate lobbies that are a five-minute outside walk apart. The property has recast itself as a business hotel by adding club floors and 10 executive rooms: enlarged studios with a common bedroom and work space. ⊠ *585 Hengfeng Lu , Zhabei District 200070* ☎ *021/6353–8008 or 800/465–4329* 🖷 *021/6354–3019* ⊕ *www. holiday–inn.com* 🖙 *481 rooms and suites* ♨ *3 restaurants, 2 coffee shops, room service, in-room data ports, in-room safes, minibars, some in-room* *fax, cable TV, 2 gyms, 2 hair salons, sauna, bowling, 2 lobby lounges, piano, baby-sitting, indoor playroom, dry cleaning, laundry service, concierge, concierge floor, Internet, business services, convention center, airport shuttle, travel services, parking (fee), no–smoking floors* ▤ *AE, DC, MC, V.*

$$ ▦ **Park Hotel** (Guoji Fandian). Once Shanghai's tallest building, the 20-story Park Hotel is now dwarfed on the Puxi skyline and eclipsed by other hotels whose glory days are present instead of past. This 1934 art deco structure overlooking People's Park still has great views and a musty charm, particularly in its restored marble lobby. Rooms are clean and bright, with prints of historic buildings from around the world. But bathrooms are tiny, and the hotel's service and facilities have definitely slipped to second-rate. ⊠ *170 Nanjing Xi Lu, Huangpu District 200003* ☏ *021/6327–5225* 🖷 *021/6327–6958* ➬ *219 rooms, 31 suites* ⚒ *3 restaurants, in-room data ports, in-room safes, minibars, cable TV, gym, sauna, hair salon, billiards, 2 bars, lobby lounge, piano, shop, dry cleaning, laundry service, concierge, Internet, business services, meeting rooms, some free parking, no-smoking rooms* ▤ *AE, DC, MC, V.*

$–$$ ▦ **Ramada Plaza.** With its ornate lobby resembling a European opera
Fodor'sChoice house, the Ramada Plaza Shanghai brings a touch of grandeur to the
★ Nanjing Road pedestrian walkway. Statues of Greek gods reign from atop intricate inlaid tables. Soaring marble columns direct the eye skyward toward a stained-glass skylight. The fair-size rooms contrast dark woods with beige walls and upholstery, and they face in toward a dramatic atrium, topped by yet another courtyard and the executive lounge. Given the lush setting and ace location, the Ramada Plaza is a good value for the money, and you can usually get a room for less than the rack rate. ⊠ *719 Nanjing Dong Lu, Huangpu District 200001* ☏ *021/ 6350–0000 or 800/854–7854* 🖷 *021/6350–6666* ⊕ *www. ramadainternational.com* ➬ *333 rooms, 36 suites* ⚒ *4 restaurants, patisserie, room service, in-room data ports, in-room safes, minibars, cable TV, gym, hair salon, massage, sauna, steam room, billiards, lobby lounge, nightclub, shops, baby-sitting, dry cleaning, laundry service, concierge, concierge floor, Internet, business services, convention center, travel services, parking (fee), no-smoking floors* ▤ *AE, DC, MC, V.*

$–$$ ▦ **Broadway Mansions Hotel.** One of Shanghai's revered old buildings, the Broadway Mansions Hotel has anchored the north end of the Bund since 1934. Although the good-size rooms were last updated in 2001, the worn wood furniture, industrial bathrooms, and steam radiators betray their age. In contrast, business rooms are strikingly modern, with a cool gray and tan interior, glass-topped desk and nightstand, and separate marble shower and tub. River-view rooms cost Y100 extra; request a higher floor to reduce the street noise. ⊠ *20 Suzhou Bei Lu, Hongkou District 200080* ☏ *021/6324–6260 Ext. 2326* 🖷 *021/ 6306–5147* ⊕ *www.broadwaymansions.com* ➬ *161 rooms, 72 suites* ⚒ *2 restaurants, café, patisserie, room service, in-room data ports, some in-room fax, some in-room safes, minibars, cable TV, gym, hair salon, massage, sauna, 2 bars, piano, baby-sitting, laundry service, concierge floor, Internet, business services, meeting rooms, airport shuttle, some free parking* ▤ *AE, DC, MC, V.*

$ ▦ **Pacific Hotel.** This 1926 property has done an admirable job of preserving its charm. In the original Italian-style front building, sixth- and seventh-floor rooms have wood floors, ornate molded ceilings, and great views of People's Park. (Bathrooms, though, are rather institutional.) The formal lobby has coffered ceilings and imposing columns. The smaller rooms in the rear building lack the fine detail and views but are still comfortable. Amenities fall short, and soundproofing could be better, but the hotel's proud history, prime location, and prices make it an appealing choice. ⊠ *108 Nanjing Xi Lu, Huangpu District 200003* ☎ *021/6327–6226* 🖷 *021/6372–3634* ⊕ *www.jjusa.com* ⟲ *161 rooms, 5 suites* ♨ *2 restaurants, room service, in-room data ports, minibars, cable TV, lobby lounge, shop, laundry service, Internet, business services, meeting rooms, travel services* ▤ *AE, DC, MC, V.*

$ ▦ **Panorama Century Court.** In a part of town dominated by historic properties, Panorama Century Court stands out for its modern facilities, competitive prices, and great Bund views from across the Waibaidu Bridge. Opened in 2000, the 32-story Accor-owned hotel attracts European tourists familiar with the brand as well as business travelers. One- to three-bedroom suites all include living rooms and tiny kitchens, but you'll have to request utensils. Standard rooms have thoughtfully designed bathrooms with handy shelves for toiletries. The well-equipped gym has one of the best views in Shanghai. ⊠ *53 Huangpu Lu, Hongkou District 200080* ☎ *021/5393–0008* 🖷 *021/5393–0009* ⊕ *www.panorama-sh. com* ⟲ *62 rooms, 92 suites* ♨ *1 restaurant, room service, in-room data ports, in-room safes, kitchens, minibars, microwaves, refrigerators, cable TV, gym, sauna, steam room, lobby lounge, library, piano, laundry facilities, laundry service, concierge, Internet, business services, meeting rooms, parking (fee)* ▤ *AE, DC, MC, V.*

¢ ▦ **Captain Hostel.** Backpackers choose Captain Hostel as much for its roof-top bar and restaurant as for its clean, bright rooms and convenient location a half-block west of the Bund. The hopping Noah's Bar on the sixth floor has views of the Pudong skyline that rival those from much pricier lodgings. The dormitories accommodate 5 to 10 people per room in bunks resembling ship's berths, in keeping with the overall nautical theme in this 1920s hotel. The 20 first-class rooms are tired but fair-sized, with TVs and private bathrooms. Bunk rooms must be paid for in cash. ⊠ *37 Fuzhou Lu, Huangpu District, 200002* ☎ *021/ 6323–5053* 🖷 *021/6321–9331* ⊕ *www.captainhostel.com.cn* ⟲ *20 rooms, 85 rooms with shared bath* ♨ *1 restaurant, cable TV in some rooms, bar, laundry facilities, Internet, meeting rooms, no-smoking rooms; no phones in some rooms* ▤ *MC, V.*

¢ ▦ **Nanjing Hotel.** A frequent choice for budget tour groups, the Nanjing Hotel is only half a block yet a world away from the modern bustle of the Nanjing Dong Lu pedestrian walkway. Step out the front door and you'll see China as the locals do: fruit vendors balancing their loads, trash men ringing their hand bells. The hotel's proximity to the metro line and the Bund compensate for the street noise and lack of views. Built in 1931, the eight-story building is dated, yet rooms are fair-sized with Internet access and a few satellite channels. ⊠ *200 Shanxi Lu, Huangpu District 200001* ☎ *021/6322–2888* 🖷 *021/6351–6520*

⊕ *www.nj-hotel.com* ⟵ *Restaurant, room service, in-room data ports, in-room safes, cable TV, minibars, shops, laundry service, Internet, business center, meeting rooms* ⊟ *AE, DC, MC, V.*

¢ ▦ **YMCA Hotel.** Its central location—within a 15-minute walk of People's Square, Xintiandi, and the Bund—makes the YMCA Hotel a top destination for budget travelers. Built in 1929 as an actual YMCA, the 11-story brick building retains some of its original features: a temple-like exterior, painted ceiling beams on the second floor. A 2003 makeover gave the small rooms an apricot-and-beige color scheme and lighter furniture. The four dormitory rooms have single beds, rather than bunks. ✉ *123 Xizang Nan Lu, Huangpu District 200021* ☎ *021/6326–1040* 🖷 *021/6320–1957* ⊕ *www.ymcahotel.com* ↩ *140 rooms, 6 suites, 4 rooms with shared bath* ⟵ *2 restaurants, coffee shop, small grocery, room service, some in-room safes, minibars, cable TV, gym (fee), hair salon, massage, billiards, Ping-Pong, recreation room, shops, laundry service, Internet, business services, meeting rooms, airport shuttle, travel services* ⊟ *AE, DC, MC, V.*

Old French Concession

$$$$ ▦ **Crowne Plaza.** This hotel on the far western side of the French Concession makes up for its out-of-the-way location with service. The staff here is among the friendliest in town and makes guests, mostly business travelers, feel at home. Rooms were updated in 2003, although bathrooms remain small. Deluxe and club rooms now sport a more contemporary look, with sleek desks and light fixtures. Superior rooms have an Asian touch, with calligraphy hung between dark-wood beams. ✉ *400 Panyu Lu, 200052* ☎ *021/6280–8888 or 800/227–6963* 🖷 *021/6280–3353* ⊕ *www.shanghai.crowneplaza.com* ↩ *467 rooms, 29 suites* ⟵ *4 restaurants, café, patisserie, room service, in-room data ports, in-room safes, minibars, indoor pool, gym, hair salon, massage, sauna, steam room, 2 bars, lobby lounge, piano, shops, baby-sitting, concierge floor, Internet, business services, convention center, airport shuttle, parking (fee), no-smoking floors* ⊟ *AE, DC, MC, V.*

$$$$ ▦ **Okura Garden Hotel.** Its park-like setting in the heart of the French Concession makes the 33-story Garden Hotel a favorite Shanghai retreat, especially for Japanese travelers familiar with the Okura Group name. The first three floors, which were once old Shanghai's French Club, have been restored, with cascading chandeliers, frescoes, and art deco details at every turn. Average-size rooms are simply furnished with silk wallpaper and European-style furniture. The romantic third-floor terrace bar overlooks the 2-acre garden, and the Japanese and French restaurants serve excellent but high-priced food. ✉ *58 Maoming Nan Lu, Luwan District 200020* ☎ *021/6415–1111* 🖷 *021/6415–8866* ⊕ *www.gardenhotelshanghai.com* ↩ *478 rooms, 22 suites* ⟵ *5 restaurants, room service, in-room data ports, in-room safes, some in-room fax, minibars, cable TV, 2 tennis courts, indoor-outdoor pool, health club, hair salon, hot tub, massage, sauna, 3 bars, lobby lounge, shops, dry cleaning, laundry service, concierge, concierge floor, Internet, business services, convention center, airport shuttle, travel services, some free parking, no-smoking floors* ⊟ *AE, DC, MC, V.*

$$$$ ⊞ **Radisson Plaza Xing Guo.** This quiet garden property was once the government-owned Xing Guo Hotel, a villa complex where Chairman Mao frequently stayed. The modern 16-story Radisson Plaza sprouted up in 2002, its garden-view rooms overlooking the central lawn and Mao's legendary Villa No. 1. The comfortable beige-tone rooms have ample work space, with two club chairs and a large desk. The Clark Hatch Fitness Center has top-name equipment, an aerobics room, and an elevated pool. However, the hotel's location in the consular district is far from the subway and most attractions. ⊠ *78 Xingguo Lu, Changning District 200052* ☎ *021/6212–9998* 🖷 *021/6212–9996 or 888/201–1718* ⊕ *www.radissonasiapacific.com* ↴ *150 rooms, 40 suites* ⌂ *2 restaurants, café, room service, in-room data ports, some in-room fax, in-room safes, minibars, cable TV, golf simulator, health club, indoor pool, hair salon, hot tub, massage, sauna, steam room, bowling, Ping-Pong, squash, bar, lobby lounge, library, shops, baby-sitting, dry cleaning, laundry service, concierge, concierge floor, Internet, business services, meeting rooms, airport shuttle, travel services, some free parking, no-smoking rooms* ▭ *AE, DC, MC, V.*

$$$$ ⊞ **Regal International East Asia Hotel.** Its exclusive Shanghai International Tennis Center is the Regal's trump card among five-star hotels. The center has 10 tournament courts as well as one of the city's best health clubs. The luxury hotel's large club rooms, updated in 2004, include a curvilinear desk and ergonomic chair and a funky chaise longue. Deluxe rooms have compact bathrooms with marble sinks and huge mirrors. The Hengshan Road metro station and bar/restaurant district are just a block away. ⊠ *516 Hengshan Lu, Xuhui District 200040* ☎ *021/6415–5588* 🖷 *021/6445–8899* ⊕ *www.regal-eastasia.com* ↴ *278 rooms, 22 suites* ⌂ *3 restaurants, coffee shop, patisserie, room service, in-room data ports, some in-room fax, in-room safes, minibars, cable TV, golf simulator, 10 tennis courts, indoor pool, health club, hair salon, hot tub, massage, sauna, steam room, billiards, bowling, Ping-Pong, squash, lobby lounge, piano, shops, baby-sitting, indoor playroom, concierge, concierge floor, Internet, business services, convention center, travel services, free parking, no-smoking floors* ▭ *AE, DC, MC, V.*

$$$–$$$$ ⊞ **88 Xintiandi.** Although it targets business travelers, 88 Xintiandi is a shopper's and gourmand's delight. The 53-room boutique hotel is in the heart of Xintiandi, its balconies overlooking the top-dollar shops and restaurants below. The rooms, all mini- or full-size suites with kitchens, are likewise upscale. Beds are elevated on a central, gauze-curtained platform; sitting areas have large TVs and DVD players. Stylish wood screens accent the rooms and common areas. Deluxe rooms and the executive lounge overlook man-made Lake Taipingqiao, and guests have access to the comprehensive Alexander City Club gym next door. ⊠ *380 Huangpi Nan Lu, Luwan District 200021* ☎ *021/5383–8833* 🖷 *021/5353–8877* ⊕ *www.88xintiandi.com* ↴ *12 suites, 41 rooms* ⌂ *1 restaurant, room service, in-room data ports, some in-room fax, in-room safes, kitchens, minibars, microwaves, refrigerators, cable TV, in-room VCRs, indoor pool, gym, bar, baby-sitting, laundry service, concierge, business services, parking (fee), no-smoking floors* ▭ *AE, DC, MC, V.*

$$$–$$$$ 🏨 **Hilton Shanghai.** Opened in 1988 as Shanghai's first five-star hotel, the Hilton remains a favorite among businessmen and airline crews. The 43-story triangular building is lower-keyed than its younger competitors, with an understated sand-tone color scheme and comfortable but not cutting-edge rooms. The huge lobby has a lounge in the front, while in the rear lies the much-lauded Italian restaurant Leonardo's and the sunlit 24-hour Atrium Café, which resembles a quiet Chinese garden. On the top floors, the conference center, Penthouse Bar, and stellar Sichuan Court restaurant all have stunning views of the ever-expanding Puxi skyline. ✉ *250 Huashan Lu, Jingan District 200040* ☎ *021/ 6248–0000 or 800/445–8667* 📠 *021/6248–3848* ⊕ *www.shanghai. hilton.com* 🛏 *692 rooms, 28 suites* ♨ *6 restaurants, café, coffee shop, grill, room service, in-room data ports, some in-room fax, minibars, cable TV, tennis court, indoor pool, health club, hair salon, hot tub, spa, sauna, Japanese baths, steam room, squash, 3 bars, lobby lounge, shops, baby-sitting, dry cleaning, laundry service, concierge, concierge floor, Internet, business services, convention center, airport shuttle, travel services, some free parking, no-smoking floors* 🖃 *AE, DC, MC, V.*

$$–$$$ 🏨 **City Hotel.** The joint-venture City Hotel almost matches the facilities but definitely lacks the polish of its brand-name competitors. Compact standard rooms have cream linens with baby-blue and pink stripes and small all-white marble bathrooms. Larger executive rooms, on the 21st through 23rd floors, have double closets, and more modern furniture and fixtures. The comprehensive City Club fitness center includes a full spa, and there's an indoor playroom for kids. Reasonably close to Huaihai Lu shops, metro line 1 and the Shanghai Exhibition Center, the hotel has equal appeal for business and leisure travelers. ✉ *5–7 Shaanxi Nan Lu, Luwan District 200020* ☎ *021/6255–1133* 📠 *021/6255–0211* ⊕ *www.cityhotelshanghai.com* 🛏 *274 rooms, 10 suites* ♨ *3 restaurants, café, room service, in-room data ports, some in-room safes, minibars, cable TV, indoor pool, health club, hair salon, sauna, spa, steam room, billiards, 2 bars, lobby lounge, piano bar, shop, baby-sitting, laundry service, Internet, business services, convention center, travel services, parking (fee), no-smoking rooms* 🖃 *AE, DC, MC, V.*

$$–$$$ 🏨 **Somerset Grand.** Designed as serviced apartments for expatriates, the Somerset Grand's suites are great for families wanting extra space plus the usual hotel amenities. The twin 34-story towers have 334 one- to three-bedroom suites, ranging from 890 to 2,500 square feet. (One-bedroom suites have only king beds.) The units feel homey, with blue-and-pink floral comforters and rugs and a small kitchen. Kids can burn off steam at the pool and play room. There's a great French restaurant and coffee shop on the grounds, plus the hotel is two blocks from the restaurants, shops, and movie theater at Xintiandi and 10 minutes to the subway. ✉ *8 Jinan Lu, Luwan District 200021* ☎ *021/6385–6888* 📠 *021/6384–8988* ⊕ *www.the-ascott.com* 🛏 *334 suites* ♨ *In-room data ports, in-room safes, kitchen, minibars, refrigerators, cable TV, 2 tennis courts, indoor pool, health club, hair salon, hot tub, massage, sauna, steam room, billiards, library, baby-sitting, playground, dry cleaning, laundry facilities, laundry service, concierge, Internet, business services, meeting rooms, travel services, parking (fee), no-smoking rooms* 🖃 *AE, DC, MC, V.*

$–$$$ 🏨 **Jinjiang Hotel.** The former Cathay Mansions, Grosvenor Gardens, and Grosvenor House, now known collectively as the Jinjiang Hotel, are among the few art deco buildings left standing in the city. It's here that President Nixon and Premier Zhou Enlai signed the Shanghai Communique in 1972. Luxury suites in the Grosvenor House start at $800 nightly. The 193 rooms in the 1929 Cathay Building are plain but fair-sized with separate showers and tubs. Deluxe rooms are more stylish. The Jin Nan Building will reopen in summer 2005 with 120 renovated budget-price standard rooms. ✉ *59 Maoming Nan Lu, Luwan District 200020* ☎ *021/6258–2582* 🖷 *021/6472–5588* ⊕ *www.jinjianghotelshanghai.com* ➳ *328 rooms, 33 suites* ♨ *5 restaurants, room service, in-room data ports, in-room safes, minibars, cable TV, indoor pool, health club, hair salon, sauna, bowling, 2 bars, lobby lounge, shops, baby-sitting, Internet, business services, convention center, airport shuttle, travel services, free parking, no-smoking rooms, no-smoking floors* ▤ *AE, DC, MC, V.*

$$ 🏨 **Jing'An Hotel.** The weekly chamber music concert in its lobby is just one example of how the Jing'An Hotel has retained its elegance and charm after 70 years. In a 1.5-acre garden, the Spanish-style main building carries the garden theme throughout its rooms. Mauve upholstery and cream wallpaper bloom with delicate floral patterns. Elaborately carved wooden door frames and lintels direct the eye upward toward the 10-foot ceilings. Facilities are lacking, but the hotel's proximity to the subway line and its French Concession setting make this oft-overlooked property a winner. ✉ *370 Huashan Lu, Jingan District 200040* ☎ *021/6248–0088* 🖷 *021/6249–6100* ⊕ *www.jinganhotel.net* ➳ *210 rooms, 17 suites* ♨ *2 restaurants, coffee shop, room service, in-room data ports, in-room safes, minibars, cable TV, gym, hair salon, massage, sauna, chess room, lobby lounge, piano bar, shops, baby-sitting, dry cleaning, laundry service, concierge, Internet, business services, meeting rooms, airport shuttle, travel services, parking (fee), no-smoking rooms* ▤ *AE, DC, MC, V.*

$–$$ 🏨 **Mason Hotel.** Although it caters to business travelers, the Mason Hotel has a convenient location for leisure travelers: steps from the Shaanxi Nan Lu metro station and surrounded by the shops of Huaihai Lu. Soundproofing blocks most—but not all—the street noise from the fairly large, simply furnished rooms, which face in toward a sunny, quiet four-story courtyard. Facilities fall a bit short, but there's a Starbucks downstairs and a cozy sunroom up top in the Avenue Joffre restaurant. ✉ *935 Huaihai Zhonglu, Luwan District 200020* ☎ *021/6466–2020* 🖷 *021/6467–1693* ⊕ *www.masonhotel.com* ➳ *115 rooms, 4 suites* ♨ *Restaurant, room service, in-room data ports, in-room safes, minibars, cable TV, gym, hair salon, billiards, lobby lounge, piano, shops, laundry service, concierge, Internet, business services, meeting rooms, free parking, no-smoking rooms* ▤ *AE, DC, MC, V.*

$–$$ 🏨 **Ruijin Hotel.** Formerly the Morriss Estate, the Ruijin Hotel showcases how opulently *taipans* (expatriate millionaire businessmen) lived in Shanghai's heyday of the 1930s. Rooms within the two preserved villas—No. 1 and Old No. 3—are rich with detail: high ceilings, ornate plaster molding, bamboo-etched glass. The two other buildings are significantly shorter on charm but still overlook the verdant grounds, which are shared with several top-notch restaurants. A hotel tower slated to open in 2006 will add 150 rooms and much-needed amenities; however, it will also result in the conversion of Villa No. 1 into a VIP villa, so reserve these rooms while you can. ⊠ *118 Ruijin Er Lu, Luwan District 200020* ☎ *021/6472–5222* 🖷 *021/6473–2277* ⊕ *www. shedi.net.cn/outedi/ruijin* 🖚 *62 rooms, 20 suites* ⌂ *Restaurant, coffee shop, room service, in-room safes, minibars, cable TV, hair salon, 2 bars, lobby lounge, shops, laundry service, Internet, business services, convention center, parking (fee), no-smoking rooms* 🖃 *AE, DC, MC, V.*

$–$$ 🖾 **Somerset Xuhui.** The family-focused facilities of the all-suites Somerset Xuhui help compensate for its location: off the subway line, halfway between Xujiahui's shops and French Concession attractions. An indoor playroom, sizeable pool, and fitness center overlooking Zhaojiabang Road provide diversion for children and adults—as does the Starbucks downstairs. There are no restaurants, just small en suite kitchens. Units range from one to three bedrooms, the latter having twin beds for kids. Cozy living rooms and huge closets help make this hotel a good spot for families in Shanghai. ⊠ *888 Shaanxi Nan Lu, Xuhui District, 200031* ☎ *021/6466–0888* 🖷 *021/6466–4646* ⊕ *www.the-ascott.com* 🖚 *167 suites* ⌂ *In-room safes, in-room data ports, kitchens, minibars, microwaves, refrigerators, cable TV, 2 tennis courts, indoor pool, health club, hot tub, massage, sauna, steam room, billiards, Ping-Pong, library, baby-sitting, playground, dry cleaning, laundry facilities, laundry service, concierge, Internet, business services, meeting rooms, travel services, parking (fee), no-smoking rooms* 🖃 *AE, DC, MC, V.*

$ 🖾 **Anting Villa Hotel.** Two blocks from the metro and the Hengshan Road nightlife district, the Anting Villa Hotel is a convenient and surprisingly quiet retreat. The cedar-shaded grounds and namesake 1934 Spanish-style villa were once home for Shanghai Mayor Chen Yi. Opened in 2000, the 10-story hotel tower has a riot of styles: bullfighter paintings, stained glass, leopard spot chairs, damask couches. Rooms in the neighboring three-story building (which lacks an elevator) appear fresher, with moss-green upholstery and dark bird's-eye maple furniture. The staff's English ability is limited; most guests are Japanese or Korean. A gym, tennis court, and pool are planned for 2005. ⊠ *46 Anting Lu, Xuhui District 200031* ☎ *021/6433–1188* 🖷 *021/6433–9726* ⊕ *www.sinohotel.com* 🖚 *135 rooms, 11 suites* ⌂ *Restaurant, café, room service, in-room safes, minibars, cable TV, hair salon, massage, piano, shops, baby-sitting, laundry service, Internet, business services, meeting rooms, travel services, free parking, no-smoking rooms* 🖃 *AE, DC, MC, V.*

$ 🖾 **Heng Shan Moller Villa.** Part gingerbread dollhouse, part castle, the Heng Shan Moller Villa has been one of Shanghai's most enchanting properties since its completion in 1936. British businessman Eric Moller built the villa to resemble a castle his daughter envisioned in a dream. The family fled Shanghai in 1941, and after 1949 the house was the Communist Youth League's headquarters. Opened as a boutique hotel in 2002, the original villa has 11 deluxe rooms and has been lushly restored with parquet floors, chandeliers, and ornately carved stairwells. Standard rooms in Building No. 2, however, are disappointingly plain. Guests have access to the neighboring Shanghai Grand Club's excellent fitness center.

✉ *30 Shaanxi Nan Lu, Jingan District 200040* ☏ *021/6247–8881 Ext. 607* 🖷 *021/6289–1020* ⊕ *www.mollervilla.com* 🛏 *40 rooms, 5 suites* ⚷ *6 restaurants, coffee shop, in-room data ports, some in-room safes, minibars, cable TV, hair salon, shop, laundry service, Internet, business services, meeting rooms, free parking* ▤ *AE, DC, MC, V.*

Hongqiao Development Zone

$$$$ 🖫 **Renaissance Yangtze.** Rebranded as Renaissance in 2001, and granted its fifth star by the National Tourism Administration of China in 2003, this hotel has become a worthy rival for the Sheraton Grand Tai Ping Yang next door. Eight executive floors cater to conventioneers and corporate types with business at INTEX and Shanghai Mart. There's a good-size gym and pool and an often-overlooked cigar bar. The hotel's long-standing reputation for top-quality catering is well preserved in its five restaurants, particularly Dynasty. Rooms are warm, with sunrise-golden comforters and drapes, vermilion club chairs, and auburn-tiled bathrooms. ✉ *2099 Yanan Xi Lu, Changning District 200336* ☏ *021/6275–0000 or 888/236–2427* 🖷 *021/6275–0750* ⊕ *www.renaissancehotels.com* 🛏 *523 rooms, 21 suites* ⚷ *5 restaurants, café, patisserie, room service, in-room data ports, in-room safes, minibars, cable TV, indoor pool, health club, hair salon, hot tub, massage, sauna, billiards, 2 bars, lobby lounge, piano, shops, baby-sitting, dry cleaning, laundry service, concierge, concierge floor, Internet, business services, convention center, travel services, some free parking, no-smoking floors* ▤ *AE, DC, MC, V.*

$$$$ 🖫 **Shanghai Marriott Hongqiao.** With only eight stories and 325 rooms, the Marriott Hongqiao feels like a boutique hotel compared to its soaring competitors in Hongqiao. Opened in 2000, the hotel transformed its top two floors into executive floors in 2003. The hotel is quiet; inside twin rooms have balconies overlooking the third-floor pool-side courtyard. Porcelain vases and Ming-influenced furniture add some Chinese flair to the generous-size rooms. The Manhattan Steakhouse serves tender, juicy steaks, while the Marriott Café has an excellent Sunday brunch. ✉ *2270 Hongqiao Lu, Changning District 200336* ☏ *021/6237–6000 or 800/228–9290* 🖷 *021/6237–6222* ⊕ *www.marriott.com* 🛏 *312 rooms, 13 suites* ⚷ *4 restaurants, patisserie, room service, in-room data ports, in-room safes, minibars, cable TV, some in-room VCRs, 1 tennis court, indoor pool, health club, hair salon, hot tub, massage, sauna, steam room, 2 bars, lobby lounge, sports bar, baby-sitting, dry cleaning, laundry service, concierge, concierge floor, Internet, business services, convention center, airport shuttle, travel services, parking (fee), no-smoking floors* ▤ *AE, DC, MC, V.*

★ $$$$ 🖫 **Sheraton Grand Tai Ping Yang.** Business travelers value the Sheraton Grand for its conscientious service and its location, 15 minutes from Hongqiao Airport and adjacent to Shanghai Mart and INTEX. Formerly the Westin, this Japanese-managed property has four club floors, one-touch service by phone, and golf privileges at Shanghai International Golf Club. Spacious standard rooms include large desks and ergonomic chairs, while plush grand rooms have oriental carpets and overstuffed chairs in the separate bed and sitting rooms. A grand staircase sweeps

A MASSAGE FOR EVERYONE

IN CHINA, A MASSAGE ISN'T AN INDULGENCE; it's what the doctor orders. According to the tenets of traditional Chinese medicine, massage can help the body's qi, or energy, flow freely and remain in balance.

Of course, where you choose to have your massage can tip the scale toward indulgence. Around Shanghai are hundreds of blind massage parlors, inexpensive no-frills salons whose blind masseurs are closely attuned to the body's soft and sore spots. At the other end of the spectrum lie the hotel spas, luxurious retreats where pampering is at a premium. Here are just a few of the massage outlets in Shanghai that can attend to your needs.

The **Banyan Tree Spa** (✉ 3F, the Westin Shanghai, 88 Henan Zhong Lu, Huangpu District ☎ 021/6335–1888), the first China outpost of this ultra-luxurious spa chain, occupies the third floor of the Westin Shanghai. The spa's 13 chambers as well as its treatments are designed to reflect wu sing, the five elemental energies of Chinese philosophy: earth, gold, water, wood, and fire. Relax and enjoy one of 10 massages (Y450–Y720), facials, body scrubs, or indulgent packages that combine all three.

With instructions clearly spelled out in English, **Double Rainbow Massage House** (✉ 47 Yongjia Lu, Luwan District ☎ 021/6473–4000) provides a cheap (Y35–Y50), non-threatening introduction to traditional Chinese massage. Choose a masseur, state your preference for soft, medium, or hard massage, then keep your clothes on for a 45- to 60-minute massage. There's no ambiance, just a clean room with nine massage tables.

Dragonfly (✉ 20 Donghu Lu, Xuhui District ☎ 021/5405–0008) is a therapeutic retreat center that has claimed the middle ground between expensive hotel spas and workmanlike blindman massage parlors. Don the suede-soft treatment robes for traditional Chinese massage (Y120), or take them off for an aromatic oil massage (Y200).

The Three on the Bund complex includes the first **Evian Spa** (✉ 3, The Bund [Zhongshan Dong Yi Lu], Huangpu District ☎ 021/6321–6622) outside of France. Its 14 theme rooms offer treatments from head to toe and nine different massages, including an Indian head massage (Y600) or a hot stone aromatherapy massage (Y900).

With its exposed wood beams, unpolished bricks and soothing fountains, the **Mandara Spa** (✉ 399 Nanjing Xi Lu, Huangpu District ☎ 021/5359–4969) in the JW Marriott resembles a traditional Chinese water town. Face, beauty, and body treatments include the spa's signature Mandara massage (Y960), a 90-minute treatment in which two therapists administer a blend of five massage styles: Shiatsu, Thai, Lomi Lomi, Swedish, and Balinese.

Ming Massage (✉ 298 Wulumuqi Nan Lu, Xuhui District ☎ 021/5465–2501) is a Japanese-style salon that caters to women, who receive a 20-percent discount daily from 11 to 2. Cross over the foot bridge to one of five small treatment rooms for a foot, body, or combination "Ming" massage (Y178).

you from the formal lobby up to the second floor and the exceptional Bauernstube deli. Giovanni's serves Italian food as impressive as its views from the atop the 27th floor. ⊠ *5 Zunyi Nan Lu, Changning District 200336* 🕾 *021/6275–8888 or 888/625–5144* 🖷 *021/6275–5420* ⊕ *www.sheratongrand-shanghai.com* ⟋ *474 rooms, 22 suites* ♧ *5 restaurants, café, coffee shop, in-room data ports, in-room safes, mini-bars, cable TV, golf privileges, pool, gym, hair salon, massage, sauna, steam room, 2 bars, lobby lounge, piano, shops, baby-sitting, dry clean-ing, laundry service, concierge, concierge floor, Internet, business ser-vices, convention center, travel services, parking (fee), no-smoking floors* 🖃 *AE, DC, MC, V.*

$$–$$$ 🏨 **Cypress Hotel.** Once part of tycoon Victor Sassoon's estate, the Cy-press Hotel's shaded, stream-laced grounds remain a tranquil retreat in noisy Shanghai. From the hotel's 149 rooms, you can look out over the garden and actually hear birdsong rather than car horns. The comfort-able, moderate-size rooms have, appropriately, a garden-green color scheme. Expansion plans will likely close the extensive health club in 2005, but you'll still be able to drop a line in the fishing pond and take a stroll over the bridges and through the woods. ⊠ *2419 Hongqiao Lu, Changning District 200335* 🕾 *021/6268–8868* 🖷 *021/6268–1878* ⟋ *141 rooms, 8 suites* ♧ *2 restaurants, room service, in-room data ports, in-room safes, minibars, cable TV, driving range, putting green, three tennis courts, indoor pool, gym, hair salon, massage, sauna, steam room, fishing, basketball, billiards, bowling, Ping-Pong, squash, bar, shop, baby-sitting, dry cleaning, laundry service, Internet, business services, meeting rooms, airport shuttle, travel services, parking (fee), no-smok-ing rooms* 🖃 *AE, DC, MC, V.*

Pudong New Area

$$$$ 🏨 **Grand Hyatt.** Occupying floors 53 through 87 of the spectacular Jin-
Fodor'sChoice mao Tower, the Grand Hyatt is the world's highest hotel. A combina-
★ tion of traditional and postmodern design, the Hyatt's interior is defined by art deco lines juxtaposed with space-age grillwork and sleek furnishings and textures. The 33-story central atrium is a marvel in itself—a seem-ingly endless cylinder with an outer-space aura. Room amenities are space age as well: CAT 5 optical lines for laptop use, Internet connections on the TV through a cordless keyboard, and three high-pressure water heads in the shower. Views from the rooms are spectacular; corner rooms have two walls of pure glass for endless panoramas of the Oriental Pearl Tower, majesty of the Bund, and expanse of the city below. ⊠ *Jinmao Dasha, 88 Shiji Dadao, Pudong 200121* 🕾 *021/5049–1234 or 800/233–1234* 🖷 *021/5049–1111* ⊕ *www.shanghai.grand.hyatt.com* ⟋ *510 rooms, 45 suites* ♧ *5 restaurants, café, coffee shop, food court, room service, in-room data ports, in-room safes, minibars, cable TV, indoor pool, health club, hair salon, spa, sauna, steam room, 3 bars, nightclub, piano bar, lobby lounge, shops, dry cleaning, laundry service, concierge, concierge floor, Internet, business services, convention center, parking (fee), some free parking* 🖃 *AE, DC, MC, V.*

★ **$$$$** 🏨 **Pudong Shangri-La.** The Shangri-La occupies one of the most prized locations in Shanghai: overlooking the Huangpu River, opposite the

Bund, near the Pearl Tower in Lujiazui. The hotel's breathtaking water's-edge views, white-glove service, and spacious rooms attract a mix of business and leisure travelers. Standard rooms alone are almost 400 square feet, with large closets and marble bathrooms. A 36-story addition scheduled for opening in spring 2005 will boost the number of rooms to nearly 1,000 and provide a more regal setting for the chain's signature Shang Palace Chinese restaurant. ⊠ *33 Fucheng Lu, Pudong 200120* ☎ *021/6882–8888 or 800/942–5050* 🖷 *021/6882–6688* ⊕ *www.shangri-la.com* ⟳ *575 rooms, 31 suites* ♨ *4 restaurants, patisserie, in-room data ports, in-room safes, minibars, cable TV, tennis court, indoor pool, gym, hair salon, hot tub, massage, sauna, steam room, lobby lounge, nightclub, shops, baby-sitting, dry cleaning, laundry service, concierge, concierge floor, Internet, business services, convention center, travel services, parking (fee), no-smoking floors* ⊟ *AE, DC, MC, V.*

★ **$$$$** 🏨 **St. Regis.** The amphitheater-like lobby of the St. Regis sets the stage for the most indulgent hotel experience in Shanghai. The 318 rooms in this 40-story red granite tower—its design lauded by *Architectural Digest*—spare no expense, with Bose wave radios, Herman Miller Aeron chairs, and rainforest showers that give you the feeling of being under a waterfall. At 500 square feet, standard rooms compare to other hotels' suites and set the bar in Shanghai. Its two women's-only floors are unique in Shanghai. Butlers address all your needs, from in-room check-in to room service. The location—15 minutes from the riverfront—is a drawback, but the fitness center and remarkable Danieli's Italian restaurant add to this pampering property's appeal. ⊠ *889 Dongfang Lu, Pudong 200122* ☎ *021/5050–4567 or 800/325–3589* 🖷 *021/6875–6789* ⊕ *www.starwood.com/stregis/index.html* ⟳ *270 rooms, 48 suites* ♨ *3 restaurants, room service, in-room data ports, some in-room fax, in-room safes, minibars, cable TV, tennis court, indoor pool, health club, hair salon, hot tub, sauna, spa, steam room, 2 bars, lounge, shops, baby-sitting, dry cleaning, laundry service, concierge, Internet, business services, convention center, travel services, parking (fee), no-smoking floors* ⊟ *AE, DC, MC, V.*

$$$–$$$$ 🏨 **Hotel InterContinental Pudong.** The *pièce de résistance* of the 24-story Intercontinental is a nearly 200-foot-high Italian Renaissance–inspired atrium that brings in natural light to the 19 guest floors, six of which are executive floors. A vivid coat of red livens up the hallways and spacious guest rooms, which all have separate tub and shower. The restaurants cater to a wide range of tastes: Japanese, Cantonese, Shanghainese, Chaozhou, Continental. The open kitchen of Level One restaurant turns out a great lunch buffet with samples of all those cuisines. ⊠ *777 Zhangyang Lu, Pudong 200120* ☎ *021/5831–8888 or 800/327–0200* 🖷 *021/5831–7777* ⊕ *www.shanghai.intercontinental. com* ⟳ *317 rooms, 78 suites* ♨ *4 restaurants, coffee shop, patisserie, room service, in-room data ports, in-room safes, minibars, cable TV, indoor pool, gym, hair salon, sauna, billiards, bar, piano, shops, baby-sitting, dry cleaning, laundry service, concierge, concierge floor, Internet, business services, convention center, parking (fee), no-smoking floors* ⊟ *AE, DC, MC, V.*

$$-$$$$ ▦ **Courtyard by Marriott Pudong.** With its moderate prices and a networking-friendly ornate lobby more in keeping with Marriott-branded hotels, the Courtyard is popular among business travelers to Pudong. The two-story lobby's intricate wood screen separates the lobby lounge from Spices Café, which serves good Thai and Western fare. Rooms, decorated in tropical floral fabrics, are compact, with little wiggle room beyond the work desk and beds. There are two executive floors, and some standard rooms have a separate tub and shower, an amenity usually reserved for higher-price lodgings. The metro line 2 into Puxi is just two blocks away. ⊠ *838 Dongfang Lu, Pudong 200122* ☎ *021/ 6886–7886 or 888/236–2427* 🖷 *021/6886–7889* ⊕ *www.marriott. com* ✇ *176 rooms, 42 suites* ⚓ *2 restaurants, room service, in-room data ports, some in-room safes, some minibars, cable TV, gym, lobby lounge, hair salon, shops, baby-sitting, dry cleaning, laundry service, Internet, business services, convention center, travel services, free parking, no-smoking rooms* ⊟ *AE, DC, MC, V.*

$$$ ▦ **Holiday Inn Pudong.** In the commercial district of Pudong, this Holiday Inn is well-situated for travelers with business in the area and just a four-block walk to metro line 2 into Puxi. Rooms are simply decorated—beige walls, bird's-eye maple furniture—but provide plenty of room to spread out your suitcases. The gym and indoor pool are quite large. For entertainment, there's a KTV (karaoke) club, a lobby piano bar and an Irish pub with Guinness and Kilkenny on tap. ⊠ *899 Dongfang Lu, Pudong 200122* ☎ *021/5830–6666 or 800/465–4329* 🖷 *021/ 5830–5555* ⊕ *www.ichotelsgroup.com* ✇ *285 rooms, 30 suites* ⚓ *3 restaurants, coffee shop, patisserie, in-room safes, minibars, cable TV, indoor pool, gym, hair salon, massage, sauna, steam room, billiards, 2 bars, piano bar, pub, baby-sitting, dry cleaning, laundry service, concierge, concierge floor, Internet, business services, convention center, travel services, parking (fee), no-smoking floors* ⊟ *AE, DC, MC, V.*

¢ ▦ **Changhang Merrylin Hotel.** The Merrylin Corporation is better known throughout China for its restaurants than its hotels. Indeed, Changhang Merrylin Hotel's exceptional Chinese restaurant overshadows its fair-size inexpensive rooms. Decor aspires to European grandeur but comes off as amusingly tacky. Reliefs and golden statues of frolicking nymphs dominate the lobby, while rooms are decked out in gold-flecked wallpaper and crackled white-painted fixtures. Service can be brusque, but the location is convenient, within three blocks of the 10-story Next Age Department Store and metro line 2 to Puxi. ⊠ *818 Zhangyang Lu, Pudong 200122* ☎ *021/5835–5555* 🖷 *021/5835–7799* ✇ *192 rooms, 32 suites* ⚓ *3 restaurants, room service, minibars, cable TV, lobby lounge, hair salon, shops, dry cleaning, laundry service, concierge, Internet, business services, meeting rooms, airport shuttle, parking (fee)* ⊟ *AE, DC, MC, V.*

NIGHTLIFE & THE ARTS

For up-to-date information about what's going on in the city, check out *That's Shanghai* and *City Weekend,* monthly and biweekly expatriate magazines available at Western bars, restaurants, and hotels throughout town; or *Shanghai Daily,* the English-language newspaper.

The Arts

Acrobatics

Shanghai Acrobatics Troupe. Considered China's best, the Shanghai Acrobatics Troupe performs remarkable gravity-defying stunts. The troupe holds court at both the Shanghai Center Theater and Shanghai Circus World, a glittering gold and green dome that seats more than 1,600 people. (☒ Shanghai Center Theater, 1376 Nanjing Xi Lu, Jingan District ☎ 021/6279–8945 ⊘ Daily 7:30 PM ☑ Y50–Y100 ☒ Shanghai Circus World, 2266 Gong He Xin Lu, Zhabei District ☎ 021/6652–7750 ☑ Y50–Y150).

Chinese Opera

Kunju Opera Troupe. Kun opera, or Kunju, originated in Jiangsu Province more than 400 years ago. Because of the profound influence it exerted on other Chinese opera styles, it's often called the mother of Chinese local opera. This troupe holds matinee performances every Saturday at 1:30 PM. Tickets cost Y20–Y50. ☒ *9 Shaoxing Lu, Luwan District* ☎ *021/6437–1012.*

Yifu Theatre. Not only Peking opera, but also China's other regional operas, such as Huju, Kunju, and Shaoxing, are performed regularly at this theater. Considered the marquee theater for opera in Shanghai, it's just a block off People's Square. Call the box office for schedule and ticket information. ☒ *701 Fuzhou Lu, Huangpu District* ☎ *021/ 6351–4668.*

Dance & Music

Shanghai Center Theater. One of the chief venues in town for quality performances, this stage serves as a home to the **Shanghai Acrobatic Troupe** and has hosted performers such as the Israel Contemporary Dance Group. The building's distinct bowed front was designed to resemble the Marriott Marquis Theater in New York's Times Square. ☒ *Shanghai Center, 1376 Nanjing Xi Lu, Jingan District* ☎ *021/6279–8663.*

Shanghai Concert Hall. City officials spent $6 million in 2003 to move this 73-year-old hall two blocks and turn the stage 180 degrees. It's the home of the Shanghai Symphony Orchestra and also hosts top-level classical musicians from around the world. ☒ *523 Yanan Dong Lu, Luwan District* ☎ *021/6386–9153.*

Shanghai Grand Stage. Built in 1975, this 12,000-seat arena usually hosts rock concerts. In 2004 the venue got a multi-million dollar facelift thanks to the return of favorite son Yao Ming in an NBA exhibition match. ☒ *1111 Caoxi Bei Lu, inside Shanghai Stadium, Xuhui District* ☎ *021/ 6473–0940.*

Shanghai Grand Theatre. The premier venue in town, this spectacular stage hosts top-billed domestic and international music and dance performances. In 2003 the theater hosted *Riverdance* and the Vienna Boys' Choir. ☒ *300 Renmin Dadao, Huangpu District* ☎ *021/6372–8701, 021/6372–8702, or 021/6372–3833.*

Shanghai Oriental Art Center. Designed to resemble a white magnolia in full bloom, the glass-shrouded Shanghai Oriental Art Center represents the blossoming of Pudong's art scene. This $94 million center is intended to rival the Shanghai Grand Theater and includes a 2,000-seat symphony hall, 1,100-seat theater, and 300-seat auditorium. ⊠ *Shiji Da Dao at Jinxiu Lu, Pudong.*

Theater

Shanghai Dramatic Arts Center. In the budding theater district along Anfu Lu, this venue presents performances of Chinese plays, as well as foreign plays in Chinese translation, such as the Royal Shakespeare Theatre Company's production of the *Merchant of Venice* in 2002. ⊠ *288 Anfu Lu, Xuhui District* ☎ *021/6473–4567.*

Shanghai Grand Theater. As the premier stage in town, the Shanghai Grand Theater hosts top national and international performances. When Broadway shows come to Shanghai—as *Cats* did in 2003 and *Sound of Music* did in 2004—they play here. ⊠ *300 Renmin Dadao, Huangpu District* ☎ *021/6372–8701, 021/6372–8702, or 021/6372–3833.*

Nightlife

Other cities in China may close down after dinner, but Shanghai never sleeps. In the wee hours of the morning, clubbers are still bar-hopping by cab between Hengshan Lu and Fuxing Park and all the hip spots in between. In the past, most partiers stopped at some point at the infamous Maoming Lu bar strip, whose seedy reputation was well deserved. But in summer 2004, city officials called off the party by imposing noise restrictions that forced many of the Maoming bars out of business or to move elsewhere. While the strip survives as a toned-down version of its former self, the spotlight is now on the new Tongren Lu bar area, near the Shanghai Center.

Despite the recent upheaval, you'll find that Shanghai's nightlife scene still adheres to certain formulas. If there's live music, it's probably a Filipino cover band. Hotel bars will likely have jazz and cigars, with optional skyline views. Gay bars will be merely hinted at, never boldly promoted. And drink prices will strike you as expensive, especially if you've been coerced into buying one for one of Shanghai's countless "drinking girls." So grab your wallet, and *ganbei!* (bottoms up!).

Bars

★ **Amber.** If you prefer a mellow evening, Amber shines as a refined, low-key lounge. A comfy white banquette rims the downstairs room, while upstairs the glow-in-the-dark tables add splashes of color to the minimalist setting. The bar's known for its creative drink specials, such as deducting your taxi fare from the cost of your first drink. ⊠ *184 Maoming Nan Lu, Luwan District* ☎ *021/6466–5224.*

Arch Bar and Café. For the artsy and intellectual crowd, head to Arch. Its location in Shanghai's only Flatiron building attracts architects and design professionals as well as people with an appreciation for this one-of-a-kind venue. ⊠ *439 Wukang Lu, Xuhui District* ☎ *021/6466–0807.*

Archie's. An inviting neighborhood bar reminiscent of *Cheers*, Archie's is a welcome escape from the madness of Xiangyang Market a block away. Drinks are cheap, and the novel glass-topped bar has an aquarium underneath. ✉ *Unit 1130, 1111 Huaihai Zonglu, Xuhui District* ☎ *021/6472–4779.*

ARK Live House. A hopping concert venue, ARK Live House has revived the rock scene in Shanghai by importing bands from Beijing, Japan, and occasionally the U.S. ✉ *House 15, North Block Xintiandi, 181 Taicang Lu, Luwan District* ☎ *021/6326–8008.*

The Blarney Stone. The friendly Irish bartenders and lively chatter make the Blarney Stone one of the best places for drinking alone in Shanghai. ✉ *5A Dongping Lu, Xuhui District* ☎ *021/6415–7496.*

Blue Frog. A Maoming Lu survivor, the Blue Frog has *branched out with new pads in the Tongren Lu bar area and the Green Sports & Leisure Center in Pudong.* Popular among Westerners, this chummy chill-out pad serves up more than 100 shots, well-mixed cocktails, and decent Western pub food. ✉ *207-6 Maoming Nanlu, Luwan District,* ☎ *021/ 6445–6334* ✉ *86 Tongren Lu, Jingan District,* ☎ *021/6247–0320* ✉ *633 Biyun Lu, Pudong,* ☎ *021/5030–6426.*

Fodor'sChoice ★ **Cotton Club.** A dark and smoky jazz and blues club, the Cotton Club is an institution in Shanghai and considered *the* place for live music. The house band is a mix of Chinese and foreign musicians with a sound akin to Blues Traveler. ✉ *8 Fuxing Xi Lu, Xuhui District* ☎ *021/6437–7110.*

Fodor'sChoice ★ **The Door.** The stunningly extravagant interior of the Door inspires admiration and distracts from the bar's overpriced drinks. Take in the soaring wood-beam ceilings, sliding doors, and museum's worth of antiques as you listen to the eclectic house band, which plays modern, funky riffs on Chinese music on the *erhu, pipa,* and other traditional instruments. ✉ *4F, 1468 Hongqiao Lu, Changning District* ☎ *021/6295–3737.*

Dublin Exchange. If you find yourself in Pudong, the Dublin Exchange is a great place for a pint. Its upmarket Irish banker's club ambience caters to the growing Wall Street that is Lujiazui. ✉ *2F, HSBC Bldg., 101 Yincheng Dong Lu, Pudong* ☎ *021/6841–2052.*

★ **Face.** The see-and-be-seen circuit in Shanghai starts at Face. Candlelighted tables outside and a four-poster bed inside are the most vied-for spots in this colonial villa with Indonesian furnishings. ✉ *Bldg. 4, Ruijin Hotel, 118 Ruijin Erlu, Luwan District* ☎ *021/6466–4328.*

Glamour Bar. For a beautiful view as well as beautiful people, go to the Glamour Bar. As the lounge for the city's top restaurant, **M on the Bund,** it enjoys the same prestige and panorama of the Bund and Pudong skyline. ✉ *7F, 20 Guangdong Lu, Huangpu District* ☎ *021/6350–9988.*

Guandii. Opened by several Hong Kong celebrities, Guandii's minimalist low-slung bar attracts hopeful star-watchers as well as flush Chinese who flash their wealth by ordering bottles of one of the 30 champagnes on the drink menu. ✉ *Fuxing Park, 2 Gaolan Lu, Luwan District* ☎ *021/5383–6020.*

House of Blues and Jazz. Black-and-white photos of blues legends look out on the performances at this unpretentious living room of a lounge. The owner—a prominent Chinese jazz musician—hosts local and international artists as well as a weekly jam session. ☒ *158 Maoming Nan Lu, Luwan District* ☎ *021/6437–5280.*

Long Bar. In the Shanghai Center, the narrow, horseshoe-shape Long Bar has a loyal expat-businessman clientele. Rousing rounds of liar's dice, a bigscreen TV, and chest-thumping conversations among executives provide the entertainment. ☒ *1376 Nanjing Xi Lu, Jingan District* ☎ *021/6279–8268.*

Malone's American Café. A magnet for Western expats and travelers, Malone's is always packed. The fun Filipino cover band, Art-7, belts out pitch-perfect versions of Van Morisson and No Doubt. TVs broadcast sporting events, and pool tables draw people upstairs to the second floor. The Shanghai Comedy Club brings in comedians one weekend each month to the makeshift third-floor stage. ☒ *255 Tongren Lu, Jingan District* ☎ *021/6247–2400.*

★ **O'Malley's.** The most beloved of Shanghai's Irish pubs, O'Malley's, has the requisite Guinness on tap and live Irish music. Its outdoor beer garden packs in the crowds in the summer and during broadcasts of European soccer and rugby matches. ☒ *42 Taojiang Lu, Xuhui District* ☎ *021/6474–4533.*

Vogue in Kevin's. At the heart of Shanghai's alternative scene, Vogue in Kevin's is a popular party and pick-up spot. The circular bar is a good perch for people watching and scoping out prospective partners. ☒ *House 4, 946 Changle Lu, Jingan District* ☎ *021/6248–8985.*

Dance Clubs

Babyface. An outpost of the popular Guangzhou nightclub, the club draws a well-dressed crowd of wannabes who don't mind waiting outside along the velvet rope before dancing to progressive house and hard trance. ☒ *180 Maoming Lu, Luwan District* ☎ *021/6445–2330.*

California Club. Celebrity guest DJs play everything from tribal to disco for the bold and beautiful crowd at this hip establishment. The club is part of the Lan Kwai Fong complex at Park 97, which also includes Baci and Tokio Joe's restaurants and ShanghART gallery. ☒ *Park 97, 2A Gaolan Lu, Luwan District* ☎ *021/5383–2328.*

Judy's Too. A veteran on the club scene, Judy's Too is infamous for its hard-partying, meat-market crowd, as portrayed in Wei Hui's racy novel *Shanghai Baby.* ☒ *176 Maoming Nanlu, Luwan District,* ☎ *021/ 6473–1417* ☒ *78-80 Tongren Lu, Jingan District,* ☎ *021/6258–0134.*

Rojam. A three-level techno behemoth, Rojam is like a never-ending rave that bulges with boogiers and underground lounge lizards from the under-30 set. ☒ *4/F, Hong Kong Plaza, 283 Huaihai Zhonglu, Luwan District* ☎ *021/6390–7181.*

Windows Too. Shanghai's budget drinking den, Windows Too packs in patrons with Y10 drinks. A hip-hop heavy rotation keeps the tiny dance floor hopping. ✉ *J104, Jingan Si Plaza, 1669 Nanjing Xi Lu, Jingan District* ☎ *021/3214–0351.*

YY's. The small, mellow YY's is a popular spot on the alternative scene; the absence of drinking girls is a clue to the core clientele. Named for the ancient Chinese *yin-yang* symbol, the club balances a quiet lounge with a techno dance floor that's popular with members of both sexes. ✉ *125 Nanchang Lu, Luwan District* ☎ *021/6466–4098.*

Hotel Bars

B.A.T.S. (Bar At The Shangri-La). Tucked away in the basement of the Shangri-La, B.A.T.S. is perhaps the best dance club in Pudong. However, the crowd ebbs and flows depending on the quality of the band. The cave-like brick-walled space has diner-style booths arranged around a large central bar. ✉ *Pudong Shangri-La, 33 Fucheng Lu, Pudong* ☎ *021/6882–8888.*

★ **Cloud 9.** Perched on the 87th floor of the Grand Hyatt, Cloud 9 is the highest bar in the world. It has unparalleled views of Shanghai from among—and often above—the clouds. The sky-high views come with sky-high prices; there's a spending minimum of Y95 per person. If you're lucky, maybe the Chinese fortune teller who makes nightly rounds of the candlelit tables will tell you that wealth is in your future. ✉ *Grand Hyatt, 88 Shiji Dadao, Pudong* ☎ *021/5049–1234.*

Jazz Bar. Within the historic and romantic Peace Hotel, this German-style pub has earned its fame due to the nightly performances (tickets, Y80) of the Peace Hotel Old Jazz Band. The musicians, whose average age is above 70, played jazz in dance halls in pre-1949 Shanghai. However, they're not quite as swingin' as in their prime, and a sense of tradition, rather than the quality of the music, has sustained these performances. ✉ *Peace Hotel, 20 Nanjing Dong Lu, Huangpu District* ☎ *021/6321–6888.*

★ **Jazz 37.** The Four Seasons' jazz bar matches its penthouse view with a stylish interior. Grab a canary-yellow leather chair by the white grand piano for some top-quality live jazz. ✉ *The Four Seasons, 500 Weihai Lu, Jingan District* ☎ *021/6256–8888.*

Patio Bar. No skyline views here, just a dazzling, dizzying view of the Grand Hyatt's soaring 33-story atrium. It's an expensive, but impressive, stop for a pre- or post-dinner drink. ✉ *Grand Hyatt, 88 Shiji Dadao, Pudong* ☎ *021/5049–1234.*

Ritz-Carlton Bar. Like an airline's first-class lounge, the Ritz-Carlton Bar is the domain of a high-flying executive clientele. Cigar smoke, specialty scotches, and jazz cap the elite atmosphere. ✉ *The Portman Ritz-Carlton, 1376 Nanjing Xi Lu, Jingan District* ☎ *021/6279–8888.*

Ye Lai Xiang. Few people know the real name of the Garden Hotel's terrace bar. Considered one of the most romantic spots in town for a drink when the weather is nice, this third-floor terrace overlooks the fountain and hotel's namesake two-acre garden. ⊠ *Okura Garden Hotel, 58 Maoming Nan Lu, Luwan District* ☎ *021/6415–1111.*

Karaoke

Karaoke is ubiquitous in Shanghai; most nights, the private rooms at KTV (Karaoke TV) establishments are packed with Shanghainese crooning away with their friends. Many KTV bars employ "KTV girls" who sing along with (male) guests and serve cognac and expensive snacks. (At some establishments, KTV girls are also prostitutes.) That said, karaoke is largely a legitimate, and fun, pastime in town.

Cash Box (Party World). This giant establishment is one of Shanghai's most popular KTV bars. Its warren of rooms is packed nightly. ⊠ *457 Wulumuqi Lu, Xuhui District* ☎ *021/6374–1111* ⊠ *208 Chongqing Nan Lu, inside Fuxing Park, Luwan District* ☎ *021/5306–3888.*

Maya. Shanghai's well-heeled hipsters favor the deluxe KTV rooms at Maya over its dance floor. Its super-stiff cocktails will turn even the meekest performer into a microphone hog. ⊠ *4-5F, Yunhai Bldg., 1333 Huaihai Zhonglu, Xuhui District* ☎ *021/6415–2281.*

SPORTS & THE OUTDOORS

Auto-Racing

Shanghai International Circuit. Shanghai made its debut on the Formula 1 circuit in 2004 with the opening of this circuit. ⊠ *Anting District* ☎ *021/6330–5555.*

Go-Carting

DISC Kart. This is definitely not your father's go-cart. A lap on a 160cc cart around the tight indoor track can, at times, seem more like a demolition derby. ⊠ *326 Aomen Lu, Jingan District* ☎ *021/6277–5641.*

Shanghai Hauge Racing Car Club. Races are a bit more civilized at this club. You are required to wear a helmet while racing its 50cc to 200cc carts around its large outdoor track. ⊠ *880 Zhongshan Bei Yi Lu, Hongkou District* ☎ *021/6531–6800.*

Golf

With its own international tournament—the Volvo China Open—and several courses designed by prestige names, Shanghai is making its mark on the golf scene. Approximately 20 clubs dot the countryside within a two-hour arc of downtown. All clubs and driving ranges run on a membership basis, but most allow nonmembers to play when accompanied by a member. A few even welcome the public. Most clubs are outside the city, in the suburbs and outlying counties of Shanghai.

Grand Shanghai International Golf and Country Club. This club has a Ronald Fream–designed 18-hole championship course and driving range. ⊠ *18 Yangcheng Zhonglu, Yangcheng Lake Holiday Zone, Kunshan City, Jiangsu Province* ☎ *0512/5789–1999.*

Shanghai Binhai Golf Club. Peter Thomson designed the Scottish links-style, 27-hole course at this club in Pudong. Another 27 holes are on the books. ✉ *Binhai Resort, Baiyulan Dadao, Nanhui County, Pudong* ☎ *021/5805–8888.*

Shanghai International Golf and Country Club. This 18-hole course designed by Robert Trent Jones Jr. is the most difficult course to get into in Shanghai. There are water hazards at almost every hole. ✉ *961 Yin Zhu Lu, Zhu Jia Jiao, Qingpu District* ☎ *021/5972–8111.*

Shanghai Silport Golf Club. This club hosts the Volvo China Open. Its 27-hole course on Dianshan Lake was designed by Bobby J. Martin; a new nine holes designed by Roger Packard opened in 2004. ✉ *1 Xubao Lu Dianshan Lake Town, Kunshan City, Jiangsu Province* ☎ *0512/5748–1111.*

Shanghai Sun Island International Club. You'll find a 27-hole course designed by Nelson & Haworth plus an excellent driving range at this club. ✉ *2588 Shantai Lu, Zhu Jia Jiao, Qingpu District* ☎ *021/5983–0888 Ext. 8033.*

Tianma Country Club. Tianma is the most accessible course to the public. Its 18 holes have lovely views of Sheshan Mountain. ✉ *3958 Zhaokun Lu, Tianma Town, Songjiang District* ☎ *021/5766–1666.*

Tomson Shanghai Pudong Golf Club. The closest course to the city center, Tomson has 18 holes and a driving range designed by Shunsuke Kato. Robert Trent Jones II has inked a deal to develop the club's second course. ✉ *1 Longdong Dadao, Pudong* ☎ *021/5833–8888.*

Health Clubs, Swimming Pools & Tennis

Most of the best health clubs and pools are at the Western-style hotels. Fees are charged for those who are not hotel guests. A few facilities outside of hotels offer day passes for Y100 to Y200.

Fitness First. This independent club is popular among the younger expats and locals. Cardio training is its strength. ✉ *Plaza 66, 1266 Nanjing Xi Lu, Jingan District* ☎ *021/6288–0152.*

Kerry Center. Fitness fanatics in town favor the gym at the Kerry Center. There are extensive classes and personal training options, well-equipped weight rooms, a swimming pool, and even a rotating rock-climbing wall. ✉ *1515 Nanjing Xi Lu, Jingan District* ☎ *021/6279–4625.*

Radisson Plaza Xing Guo. The Clark Hatch gym at the Radisson is run by an American manager and has top-name equipment, an aerobics studio, a pool, even a bowling alley. Nonmembers and nonguests pay a Y200 day rate. ✉ *78 Xingguo Lu, Changning District* ☎ *021/6212–9998.*

Shanghai Hilton. The Spa here has an elevated swimming pool; weight room; tennis, racquetball, and squash courts; and a full schedule of aerobics, yoga, and other classes. The day rate for nonguests and nonmembers is a prohibitive Y480. ✉ *250 Huashan Lu, Jingan District* ☎ *021/6248–0000.*

Skiing

Shanghai Yin Qi Xing Indoor Skiing Site. This innovative indoor venue brings winter fun to Shanghai's tropical climes. The world's second largest indoor ski run, the gentle 4,100-foot slope is good for beginners, who can take snowboarding or skiing lessons in Chinese or Japanese. ✉ *1835 Qixing Lu, Minhang District* ☎ *021/6478–8666.*

Soccer

Shanghai Stadium. The overwhelmingly grandiose, UFO-like Shanghai Stadium seats 80,000 spectators and holds athletic events, especially soccer matches, regularly. ✉ *666–800 Tianyaoqiao Lu, Xuhui District* ☎ *021/6426–6888 Ext. 8268.*

SHOPPING

You can accomplish most of your souvenir shopping in Shanghai at two stops. The shops around Yu Garden are convenient for traditional Chinese gifts: chopsticks, name chops (seals with your name engraved in Chinese and English), painted bottles, silk, pearls, and teapots. Xiangyang Market is knockoff central, with watches, bags, shoes, and clothes galore. The clothing sold here is made for export, so you're more likely to find items that fit. Most department stores don't carry Western-sized clothing, and those that do will likely hand you an XXXL to try on, so prepare your ego for the bruising.

While prices are fixed at government-owned stores and most malls, never accept the first price (or even the first counteroffer) at markets and small stores. Bargaining is a full-contact sport in Shanghai, with as many bluffs, blitzes, and strategies as an NFL playbook. Decide what your desired final price is, then start negotiations at 15% to 25% of the asking price. If the vendor's not budging, walk away; he'll likely call you back.

Major Shopping Districts

Huaihai Zhonglu

Huaihai Zhonglu in Puxi is shopping for the middle-class masses. Retail stores for such Asian brands as Baleno dominate the seemingly endless strip mall.

Nanjing Dong Lu

Shanghai No. 1 Department Store anchors the row of Chinese department stores along the Nanjing Dong Lu pedestrian walkway, which stretches from just east of People's Square to a few blocks west of the Bund.

Nanjing Xi Lu

Nanjing Xi Lu, around the Shanghai Center in Puxi's city center, is Shanghai's equivalent of New York's Fifth Avenue. Plaza 66, CITIC Square, and Westgate Mall are home to the big-name brands—Prada, Burberry, and Versace—copied shamelessly at Xiangyang Market.

Taikang Lu

Taikang Lu in Puxi has become Shanghai's Soho. International designers and artists have settled into the lofts and lanes along this short stretch of street.

Xujiahui

The megamall corner at Xujiahui in Puxi looks straight out of Tokyo. The cavernous domed Grand Gateway holds center court, flanked by Metro City, Oriental Shopping Center, and Huijin Department Store.

Other Shopping Districts

Even outside the malls, Shanghai's shopkeepers of a feather tend to flock together. Shanghai's book street, **Fuzhou Lu**, is a few blocks south of and parallel to the Nanjing Dong Lu pedestrian walkway in Puxi. For furniture warehouses, wander **Wuzhou Lu**, in western Puxi. For greatly discounted children's clothing and shoes, hit the underground mall at **10 Puan Lu**, a few blocks north of Xintiandi in Puxi. You'll find *qipao* (traditional Chinese dress) shops aplenty on **Changle Lu** between Maoming Nan Lu and Shaanxi Nan Lu, two streets that also are home to dozens of tiny boutiques in the blocks just north and south of Huaihai Lu.

Department Stores & Malls

Grand Gateway. Look for the dome; beneath you'll find more than 1.4 million square feet of shopping and entertainment, including a theater, restaurants, and floor after floor of clothing stores. ⊠ *1 Hongqiao Lu, Xuhui District* ☎ *021/6407–0115.*

Plaza 66. Home of the elite brands that are copied so shamelessly at Xianyang Market, Plaza 66 is where you can buy real Prada, Piaget, and Versace. Most of the mall's customers are strictly window shoppers. ⊠ *1266 Nanjing Xi Lu, Jing'an District* ☎ *021/5306–8888.*

Shanghai Hongqiao Friendship Shopping Centre. Huge Dior and Lacoste signs on the mall's marquee provide a clue that Western brands are the focus of this state-owned shopping center, which also has a large import grocery store. ⊠ *6 Zunyi Lu, Changning District* ☎ *021/6270–0000.*

Shanghai No. 1 Department Store. Shanghai's largest state-owned store attracts masses of Chinese shoppers, especially on weekends. It sells everything from porcelain dinnerware to badminton racquets. ⊠ *830 Nanjing Dong Lu, Huangpu District* ☎ *021/6322–3344.*

Super Brand Mall. The 10-story Super Brand Mall has promise in the underdeveloped Pudong shopping scene. You'll find a movie theater, a huge Lotus Supermarket in the basement, a substantial food court, and outlets for several of Shanghai's popular restaurants, such as **South Beauty**. ⊠ *168 Lujiazui Lu, Pudong* ☎ *021/6887–7888.*

Westgate Mall. Quality Chinese restaurants and a movie theater help make Westgate a well-rounded mall. Its anchor store is **Isetan**, a fashionable Japanese-run department store that carries such brands as Lancôme, Clinique, Benetton, Esprit, and Episode. ⊠ *1038 Nanjing Xi Lu, Jing'an District* ☎ *021/6322–3344.*

Markets

Bargaining is an inescapable part of the sales ritual in markets. Remember that vendors inflate their first offers, expecting to negotiate. Don't be afraid to counter-offer a price less than half the amount of the first offer. And shop around, many vendors stock identical items.

Antiques Market of Shanghai Old Town God Temple (Huabao Building). Tucked in the basement of this cornerstone building at Yu Garden, this market is a convenient, albeit higher priced, stop for antiques. You'll find 250 booths selling ivory, jade, porcelain, and other collectibles, all at negotiable prices. ⊠ *Yu Garden, 265 Fangbang Zhonglu, Huangpu District* ☎ *021/6355–9999.*

Cang Bao Antiques Building (Cang Bao Lou). During the week, you can browse four floors of booths that sell everything from Mao paraphernalia to real and fake antique porcelain. On Sunday, the action starts far before sunrise when, according to a local saying, only ghosts should be awake, hence the market's nickname: "ghost market." Hawkers from the provinces arrive early to lay out their goods on the sidewalk or inside on the fourth floor. Ivory, jade, and wood carvings are among the many goods sold here, all at negotiable prices. ⊠ *457 Fangbang Zhonglu, Huangpu District.*

★ **Dongjiadu Lu Fabric Market.** You'll find everything you need to make a garment: buttons, Chinese knots, even the tailors themselves. (Try Shirly at stall 220.) More than 250 vendors sell fabrics from cashmere to leather to silk of all kinds. There's Thai silk at stall 154, double-sided cashmere in winter and linen in summer at stall 164. All prices are negotiable. Try to shop here in the morning, before the temperatures and crowds become unbearable. ⊠ *118 Dongjiadu Lu, by Zhongshan Nan Lu, Huangpu District* ☉ *Daily 9–5.*

Fodor's Choice **Dongtai Lu Antiques Market.** Outside antiques stalls line six blocks and ★ sell everything from Buddha statues to Mao posters to Victrolas. While the chances of finding a real antique among the reproductions are slim, it's fun scavenging among the shelves to see what you can unearth. You'll see the same "jade" bowls and porcelain vases in multiple stalls, so if your first bargaining attempt isn't successful, you'll have another opportunity a few stores down. Prices have shot up over the years and fakes abound, so bargain hard and with the knowledge you're likely getting a curio rather than a true collectible. ⊠ *Off Xizang Lu, Huangpu District.*

Pearl's Circles. One of Shanghai's two large pearl markets is across the street from Yu Garden in the First Asia Jewelry Plaza. ⊠ *First Asia Jewelry Plaza, 3rd floor, 288 Fuyou Lu, Huangpu District.*

Pearl City. Several dozen vendors sell and repair pearl jewelry at this market in the heart of the Nanjing Road pedestrian walkway. ⊠ *2nd and 3rd floors, 558 Nanjing Dong Lu, Huangpu District.*

Qi Pu Clothing Wholesale Market. The vendors from Xiangyang Market come here in the mornings to stock up their stalls. You're better off coming after lunch to browse your way through these huge buildings. Jeans, bags, shirts, and shoes are of lower quality but bargain priced, even before you start dickering. ⊠ *168 and 183 Qipu Lu, by Henan Bei Lu, Zhabei District* ☎ *021/5102–0001.*

★ **Xiangyang Market.** Shanghai's headquarters for knockoff items, Xiangyang Market sells it all. In addition to souvenir T-shirts and silk duds, you'll find designer-label purses, jackets, watches, and clothing. Some are real—seconds or swiped from the factory in China—but most are copies, so check all purchases carefully for flaws before agreeing on a price. ⊠ *999 Huaihai Zhonglu, bordered by Huaihai Zhonglu, Fenyang Lu, Shaanxi Nan Lu and Nanchang Lu, Xuhui District.*

Zhonghua Xin Lu Market. Shanghai's biggest flea market attracts private hawkers whose goods lean more toward second-hand than antiques, with a lot of used tools, clothes, and appliances for sale. ⊠ *100 Hengfeng Lu, Zhabei District.*

Specialty Stores

Antiques & Furniture

Antiques markets, shops, and furniture warehouses abound in Shanghai, as increasing numbers of foreigners, lured by news of great deals, flock to the city. Great deals, however, are gradually becoming only good deals. Note that fake antiques are often hidden among real treasures and vice versa. Also be aware of age: the majority of pieces date from the late Qing Dynasty (1644–1911); technically, only items dated after 1795 can be legally exported. When buying antique furniture, it helps to know age, of course, and also what kind of wood was used. Although the most commonly used was elm, woods ranging from camphor to mahogany can be found in Chinese antiques. All shops will renovate any pieces you buy, and most can arrange international shipping.

Henry Antique Warehouse. This company has the unique honor of being a Chinese antique furniture research, teaching, and training institute for Tongji University. Part of the showroom often serves as an exhibition hall for the modern designs created jointly by students and the warehouse's 50 craftsmen. On average, the showroom has 2,000 pieces on display, ranging from altar tables to 1920s art deco bedroom furniture. ⊠ *3F, Building 2, 389 Hongzhong Lu, off Wuzhong Lu, Minhang District* ☎ *021/6401–0831.*

★ **Hu & Hu Antiques.** Co-owner Marybelle Hu worked at Taipei's National Palace Museum as well as Sotheby's in Los Angeles before opening this shop with sister-in-law, Lin, in 1998. Their bright, airy showroom contains not only such furniture as Tibetan chests but also a large selection of accessories, from lanterns to moon-cake molds. Their prices are a bit higher than their competitors, but so is their standard of service. ⊠ *1685 Wuzhong Lu, Minhang District* ☎ *021/6405–1212.*

Madame Mao's Dowry. From Depression-era glass to Cultural Revolution propaganda posters, this boutique's eclectic collection chronicles the past century of Shanghai's turbulent history. ⊠ *70 Fuxing Xi Lu, Xuhui District* ☎ *021/6437–1255.*

Shanghai Antique and Curio Store. For a government-owned shop, this gallery has some unique pieces: wooden altar sculptures, expertly painted fans, cloisonné-inset screens. There's no bargaining, but you're sure not to get a fake, and the receipts are official. ⊠ *200–242 Guangdong Lu, Huangpu District* ☎ *021/6321–5868.*

Asian View. A long-time favorite among expats for Chinese furniture, Alex Zheng has broadened his focus with his new store devoted to furnishings from throughout Asia. Reasonably priced and beautifully made tables, beds, and accessories from Indonesia, India, Malaysia, and Thailand fill the 4,000-square-foot showroom. ⊠ *233 Shaanxi Nan Lu, Luwan District* ☎ *021/6474–1051.*

Arts & Crafts/Galleries

Arts and Crafts Research Institute. Shanghai artisans create pieces of traditional Chinese arts and crafts right before your eyes at this institute. You can purchase everything from paper cuts to snuff bottles, although at prices higher than you'll pay at the stalls around Yu Garden. ⊠ *79 Fenyang Lu, Xuhui District* ☎ *021/6437–0509* 🖘 *Y8.*

Art Scene. A 1930s French Concession villa serves as a beautiful, albeit contrasting, backdrop for this gallery's contemporary Chinese artwork. Like the established and emerging artists it represents, the gallery is making a name for itself internationally, having participated in Art Chicago and the San Francisco International Art Exposition. ⊠ *No. 8, Lane 37, Fuxing Xi Lu, Xuhui District* ☎ *021/6437–0631.*

Eddy Tam's Gallery. Inexpensive picture framing is one of Shanghai's best-kept shopping secrets. While its frame selection is somewhat limited, this skilled shop does attractive, inexpensive custom framing work. It also sells original peasant paintings, shadowboxed Chinese mementos, and other artwork. ⊠ *20 Maoming Nan Lu, Luwan District* ☎ *021/ 6253–6715.*

Elegance Art Studio. David Yang's beautiful silk photo albums, CD cases, and notebooks are sold at many of Shanghai's five-star hotels and in American boutiques. You can buy from him directly at his home studio at discounted prices. Call ahead for an appointment. ⊠ *Building 10, Suite 201, 350 Guiping Lu, Minhang District* ☎ *021/6485–8720.*

Friendship Store. This state-owned chain for foreigners started in major Chinese cities as a sign of friendship when China first opened to the outside world. It's touristy but a good quick source of Chinese silk clothes, snuff bottles, carpets, calligraphy, jade, porcelain, and other traditional items that are certified as authentic, and therefore priced accordingly. The current location, opened in late 2003, is half the original's size but includes a mix of domestic and imported food products—including Starbucks, which has a kiosk on the first floor. There's no bargaining, but there are occasional sales. ⊠ *65 Jingling Xi Lu, Huangpu District* ☎ *021/6337–3555.*

Harvest Studio. China's Miao minority is highly regarded for its embroidery. This studio sells Miao embroidered pillows, purses, and clothing as well as the silver jewelry that traditionally adorns the Miao ceremonial costume. ✉ *Room 118, 3, Lane 210, Taikang Lu, Luwan District* ☎ *021/6473–4566.*

Fodor'sChoice **Shanghai Museum Bookshop.** In the museum's comprehensive gift shop,
★ you'll find everything from postcards and pearls to reproductions of the museum's porcelains. Its large book section has coffee table books as well as titles on Chinese art and culture. ✉ *Shanghai Museum, 201 Renmin Dadao, Huangpu District* ☎ *021/6372–3500.*

ShanghART. The city's first modern art gallery, ShanghART is *the* place to check out the work of art-world movers and shakers such as Ding Yi, Xue Song, and Shen Fan. Here you can familiarize yourself with Shanghai's young contemporary avant-garde artists, who are garnering increasing international attention. ✉ *Park 97, 2 Gaolan Lu, Luwan District* ☎ *021/6359–3923 or 139/1747–857* 🖷 *021/6359–3923.*

Simply Life. Dress up your table with Simply Life's tasteful Asian-influenced tableware and silk accessories (many of which are copied and sold cheaper at the local markets). You'll find gold and red lacquerware, hand-painted bone china, Thai silverware, and silk placemats. ✉ *1-2F, Xintiandi South Block, Building 5, 123 Xingye Lu, Luwan District* ☎ *021/6387–5100.*

Carpets
Beijing has always been a better place to buy Chinese rugs, but Shanghai has a few shops that sell silk and wool carpets.

Bokhara Carpets. This small store specializes in hand-made wool carpets from Iran and Turkmenistan. It advertises heavily in expat circles, so prices are on the high side. ✉ *679 Xianxia Lu, Changning District* ☎ *021/6290–1745.*

Tom's Gallery. The carpet gallery at the back of this antiques store sells three varieties of carpets: high-quality silk carpets from Henan Province, wool carpets from Xinjiang, and lower-priced fashion rugs from Qinghai. ✉ *325-1 Huashan Lu, Jingan District* ☎ *021/6209–9058.*

Chinese Medicine
Lei Yun Shang. Founded in Suzhou in 1662, this pharmacy first opened its doors in Shanghai in 1860. Most transactions still take place at the old-fashioned wooden pharmacy counter. There's a 24-hour service counter for emergencies. ✉ *2 Huashan Lu, Jingan District* ☎ *021/6217–3501.*

Shanghai No. 1 Dispensary. Claiming to be China's largest pharmacy, the state-run No. 1 Dispensary has 12 locations in Shanghai. Its flagship store on Nanjing Dong Lu carries Eastern and Western medicines from ginseng to hairy antler, aspirin to acupuncture needles. ✉ *616 Nanjing Dong Lu, Huangpu District* ☎ *021/6322–4567.*

Clothing

Feel. The qipao may be a traditional Chinese dress, but Feel proves with its original designs that it's a style for modern times as well. The staff will alter its styles to fit your frame. ⊠ *No. 2, Lane 210, Taikang Lu, Luwan District* ☎ *021/5465–4519.*

insh (In Shanghai). The whimsical graphics on In Shanghai's T-shirts capture the city's traditional and modern cross currents. One T-shirt has a list of Shanghainese taxi directions; another transforms traditional Chinese gowns into a windmill. These popular shirts make great souvenirs; they're sold at the Xintiandi gift shop as well as the Pudong International Airport. ⊠ *306-310, No. 3, Lane 210, Taikang Lu, Luwan District* ☎ *021/6473–1921.*

Shanghai Tang. This trés chic expensive boutique started in Hong Kong and opened its Shanghai branch in late 2003. Its trademark neon-colored silks come in every form, style, and size: *qipaos* and bags for the ladies, jackets for the men, plus accessories and home furnishings. ⊠ *Promenade, Shop E, 59 Maoming Nan Lu, Luwan District* ☎ *021/5466–3006.* ⊠ *House 15, North Block, Xintiandi, 181 Taicang Lu, Luwan District,* ☎ *021/6384–1601.*

Supermarkets & Drug Stores

Carrefour. The Gubei branch of this French grocery chain is one of the most comprehensive supermarkets in the city. Health and beauty, housewares, clothes, and electronics are on its first level, with food and beverage on the second. ⊠ *268 Shuicheng Nan Lu, Changning District* ☎ *021/6278–1944.*

City Supermarket. The city's premier import grocery store, City Supermarket, can be counted on for products you can't find anywhere else—at sky-high prices you won't see elsewhere. You'll find surprises on every aisle: nylons, laundry detergent, corkscrews, even baby food. ⊠ *Shanghai Center, 1376 Nanjing Xi Lu, Jingan District* ☎ *021/6279–8018* ⊠ *BF, Hong Kong New World Department Store, 939 Huaihai Zhonglu, by Shaanxi Nan Lu Luwan District* ☎ *021/6474–1260.*

Watson's. The Walgreens of China, Watson's has everyday health and beauty items: shampoo, soap, nail polish remover. ⊠ *787–789 Huaihai Zhonglu, Luwan District* ☎ *021/6431–8650.*

Fabrics & Tailors

China is famous for its silk, but some unscrupulous vendors will try to pass off synthetics at silk prices. Ask the shopkeeper to burn a small scrap from the bolt you're considering. If the burnt threads bead up and smell like plastic, the fabric is synthetic. If the threads turn into ash and smell like burnt hair, the fabric is real silk. (The same goes for wool.) For brocade silk, fair market prices range from Y30 to Y40 a meter; for synthetics, Y10 to Y28. You'll pay more in retail shops.

Tailors usually charge a flat fee and require a deposit, with the balance paid upon satisfactory completion of the garment. If you can, bring in a picture of what you want made or an existing garment for them to copy. Try to allow enough time for an initial and follow-up fitting. Tailors are accustomed to working with Chinese bodies and may need to adjust the garment a bit more to achieve a proper fit on larger Western frames.

Dave's Custom Tailoring. Its English-speaking staff and skilled tailoring make Dave's a favorite among expat and visiting businessmen. The shop specializes in men's dress shirts and wool suits, which require 10 days and two fittings to complete. The store moved from its popular Shanghai Center location in 2004; although another tailor has filled the space, the original Dave—owner Dave K. C. Shiung—can only be found at the shop on Wuyuan Lu. ⊠ *No. 6, 288 Wuyuan Lu, Xuhui District* ☎ *021/5404–0001.*

Hanyi. A well-respected qipao shop, Hanyi has a book of styles that its tailors can make in three days or more complex, finely embroidered patterns that require a month for proper fitting. Prices range from Y1,000 to Y1,800. ⊠ *217–221 Changle Lu, Luwan District* ☎ *021/5404–4727.*

Silk King (Shanghai Silk Commercial Company). Silk King is respected for its quality silk and wool. Prices start at Y68 per meter. Staff tailors can transform that silk into qipaos for Y500 to Y700. ⊠ *139 Tianping Lu, Xuhui District* ☎ *021/6282–5013* ⊠ *590 Huaihai Zhonglu, Luwan District* ☎ *021/6372–0561* ⊠ *1226 Huaihai Zhonglu, Xuhui District* ☎ *021/6437–3370.*

Tailor Chen. One phone call will bring the English-speaking Mr. Chen to your hotel room for measurements. He's known for his women's suits and qipaos. ☎ *021/5218–0621.*

Jewelry

Many freshwater pearls sold in Shanghai are grown in nearby Suzhou; seawater pearls come from Japan or the South Seas. The price of a strand of pearls depends on several factors. The longer the strand and bigger the pearl, the higher the price. High quality pearls have a shiny, clear luster and are uniform in size, color, and roundness on the strand. Real pearls are cool to the touch and feel gritty if you bite them. In most shops, you can bargain down the price 15% to 50%, with the clasp often negotiated separately.

★ **Amy's Pearls and Jewelry.** Friendly owner Amy Lin has sold pearls to European first ladies and American presidents but treats all her customers like royalty. Her shop just outside the west gate of Xiangyang Market has inexpensive trinket bracelets, strings of seed pearls, and stunning Australian seawater pearl necklaces. ⊠ *77 Xiangyang Nan Lu, Xuhui District* ☎ *021/5403–9673.*

Lilli's. Perhaps the best jewelry designer in town, Lilli's is known for refashioning old pieces into new styles. You'll find pearls, dainty silver bracelets with Chinese characters, and mah johngg tile bracelets. There's a pricey selection of swank silk photo albums and purses. ⊠ *Suite 1D, Maosheng Mansion, 1051 Xinzha Lu,, Jingan District* ☎ *021/6215–5031* ⊠ *Suite 605, Shanghai Center, 1376 Nanjing Xi Lu, Jingan District* ☎ *021/6279–8987* ⊠ *The Gatehouse, Dong Hu Villas, 1985 Hongqiao Lu, Changning District* ☎ *021/6270–1585.*

Ling Ling Pearls & Jewelry. Ling Ling sells traditional pearl necklaces at every price point; bargaining can net you 40% to 50% off the price. Its inexpensive fashion jewelry stands out for being hipper than the competition. ⊠ *2F, Pearl City, 558 Nanjing Dong Lu, Huangpu District* ☎ *021/6322–9299.*

Ru Pei Pei. With a reputation for high quality and many pieces combining diamonds with South Sea pearls, Ru Pei Pei is at the pricier end of pearl shops. Among the store's more moderately priced fashion jewelry are trendy pearl-banded watches, coral bracelets, onyx earrings, and other semi-precious stones. ⊠ *Suite 23, 2F, Pearl City, 558 Nanjing Dong Lu, Huangpu District* ☎ *021/6711–7435.*

Tea

Shanghai Huangshan Tea Company. Its nine shops around Shanghai sell traditional Yixing tea pots as well as a huge selection of China's best teas by weight. The higher the price, the better the tea. ⊠ *853 Huaihai Zhonglu* ☎ *021/6545–4919.*

Tianshan Tea City. More than 300 vendors occupy the three floors of Tianshan Tea City. You can buy such specialties as West Lake dragon well tea and Wuyi red robe tea as well as a porcelain tea set to serve it in. ⊠ *518 Zhongshan Xi Lu, Changning District* ☎ *021/6259–9999.*

SHANGHAI A TO Z

To research prices, get advice from other travelers, and book travel arrangements, visit www.fodors.com.

ADDRESSES

Shanghai is loosely laid out on a grid. Major east–west roads divide the city into *bei* (north), *zhong* (middle), and *nan* (south) sections, and north–south roads divide the city into *dong* (east), *zhong* (middle), and *xi* (west) segments. Xizang Lu, Beijing Lu, and Yanan Lu are the demarcation points for most surface streets in the city center. Puxi's main east–west roads are named for Chinese cities; some north–south streets are named for Chinese provinces.

AIR TRAVEL

Many offices of international carriers are represented in the Shanghai Center and Shanghai's western hotels. Major foreign airlines that serve Shanghai are: Aeroflot, Air Canada, Air France, Asiana, Dragon Airlines, Japan Airlines, Lufthansa, Malaysian Airlines, Northwest Airlines, Qantas, Singapore Airlines, Thai Airways, and Virgin Atlantic Airways.

Domestic carriers that connect international destinations to Shanghai include Air China and China Eastern Airlines.

Although several regional carriers serve Shanghai—Shanghai Airlines, China Southern, Shenzhen Airlines—China Eastern Airlines dwarfs them all. It's the main Chinese carrier connecting Shanghai to the rest of China. Beijing is by far the most popular destination, with 35 flights daily, the majority out of Hongqiao International Airport.

⚡ Carriers Aeroflot ✉ Shanghai Center, 1376 Nanjing Xi Lu, Jingan District ☎ 021/6279-8033. **Air Canada** ✉ United Plaza, 1468 Nanjing Xi Lu, Jingan District ☎ 021/6279-2999. **Air China** ✉ 600 Huashan Lu, Jingan District ☎ 021/5239-7227 or 021/6269-2999. **Air France** ✉ Novel Plaza, 128 Nanjing Xi Lu, Huangpu District ☎ 021/6380-6688. **Asiana** ✉ Rainbow Hotel, 2000 Yanan Xi Lu, Changning District ☎ 021/6219-4000. **China Eastern Airlines** ✉ 200 Yanan Xi Lu, Jingan District ☎ 021/6247-5953 domestic, 021/6247-2255 international or 95108. **China Southern Airlines** ✉ 227 Jiangsu Lu, Changning District ☎ 021/6226-2299. **Dragon Airlines** ✉ Shanghai Plaza, 138 Huaihai Zhonglu, Luwan District ☎ 021/6375-6375. **Japan Airlines** ✉ Plaza 66, 1266 Nanjing Xi Lu, Jingan District ☎ 021/6288-3000. **Lufthansa** ✉ Puxiang Plaza, 1600 Shiji Dadao, Pudong ☎ 021/5831-4400. **Malaysian Airlines** ✉ Shanghai Center, 1376 Nanjing Xi Lu, Jingan District ☎ 021/6279-8607. **Northwest Airlines** ✉ Shanghai Center, 1376 Nanjing Xi Lu, Jingan District ☎ 021/6884-6884. **Qantas** ✉ Shanghai Center, 1376 Nanjing Xi Lu, Jingan District ☎ 021/6279-8660. **Shanghai Airlines** ✉ 212 Jiangnan Lu, Jingan District ☎ 021/6255-8888. **Shenzhen Airlines** ✉ Suite 1107, 2088 Huashan Lu, Xuhui District ☎ 021/5298-0092. **Singapore Airlines** ✉ Kerry Center, 1515 Nanjing Xi Lu, Jingan District ☎ 021/6289-1000. **Thai Airways** ✉ Kerry Center, 1515 Nanjing Xi Lu, Jingan District ☎ 021/5298-5555. **United Airlines** ✉ Room 3301-3317, 33F, Shanghai Central Plaza, 381 Huaihai Zhonglu, Luwan District ☎ 021/3311-4567. **Virgin Atlantic Airways** ✉ 12 The Bund [Zhongshan Dong Yi Lu], Huangpu District ☎ 021/5353-4600.

AIRPORTS

Most international flights and larger airplanes serving Beijing and other major Chinese cities are routed through the ultramodern Pudong International Airport (PVG), which is across the river east of the city center. Hongqiao International Airport (SHA), in western Shanghai about 15 km (9 mi) from the city center, receives most domestic flights, especially those to smaller city airports. A taxi ride between the two airports will cost you about Y250 and take approximately 90 minutes. Shuttle buses between the airports cost Y30 and take much longer.

⚡ Airport Information Hongqiao International Airport ☎ 021/6268-8918 Ext. 2 for 24-hr airport information. **Pudong International Airport** ☎ 021/3848-4500 Ext. 2.

TRANSFERS Depending on the traffic, the trip between Hongqiao International Airport and the city center can take anywhere from 30 minutes to an hour. Pudong International Airport is 60 to 90 minutes from the city center.

Plenty of taxis are available at the lines right outside both the international and domestic terminals of both airports. Don't ride with drivers who tout their services at the terminal entrances; their cars don't have meters, and they'll try to charge you exorbitant rates. Taxis from Pudong to the city center cost Y120–Y150. From Hongqiao to the city center, it should cost Y50–Y70, plus a Y15 toll for the Yanan Elevated Road.

Pudong Airport Shuttle Buses link the airport with a number of hotels and major sites in the city center. The trip takes about 1½ hours and costs about Y19–Y30, depending on the destination. A shuttle also runs between Pudong and Hongqiao airports and costs Y30. From Hongqiao, Bus 925 runs to People's Square, but there's little room for luggage. It costs Y4. Many hotels have shuttle or car transfers available as well.

The high-speed maglev train, the city's showpiece, covers the 30 km (19 mi) between Pudong International Airport and Longyang Lu subway station in a mere eight minutes. The entrance to the platform is on the airport's second floor. Tickets cost Y50 one-way. The train operates weekdays 8:30 AM–12:30 PM, and weekends 8:30 AM–5:30 PM.

🚊 **Dazhong Taxi Company** ☎ 021/82222. **Jinjiang Taxi** ☎ 021/6275-8800. **Maglev Train** ✉ Longyang Lu Station, 2100 Longyang Lu ☎ 021/2890-7777. **Pudong Airport Shuttle Buses** ☎ 021/6834-6612. **Qiangsheng Taxi** ☎ 021/6258-0000.

BIKE TRAVEL

Shanghai's frenzied traffic is not for the faint-of-heart cyclist. If you wish to explore the city on wheels, consider a ride through the old lanes of the French Concession, with its marvelous 1930s houses that have managed thus far to escape the wrecking ball. Pudong roads have far less traffic but also less scenery.

Rental options are few in Shanghai; the going rental rate is Y150 per day. It's not much more expensive to buy yourself a bike, but local laws, not always enforced, require all bikes to be registered and licensed.

🚲 Bike Rentals **Bohdi Bikes** ✉ Room 406, No. 59, 710 Dingxi Lu, Changning District ☎ 021/3226-0000 ⊕ www.bohdi.com.cn.

BOAT & FERRY TRAVEL

There are more than 20 ferry lines between Pudong and Puxi. The most convenient ferry for tourists runs daily between the Bund in Puxi and Pudong's terminal just south of the Riverside Promenade. There are no seats, merely an empty lower deck that welcomes the masses with their bikes and scooters. The per-person fare is Y.5 (5 *jiao* or 50 *fen*) each way. The ferries leave the dock every 10 minutes, 24 hours a day.

The Shanghai Ferry Company runs a weekly ferry between Shanghai and Osaka, Japan. The ferry, which has restaurants, a game room, and even karaoke on board, leaves from Waihongqiao Harbor every Tuesday at 11 AM and arrives in Osaka at 9 AM the following Thursday. Tickets can be booked through the company or through China International Travel Service (CITS), the government tourism office. The China-Japan International Ferry Company also launches one ship from Shanghai's Waihongqiao Harbor every Saturday, alternating between Osaka and Kobe in Japan. The journey takes approximately two days. Tickets can be booked through the company or through CITS.

Most domestic boats leave from the Shiliupu Passenger Terminal for such destinations on the Yangzi River (Changjiang) as Wuhan and Chongqing; coastal cities such as Nantong, Dalian, and Ningbo; and the outlying island of Putuoshan. All domestic tickets can be purchased through CITS. There's a wide range of boats, although most domestic boats are not luxurious. They do, however, have different levels of berths, the most comfortable being first class.

🚢 Boat & Ferry Information **China-Japan International Ferry Company** ✉ 908 Dongdaming Lu, Hongkou District ☎ 021/6595-7988. **CITS** ✉ 1277 Beijing Xi Lu, Jingan District ☎ 021/6289-8899. **Ferry passenger information** ☎ 021/6326-3560. **Pudong-Puxi ferry** ✉ Puxi dock, the Bund at Jinling Lu, Huangpu District ✉ Pudong dock, 1 Dongchang Lu, south of Binjiang Da Dao, Pudong ☎ 021/6321-6547. **Shanghai Ferry Company** ✉ 908 Dongdaming Lu, Hongkou District ☎ 021/6537-5111. **Shiliupu Passenger Terminal/boat information** ✉ Zhongshan Dong Lu south of the Bund, Huangpu District ☎ 021/6326-0050. **Waihongqiao Harbor/boat information** ✉ 100 Yangshupu Lu, Hongkou District ☎ 021/6595-9529.

BUS TRAVEL

TO SHANGHAI Getting to and from Shanghai by bus is usually less convenient than by train. Be sure to compare train fares and schedules before taking the bus. Regular buses, most of which are uncomfortable, run from the long-distance bus stations and are acceptable for shorter trips to places such as Hangzhou and Suzhou (there are hourly departures) and other destinations in Jiangsu and Zhejiang provinces. With several stations scattered around town, it can be difficult to know which buses leave from where. Things should be simpler once a four-story bus terminal opens in 2005 adjacent to the Shanghai Railway Station, replacing many smaller terminals. In conjunction, the city also plans to open more than 200 bus-ticket kiosks around the city. Among the existing stations, the main one is on Hengfeng Lu near the Railway Station.

🚍 Bus Information Bus hotline (operators speak Chinese only) ☎ 021/96850 or 021/5631-0327. **Long-distance bus stations** ✉ High Speed Passenger Transport, 270 Hengfeng Lu, Zhabei District ☎ 021/6317-3912 ✉ North Bus Station, 80 Gongxin Lu, Zhabei District ☎ 021/5663-0230 ✉ Renmin Lu Station, 31 Renmin Nan Lu, Huangpu District ☎ 021/5782-0748.

WITHIN SHANGHAI Many Shanghai buses have air-conditioning and plenty of seats. Much of the fleet, though, is still very old and uncomfortable, primarily standing-room only, and extremely inconvenient. Although the network canvasses the whole town, you'll often have to change buses several times to reach your destination. During busy traffic hours the buses are unbelievably crowded, and in the frenzy you may get carried past your stop.

One exception to the above is Bus 911, a double-decker bus running down Huaihai Lu through the old French Concession. It's a pleasant ride, as the vehicles on this line are imported from Hong Kong and have many seats. From the top deck, you have a great view over the compound walls of the beautiful old Shanghai buildings that line the thoroughfare. Fares on this bus line will run you a few yuan, depending on how far you take it. The line starts at the Laoshi Men (Old City Gate) on Renmin Lu, just north of Yu Garden.

FARES & SCHEDULES On most buses the fare for any stop on the line is Y2 for air-conditioned buses, Y1 for those without air-conditioning. Most buses run from 5 or 5:30 AM to 11 PM.

🚍 Local Bus Information Passenger hotline ☎ 021/96900.

CAR TRAVEL

Highways connect Shanghai to neighboring cities such as Suzhou and Nanjing in the west, and Hangzhou in the south. However, due to government restrictions, it's virtually impossible for nonresidents of China to drive. You can, however, hire a car and driver through your hotel's transportation service or through Hertz or Avis, both of which have several locations throughout the city.

Avis ☎ 021/6241-0215. **Hertz** ☎ 021/6252-2200.

CONSULATES

Australia Australian Consulate ✉ 22F, CITIC Square, 1168 Nanjing Xi Lu, Jingan District ☎ 021/5292-5500 🖷 021/5292-5511.

Canada Canadian Consulate ✉ Tower 4, Suite 604, Shanghai Center, 1376 Nanjing Xi Lu, Jingan District ☎ 021/6279-8400 🖷 021/6279-8401.

New Zealand New Zealand Consulate ✉Qihua Dasha, 15th floor, 1375 Huaihai Zhong Lu, Xuhui District ☎ 021/6471-1108.

United Kingdom British Consulate ✉ Suite 301, Shanghai Center, 1376 Nanjing Xi Lu, Jingan District ☎ 021/ 6279-7650 ✉ Visa and Consular Sections, Suite 715, Shanghai Center, 1376 Nanjing Xi Lu, Jingan District ☎ 021/6279-8130.

United States United States Consulate ✉ 1469 Huaihai Zhong Lu, Xuhui District ☎ 021/6433-6880, 021/6433-3936 for after-hours emergencies 🖷 021/6433-1576 ✉ Citizen Services Section, Westgate Mall, 8th floor, 1038 Nanjing Xi Lu, Jingan District ☎ 021/3217-4650.

DISCOUNTS & DEALS

For Y70 (a saving of Y15), you can buy a combined ticket for the Shanghai Museum, Shanghai Grand Theater, and Shanghai Urban Planning Exhibition Center; the pass is available at any of the three sites. The Y280 Enjoy card, available through the Enjoy Web site, entitles you to discounts at participating restaurants, bars, and shops around town.

Enjoy ☎ 021/6431-6764 ⊕ www.enjoyshanghai.com.

EMERGENCIES

In a medical emergency don't call for an ambulance. The Shanghai Ambulance Service is merely a transport system that takes you to the closest hospital, not the hospital of your choice. If possible, take a taxi to the hospital; you'll get there faster.

International SOS 24-hour Alarm Center has information on emergency evacuations. Lifeline, a nonprofit support group for expatriates, operates a counseling hotline daily noon–8 PM.

The clinics and hospitals listed below have a limited number of English-speaking doctors on hand. At most hospitals, few staff members will speak English.

Dentists Cidi Dental Clinic ✉ 821 Yanan Zhong Lu, Jingan District ☎ 021/6247-0709. **DDS Dental Care** ✉ 1 Taojiang Lu, Xuhui District ☎ 021/6466-0928. **Orthodontics Asia** ✉ 3F, Ciro's Plaza, 388 Nanjing Xi Lu, Huangpu District ☎ 021/6473-7733. **World Link Dental Center** ✉ Mandarin City, 1F, Unit 30, 788 Hongxu Lu, Minhang District ☎ 021/6405-5788.

Doctors World Link Medical Center ✉ Room 203, West Tower, Shanghai Center, 1376 Nanjing Xi Lu, Jingan District ☎ 021/6279-7688 ✉ Hongqiao Clinic ✉ Mandarin City, 1F, Unit 30, 788 Hongxu Lu, Minhang District ☎ 021/6405-5788 ✉ Specialty and Inpatient Center, 3F, 170 Danshui Lu, Luwan District ☎ 021/6385-9889.

⚠ Emergency Services Fire ☏ 119. **International SOS 24-hour Alarm Center** ☏ 021/ 6295-0099. **Police** ☏ 110 or 021/6357-6666 (English). **Shanghai Ambulance Service** ☏ 120.

⚠ Hospitals Huadong Hospital ✉ Foreigners' Clinic, 2F, 221 Yanan Xi Lu, Jingan District ☏ 021/6248-3180 Ext. 30106. **Huashan Hospital** ✉ Foreigners' Clinic, 15F, 12 Wu-lumuqi Zhong Lu, Jingan District ☏ 021/6248-3986, 021/6248-9999 Ext. 2531 for 24-hour hotline. **Shanghai East International Medical Center** ✉551 Pudong Nan Lu, near Pudong Dadao, Pudong ☏ 021/5879-9999. **Shanghai United Family Hospital** ✉ 1111 Xianxia Lu, Changning District ☏ 021/6291-1635.

⚠ Hot Line Lifeline ☏ 021/6279-8990.

⚠ 24-Hour Pharmacy Shanghai Wu Yao Pharmacy ✉ Celebrity Garden, 201 Lian-hua Lu, Changning District ☏ 021/6294-1403.

ENGLISH-LANGUAGE MEDIA

English-language city magazines such as the biweekly *City Weekend* and monthly *That's Shanghai* are the most widely available independent publications in town, distributed through local bars, restaurants, and shops; they provide information on restaurants, cultural venues, and events. The state-owned *Shanghai Daily* publishes world, national, and business news, while the weekly *Shanghai Star* is more feature-heavy. English-language books and periodicals are harder to come by; you can buy them at the Foreign Language Bookstore (also known as Shanghai Book Traders), Shanghai City of Books (also known as the Shanghai Book Mall), City Supermarket, and the high-end Western hotels.

⚠ English-Language Bookstores City Supermarket ✉ Shanghai Center, 1376 Nan-jing Xi Lu, Jingan District ☏021/6279-8018. **Foreign Language Bookstore** ✉390 Fuzhou Lu, Huangpu District ☏ 021/6322-3200 ⊕ www.sbt.com.cn. **Shanghai City of Books** ✉ 465 Fuzhou Lu, Huangpu District ☏ 021/6391-4848.

RADIO &
TELEVISION
Most Western hotels have satellite TV, with CNN, BBC, and HBO in addition to the standard Chinese stations. As for radio, there's an English-language music program on 101.7 FM two times daily: 2 PM–3 PM and 8 PM–9 PM.

MAIL & SHIPPING

Shanghai's main post office is at 276 Sichuan Bei Lu, but there are branches all over town. Look for the green English CHINA POST signs. The Shanghai Center branch has the best English service; the Xintiandi location even has a small postal museum.

Most major hotels have in-room Internet access, and there are numerous Internet cafés around town. Eastday Bar is the largest chain, with approximately 240 Internet cafés.

⚠ Post Offices Main post office ✉ 276 Sichuan Bei Lu, Hongkou District ☏ 021/ 6306-0438. **Post office information** ☏ 021/6393-6666 Ext. 00. **Shanghai Center post office** ✉ Shanghai Center, 1376 Nanjing Xi Lu, Jingan District ☏ 021/6281-7434. **Xintiandi post office** ✉ 123 Xinye Lu, Huangpu District ☏ 021/6385-7449.

MONEY MATTERS

The best places to convert your money into yuan are at your hotel's front desk or a branch of a major bank, such as Bank of China, CITIC, or HSBC. You'll need to present your passport to do so.

ATMs are widespread, but not always reliable. Although you'll incur an extra fee, run a balance inquiry first; if the connection goes through, then make your withdrawal.

⚑ Currency Exchange Bank of China ⊠ 23 The Bund (Zhongshan Yi Lu), Huangpu District ☎ 021/6329-1979. **HSBC** ⊠ Shanghai Center, 1376 Nanjing Xi Lu, Jingan District ☎ 021/6279-8582.

PASSPORTS & VISAS

To extend your visa or ask for information about your status as an alien in China, stop by the Public Security Bureau Division for Aliens, which is open weekdays 9 to 11:30 and 1:30 to 4:30. The office is extremely bureaucratic, and the visa officers can be difficult. Most of them can speak English. It's usually no problem to get a month's extension on a tourist visa. You'll need to bring in your passport and your registration of temporary residency from the hotel at which you're staying. If you are trying to extend a business visa, you'll need the above items as well as a letter from the business that originally invited you to China saying it would like to extend your stay for work reasons. Rules are always changing, so you will probably need to go to the office at least twice to get all your papers in order.

⚑ Public Security Bureau Division for Aliens ⊠ 333 Wusong Lu, Huangpu District ☎ 021/6357-6666.

SIGHTSEEING TOURS

BOAT TOURS A boat tour on the Huangpu River affords a great view of the Pudong skyline and the Bund. Huangpu River Cruises launches several small boats for one-hour daytime cruises as well as its unmistakable dragon boat for two night cruises. The company also runs a 3½-hour trip up and down the Huangpu River between the Bund and Wusong, the point where the Huangpu meets the Yangzi River. You'll see barges, bridges, and factories, but not much scenery. All tours depart from the Bund at 239 Zhongshan Dong Lu. You can purchase all tickets at the dock or through CITS; prices range Y35–Y90.

Shanghai Oriental Leisure Company runs 40-minute boat tours along the Bund from the Pearl Tower's cruise dock in Pudong. Daytime cruises cost Y40, nighttime Y50. Follow the brown signs from the Pearl Tower to the dock.

⚑ Fees & Schedules CITS ⊠ 1277 Beijing Xi Lu, Jingan District ☎ 021/6289-8899. **Huangpu River Cruises** ⊠ 239 Zhongshan Dong Er Lu (the Bund), Huangpu District ☎ 021/6374-4461. **Shanghai Oriental Leisure Company** ⊠ Oriental Pearl Cruise Dock, 1 Shiji Dadao, Pudong ☎ 021/5879-1888 Ext. 80435.

BUS TOURS Grayline Tours has escorted half- and full-day coach tours of Shanghai as well as one-day trips to Suzhou, Hangzhou, and other nearby waterside towns. Prices range from Y289 to Y1,323.

Jinjiang Tours runs a full-day bus tour of Shanghai that includes the French Concession, People's Square, Jade Buddha Temple, Yu Garden, the Bund, and Pudong. Tickets cost Y250 and include lunch. Small groups can arrange for a tour by car with an English-speaking guide.

The Shanghai Sightseeing Bus Center has more than 50 routes, including 10 tour routes that make a circuit of Shanghai's main tourist attractions. There are also one-stop itineraries and weekend overnight trips to sights in Zhejiang and Jiangsu provinces. One-day trips range from Y30 to Y200; overnight trips cost as much as Y400. You can buy tickets up to a week in advance. The main ticket office and station, beneath Staircase No. 5 at Shanghai Stadium, has plenty of English signage to help you through the ticketing process.

🛈 Fees & Schedules **Grayline Tours** ✉ 2 Hengshan Lu, Xuhui District ☏ 135/1216–9650 ⊕ www.grayline.com. **Jinjiang Tours** ✉ 161 Chang Le Lu, Luwan District ☏ 021/6415–1188. **Shanghai Sightseeing Bus Center** ✉ No. 5 Staircase, Gate 12, Shanghai Stadium, 666 Tianyaoqiao Lu, Xuhui District ☏ 021/6426–5555.

SUBWAY TRAVEL

The Shanghai subway is constantly being expanded. So far, three lines are fully operational and nine more are planned. With Shanghai's traffic-choked streets, it is by far the quickest way to get to most places. Stations are clean and fairly well signed in English, although not all exit signs list their corresponding streets. In-car announcements for each station are given in both Chinese and English. The subway is not too crowded, except at rush hour.

Pick up a subway or city map at your hotel; at most stations, you won't find an English-language route map until after you've bought your ticket and cleared the turnstile. Ticket machines have instructions in English; press the button for the fare you want (Y2–Y4), then insert your coins. You can get change at the adjacent booth. Keep your ticket handy; you'll need to insert it into a second turnstile as you exit at your destination.

Line One travels between Xinzhuang and the Shanghai Railway Station, with stops in the French Concession at Hengshan Lu, Changshu Lu, Shaanxi Nan Lu, and Huangpi Lu. It intersects with Line Two at People's Square, a labyrinth of a station with two levels and 20 exits. Line Two, which will eventually link Hongqiao International Airport with Pudong International Airport, currently runs from Zhongshan Gongyuan in Puxi to Zhangjiang Station in Pudong. Stops in the city center include Jingan Temple and Shimen Yilu, with the Henan Zhong Lu station right at the entrance to the Nanjing Dong Lu pedestrian walkway. A light rail line, called the Pearl Line, will eventually circle the city, with twin tunnels under the Huangpu River. For now, it runs from the South Railway Station to Jiangwan Town.

FARES & SCHEDULES Trains run regularly, with three to six minutes between trains on average. Service on Line One begins at around 5:20 AM and ends at about 11:30 PM. Line Two opens at 6:30 AM and closes just before 11 PM. The Pearl Line operates from around 6:20 AM to 10:15 PM. Tickets cost Y2–Y6, and there's no charge to change trains.

🛈 **Passenger information** ☏ 021/6318–9000.

TAXIS

Taxis are plentiful, easy to spot, and by far the most comfortable way to get around Shanghai. Almost all are Volkswagen Santanas or Passats, and they come in a rainbow of colors: teal, green, yellow, red, dark blue, and white. They are all metered. You can spot the available ones by looking in the front window for a small lit-up sign glowing on the passenger side. The fare starts at Y10 for the first 2 km (1 mi), with each kilometer thereafter costing Y1. After 11 PM, the base fare is Y13, with each kilometer thereafter costing Y2.6; the price per kilometer jumps to Y3.9 after you've gone 10 km (6 mi). You also pay for waiting time in traffic.

Cabs can be hailed on the street or called for by phone. If you're choosing a cab from a queue, peek at the driver's license on the dashboard. The lower the license number, the more experienced the driver. Drivers with a number below 200,000 (out of a possible 260,000) can usually get you where you're going. Stars on the license are awarded for professional or courteous service.

Most cab drivers don't speak English, so it's best to give them a piece of paper with your destination written in Chinese. (Keep a card with the name of your hotel on it handy for the return trip.) Hotel doormen can also help you tell the driver where you're going. It's a good idea to study a map and have some idea where you are, as some drivers will take you for a ride—a much longer one—if they think they can get away with it.

7 Taxi Companies **Dazhong Taxi Company** ☎ 021/82222. **Jinjiang Taxi** ☎ 021/6275-8800. **Qiangsheng Taxi** ☎ 021/6258-0000.

TELEPHONES
7 **Local directory assistance** ☎ 114. **Time** ☎ 117. **Weather** ☎ 121.

TRAIN TRAVEL
Shanghai is connected to many destinations in China by direct train. The Shanghai Railway Station is in the northern part of the city; a second key station will open in southwest Shanghai, in Xuhui District, in spring 2006. Currently, several trains a day run from the railway station to Suzhou, Hangzhou, Nanjing, and other nearby destinations. The best train to catch to Beijing is the overnight express that leaves around 6 PM and arrives in Beijing the next morning. The express train for Hong Kong departs around noon and arrives at the Kowloon station 24 hours later.

You can buy train tickets at CITS, but a service fee is charged. Same-day, next-day, and sometimes third-day tickets can also be easily purchased at the ticket office on the first floor of the Longmen Hotel, on the western side of the train station.

7 Train Information **Shanghai Railway Station** ✉ 303 Moling Lu, Zhabei District ☎ 021/6317-9090. **Ticket office** ✉ 777 Hengfeng Lu, Zhabei District ☎ 021/6356-0051.

TRAVEL AGENCIES
The agencies below are accustomed to dealing with expatriates and English-speaking visitors; they can arrange both domestic and international travel. For additional agents, check out the travel section of *That's Shanghai.*

7 Agencies **American Express** ✉ Shanghai Center, 1376 Nanjing Xi Lu, Jingan District ☎ 021/6279-8082. **China International Travel Service** (CITS) ✉ 1277 Beijing Xi Lu, Jingan District ☎ 021/6289-8899. **Great West Travel** ✉ Room 660, East Tower, Shanghai Center, 1376 Nanjing Xi Lu, Jingan District ☎ 021/6279-8489 ⊕ www.great-west-travel.com. **Huating Overseas Tourist Company** ✉ 4F, 501 Wulumuqi Bei Lu, Jingan District ☎ 021/6249-1234. **Polo Air** ✉ Suite 4107A, Plaza 66, 1266 Nanjing Xi Lu, Jingan District ☎ 021/6288-1555.

VISITOR INFORMATION

🛈 Community Organizations **American Chamber of Commerce** ☎ 021/6279-7119. **Australia Chamber of Commerce** ☎ 021/6248-8301. **British Chamber of Commerce** ☎ 021/6218-5022. **Canadian Business Forum** ☎ 021/6279-8400. **Hong Kong Chamber of Commerce** ☎ 021/5306-9533. **Jewish Community of Shanghai** ☎ 021/6278-0225. 🛈 Tourist Information **China International Travel Service** ✉ 1277 Beijing Xi Lu, Jingan District ☎ 021/6279-8899. **Shanghai Tourist Information Services** ✉ Yu Garden, 159 Jiujiaochang Lu, Huangpu District ☎ 021/5355-5032 ✉ Hongqiao International Airport ☎ 021/6268-8899. **Spring Travel Service** ☎ 021/6252-0000 Ext. 0. **Tourist Hotline** ☎ 021/6439-0630 or 021/6439-8947.

SIDE TRIPS FROM SHANGHAI
SUZHOU, ZHOUZHUANG, AND HANGZHOU

4

ADMIRE PERFECTION IN DESIGN
at the Master of the Nets Garden ⇨*p.175*

EAT YOUR GREENS AND ROCKS AND TREES
at Deyuelou restaurant ⇨*p.178*

TAKE A SERENADED GONDOLA RIDE
along the canals of Zhouzhuang ⇨*p.186*

EXPLORE GARDEN PATHS
around idyllic West Lake ⇨*p.188*

HIKE UP TO THE PAVILIONS
on Solitary Hill Island ⇨*p.188*

WALK AMID THE BAMBOO TREES
of the Shangri-La Hotel Hangzhou ⇨*p.195*

Revised by
Kristin Baird
Rattini

IT'S EASY TO GET SHANGHAI FATIGUE. The traffic, crowds, smog, and go-go pace of China's largest city can wear you down and leave you longing for someplace greener, more laid-back, and more reflective of China's past rather than its surge toward the future. Water towns are the quickest escape. These living history museums along eastern China's vast canal system lie within a two-hour arc of Shanghai, down country roads and past fields still worked by hand, as they have been for centuries. City dwellers flock to the water towns to admire the ancient houses and simpler way of life—but then return to modernity and their own homes in time for dinner. Farther afield, the lakes, hills, gardens, and streams of eastern China provide a scenic reminder that Shanghai's urban canyon is not a natural, but a human-made, wonder, and that there are places where the greatest heights are peaks rather than skyscrapers.

About the Restaurants & Hotels

Despite the fact that they are often portrayed as quaint, scenic marvels, Hangzhou and Suzhou are huge cities with several million residents. Western hotel chains are in both markets and cater as much to business travelers as to tourists. A few exceptional local hotels rival the quality standards of their foreign competitors; however, most are less-refined budget properties with fewer amenities.

Mom-and-pop Chinese restaurants are the rule in the water towns. In Suzhou, the focus is on its storied centuries-old restaurants along Guanqian Jie; the few non-Chinese outlets (that aren't fast food) are found in hotels. Hangzhou's dining scene has progressed much farther; you'll find everything from tiny noodle shops to expensive Cantonese shark's-fin restaurants to outposts of Italian and Thai chains from Shanghai and Hong Kong.

WHAT IT COSTS In Renminbi (Yuan)				
$$$$	**$$$**	**$$**	**$**	**¢**
RESTAURANTS over Y165	Y100–Y165	Y50–Y100	Y30–Y50	under Y30
HOTELS over Y1800	Y1400–Y1800	Y1100–Y1400	Y700–Y1100	under Y700

Restaurant prices are per person for a main course at dinner, excluding tax and tips. Hotel prices are for a standard double room, excluding 10%–15% service charge.

Timing

The weather is at its best in spring and autumn, but these are also the busiest tourist seasons. The roads leading to Suzhou and Zhouzhuang clog with traffic during the Qing Ming festival, when Chinese families visit their ancestors' graves at the dozens of cemeteries in Jiangsu Province; the festival runs March 15–April 15, but its peak is April 5. Hangzhou is one of China's most heavily visited cities; reservations for hotels are recommended any time of year but are absolutely essential during holidays and on spring and autumn weekends, when crowds from outlying regions descend on the city. If possible, visit Zhouzhuang during the week; the town is packed on weekends and national holidays.

SUZHOU

Approximately 1½ hrs west of Shanghai on Shanghai–Nanjing rail line.

If the renowned gardens of Suzhou form a thriving monument to the city's past, the passages leading up to them speak of a time of transition. Entire blocks of old-style houses still line some of the city's canals. Decorated gates and doorways from centuries ago catch the eye, but they now lead into shops selling silk and cashmere in Chinese and Western styles; the ramshackle houses from past eras border tall office buildings and shiny new hotels; and the traditional-style sloping, tiled roofs often sit atop structures built in the last few years. This mixture of old styles with new makes Suzhou's central districts a pleasure to explore.

Suzhou's many canals once formed the basis of its economy. Now falling into disuse, the waterways still line many a lamplighted street. These canals, however, are really only the younger cousins of the Grand Canal (Da Yunhe), which passes through the outskirts of town. Just 5 km (3 mi) south of the city is the Precious Belt Bridge (Baodai Qiao), one of the most famous and grandiose bridges on the canal. The canal used to be a main transportation route for eastern China but has been gradually replaced with newer, faster modes.

Suzhou's fabulous gardens set a style and standard for gardens throughout the country. They exemplify the delicate balance among the four traditional elements of Chinese gardens: plants, rock, water, and buildings. The gardens were created by retired officials and unaffiliated literati as places in which to read and write poetry and philosophy, to stroll and drink with their friends, and to meditate and spend quiet hours. The attraction of these gardens goes beyond the mazes of bizarre rock formations or thoughtfully arranged vegetation; rather, each garden is meant to be enjoyed for its overall atmosphere, as well as for its unique style and layout. It's lovely to simply sit in a teahouse near a pond and feel the peaceful breeze as you watch it ruffle the water, carrying fragrances with it. Pathways lead, perhaps, to an artfully planted tree winding its way up the garden wall, a glimpse of lake from a small human-made cave, or a pavilion displaying Qing Dynasty tree-root furniture. Every plant, rock, bit of water, piece of furniture, wall, and even fish has been carefully created or chosen for its individual shape, color, shadow, and other characteristics and for the way each blends with the whole at different times of the day and year. Although spring is considered prime viewing time, each season works its own magic.

a good walk

Starting where Renmin Lu meets Xibei Jie in the northern section of town, check out the **Suzhou Silk Museum ❶** ▶ and the tall **North Temple Pagoda ❷**, with views of the city. Walk east along Xibei Jie, with its traditional-style fronts and shops, until you come to the **Suzhou Museum of Arts & Crafts ❸**. A few blocks down, as the street changes names to Dongbei Jie, you'll come to the **Suzhou History Museum ❹** and the **Humble Administrator's Garden ❺**, Suzhou's largest garden. Head south along Yuanlin Lu, checking out the silk shops that line the street. **Lion's Grove Garden ❻**, filled with caves, will be on your right about halfway down the short street. At the

Numbers in the text correspond to numbers in the margin and on the Shanghai Side Trips, Suzhou, Zhouzhuang, and Hangzhou maps.

4

If you have
2 days

Take a bus or train from Shanghai to **Suzhou** ❶–⓮ ➤ and spend your first day exploring the town's renowned gardens. Take a late train or, if you're more adventurous, the overnight ferry down the Grand Canal to **Hangzhou** ㉓–㊳. Start your visit at West Lake, at the center of the city, and move out to explore the town's pagodas, museums, and other sights.

If you have
5 days

Take a day trip via bus to **Zhouzhuang** ⓯–㉒ ➤ for a glimpse of life in China's water towns. On Day 2, take a train from Shanghai to **Suzhou** ❶–⓮. Spread out your walking tour of the town's famous gardens over two days, allowing you more leisure time to linger among the blooms as well as time in between the stops to shop for silk, Suzhou's specialty. Enjoy dinner at one of the centuries-old restaurants on Guanqian Jie, then catch the traditional music performance at the **Master of the Nets Garden** ❽. From Suzhou, take a late train or the overnight ferry down the Grand Canal to **Hangzhou** ㉓–㊳. Focus on the attractions around West Lake, including a boat ride out to **Three Pools Reflecting the Moon** ㉕. Wrap up your first day by watching the sunset from **Evening Sunlight at Thunder Peak Pagoda** ㉙, then dine at one of the nearby restaurants along Nanshan Lu. The next day, explore the sights farther out in the countryside, especially the **Temple of the Soul's Retreat** ㉝, before catching the train back to Shanghai.

---

end of the street, turn right and then left onto Lindun Lu. Follow Lindun Lu south to Guanqian Jie and turn right to reach the **Temple of Mystery** ❼, an ancient temple in a busy market square.

Continue south on Lindun Lu to its end at Ganjiang Donglu. Make a slight jog left and follow Fenghuang Jie south to Shiquan Jie, turning left for the small, exquisite **Master of the Nets Garden** ❽. Exit the garden and head west on on Shiquan Jie to Renmin Lu; turn left again and follow it to **Blue Wave Pavilion** ❾, a large garden off the street to the left. From here, you can continue south on Renmin Lu, turn right at Xinshi Lu and walk west for three long blocks. Turn left on Dongda Jie to reach the **Pan Gate** ❿. Or head back up Renmin Lu, just north of Ganjiang Lu, to visit one of Suzhou's younger gardens, **Joyous Garden** ⓫. Take a bus or taxi north and west across the city moat and a branch of the Grand Canal to the large, well-designed **Lingering Garden** ⓬. Just to the west, at the end of Liuyuan Lu, is the Buddhist **West Garden Temple** ⓭. From this temple, take another taxi or the No. 1 bus to **Tiger Hill** ⓮, a large park north of the city with a leaning pagoda.

TIMING   The most leisurely way to do this walk is to spread it out over two days. Most of the sights have English signs, but they're often poorly placed off the main roads, so you may have to seek them out.

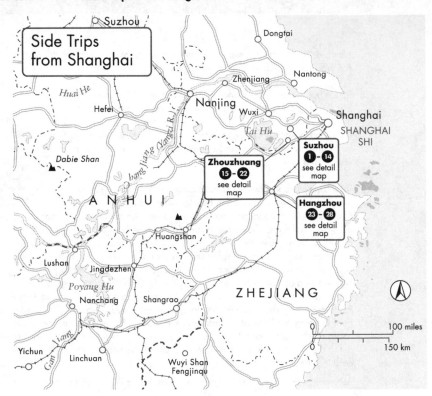

Side Trips from Shanghai

Suzhou

Dongtai

Zhenjiang   Nantong

Nanjing   Wuxi   Shanghai

Huai He   Hefei   *Tai Hu*   SHANGHAI SHI

Jiang (Yangtze R.)

Zhouzhuang 15 - 22 see detail map

Suzhou 1 - 14 see detail map

Hangzhou 23 - 28 see detail map

Dabie Shan

A N H U I

Huangshan

Lushan   Jingdezhen

Poyang Hu   Z H E J I A N G

Nanchang   Shangrao

Gan Jiang

Yichun   Linchuan   Wuyi Shan Fengjinqu

| 0 | 100 miles |
| 0 | 150 km |

What to See

9 **Blue Wave Pavilion** (Canglang Ting). First built in 1045, Blue Wave Pavilion is the oldest existing garden in Suzhou. Of the four components of Suzhou-style gardens, it relies most heavily on rocks and structures for its charm. A maze of oddly shaped doorways circles a central rocky hill. From atop the hill you can see the adjacent canal. A path here leads down through a human-made cave to a small stone picnic table. The **Pure Fragrance Pavilion** showcases Qing Dynasty furniture at its most extreme; the entire suite is created from gnarled, knobby Fujian banyan root. ⊠ *Off Renmin Lu between Shiquan Jie and Xinshi Lu* ☎ *0512/ 6519–4375* 🎫 *Y20* ☉ *Daily 7:30–5:30, last ticket sold at 5.*

5 **Humble Administrator's Garden** (Zhuo Zheng Yuan). This 10-acre garden, **Fodor'sChoice** Suzhou's largest, was built in 1509 by Wang Xianjun, an official dismissed ★ from the imperial court. He chose the garden's name from a line in a Tang Dynasty rhapsody. The line of poetry, reading "humble people govern," seems like a clever bit of sarcasm when considered in conjunction with the grand scale of this private garden—perhaps explaining Wang's un-suitability for public life. East and west sections (the latter with a collection of 700 bonsai trees) flank the garden's centerpiece: its central pond. Lily pads float on the surface, forsythias skirt the edge, walkways zig-zag across the corners and a series of open-air pavilions perfectly frame the scene, which retains a timeless tranquility despite the throngs passing through the tableau. ✉ *178 Dongbei Jie* ☎ *0512/6751–0286* 🚌 *Y70* ⏱ *Mar.–Oct., daily 7:30–5; Nov.–Feb., daily 7:30–5.*

⓫ **Joyous Garden** (Yi Yuan). Built in 1874, Joyous Garden is the youngest garden in Suzhou, and it pleasantly blends pavilion and rockery, court-yard and pond. An on-site nursery shelters fledgling blooms. The most unusual feature among the many corridors in the garden is an oversize mirror. Inspired by a tale of Bodhidharma (founder of Zen Buddhism), who stared at a wall for years to find enlightenment, the garden's founder hung the mirror opposite a pavilion, so that the building could contemplate its reflection. At night, the garden doubles as a popular tea-house. ✉ *343 Renmin Lu* ☎ *0512/6524–9317* 🚌 *Y15, 7:30 AM–5 PM; Y20, 5 PM–2 AM, Y45 with tea* ⏱ *Daily 7:30 AM–2 AM.*

⓬ **Lingering Garden** (Liu Yuan). Created during the Ming Dynasty, Liu Yuan has since become one of Suzhou's most famous gardens. True to its name, the five-acre garden has many pavilions and courtyards in which visitors linger. The **Mandarin Duck Hall** is particularly impressive, with a lovely moon gate engraved with vines and flowers. Follow the zigzag corridors and walkways inlaid with stone cranes and flowers to the back of the gar-den to view the garden's centerpiece: the nearly 70-foot-tall rock that is said to have come from Tai Lake (Tai Hu). ✉ *80 Liuyuan Lu* ☎ *0512/ 6533–7903* 🚌 *Y40* ⏱ *Daily 7:30–5:30, last ticket sold at 5.*

❻ **Lion's Grove Garden** (Shizi Lin). A labyrinth of human-made caves sur-rounds a small scenic lake at this garden. Illusions of space are expertly created here: the divided wall and the positioning of the pavilions make the garden seem more spacious than it really is. You can get a wide view of the garden walking the paths around the lake. The cave maze brings your attention to minute landscaping details. If you look closely at the rocks, you may see the source of the garden's name—they are said to resemble lions. At the garden's exit is a small marketplace with antique replicas and silks of all sorts. ✉ *23 Yuanlin Lu* ☎ *0512/6727–8316* 🚌 *Y20* ⏱ *Mar.–Oct., daily 7:30–5:30; Nov.–Feb., daily 8–5.*

❽ **Master of the Nets Garden** (Wangshi Yuan). Despite its comparatively small size, Wangshi Yuan, with its subdued beauty, is perhaps the most in-teresting garden in a city famous for them. All of the elements of the Suzhou style are here—artificial rock hills, an abundance of flora, pavil-ions overlooking a central pond—in seemingly perfect balance, as if this were the culmination of the art of garden design. The park was origi-nally constructed in the 12th century, and reworked in the 18th. The **Dianchun Yi** (Spring Cottage) was reproduced for an exhibition in the Metropolitan Museum of Art in New York. From mid-March to mid-November, the grounds serve as a concert hall for evening performances of traditional Chinese music. ✉ *Shiquan Jie* ☎ *0512/6529–3190* 🚌 *Y30; Y60 for evening performances* ⏱ *Daily 7:30–5, last ticket sold at 4:30; evening performances mid-March–mid-November, daily 7:30–10.*

Fodor'sChoice
★

❷ **North Temple Pagoda** (Beisi Ta). One of the symbols of ancient Suzhou, Beisi Ta towers over the old city. This complex has a 1,700-year history, dating to the Three Kingdoms Period (3rd century AD). The wooden pagoda

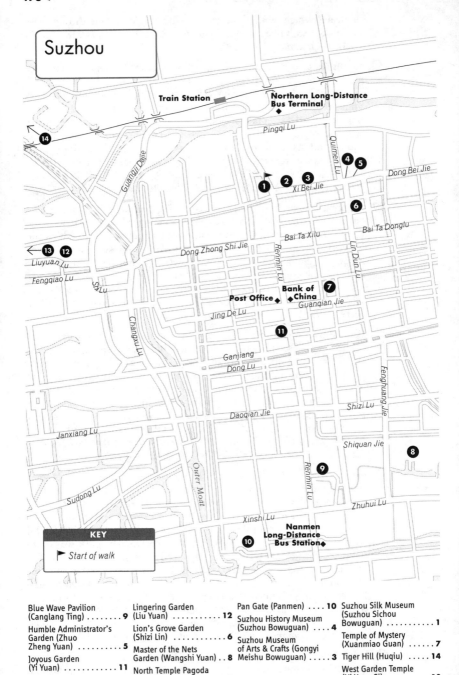

Suzhou

Train Station

Northern Long-Distance Bus Terminal

Pingqi Lu

KEY

⚑ Start of walk

has been renovated several times and stands nine stories, or approximately 2,500 feet high, with windows and balconies on each floor. You can climb as high as the eighth floor to get what might be the best view of Suzhou. Within the grounds are also the Copper Buddha Hall and Plum Garden, which, built in 1985, lacks the history and the complexity of Suzhou's other gardens. ⊠ *Xibei Jie and Renmin Lu* 🕾 *0512/6753–1197* 🚃 *Y15* ⊘ *Mar.–Oct., daily 7:45–6; Nov.–Feb., daily 7:45–5:30.*

❿ **Pan Gate** (Panmen). An early-morning visit to the grounds of the Pan Gate adds wonderful local color to this Suzhou landmark. Women practice sword tai chi around the base of the seven-story **Radiant Light Pagoda** (Ruiguang Ta), while old men walk backwards (believing this to keep them healthy) across **Wumen Bridge** and along the ramparts of the Pan Gate. The rare side-by-side stone land and water gates, which date to 1351, protected the city from potential invaders who plied the Grand Canal. There's now a teahouse here to protect visitors from thirst. The nicely landscaped grounds include a bell tower and a pavilion overlooking a pond. ⊠ *1 Dongda Jie* 🕾 *0512/6519–3054* 🚃 *Y20, Radiant Light Pagoda, Y6* ⊘ *Daily 8–5.*

❹ **Suzhou History Museum** (Suzhou Bowuguan). This humble museum will meet with greatness in 2005, when a new facility designed by Suzhou's favorite son, architect I. M. Pei, is scheduled to open to much fanfare. The new museum's 70,000 square feet of gallery space will house, among other items, the original museum's core collection of tools, funeral pots, and other artifacts dating to 5,000 BC. The grounds include an art gallery and a classic opera hall with walls inscribed with calligraphy and flowers. The traditional courtyard home of Taiping leader Li Xiucheng is next door. ⊠ *204 Dongbei Jie* 🕾 *0512/6754–1534* 🚃 *Y10* ⊘ *Daily 8:15–4:15.*

★ ❸ **Suzhou Museum of Arts & Crafts** (Gongyi Meishu Bowuguan). A former courtyard home houses this wonderful museum showcasing a "best of" Suzhou's best-known handicrafts: double-sided silk embroidery, elaborate carvings, musical instruments, and traditional paintings. The works are stunning in their complexity. A 6-foot-wide, 5-foot-tall embroidered portrait of Mao took 4,000 days to complete. What started as a ton of jadeite was whittled down over two years to a delicate folding fan just 4 millimeters thick in places. The gift shop, at the far back of the property, sells an excellent selection of souvenirs—from painted bottles to embroidery to silk—at negotiable prices. ⊠ *8 Xibei Jie* 🕾 *0512/6753–4874* 🚃 *Y15* ⊘ *Daily 9–5, last ticket sold at 4:30.*

▶ ❶ **Suzhou Silk Museum** (Suzhou Sichou Bowuguan). From silkworm to sales rack, the Silk Museum covers all stages of silk production, one of Suzhou's claims to fame. A sculpted wall depicting silk-trade merchants starts you on your journey through the museum. Display cases, with English and Chinese signage, house original and reproduction silk pieces from the past 3,000 years. Of particular interest are the half-dozen old looms, which resemble medieval torture devices. The museum store sells an exhaustive variety of marked-up adult and children's silk clothing. ⊠ *2001 Renmin Lu* 🕾 *0512/6753–6506* 🚃 *Y7* ⊘ *Daily 9–5:30, last ticket sold at 5.*

❼ Temple of Mystery (Xuanmiao Guan). One of the most well-preserved old-style temples, the Temple of Mystery backs a large market square, which used to be temple grounds. Founded in the third century, the Taoist temple has undergone fewer restorations than most its age, still retaining parts from the 12th century. The main building, **Sanqing Dian,** is one of the largest and oldest wooden structures in China. Fortunately, it suffered very little damage in the Cultural Revolution. ⊠ *Guanqian Jie* ☎ *No phone* 🎟 *Y15* ⊘ *Daily 7:30–4:45.*

⑭ Tiger Hill (Huqiu). About 5 km (3 mi) northwest of the city center is this park, home of the tomb of Helu, the supposed founder of the city. According to legend, a white tiger appeared here three days after Helu was interned, hence the name. Atop the hill stands the 98-foot-tall **Leaning Pagoda** (Xia Ta), Suzhou's version of the Leaning Tower of Pisa, tilting at a 15° angle. An interpreter's stand at the entrance gate can pair you up with an English-speaking guide. ⚑ *Huqiu Lu, north of city* ☎ *0512/ 6723–1305* 🎟 *Y50* ⊘ *Mar.–Oct., daily 7:30–6; Nov.–Feb., daily 7:30–5:30.*

⑬ West Garden Temple (Xi Yuan Si). This active Buddhist temple was originally constructed in the Yuan Dynasty (1279–1368), but was destroyed in the mid-19th century during the Taiping Rebellion and rebuilt in the late 19th century, during the Qing Dynasty. Several new buildings have been added since that time. Of particular interest is the **Wubai Luohan Tang** (Hall of 500 Arhats), which houses 500 gold-painted statues of arhats, each with its own peculiar expression. Behind the main temple is the large, open garden, which has several ponds and a bonsai yard. ⊠ *8 Xiyuan Lu, down the street from Liu Yuan* ☎ *0512/6531–3361 Ext. 0* 🎟 *Y15* ⊘ *Daily 8–5:30, last ticket sold at 5.*

Where to Stay & Eat

Many of Suzhou's centuries-old restaurants line Guanqian Jie.

★ **$–$$$** ✕ **Deyuelou.** For more than 400 years this restaurant has been serving Suzhou-style food, including fish dishes, local-style dim sum, and a particularly tasty *deyue tongji* (braised chicken). It also specializes in an attractive type of food presentation, the ancient art of "garden foods"—an assortment of dim sum specialties arranged to resemble gardens, with foods portraying flowers, trees, and rocks. ⊠ *27 Taijian Nong* ☎ *0512/ 6522–6969* ▭ *AE, MC, V.*

★ **¢–$$** ✕ **The Pine and Crane** (Songhelou). With more than two centuries of history, the Pine and Crane is one of Suzhou's most famous restaurants. It serves Suzhou specialties and catches from the river that in the old days were actually eaten on riverboats during banquet cruises—hence their popular designation as "boat food." The recommended dish here is the *songshu guiyu,* or "squirrel-shaped Mandarin fish" (don't let the English translation turn you off). The restaurant has nine dining halls decorated with Suzhou regional arts and calligraphy. ⊠ *18 Taijian Nong* ☎ *0512/6523–3270* ▭ *AE, MC, V.*

¢–$ ✕ **Huangtianyuan.** Although there's a dining room upstairs, the heart of Huangtianyuan is the first-floor cafeteria, where you purchase tickets and present them at different windows for various dishes, including stews, spring rolls, and dim sum. In business since 1821, the restaurant portion claims to have originated the Suzhou speciality of *mifen*—gluten cakes made by pounding rice to a fine paste. There's a takeout counter for these delicacies along one side of the cafeteria. Other house specialties include *babao fan* (syrupy rice with nuts and fruit) and meat- or sweets-filled *tang tuan* (dim sum with skin made of thick mifen dough). The menu changes with each season. ✉ *86 Guanqian Jie* ☎ *0512/6727–7033* ▤ *No credit cards.*

$$$–$$$$
Fodor'sChoice
★
🏨 **Sheraton Suzhou Hotel & Towers.** With its three-story pagoda lobby, beautiful garden grounds, and traditional-style white buildings with upturned eaves, the Sheraton is a landmark in itself that seamlessly matches its surroundings. The two-story stone entrance is modeled after the city's Pan Gate, which lies just behind the hotel. The large rooms have plush beds and separate showers and tubs; you can order an aromatherapy bath to be drawn. The fitness center includes a stunning indoor Roman pool, its fiery red-and-gold-tile waterfall sharply contrasting with the turquoise-glazed pool. The Garden Brasserie has a great Asian buffet, and high tea is served on weekends. ✉ *388 Xinshi Lu, 215007* ☎ *0512/6510–3388* 🖷 *0512/6510–0888* ⊕ *www.sheraton-suzhou. com* ⤳ *370 rooms, 30 suites* 🍴 *3 restaurants, patisserie, room service, in-room data ports, some in-room faxes, minibars, cable TV, golf privileges, tennis court, indoor-outdoor pool, health club, hot tub, massage, sauna, steam room, bicycles, bar, lobby lounge, piano, shop, baby-sitting, dry cleaning, laundry service, concierge, concierge floor, Internet, business services, convention center, travel services, no-smoking rooms, no-smoking floors* ▤ *AE, DC, MC, V.*

★ **$–$$**
🏨 **Gloria Plaza Hotel Suzhou.** From the watercolor paintings lining the halls to the cascading waterfall windows of its Sampan Restaurant, the Gloria Plaza Hotel stands out as an inviting property. The large, standard rooms dwarf the furniture inside; rooms on the Plaza Floor fill the space better by adding a valet and pull-out couch. The service is attentive; the lobby staff, for example, is diligent in offering assistance. The hotel is a five-minute walk from Guanqian Jie's shops and restaurants. ✉ *535 Ganjiang Donglu, 215006* ☎ *0512/6521–8855* 🖷 *0512/ 6521–8533* ⊕ *www.gphsuzhou.com* ⤳ *281 rooms, 13 suites* 🍴 *2 restaurants, room service, in-room data ports, in-room safes, minibars, cable TV, some in-room VCRs, putting green, gym, hair salon, massage, sauna, steam room, Ping-Pong, lobby lounge, shops, baby-sitting, laundry service, concierge, concierge floor, Internet, business services, convention center, travel services, no-smoking rooms* ▤ *AE, DC, MC, V.*

¢–$
🏨 **Lexiang Hotel.** Amenities are few, but the location of this budget hotel that caters mostly to Chinese guests is excellent—down the street from the Joyous Garden and a block from the Temple of Mystery. And despite being in the middle of the Guanqian Jie shopping-and-entertainment district, the hotel is surprisingly quiet. Third-floor rooms are stunning, with sleek entertainment centers and sliding wood screens dividing the bathroom from the bedroom. ✉ *18 Dajing Xiang, 215005* ☎ *0512/6522–2815* 🖷 *0512/6523–7625* ⤳ *195 rooms, 5 suites* 🍴 *2 restaurants, in-room data ports, in-room safes, minibars, cable TV, hair salon, sauna, lobby lounge, piano, shops, laundry service, business services, meeting rooms, no-smoking rooms* ▤ *AE, DC, MC, V.*

¢–$ ▢ **Nanyuan Guest House.** Its 10 acres off Shiquan Jie make the Nanyuan a garden in itself, but the guest house's greater selling point is its location two blocks from Suzhou's famous Master of the Nets Garden. The apricot and mauve rooms, which are scattered among six buildings, show their age, with worn carpets and trim; bathrooms are a bit brighter with silver and pearl wallpaper. At this writing the Nanyuan was undergoing significant renovations to add a gym and 200 new rooms. ⊠ *249 Shiquan Jie, 215006* ☎*0512/6519–7661 Ext. 3101* 🖷*0512/6519–8806* ◁*93 rooms, 7 suites* ◊ *2 restaurants, coffee shop, room service, minibars, cable TV, hair salon, massage, sauna, bar, shops, laundry service, Internet, business services, meeting rooms, travel services* ▭ *AE, DC, MC, V.*

¢–$ ▢ **Suzhou Hotel.** Its location—15 acres on Shiquan Jie—is the main attraction of the Suzhou Hotel. It's a short walk from the Master of the Nets Garden and a stretch of restaurants and silk and cashmere stores along Shiquan Jie. Creams and grays decorate the fair-sized but tired standard rooms. In the Chinese-style suites, a moon gate separates the beds from the sitting area. This spot is popular with Chinese tour groups. At this writing the hotel was undergoing a substantial renovation of its facilities. ⊠ *115 Shiquan Jie, 215006* ☎ *0512/6520–4646* 🖷 *0512/6520–4015* ⊕ *www.suzhou-hotel.com* ◁ *283 rooms, 23 suites* ◊ *16 restaurants, room service, minibars, cable TV, gym, hair salon, massage, sauna, Ping-Pong, lobby lounge, piano, shops, playground, dry cleaning, laundry service, business services, convention center, free parking, no-smoking floors* ▭ *AE, MC, V.*

¢ ▢ **Nanlin Hotel.** Although its sprawling lobby and spiral marble staircase make a grand first impression, the Nanlin Hotel is definitely a budget hotel, not a luxury one. Rooms are plain, with dated furnishings. It's within walking distance of the Master of the Nets Garden and Blue Wave Pavilion, yet the hotel is off the tourist track, down a hard-to-find lane, which makes this a fairly quiet property. ⊠ *20 Gunxiu Fang, Shiquan Jie, 215006* ☎ *0512/6519–4641* 🖷 *0512/ 6519–1028* ⊕ *www.nanlinhotel.com.cn* ◁ *252 rooms, 5 suites* ◊ *Restaurant, coffee shop, room service, cable TV, indoor pool, gym, hair salon, massage, sauna, Ping-Pong, lobby lounge, shops, dry cleaning, laundry service, Internet, business services, meeting rooms, no-smoking rooms* ▭ *AE, DC, MC, V.*

Nightlife & the Arts

Apart from karaoke clubs and hotel lounges, there are few bars to speak of in Suzhou.

Mid-March to mid-November, the Master of the Nets Garden (Wang-shi Yuan) has **traditional opera and music performances** (⊠ Shiquan Jie ☎ 0512/6826–7737) every night from 7:30 to 10; the cost is Y60. The show presents a taste of various scenes from opera, as well as an opportunity to hear classical Chinese instruments. It can be a bit crowded during the peak tourist season. The beautiful location, however, makes the performance a uniquely enjoyable experience. Check at the entrance gate of the garden or with CITS (the tourism office, at 18 Dajing Xiang) about times and tickets.

Wuyuegong Restaurant Theater stages a **show of Wu culture** (✉ Suzhou Hotel, 115 Shiquan Jie ☎ 0512/6519–2556) every evening at 6:30. The hour-long song-and-dance program features Kun opera, acrobatics, and a river-village dance. Tickets range from Y80, which includes tea, to Y150, which includes a dinner of traditional Suzhou "boat food."

Shopping

Districts around the gardens and temples teem with silk shops and outdoor markets. If you're up for a 20-minute taxi ride north of town, you'll have your pick of freshwater pearls at the 1,200 shops in **China Pearl City** (✉ Zhengzhu Lu, Weitang Town). **Wangshi Pearl Company** (✉ 69-C Zhengzhu Lu ☎ 0512/6540–6999) has an especially nice selection of strands of freshwater pearls and fashionable jewelry at low prices. The shop has a loyal clientele of expat women in Shanghai.

The **Dong Wu Silk Weaving Mill** (✉ 540 Renmin Lu ☎ 0512/6727–4691) has been selling export-quality silk for a century. Its silk underwear and 100% silk brocade are top sellers. The **Friendship Store** (✉ 433 Renmin Lu ☎ 0512/6523–7090) carries local products made of silk, wood, and jade. The **Suzhou Antiques Store** (✉ 328 Renmin Lu, near Leqiao Bridge ☎ 0512/6522–8368) has been selling antiques, calligraphy, jades, and other "cultural products" since 1956. With its large selection of silk clothing, the **Suzhou Silk Museum Shop** (✉ 2001 Renmin Lu ☎ 0512/6753–4941), while pricey, is the best reason to visit the museum. For local artwork and calligraphy, visit the **Wumen Artstore** (✉ 105 Liuyuan Lu ☎ 0512/6533–4808).

Suzhou A to Z

To research prices, get advice from other travelers, and book travel arrangements, visit www.fodors.com.

The most comfortable and convenient way to get to Suzhou from Shanghai is by train.

AIR TRAVEL

Since Suzhou does not have an airport, international flights go through Shanghai's Pudong International Airport (PVG), domestic flights through the Nanjing (NKG) or Shanghai Hongqiao (SHA) airports. In Suzhou, CITS can arrange plane tickets. You also can contact the Civil Aviation Administration of China office for flight information or get in touch with the China Eastern Airlines office in Suzhou.

🚹 **Civil Aviation Administration of China (CAAC)** ✉ 85 Renmin Lu ☎ 0512/6510–4881. **China Eastern Airlines** ✉ 114 Ganjiang Xilu, Suzhou ☎ 0512/6522–2788. **CITS** ✉ 18 Dajing Xiang, Guanqian Jie ☎ 0512/6522–1012 Ext. 2010.

AIRPORT TRANSFERS From Hongqiao International Airport, buses depart hourly between 10 AM and 8 PM to Suzhou. Tickets cost Y50. A long-distance bus connects Pudong International Airport to Suzhou. It leaves the airport every hour between 10 AM and 6 PM. Tickets cost Y82. From Nanjing's Lukou Airport, you'll have to take a taxi; buses and trains run only from Nanjing's city center.

🚌 Hongqiao Airport Long Distance Bus ☎ 021/6268-8899. Pudong Airport Long Distance Bus ☎ 021/6834-5743.

BIKE TRAVEL

Suzhou's crowded streets can be perilous for casual bike riders, but you may make better time on two wheels instead of four. The Sheraton Suzhou rents bicycles, and you'll also find stands near the Master of the Nets Garden and on Renmin Lu between the train station and North Temple Pagoda.

🚲 Bike Rentals **Sheraton Suzhou Hotel & Towers** ✉ 388 Xinshi Lu ☎ 0512/6510-3388.

BOAT & FERRY TRAVEL

The overnight boat trip from Suzhou to Hangzhou along the Grand Canal takes you through some great countryside scenery between two of China's prettiest cities. The boat leaves Suzhou at 5:30 PM and arrives in Hangzhou the next morning at around 6:30 AM. Tickets can be purchased through your hotel, a travel agent, or at the Suzhou Ferry Terminal, on the south side of Suzhou near the old city gate.

🚢 Boat & Ferry Information **Suzhou Ferry Terminal** ✉ 2 Renmin Lu, at Renmin Bridge ☎ 0512/6520-8484.

BUS TRAVEL

TO SUZHOU Buses travel frequently from Shanghai to Suzhou. Return buses to Shanghai depart from the Northern Long-Distance Bus Terminal, which is next to the train station. From the Nanmen (South Gate) Long-Distance Bus Station, buses travel to Hangzhou as well as other Jiangsu destinations. Wherever you travel, it's best to have the name of your destination written in Chinese to avoid misunderstanding. Buses are the most convenient choice for short trips, like from Suzhou to Wuxi. Otherwise, trains are more comfortable.

🚌 Bus Depots **Nanmen Long-Distance Bus Station** ✉ Southern tip of Renmin Lu, by Renmin Bridge ☎ 0512/6520-4867. **Northern Long-Distance Bus Terminal** ✉ 29 Xihui Lu ☎ 0512/6526-1893.

WITHIN SUZHOU While several of Suzhou's bus routes stop at popular gardens, there are no English maps or schedules available to help you sort out routes and times. Ask your hotel's concierge for assistance. In general, bus route No. 2 is the most convenient route. It starts at the train station, travels along Renmin Lu, stops at both the Humble Administrator's Garden and the Master of the Nets Garden before heading out to Tiger Hill.

The fare for sightseeing buses is Y2, or Y3 for air-conditioned buses. Regular public buses are Y1, Y2 for air-conditioned buses.

🚌 Bus Information **Suzhou Bus Information** ☎ 0512/6525-2155.

EMERGENCIES

Ambulances are merely a transport service; the attendants do not provide medical care. You're better off taking a taxi directly to the hospital.

🚨 Emergency Services **Ambulance** ☎ 120. **Police** ☎ 110.

🏥 Hospitals **No. 1 Affiliated Hospital of Suzhou University** ✉ 96 Shizi Jie ☎ 0512/6522-3637. **People's Hospital No. 2** ✉ 26 Daoqian Jie ☎ 0512/6521-4726.

TAXIS

Traveling by taxi is a slow proposition in Suzhou; the clogged streets can double or even triple your estimated travel times. However, you'll likely need a taxi to shuttle between some of the city's more far-flung sights.
🚩 Taxi Companies **Datong Auto Renting Service Company** ☎ 0512/6752-6666. **Xiantong Auto Renting Service Company** ☎ 0512/6752-8826.

TOURS

Major hotels as well as Suzhou China International Travel Service (CITS) can often arrange for a tour guide. CITS charges Y300 for an English-speaking guide. Individuals may offer you day tours; just make sure the price is set and the guide's English is good enough to make it worthwhile.
🚩 **Suzhou China International Travel Service** ✉ 18 Dajing Xiang, Guanqian Jie ☎ 0512/6522-1012 Ext. 2010.

TRAIN TRAVEL

Trains travel hourly between Suzhou and Shanghai's main train station, although a few use the smaller Shanghai West Station. The trip takes between 40 minutes and an hour. Suzhou's train station is on the north side of town.
🚩 Train Station **Suzhou Train Station** ✉ 27 Chezhan Lu ☎ 0512/6702-1252.

TRAVEL AGENCIES

🚩 Agencies **Suzhou China International Travel Service** ✉ 18 Dajing Xiang, Guanqian Jie ☎ 0512/6522-1012 Ext. 2010. **Suzhou Overseas Tourist Corporation** ✉ 195 Shiquan Jie ☎ 0512/6515-0177.

VISITOR INFORMATION

🚩 Tourist Information **Suzhou China International Travel Service** ✉ 18 Dajing Xiang, Guanqian Jie ☎ 0512/6522-1012 Ext. 2010. **Tourist Information Hot Line** ☎ 0512/6520-3131.

ZHOUZHUANG

90 mins west of Shanghai by bus, 45 mins southeast of Suzhou by bus.

More than 2.5 million visitors head to the water village of Zhouzhuang each year to catch a glimpse of the China that was. Its 14 arched stone bridges, crisscrossing canals, narrow lanes, and centuries-old houses evoke the quaint river life depicted in traditional Chinese paintings throughout the ages. The town dates to the 12th century, when Shen Wansan, a wealthy bureaucrat, diverted water from the Baixian River to create its canals. Two-thirds of the town's tile-roof wooden houses skirting the canals date to the Ming (1368–1644) and Qing (1644–1911) dynasties, when they were built as mansions for the rich.

Today, the ramshackle houses are occupied by poorer folk, for whom Zhouzhuang's development into a tourist destination has been a mixed blessing. Many were forced from their homes to make way for the hundreds of restaurants and shops occupying the ½ square km (⅕ square mi) that makes up the old town. But you'll hear others singing the town's official song, "New Zhouzhuang is Good," as they steer tourists in gondolas along the town's canals.

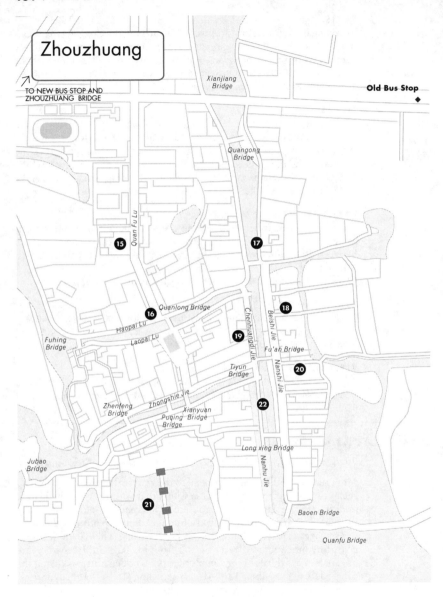

Zhouzhuang

TO NEW BUS STOP AND
ZHOUZHUANG BRIDGE

Xianjiang Bridge

Old Bus Stop

Quangong Bridge

Quan Fu Lu

15

17

Quanlong Bridge

16

Haopai Lu

Laopai Lu

18

Beishi Jie

Chenhuangdi Jie

Fu'an Bridge

Fuhing Bridge

19

Nanshi Jie

20

Tiyun Bridge

Zhenfeng Bridge

Zhongshie Jie

Xianyuan Bridge

Puqing Bridge

22

Jubao Bridge

Long xing Bridge

Nanhu Jie

21

Baoen Bridge

Quanfu Bridge

Most tour buses drop you at the main parking lot a mile from the main gate. English signs point the way to Zhouzhuang's landmarks, so you can hoof it through the new Zhouzhuang (which utterly lacks the charm of its predecessor) or haggle for a ride on a pedicab. One of the first things you'll pass on the way to the old town is an "ancient memorial archway"—which is actually new. Beside this arch is a **ticket window**, where you can purchase a pass that covers all of the major sights of the old town. ⊠ *Quanfu Lu* ☎ *0512/5721–7213 ticket office, 0512/ 5721–1654 general information* ⊕ *www.zhouzhuang.net* 🎟 *Y60 for pass for Zhouzhuang's sights* ☉ *7 AM–6:30 PM.*

⑮ Full Fortune Pagoda (Quanfu Ta), a five-story, 100-foot-tall tower, serves as a symbol of the old town, but it's surprisingly new: it was built in 1987. It's one of the first landmarks you'll pass on the way to the old town from new Zhouzhuang. Unfortunately, you can only admire it from the outside. ⊠ *Quanfu Lu.*

⑯ The **Museum of Zhouzhuang** (Zhouzhuang Bowuguan) is worth a stop for its long scroll painting, a 100-foot-long landscape of Zhouzhuang completed over six months by 30 artists in 1998. Another noteworthy exhibit is a collection of 5,000-year-old artifacts unearthed from nearby Tai Lake (Tai Hu). The museum is to the right of the white-marble carving of Zhouzhuang that marks the entrance to the first canal. ⊠ *Laopai Lu at Quanfu Lu.*

⑰ Zhouzhuang is known for its ancient stone bridges, particularly the **Double Bridge** (Shuang Qiao), which consists of two arched bridges—Shi De and Yong An—that resemble an ancient Chinese key. It was built between 1513 and 1619. Artist Chen Yifei painted the bridge in a work called "Memory of Hometown," which was purchased by industrialist Armand Hammer and presented to China's then-leader, Deng Xiaoping, in 1985. The donation put Zhouzhuang in the national—and world—spotlight.

⑱ Built between 1436 and 1449, the **Zhang Residence** (Zhang Ting), also

Fodor'sChoice called Jade Swallow Hall (Yuyan), is the oldest building in Zhouzhuang

★ open to the public. The 18,000-square-foot property comprises six courtyards and 70 rooms. The Big Chamber is noteworthy for its wooden drum foundation, a rare surviving example of a traditional Ming architectural style. But this chamber is formal and cold in comparison to the dark rosewood recreation room, where tea tables, a zither, and a mah-jongg table speak of past amusements. The study room is lovely, too, with latticed windows overlooking a rear courtyard through which the Ruojing River runs. Today, this small side canal and a turnabout pond are used more by geese than by boats. For a separate Y10 fee, you can tour the **Roundabout Building,** the upstairs personal chambers of the Zhang Residence. The master bedroom is the grandest, with a red-and-gold wooden bed chamber covered with elaborate tapestries and carved panels of fish, vases, and gods. ⊠ *Beishi Jie, south of Double Bridge.*

⑲ An antiquer's dream, the **Folk Collection Hall** (Tianxiaode) is bursting at the seams with more than 200,000 items assembled over 30 years. Han Dynasty coins, ivory chopsticks, porcelain, opium pipes, embroidered slippers, and much, much more pack dozens of display cases in the warren of rooms. ⊠ *Chenhuangdi Jie, north of Fu'an Bridge.*

㉒ Just inside the **Shen Residence** (Shen Ting) is a framed work of calligraphy by architect I. M. Pei that reads "Zhouzhuang is a national treasure." The Shen Residence is a town treasure, dating to 1742. Most visitors overlook the estate's true front entrance; it's not the tearoom but the water gate along the canal, with a wharf for docking barges. Among the more than 100 rooms, **Song Mao Hall** is the most glorious, with phoenix, crane, and dragon carvings on its beams and a full suite of oversize Qing-style furniture. Look for the faded but elegant poems and landscape paintings on the door panels in the Big Chamber. ⊠ *Nanshi Jie, southeast of Fu'an Bridge.*

★ **㉑** Zhouzhang is named for Zhou Digong, a devout Buddhist who in 1086 donated his 32 acres to the **Full Fortune Temple** (Quanfu Si). Here, 21 gold Buddhas, plus a 15-foot-tall bronze one, watch over the lovely temple grounds, which circle a large pond. An arch bridge and zigzag corridors connect the halls and gazebos that stand as islands. It's a tranquil spot to sit and listen to birds chirping or admire the flowers in **Nanhu Garden.** ⊠ *Off Nanhu Jie, south end of town.*

㉒ A **gondola ride,** available at the **Boat Hall** (Chuan Matou), is a must in Zhouzhuang. The price is Y80 per boat, regardless of the number of passengers, and the ride is worth the fee. Blue-smocked women serenade you as they steer the long tillers mounted on the stern. After passing under the Double Bridge and several other stone bridges, the boat drops you off at the Museum of Zhouzhuang. ⊠ *Xiwan Lu, south of Fu'an Bridge* ⊡ *Y80.*

Where to Stay & Eat

Most people visit Zhouzhuang as a day trip, but there are a few budget hotels in the area. Restaurants are largely mom-and-pop operations—some of them on floating barges—with a live tank, a few tables, and a view of the canal. Zhouzhuang's culinary specialties are pickled vegetables, three-flavor meatballs, and Wansan pork tendon, a crispy glazed pork hindquarter for sale at dozens of stores throughout town.

¢–$$ ✕ **Shenting Restaurant.** Don't let the "steamed bad-smelling bean curd" on the menu stop you from eating at Shenting, also known as Shen House Restaurant. It serves Zhouzhuang classics like Wansan pork as well as a good selection of seafood and cold dishes. ⊠ *Beishi Jie, north of Fu'an Bridge* ☎ *0512/5721–7203* ⚑ *Reservations not accepted* ▭ *No credit cards.*

¢–$$ ✕ **Wanxian Restaurant.** Founded in the late 19th century, Wanxian is a landmark in Zhouzhuang. Steamed seafood—eel, turtle, fish, shrimp—dominates the menu. Tables beside the open latticed windows on the second floor provide a good perch for people-watching. ⊠ *Xiwan Jie, south of Fu'an Bridge* ☎ *0512/5721–2315* ⚑ *Reservations not accepted* ▭ *No credit cards.*

¢ ⊞ **Zhouzhuang Hotel.** Among Zhouzhuang's limited lodging options, this hotel has the highest standards and best facilities. There are two restaurants, one serving Chinese and the other Western food, plus a tiny gym. Fair-sized rooms are simple but clean, with robes for lounging. The hotel is just a two-block walk from the old town's main gate. ✉ *108 Quanfu Lu, Zhouzhuang Town, Kunshan City 215325* ☎ *0512/5721–6666* 📠 *0512/5721–6698* ⊕ *www.zhouzhuanghotel.com* 🛏 *97 rooms, 11 suites* ♨ *2 restaurants, grocery, in-room data ports, minibars, cable TV with movies, gym, hair salon, sauna, Ping-Pong, bar, shop, laundry service, business center, meeting rooms* 🖃 *MC, V.*

Zhouzhuang A to Z

To research prices, get advice from other travelers, and book travel arrangements, visit www.fodors.com.

BUS TRAVEL

Buses are the most convenient way to travel between Shanghai and Zhouzhuang; public and sightseeing buses make the round-trip several times daily. Public buses run a half-dozen times each day between Shanghai and Zhouzhuang. They depart from Shanghai's north bus station on Gongxin Lu, near Shanghai Railway Station. The fare is Y22 each way. Eight tour buses depart daily for Zhouzhuang from the Shanghai Sightseeing Bus Center at Shanghai Stadium. Tickets cost Y110 for round-trip transportation and admission to Zhouzhuang.

🚍 **North Bus Station** ✉ 80 Gongxin Lu, Zhabei District, Shanghai ☎ 021/5663–0230. **Shanghai Sightseeing Bus Center** ✉ No. 5 Staircase, Gate 12, Shanghai Stadium, 666 Tianyaoqiao Lu, Xuhui District, Shanghai ☎ 021/6426–5555.

PEDICAB TRAVEL

Hundreds of pedicabs line the streets near the main parking lot where most tour buses drop passengers off. Be prepared to haggle; Y4 should get you into the old town.

TOURS

Jin Jiang Optional Tours Center runs bus tours to Zhouzhuang and neighboring Grandview Garden Friday–Monday and Wednesday. The Y380 fee includes round-trip transportation, admission fees, lunch, and an English-speaking guide.

🚍 **Jin Jiang Optional Tours Center** ✉ Jinjiang Tower, 161 Changle Lu, Luwan District, Shanghai ☎ 021/6415–1188 Ext. 80160.

HANGZHOU

2–3 hrs southwest of Shanghai by train or express bus.

The southern terminus of the Grand Canal in Zhejiang Province, Hangzhou was destined for greatness as an economic center from the canal's completion in AD 609. In 1126 the Song Dynasty fled south from Kaifeng, in Henan Province, to Hangzhou to escape the Jurchen invaders. The era that ensued, later known as the Southern Song, witnessed the rise of Hangzhou's cultural and administrative importance. Its proximity not only to the canal but also to river and ocean, as well as the unusual fertility of its environs, made Hangzhou the hub of southern Chinese culture. By the 13th century the city had a population of between 1 and 1.5 million people.

From 1861 to 1863 Hangzhou was occupied by the Taiping forces, and in the ensuing battles with the imperial forces, the city, along with its cultural artifacts and monuments, was largely destroyed. As the center of so much traditional and imperial history, Hangzhou was also a natural target during the Cultural Revolution, when Red Guards smashed to bits much of what had survived the previous century's turmoil. Many of the city's monuments have been repaired or reconstructed, and even the Red Guards couldn't destroy West Lake, which lends Hangzhou much of its romantic beauty. The lake provides a setting of serenity rarely seen in a Chinese city. A little way outside the city, you can visit the plantations that produce the area's famous Long Jing tea, or stroll in forested hills to take in the views of the surrounding area.

The best way to explore Hangzhou's sights is to start at the lake, which is the effective center of town. From the lake you can go on to visit the city proper and then move out to the less populous region to the southwest.

❷❸ Hangzhou culture revolves around **West Lake** (Xihu). The lake was originally a lagoon, cut off from the nearby river, until the local government began taking steps to clear the lake's waters. For several years the government has been pumping water from the nearby Qiantang River into the lake, and with the periodic dredgings of the lake floor and the daily skimmings of its surface, the lake is clearer and cleaner than it's been in centuries.

Parks and a paved waterfront walkway ring most of the lake, and an electric tram shuttles passengers on a 1-km (½-mi) shoreline tour for Y40. You can pick up the tram by the boat ticket office on the Hubin Lu pedestrian walkway or in the Orioles Singing in the Willow Waves park. Particularly scenic are the garden-lined promenades of **Nanshan Lu Park** and the **Hubin Lu pedestrian walkway.** The lake is crossed by two pedestrian causeways: the **Baidi** (named for the famed Tang Dynasty poet Bai Juyi) and the **Sudi** (named for the Song Dynasty poet Su Dongpo). Both walkways are lined with willow and peach trees, flowers, and benches, and are closed to automobiles, making them ideal for strolling or bicycle riding.

Small private boats, some of which look like science-fiction inventions, are moored around the lake. You can dictate the itinerary and negotiate the price; Y45 per person for an hour-long tour is the going rate. Private paddleboats are also available. Officially run multiseat boats leave every half hour or so to the lake's islands from a pier on the Hubin Lu pedestrian walkway near the Hangzhou Overseas Chinese Hotel (at 39 Hubin Lu); the cost is Y45 per adult per hour.

❷❹ **Solitary Hill Island** (Gushan), reached by Baidi causeway, is West Lake's largest island. It's the site of **Zhongshan Park** (Zhongshan Gongyuan), a small but lovely park centered on a pond and several pavilions. From here, you can follow the path up the hill to the **Seal Engraver's Society** (Xileng Yinshe; ☎ No phone ⛵ Free). This was once the headquarters of a professional seal-carving operation. Today, several pavilions and corridors—open-air structures open around the clock—still house examples of carvings, including an engraved monument dating from nearly 2,000 years ago. The trip up the hill to the society is worth it, even if you're not interested in Chinese stamps. A beautiful garden in front of the society's buildings has some of the best views of West Lake in all of Hangzhou.

Solitary Hill Island's **Zhejiang Provincial Museum** (Zhejiang Bowuguan) houses an excellent collection of bronzes from the Shang and Zhou dynasties (1600 BC–221 BC), natural-history and ceramics exhibits, and a gallery for local contemporary art. ⊠ *25 Gushan Lu* ☎ *0571/8797–1177* ⊕ *www.zhejiangmuseum.com/ehome.html* 🎟 *Y10 museum, Y8 art gallery, Y15 combined ticket* ⊙ *Mon. noon–4:30; Tues.–Sun. 8:30–4:30.*

need a break? Adjacent to the Seal Engraver's Society is a small **souvenir shop** that serves tea. Order a cup and have a seat on the hilltop veranda. The view, especially at sunset, should reveal why the Chinese have loved this spot for centuries.

㉕ Just off the banks of Solitary Hill Island is the small man-made island of **Three Pools Reflecting the Moon** (Santan Yinyue). On the island are numerous ponds connected by small bridges and dotted with pavilions. Off the island's southern shore are three stone pagodas. During the autumn moon (August), fires are lit in the pagodas. The moonlight reflects three golden disks into the water, hence the name. Official multiseat boats travel to the island from Solitary Hill Island. 🎟 *Y20, boats from Solitary Hill Island Y35 (includes admission).*

㉖ Near Solitary Hill Island stands the **Yue Fei Mausoleum** (Yue Fei Mu), a temple built to honor the Song general Yue Fei (1103–42), a commander against the Jurchen invaders. A jealous courtier convinced the emperor that the loyal Yue Fei was a traitor, and the emperor ordered him executed. Before submitting himself to the emperor's will, Yue Fei had the words LOYAL TO THE LAST tattooed on his back. Twenty years later he was rehabilitated and deified and is now one of China's national heroes, a symbol of patriotic duty. The temple wall replicates the tattooed inscription, while a statue of the traitorous courtier kneels in shame nearby. Traditionally, you're supposed to spit on statues of traitors, but a sign near the statue asks visitors to refrain. ⊠ *Beishan Lu, west of Solitary Hill Island* 🎟 *Y25* ⊙ *Daily 7:30–5:30.*

㉗ **Precious Stone Hill** (Baoshi Shan), with its famous **Protecting Chu Pagoda** (Baochu Ta), can be seen on the north side of West Lake from just about anywhere on the lake. It's well worth your time to spend a morning or afternoon exploring the hill. Numerous paths, both paved and unpaved, lead from the lakeside up to the hilltop, from which you can not only see all of West Lake, but also a good part of Hangzhou. The original pagoda was built about AD 970; the present structure dates from 1933. The hill is also dotted with Buddhist and Taoist shrines and temples—some impressive, others not so—as well as some mysterious caves. In the summer, locals often gather in the bigger caves for picnics or cards to escape the heat. ⊠ *Shuguang Lu* 🎟 *Park, free; pagoda, Y15* ⊙ *Daily 7:30–dusk.*

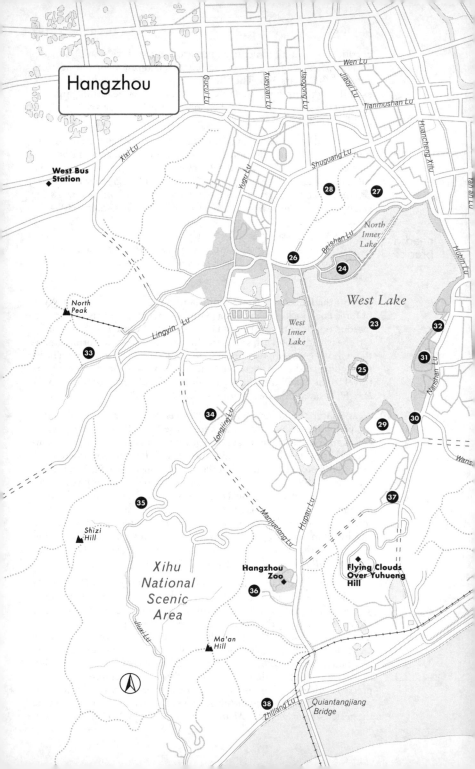

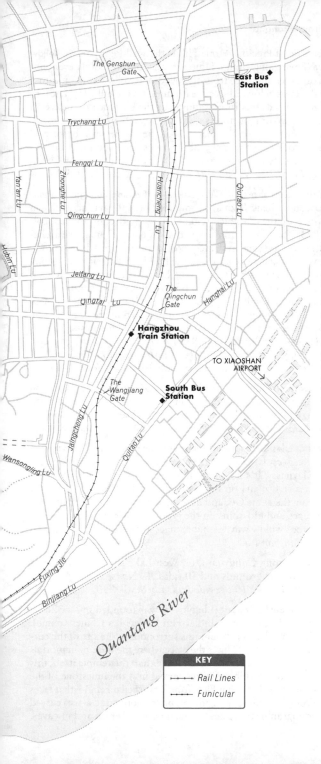

㉘ On the back side of Precious Stone Hill is the well-kept park of **Yellow Dragon Cave** (Huanglong Dong), famous for its (purportedly) never-ending stream of water spurting from the head of a yellow dragon into a pond several meters below. Above the fountain on the hillside is another yellow dragon's head, this time standing at the entrance to a cave. A bronze statue of two dragon angels stands before a bamboo groove with rare "square bamboo." As the placard for the statue says, be sure to "touch the buttocks" of these cherublike imps for good luck. There's also a stage where, twice a day, free Yue Opera performances are held. ✉ *Shuguang Lu* ☎ *0571/8798–5860* 💲 *Y15* ◷ *Daily 7:30–5:30.*

㉙ On the southeastern shore of West Lake, the **Evening Sunlight at Thunder Peak Pagoda** (Leifeng Xizhao), completed in 2002, has arisen like a phoenix from atop the crumbled remains of its predecessor, which collapsed in 1924. The foundation dates to AD 976 and is an active archeological site, where scientists uncovered a miniature silver pagoda containing what is said to be a lock of the Buddha's hair; it's on display in a separate hall. You can watch the dig before climbing (or riding an elevator part way) up five stories, each with remarkable paintings and carvings. Most noteworthy is a vast carved tableau from the Chinese opera *White Snake,* whose heroine was imprisoned in the pagoda. The view of the lake is breathtaking, particularly, as the name suggests, at sunset. ✉ *15 Nanshan Lu* ☎ *0571/8796–4515* ⊕ *www.leifengta.com. cn* 💲 *Y40* ◷ *May–Oct., daily 8 AM–10 PM; Apr. and Nov., daily 8 AM–9 PM; Dec.–Mar., daily 8–5:30; last admission 30 mins before closing.*

FodorśChoice
★

㉚ **Hangzhou Aquarium** (Hangzhou Haidi Shijie), or Underwater World, on West Lake's eastern shore, is a small but well-designed aquarium with a walk-through glass tunnel in its main tank and several hands-on exhibits. ✉ *49 Nanshan Lu* ☎ *0571/8706–9500* 💲 *Y50* ◷ *Daily 8:30–5.*

★ ㉛ The peaceful **Orioles Singing in the Willow Waves** (Liulang Wenying), a 51-acre park on West Lake's eastern shore, was an imperial garden during the Song Dynasty. It's a wonderful place to relax on a bench or in the grass and watch boats on the lake, school children on field trips, old men playing the game Go, and amateur photographers framing the countless bridges and blossoms on the grounds. Orioles still sing here, though not in the "willow waves," but in cages scattered among the park's pavilions. ✉ *Nanshan Lu.*

㉜ **Children's Park** (Ertong Gongyuan), on West Lake's eastern shore, is a kitschy park with playgrounds and 50 rides. ✉ *Nanshan Lu* ☎ *0571/ 8798–1770* 💲 *Y3; Y1–Y10 per ride* ◷ *Daily 8:30–4:30.*

㉝ The **Temple of the Soul's Retreat** (Lingyin Si) was founded in AD 326 by Hui Li, a Buddhist monk from India (Hui Li was his Chinese name). Reportedly, he looked at the mountains surrounding the site of the current temple and exclaimed, "This is the place where the souls of immortals retreat," hence the name. Perhaps even more than the temple itself, this site is famous for the Buddhist figures carved into the limestone of the mountain—named the **Peak that Flew from Afar** (Feilai Feng)—that faces the temple. From the 10th to the 14th centuries, monks and artists carved 338 stone iconographical images on the mountain's face and in caves.

FodorśChoice
★

Unfortunately, the destruction wrought by the Red Guards in Hangzhou during the Cultural Revolution is nowhere more evident than here, even though admirable attempts have been made to restore much that was damaged.

The temple itself, across from the Buddhist carvings, is one of China's ten large Zen (Chan) Buddhist temples and is definitely worth visiting. However, as one of Hangzhou's most popular attractions, the temple is always crowded. Avoid the place on weekends and holidays if possible. ⊠ *Lingyin Si Lu, west of the city* ☎ *0571/8796–9691* 🔄 *Park Y25, temple Y20* ⊙ *Park daily 5:30 AM–6 PM; temple daily 7–5.*

③④ The **China Tea Museum** (Zhongguo Cha Ye Bowuguan), west of the lake, explains the history, growing practices, and serving customs tied to this national drink. ⊠ *Longjing Lu, Shuangfeng Village* ☎ *0571/8796–4221* 🔄 *Free* ⊙ *Daily 8:30–4:45.*

③⑤ A short ride southwest of the lake takes you to the **Dragon Well Tea Park** (Longjing Wencha), where you can buy the local Long Jing green tea from people who are serious about quality. The park, set amid tea plantations, is the site of the well from which water for the best tea is drawn. Tea sellers may invite you to taste the tea, often at their homes. The prices seem ridiculous until you take a sip: there really is a difference. However, be sure to bargain for a good price. Tea picked from the season's first crop, between April 5 and 21, is the most expensive. The lowest-grade tea leaves can be had for Y5 to Y7 an ounce, while top-quality longjing tea leaves average Y100 to Y125 an ounce. ⊠ *Longjing Lu* 🔄 *Y10* ⊙ *Daily 7:30–5:30.*

③⑥ Almost directly south of the lake, about 15 minutes by bus, the **Running Tiger Dream Spring** (Hupao Meng Quan) has a temple built on a dream. According to legend, Qi Gong, a traveling monk, decided this setting would be perfect for a temple, but as there was no stream or other water in the place, he couldn't build one. Sleeping on the ground, he dreamed that two tigers came and tore up the earth around him. When he awoke, he was lying next to the stream that they had dug for him. He duly built the temple. The grounds have a bamboo grove, a nondescript teahouse, a modern statue of the dreamer with his tigers, and an intriguing "dripping wall." This cutout part of the mountainside is so porous and moist that it exudes water from its surface. Many locals come here to fill their water jugs, believing the water has special qualities—and it does. If you don't believe it, ask one of the people working in the temple souvenir shop to float a coin on the surface of the water to prove it. ⊠ *Hupao Lu, south of West Lake* 🔄 *Y15* ⊙ *Daily 6:45 AM–6 PM.*

③⑦ At the **China National Silk Museum** (Zhongguo Sichou Bowuguan), well-curated galleries, signed in Chinese and English, explore the history of the "queen of fibers." On display are weaves and samples—some replicas, some real—of Chinese silk clothing worn during different dynasties. Upstairs there's an art gallery. The first-floor shop sells clothing and silk by the meter. The museum is south of the lake, on the road to Jade Emperor Hill. ⊠ *73-1 Yuhuangshan Lu* ☎ *0571/8706–2129* 🔄 *Free* ⊙ *Daily 8–6.*

A few miles south of the city, atop **Moon Mountain** (Yuelin Shan) and overlooking the banks of the Qiantang River, stands the impressive

38 Pagoda of Six Harmonies (Liuhe Ta). From the outside, it seems as if this structure has more floors than it does; there are actually seven stories, and you can climb to the top for great views of the river. On the 18th day of the eighth lunar month, the pagoda is packed with people, all wanting the best seat for "Qiantang Reversal." On this day the flow of the river reverses itself, creating large waves that for centuries have delighted observers. Behind the pagoda is an extensive park with a pagoda exhibition: expert re-creations of a hundred or so miniature pagodas, representing every Chinese style, are on permanent display here. ☒ *Fuxing Jie, south of Hangzhou* ☒ *Y20; Y10 to climb pagoda* ☎ *0571/ 8659–1401* ☉ *Daily 6–6.*

Where to Stay & Eat

At this writing, several hotels were under construction as a result of the selection of Hangzhou to host the 2006 World Leisure Expo. The added competition has put pressure on existing hotels to upgrade facilities or drop prices—meaning there are bargains to be had, especially among the older Chinese hotels whose facilities can't match the newcomers.

The city's dining scene, likewise, is on the rise. Along the eastern shore of West Lake lies Xihu Tiandi—"West Lake Heaven on Earth"—an upscale dining and shopping complex patterned on Shanghai's Xintiandi. Along the surrounding Nanshan Lu bar and restaurant district, you'll find good Indian, Italian, Thai, and Continental fare.

★ **$–$$$**   ✕ **Louwailou Restaurant.** Founded in 1848, this restaurant on the banks of West Lake is Hangzhou's most famous—and therefore a bit overrun with tourists during peak season. Among the Hangzhou specialties served here are a shrimp dish made with Long Jing tea leaves and West Lake vinegar fish, a delicate, tart dish celebrated in a poem painted on the restaurant's wall. The fish dishes are made with fish raised in a small sectioned-off area of West Lake in front of the restaurant. Ask for a table upstairs in the Russian Hall, a formal dining room with large windows overlooking the lake. ☒ *30 Gushan Lu* ☎ *0571/ 8796–9023* ▤ *AE, MC, V.*

$$ ✕ **Haveli.** Haveli brings an authentic taste of India to Hangzhou, with a short but solid list of classic dishes: samosas, lamb vindaloo, and chicken *makhni* (chicken cooked with butter), plus fantastic mango lassis. The artful use of gauze curtains as dividers among the candlelighted tables makes the restaurant feel intimate rather than small; a high peaked ceiling with exposed wood beams also opens up the room. A large patio handles the overflow, but if you dine outdoors you'll miss the belly dancer who performs nightly. ☒ *77 Nanshan Lu* ☎ *0571/8707–9677* ⌲ *Reservations essential* ▤ *AE, DC, MC, V.*

¢–$$ ✕ **Zhiweiguan Restaurant.** The first floor here is a pay-as-you-go dim sum cafeteria. With no English menus you'll need to rely on body language to order a bamboo steamer of their famous dumplings. The second and fourth floors offer a much more pleasant dining experience (with English menus), especially the peaceful dining room just off the banquet room on the fourth floor. Try the West Lake beef soup, the Zhiwei duck, or Dongpo pork, a Hangzhou delicacy. ⊠ *83 Renhe Lu* ☎ *0571/ 8706–5871* ⊟ *No credit cards.*

$$$–$$$$ ⊡ **Hyatt Regency Hangzhou.** After a delay of several years, the long-anticipated Hyatt Regency is slated to open its doors in June 2005. Its location along the Hubin Lu pedestrian walkway ensures that most rooms will have lake views. Facilities will include an alfresco café, a tea shop, a day spa, and programs for kids. ⊠ *28 Hubin Lu, 310006* ☎ *0571/ 8779–1234* ᐁ *0571/8779–1818* ⊕ *http://hangzhou.regency.hyatt.com* ↩ *350 rooms, 20 suites* ◊ *Restaurant, café, tea shop, room service, in-room data ports, in-room safes, minibars, cable TV, tennis court, golf privileges, indoor pool, gym, sauna, spa, steam room, 2 bars, shops, children's programs (ages 1–12), dry cleaning, laundry service, concierge, business services, convention center, no-smoking rooms* ⊟ *AE, DC, MC, V.*

$$$–$$$$ ⊡ **Radisson Plaza Hotel Hangzhou.** Located in the business district, the Radisson Plaza has the right blend of facilities and comfort for its predominantly corporate clientele. Warm wood-paneled landings lead to soothing rooms—only 15 per floor—decorated with soft beiges and plush carpets. King-size rooms have separate showers and tub. Lake views are possible only if you crane your neck. The decent-size gym has separate cardio and weight rooms overlooking a garden. There are three executive floors, and the Unkai Sushi and Summer Palace restaurants are nice spots for business dinners. ⊠ *333 Tiyuchang Lu, 310006* ☎ *0571/ 8515–8888* ᐁ *0571/8515–7777* ⊕ *www.radisson.com/hangzhoucn* ↩ *239 rooms, 45 suites* ◊ *5 restaurants, patisserie, room service, in-room data ports, in-room safes, some kitchenettes, minibars, some microwaves, cable TV, indoor pool, gym, hair salon, hot tub, massage, sauna, steam room, bicycles, billiards, bowling, 3 bars, lobby lounge, piano, shops, baby-sitting, dry cleaning, laundry service, concierge, concierge floor, Internet, business services, convention center, airport shuttle, travel services, no-smoking rooms, no-smoking floors* ⊟ *AE, DC, MC, V.*

$$$–$$$$
Fodor's Choice
★ ⊡ **Shangri-La Hotel Hangzhou.** The best hotel in Hangzhou, the Shangri-La, once the site of the Feng Lin Temple, is a scenic and historic landmark. The hotel's 40 hillside acres of camphor and bamboo trees merge seamlessly into the nearby gardens and walkways surrounding West Lake and Solitary Hill Island. Spread over two wings, the large rooms have a formal air, with high ceilings and heavy damask couches and bedspreads. Request a room overlooking the lake; the Horizon Club's patio has the best views. The health club and restaurants are all top caliber. ⊠ *78 Beishan Lu, 310007* ☎ *0571/8797–7951* ᐁ *0571/8707–3545* ⊕ *www. shangri-la.com* ↩ *355 rooms, 28 suites* ◊ *3 restaurants, room service, in-room data ports, in-room safes, minibars, cable TV, tennis court, indoor pool, gym, hair salon, hot tub, massage, sauna, steam room, bicycles, billiards, bar, lobby lounge, shops, baby-sitting, dry cleaning, laundry service, concierge, concierge floor, Internet, business services, convention center, airport shuttle, travel services, no-smoking rooms* ⊟ *AE, DC, MC, V.*

★ **$$–$$$** ⊡ **Sofitel Westlake Hangzhou.** A stone's throw from West Lake and Xihu Tiandi, the Sofitel has made waves on the lodging scene since quietly opening in late 2003. Brown-gauze curtains and etched-glass-and-wood columns divide the distinctive lobby, with its gold-and-black mural of three Hangzhou landmarks: Pagoda of Six Harmonies, Protecting Chu Pagoda, and Evening Sunlight at Thunder Peak Pagoda. The rooms—most of which have lake views—are thoughtfully designed, with sleek oval desks, gauze-covered headboards, and a glass privacy screen in the bathrooms. The roman-style pool overcomes its drab basement location. ✉ *333 Xihu Dadao, 310002* ☎ *0571/8707–5858* 📠 *0571/8707–8383* ⊕ *www.accor.com* ⇆ *186 rooms, 15 suites* ⚴ *4 restaurants, room service, in-room data ports, in-room safes, minibars, cable TV with movies, indoor pool, gym, hair salon, massage, sauna, spa, bar, lobby lounge, piano, shops, dry cleaning, laundry service, concierge, concierge floor, Internet, business services, convention center, airport shuttle, no-smoking rooms* ▭ *AE, DC, MC, V.*

$$ 🏨 **World Trade Center Grand Hotel Zhejiang.** Although it targets conventioneers, this hotel is a great choice for leisure travelers, too. The two-story gym, complete with a spa, is a strong selling point; its spectacular 20-meter indoor pool has a swim-up bar. Entertainment options range from karaoke to high tea to mah-jongg. The fair-sized rooms are well maintained and have nice views of Precious Stone Hill, a few minutes' walk away. Staff members at the front desk, though harried, are efficient and have a decent command of English. The hotel is known for its art and antiques collection, on display throughout the halls and lobby. ✉ *122 Shuguang Lu, 310007* ☎ *0571/8799–0888* 📠 *0571/8795–0050* ⊕ *www.wtcgh.com* ⇆ *360 rooms, 33 suites* ⚴ *5 restaurants, patisserie, room service, in-room data ports, some in-room faxes, minibars, cable TV with movies, tennis court, indoor pool, health club, hair salon, hot tub, sauna, spa, billiards, Ping-Pong, squash, lobby lounge, library, nightclub, baby-sitting, dry cleaning, laundry service, concierge, concierge floors, Internet, business services, convention center, no-smoking rooms* ▭ *AE, DC, MC, V.*

$–$$ 🏨 **Dragon Hotel.** Within walking distance of Precious Stone Hill and the Yellow Dragon Cave, this hotel stands in relatively peaceful and attractive surroundings. It's a large hotel, but seems smaller because the buildings are spread around peaceful courtyards with ponds, a waterfall, and a gazebo. Two towers house the fair-sized guest rooms, which are decorated in pale greens and blues; the cream wallpaper is peeling in places. Although it has plenty of facilities, the hotel lacks the polish of its Western competitors and the next-door World Trade Center Grand Hotel. ✉ *120 Shuguang Lu, 310007* ☎ *0571/8799–8833* 📠 *0571/8799–8090* ⊕ *www.dragon-hotel.com* ⇆ *468 rooms, 28 suites* ⚴ *3 restaurants, room service, in-room data ports, in-room safes, minibars, cable TV, tennis court, pool, gym, hair salon, hot tub, massage, sauna, bicycles, lobby lounge, shops, baby-sitting, dry cleaning, laundry service, concierge, Internet, business services, convention center, travel services, no-smoking rooms, no-smoking floors* ▭ *AE, DC, MC, V.*

$–$$ 🏨 **Lakeview Hotel.** True to its name, the Lakeview Hotel has good views of West Lake from its corner at the lake's northeastern shore. The top-floor Solmer Restaurant, in particular, is a great vantage point for watching the sun set over the lake. A blue-and-gray color scheme decorates the rooms, and the furniture has some nice inlaid detailing. The hotel is popular with domestic and Japanese travelers, for whom state-of-the-art, heated Japanese toilets have been installed in the bathrooms. The staff's English is shaky, but the hotel is marketing itself more toward Westerners. ⊠ 2 *Huancheng Xilu, 310006* ☎ *0571/8707–8888* 🖷 *0571/8707–1350* ⊕ *www.lakeviewhotelhz.com* ➯ *347 rooms, 14 suites* ⚫ *3 restaurants, room service, in-room data ports, in-room safes, minibars, cable TV, indoor pool, gym, hair salon, massage, sauna, bicycles, billiards, lobby lounge, piano, shops, baby-sitting, dry cleaning, laundry service, concierge, meeting rooms, travel services, no-smoking rooms* ⊟ *AE, DC, MC, V.*

¢ 🖭 **Hangzhou Overseas Chinese Hotel.** In spite of its name, this budget hotel welcomes visitors of any origin, although the staff's English skills are shaky. Its location is the main draw, just steps from West Lake and the Hubin Lu pedestrian walkway. Rooms on the fifth floor have the best lake views. Modern beige wallpaper and carpeting help brighten the fairly large rooms but can't hide the cracked walls and scratched woodwork in this older state-owned hotel. You can hire a car and driver here to tour the outlying area. ⊠ *39 Hubin Lu, 310006* ☎ *0571/8707–4401* 🖷 *0571/8707–4978* ➯ *218 rooms, 21 suites* ⚫ *2 restaurants, in-room safes, minibars, hair salon, massage, sauna, 2 bars, shops, baby sitting, laundry service, business services, meeting rooms, travel services* ⊟ *AE, DC, MC, V.*

Nightlife & the Arts

Nanshan Lu is the epicenter of Hangzhou's nightlife scene. The laidback **Kana Pub** (⊠ 152 Nanshan Lu ☎ 0571/8706–3228) is the highlight of the strip and an expat favorite for its well-mixed cocktails, live music, and the hospitality of its owner. The warm, muted, brown-and-yellow interior of **Paradise Rock** (⊠ 39 Hubin Lu, next to Hangzhou Overseas Chinese Hotel ☎ 0571/8707–4401), a British-style pub, is perfect for light drinks and conversation. The friendly staff at the **Shamrock** (⊠ 70 Zhongshan Zhonglu ☎ 0571/8702–8760), Hangzhou's first Irish pub, serves Guinness and Kilkenny pints, bottled-beer specials, and great food.

Yue Opera performances take place daily from 8:45 AM to 11:45 AM and 1:45 PM to 4:45 PM at the **Huanglong Dong Yuanyuan Mingshu Yuan theater** (⊠ 16 Shuguang Lu ☎ 0571/8798–5860), at the Yellow Dragon Cave. The performances are free, but you must pay the Y15 park admission.

Shopping

The best souvenirs to buy in Hangzhou are green tea and silk, but all sorts of wooden crafts, silk fans and umbrellas, and antiques are available in small shops sprinkled around town. For the best Longjing tea, head to the tea plantations at Dragon Well Tea Park. Around town, especially along Yanan Lu, you can spot the small tea shops by the large woklike tea roasters at each store's entrance.

China Silk City (Zhongguo Sichou Cheng; ⊠ 253 Xinhua Lu, between Fengqi Lu and Tiyuchang Lu) sells silk ties, pajamas, and shirts, plus silk straight off the bolt. The **Xihu Longjing Tea Company** (⊠ 602 Fengqi Lu ☎ 0571/8510–3878) has a nice selection of Longjing Tea.

Although it has been relocated several times, Hangzhou's **night market** (⊠ Renhe Lu east of Huansha Lu) is still thriving. Merchants sell silk clothing and accessories of every kind—ties, scarves, pillow covers—as well as knockoff purses, silver jewelry, and alleged antiques. You'll find the same items at multiple stalls, so don't hesitate to walk away if the price isn't right. It's open nightly 6 PM–10:30 PM.

Hangzhou A to Z

To research prices, get advice from other travelers, and book travel arrangements, visit www.fodors.com.

AIR TRAVEL
There are more than 30 regular flights (often daily, depending on the season) between Hangzhou and major Chinese cities, plus international flights to Tokyo, Osaka, Seoul, and Bangkok. You can contact the CAAC office for flight information. Dragonair runs two daily flights between Hangzhou and Hong Kong.

🚹 **CAAC** ⊠ 160 Tiyuchang Lu ☎ 0571/8515-4259. **Dragonair** ⊠ 5F, Radisson Plaza Hotel Hangzhou, 333 Tiyuchang Lu ☎ 0571/8506-8388.

AIRPORTS
Hangzhou's Xiaoshan International Airport (HGH) is 15 km (9 mi) from downtown. Most international travelers fly into Shanghai's Pudong International Airport (PVG), a 2½-hour drive to the northeast.

🚹 Airport Information **Xiaoshan International Airport** ☎ 0571/8666-1236 Ext. 3.

TRANSFERS Major hotels provide limo service to and from Xiaoshan International Airport. The taxi ride between the airport and downtown costs around Y120. Several public bus routes connect the airport to city locations. The fare costs Y1, or Y2 for an air-conditioned bus. A bus leaves daily for the airport from the CAAC office every 40 minutes during the day for about Y15.

From Shanghai's Hongqiao International Airport you can take a long-distance bus to Hangzhou; there are eight departures between 10 AM and 7:30 PM, and tickets cost Y85. Pudong International Airport also has long-distance bus service to Hangzhou. There are six departures between 10 AM and 7 PM; tickets cost Y100.

🚹 **CAAC Office** ⊠ 160 Tiyunchang Lu ☎ 0571/8515-4259. **Hongqiao Airport Long Distance Bus** ☎ 021/6268-8899. **Pudong Airport Long Distance Bus** ☎ 021/6834-5743.

BIKE TRAVEL
Traffic makes biking a dodgy endeavor in downtown Hangzhou. However, the two West Lake causeways, Baidi and Sudi, are closed to automobile traffic and perfect for cycling. Major hotels have bike rentals, as does the Orioles Singing in the Willow Waves park and a small stall on Solitary Hill Island. Rental rates are Y8–Y30 per hour, with a deposit of Y100–Y300 usually required.

BOAT & FERRY TRAVEL
You can travel overnight between Hangzhou and Suzhou on the lovely Grand Canal. Tickets are available at the Hangzhou Wulingmen Dock.

The boat departs daily from Hangzhou at around 5:30 PM and arrives in Suzhou the next morning at 7 AM.

You can rent a two- or four-seat paddleboat for use on West Lake, but you won't be able to dock at the islands. Official boats run to Three Pools Reflecting the Moon island from Solitary Hill Island whenever they have enough passengers—usually about every 40 minutes. Walking around the lake, you'll be approached by vendors selling rides on private four-seaters. These are more expensive but quieter and will go wherever you want. The going rate is Y45 per person for an hour ride.
Boat & Ferry Information Hangzhou Wulingmen Dock ⊠ 238 Huangcheng Beilu ☎ 0571/8515-3185.

BUS TRAVEL

TO HANGZHOU The bus hub of Zhejiang Province, Hangzhou has several bus stations. The East Bus Station is the town's biggest, with several hundred departures per day to cities as far away as Beijing and closer destinations like Suzhou. Buses to Suzhou and Shanghai leave every 20 minutes from the East Station. The West Bus Station has several buses daily to the nearby mountain area of Huangshan, in Anhui Province. Make sure you check with your hotel or travel agent about which bus station you need to use.
East Bus Station ⊠ 215 Liangshan Xilu ☎ 0571/8696-4011. **West Bus Station** ⊠ 89 Tianmushan Lu ☎ 0571/8502-1941. **Bus Information** ☎ 0571/8604-6666.

WITHIN Nearly every street in Hangzhou except the causeways has bus stops;
HANGZHOU the buses come frequently and cost Y1, or Y2 for air-conditioned buses. However, you'd be lucky to find an uncrowded bus anytime before 9 PM. If you're willing to brave the crowds, though, ask at your hotel desk or the Zhejiang Foreign Language Bookstore (446 Yanan Lu) about English-language bus maps. The most popular tourist route is No. 507, which runs along the north side of the lake on its way to the Temple of the Soul's Retreat. No. 508 heads to the Dragon Well Tea Park plantations from the zoo.

Tourist trolleys shuttle passengers among West Lake tourist sights, the train station, and downtown stops. Route 1 runs between Temple of the Soul's Retreat and Wu Hill, with stops along the east side of the lake. Route 9 travels a circular route along the northeastern shore, starting and ending at Yellow Dragon Cave, with stops at the Botanical Garden, two lakeshore parks, and Yue Fei Mausoleum. Prices range from Y1 to Y5. Most trolleys operate daily 8–5:30.
Hangzhou Public Bus Transport Corporation ☎ 0571/8519-1122.

ENGLISH-LANGUAGE MEDIA

Many hotels provide copies of *In Touch Zhejiang*, a bimonthly magazine with hotel, restaurant, and nightlife listings.
English-Language Bookstores Zhejiang Foreign Language Bookstore ⊠ 446 Yanan Lu ☎ 0571/8506-9826.

EMERGENCIES

Ambulances are merely a transport service; the attendants do not provide medical care. Instead, take a taxi directly to the hospital.
Emergency Services EMS ☎ 120. **Police** ☎ 110.

Hospitals **Hangzhou Red Cross Hospital** ✉ 38 Huancheng Donglu ☎ 0571/8518-6042 or 0571/8518-3137. **Run Run Shaw Hospital** (Shao Yifu Hospital) ✉ 3 Qingchun Donglu ☎ 0571/8609-0073. **Zhejiang Medical University Affiliated Hospital No. 1** ✉ 79 Qingchun Lu ☎ 0571/8723-6756.

TAXIS

Cabs are in great supply in Hangzhou; the metallic green ones are considered the most reliable. The base fare is Y10 for 4 km (2½ mi), Y2 for each subsequent kilometer up to 8 km (5 mi), then Y2.4 per kilometer. Beware of drivers who take the scenic route instead of the straight one.

Taxi Company **Zhejiang Overseas Tourist Taxi Company** ☎ 0571/8707-8855.

TOURS

Hotels can set up tours for interested groups. The business center of the Shangri-La Hotel Hangzhou offers half- and full-day tours at prices ranging from Y110 to Y650 per person, depending on the size of the group. Zhejiang China International Travel Service (CITS) charges Y440 for a full-day tour that includes a car and an English-speaking guide; the fare covers as many passengers in your group that can fit in the car. Hawkers or taxi drivers at the train station or in front of your hotel may offer tours; although these guides can be as good as the official ones, their English is often minimal.

Shangri-La Hotel Hangzhou business center ✉ 78 Beishan Lu ☎ 0571/8797-7951 Ext. 24. **Zhejiang China International Travel Service** ✉ 1 Shihan Lu ☎ 0571/8505-9025.

TRAIN TRAVEL

Train travel between Shanghai and Hangzhou is quick and convenient—there are seven express trains daily in each direction, and the trip takes two hours. The train station is crowded and difficult to manage, but hotel travel desks can often book tickets for you for a small fee.

Hangzhou train station ✉ 1 Tiancheng Lu ☎ 0571/8782-9418. **Train-ticket booking Hot Line** ☎ 0571/8782-9983.

TRAVEL AGENCIES

Many hotels have their own travel agencies and offer visitor information.

Agencies **Hangzhou Overseas Tourist Co.** ✉ 239 Xihu Dadao ☎ 0571/8770-9770. **Zhejiang China International Travel Service** ✉ 1 Shihan Lu ☎ 0571/8505-9025.

VISITOR INFORMATION

Tourist Information **Hangzhou Travel and Tourism Bureau** ✉ 3 Huanglong Dong ☎ 0571/8796-2723. **Travel-information hot line** ☎ 0571/96123. **Zhejiang China International Travel Service** ✉ 1 Shihan Lu ☎ 0571/8505-9025.

UNDERSTANDING BEIJING & SHANGHAI

BEIJING AT A GLANCE

Fast Facts

Type of government: Independent unit administered directly by the national Communist government, with a mayor and deputies appointed by the Beijing Municipal People's Congress, assembled through local elections every five years.
Population: 13.8 million
Population Density: 812 people per square km (2,102 people per square mi)

Language: Mandarin (official), Putonghua (Beijing dialect)
Literacy: 95%
Ethnic groups: Han 96%; Hui, Man, Mongolian, and other minorities 4%

I don't know exactly what democracy is. But we need more of it.
— Anonymous Chinese student, during protests in Tiananmen Square, 1989

Geography & Environment

Latitude: 39° N (same as Ankara, Turkey; Lisbon Portugal; Sacramento, California)
Longitude: 116° E (same as Perth, Australia)
Elevation: 63 meters (209 feet)
Land area: 17,000 square km (6,564 square mi)
Terrain: Bordered by mountains in the west, north, and northeast, with the vast North China Plain to the south; highest point, Mount Lingshan, 2,303 meters (7,556 feet)
Natural hazards: Earthquakes, fires, sandstorms

Environmental issues: Air pollution from the burning of coal has reached a critical point and city officials have created 40 "coal-free zones" in the city. Vehicle emissions are contributing to poor air quality as well. The city has converted many official gasoline vehicles to natural gas; there are also plans for natural gas pipelines' that would reduce reliance on coal. Water shortages are a persisting problem, as is a lack of wastewater treatment capacity.

Economy

Per capita income: 13,883 yuan ($1,786)
Unemployment: 1.4%
Work force: 7 million

Major industries: Chemicals, electronic equipment, heavy machinery, iron- and steelworks, petrochemicals, plastics, railroads, synthetic fibers, textiles

Did You Know?

• Known as "the navel of China," 98-acre Tiananmen Square is the world's largest square. It's also home to the largest building used for theatrical performances in the world, the National People's Congress Building.

• Calling Beijing "Peking" isn't just wrong, it's a linguistic anachronism. During the Qing Dynasty the "k" sound in Mandarin became a "j" sound, transforming the pronunciation of the name French missionaries heard as "Peking."

• Beijing's biggest export is mobile phones. In 2003, the city shipped 12.5 million of them, worth $1.2 billion.

• The largest dancing dragon in the world was brought to life near Beijing in 2000. It took 3,200 people to get the 10,000 foot beast to dance.

• There are 84,000 guest rooms in Beijing. By comparison, New York has 66,000 rooms.

• Beijing University's library is the largest academic library in China, with more than 4 million volumes, 25 percent of which are thread-bound.

• With more than 1,630 vehicles, Beijing has the largest fleet of natural-gas buses in the world.

SHANGHAI AT A GLANCE

Fast Facts

Nickname: Pearl of the Orient, Paris of China

Type of government: One of four municipalities in China directly administrated directly by the central Communist government

Population: 7.5 million (city); 16.7 million (metro)

Population Density: 1,518 people per square km (3,795 people per square mi)

Language: Mandarin Chinese (official), Shanghainese (dialect of Wu Chinese)

Ethnic groups: 99.5% han; Hui, Man, Mongolian, other 0.5%

Religion: Buddhist and Taoist 98%; Christian 1%; other 1%

Of all the inventions that have helped to unify China, perhaps the airplane is the most outstanding. Its ability to annihilate distance has been in direct proportion to its achievements in assisting to annihilate suspicion and misunderstanding.
— Madame Chiang Kai-shek (b. 1897), Chinese sociologist, in the *Shanghai Evening Post*, March 12, 1937.

Geography & Environment

Latitude: 31° N (same as Austin, Texas; Jerusalem, Israel)

Longitude: 121° E (same as Manila, Philippines)

Elevation: 7 meters (26 feet)

Land area: 6,218 square km (2,400 square mi) (city); 11,000 square km (4,400 square mi) (metro)

Terrain: Chang Jiang delta, facing the East China Sea (part of the Pacific Ocean); the city straddles the Huangpu River.

Natural hazards: Earthquakes, floods, tsunamis, typhoons.

Environmental issues: Sewage and industrial pollution along the Yangzi River are causing toxic algae and other problems along the east coast. Shanghai's air is considered heavily polluted by U.S. standards. The government is working to get older cars and motorcycles off the road, replacing them with LPG and electric buses and taxis. Coal-fired power plants are also being replaced with natural gas plants, to reduce emissions. Sufficient supply of clean water is a persistent concern; residents have about one-tenth of the fresh water available in most cities worldwide.

Economy

Per capita income: 14,867 yuan ($1,795)

Unemployment: 4.9%

Major industries: Aircraft, chemicals, consumer goods, diamond-processing operations, electrical, electronic, and computer equipment, gas-extracting, heavy machinery, motor vehicles, oil-refining, pharmaceuticals, plastics, publishing, shipbuilding, steelworks, textile mills, tractors, turbines.

Did You Know?

• The name Shanghai means "on the sea."

• At 1575 feet high, Shanghai's Jin Mao Tower is the third-tallest building in the world. It also contains the world's highest hotel, on its 53rd through 87th floors.

• To "shanghai" someone means to put them aboard a ship by force. The word comes from 19th-century scams to secure sailors for voyages to eastern Asia. It may be the only city name turned into a verb worldwide.

• American visitors with layovers in Pudong or Honqiao airports can look around the city for 48 hours without a Chinese visa.

• One of the biggest annoyances for Shanghai residents is noise pollution. Government officials are bombarded with complaints about the loud combination of traffic, construction, and narrow streets throughout the city.

• Shanghai is fighting a never-ending battle with silt. The Yangzi deposits enough to extend the city's shoreline by 25 feet every year.

• Like to shop with 1.07 million people in one store in one day? Then head for the Nextage Shanghai, which set a world record with that number of daily shoppers in 1995.

CHINA'S DANCE

APED TO AN OLD SHOP WINDOW in Suzhou, a city more than 2,500 years old with its walls still intact, is an advertisement for cellular phones: a young Chinese woman holds a phone to her ear as she stands on the Great Wall, the long structure twisting off into the distance behind her. "Get connected," says the ad. "This is the new China."

Bamboo scaffolding and gleaming department stores, construction cranes looming over wooden villages, KFC and chopsticks, yak herders and cell-phone abusers within miles of each other, communism and capitalism coexisting—China has more paradoxes than it has dialects. To visit China now is to witness a country revolutionizing itself in the cities and struggling to stay alive in the countryside.

The fourth-largest country in the world, holding the world's largest population, China is chiefly challenged by questions of cohesiveness—how to bring a country speaking hundreds of different dialects together under one rule. Beginning with the Zhou Dynasty (1100–771 BC), Chinese governors held the country together not only by force but by claiming a heaven-sent legitimacy known as the Mandate of Heaven. The mandate was a convenient claim of legitimacy, as anyone who led a successful rebellion could assert his victory was predicated upon the support of the gods. The traditional belief was that heaven would demonstrate disapproval of evil rulers through natural disasters like droughts and earthquakes, disease, and floods.

Today, as China's mesh of socialist and capitalist policies brings instability to the country, it is becoming unclear who holds the mandate. Are the heirs to Mao's revolution the conservative members of the Communist Party, or are President Hu Jintao and other reformers intent on imbuing the national economy with a capitalist bent? Whatever the case, it's clear that as the country continues to modernize, especially with Hong Kong under its belt, communism appears to be taking the back seat to a still undefined front seat, neither capitalism in a Western sense nor communism as in the years of Mao. The Chinese government has found itself in an awkward situation. If it tries to clamp down, it will surely lose in the race for modernization. If it allows modernization to continue, its control is inevitably weakened.

Ranging from the Three Gorges Dam, a colossal project that is uprooting 2 million people, to the perpetual construction of skyscrapers crowding the cities' skylines, the Chinese landscape is quickly changing. In some respects, it's as if the people had been plucked from their traditional homes and transported 100 years into a future. Foreign companies and joint ventures have demanded that single men and women climb a corporate ladder at an accelerated pace; eating habits have changed from family style to a quick bite at McDonald's; grocery stores have begun to replace outdoor markets; bars and discos stay open all night. The country has become more modern, but what does that mean to a nation that looks back on more than 5,000 years of history?

HE ANCIENT PHILOSOPHY OF Confucianism laid a foundation for Chinese ethics and morals that still survives today, teaching respect, selflessness, obedience, and a sense of community. Unlike Americans, who prize their individuality and independence, the Chinese believe it is important to stay within and abide by a community. Shame is considered a much graver emotion than guilt: the Chinese judge themselves according to how they believe they are perceived by those whom they love and respect. As a new generation works the corporate life in cities away from home, how this undeniably Chinese characteristic will be affected is the subject of much debate.

The Chinese believe that, no matter where you were born, where you live, or what your native tongue, if you have Chinese ancestry, you are still Chinese. Their sense of pride about emerging as a colossal force in the global economy is combined with a deep sense of race that holds the country tentatively together. Paradoxically, China is busy buying up Western products, from french fries to Hollywood action movies. Nike is cool. Madonna is hip. This external desire for Western style coexists comfortably, though ironically, with a perennial internal nationalism. The Chinese have so internalized their landscape that, for example, the TV tower in Shanghai is for them comparable to the Jade Buddha Temple down the street as a sight not to be missed; advertisements in subway stations are celebrated as a new form of artistic expression; the elderly happily practice tai chi to the beat of rock music.

More than 70% of the mainland population lives along the eastern seaboard, leaving the westernmost provinces barren and nearly vacant, in part because only 20% of China's land is arable. In the 1970s peasants' lifestyles improved as a result of Deng Xiao Ping's policy of allowing profit after government quotas had been met, but small plots of land and an ever-increasing population meant the new policy only provided limited relief. People still flock to the cities, creating a large homeless population. Although China appears to be overhauling itself, many residents of the smaller cities and villages are still living the way they did 100 years ago. As in other countries experiencing rapid development, there is a profound division between the growing middle class and unemployed farmworkers.

Excursions to small towns reveal just how much China relies on basic human power. Farm laborers stand up with their tools and wave as a train passes, a girl wearing a Nike jacket carries buckets swinging from a yoke over her shoulders, herds of sheep carry goods down dirt roads into the village center, local buses are crowded full of men and women carrying raw animal furs, and everywhere cycles of every description carry people and goods. Even in the cities, a surplus of men work with hammer and nail to build a skyscraper. Perhaps these images will disappear in a few years, but for now they reveal a country in the throes of revolution still holding on quite tightly to tradition.

During a visit to China, often the best moments are the ones you invent on your own, not what the hotel or the China International Travel Service (CITS) recommends. In this way you can enjoy China's hidden secrets—nature walks, bustling markets, small villages. Of course, the consequence of making up your own itinerary is having to follow a very cryptic and archaic route, one where the roads may not be paved, the train does not show up, hotels are not where they are supposed to be, and People's Liberation Army officers creep up out of nowhere. There is little peace, little comfort, and incredible markups for foreigners; keep an open mind and an adventurous spirit.

—Angela Yuan

RELIGION IN CHINA

ALTHOUGH CHINA IS OFFICIALLY ATHE-IST, it has historically adopted a pragmatic and eclectic attitude toward belief systems, and it has incorporated Taoism, Buddhism, Islam, and Christianity into its societal fabric. Indeed, the typical Chinese philosophy is a rich tapestry of Confucianism, Taoism, and Buddhism. In theory, Chinese have the freedom of religious belief, and their religious activities are protected by the Constitution. However, there are only two government-sanctioned sects of Christianity—the Catholic church without ties to Rome and the "Three-Self-Patriotic" Protestant church. Other "unauthorized" churches exist in many parts of China, where the local governments may tolerate them, attempt outright to control them, or offer them treatment that falls somewhere between the two.

Because of the hodgepodge of beliefs, it is difficult to pigeonhole people as belonging to any one religion. However, official figures put Buddhism in the forefront, with an estimated 100 million adherents. Traditional Taoism also is practiced. Official figures indicate there are 18 million Muslims, 10 million Protestants, and 4 million Catholics; unofficial estimates are much higher.

Religion often follows ethnic divisions. Hui, Uygur, Kazak, Kirgiz, Tatar, Ozbek, Tajik, Dongxiang, Salar, and Bonan, for example, follow Islam. Tibetans, Mongolians, Lhobas, Moinbas, Tus, and Yugurs subscribe to Lamaism (Tibetan Buddhism), while Dai, Blang, and Deang are largely Hinayana Buddhist. Many Miao, Yao, and Yi are Catholic or Protestant; Han are mainly divided among Buddhism, Protestantism, Catholicism, or Taoism.

Taoism

Taoism developed from the philosophical and naturalist text, the *Tao Te Ching*, believed to have been written by Lao Tzu, a contemporary of Confucius in the first century BC. Taking form in the second century, Taoism is one of two belief systems indigenous to China. Lao Tzu and his followers emphasized individual freedom, laissez-faire government, human spontaneity, and mystical experience. The goal of Taoism is to attain balance and harmony with nature and spiritual forces, as well as within oneself. Tao, the Way, is the journey to understanding the unseen reality behind appearances.

Confucianism

Confucianism, the other indigenous Chinese belief system, provided a large part of the foundation of the Chinese society and culture. Confucius (K'ung Fu-tzu) was a philosopher who lived from 551 to 479 BC. His philosophies shaped the mores and behaviors of the Chinese for nearly 2,000 years. Confucius believed that moral behavior stemmed from the fulfillment of traditional roles and hierarchies. He defined five basic relationships, which he called *wu lun*. Each relationship represents a reciprocal obligation.

- Emperor to Subject—An emperor must show his subjects kindness; a subject must be loyal.

- Father to Son—A father must provide protection and favor to his son; the son reciprocates with respect and obedience.

- Husband to Wife—A husband has the obligation to provide for his wife; a wife respectfully submits.

- Older brother to Younger brother—The older brother cares for his younger brother; the younger brother models himself after his older brother.

- Friend to Friend—The relationship between friends is one of mutual trust.

From this basic framework come ideas of hierarchy, group orientation, and respect for age and tradition. It's important to remember that the basis of this system is not the subjugation of one person by another. It is concern for one person by another. According to Confucian thought, when one's basic motivation is the well-being of another person, then one's behavior is moral.

Buddhism

Buddhism was begun in India by Siddhartha Gautama, a prince turned teacher and philosopher. The name Buddha means "awakened" or "enlightened." The ideals of Buddhism focus on achieving freedom from the cycle of death and rebirth and thereby entering into Nirvana, perfect and total peace and enlightenment.

The centerpiece of Buddhism is the Four Noble Truths:

• Life is suffering

• Desire is the cause of suffering

• When you cease to desire, you eliminate suffering

• Desire, and thus suffering, can be eliminated by following the Middle Way and the Eightfold Noble Path

The Middle Way is exactly that: a way of life that exists between the wanton sating of desire and zealous self-denial. The Eightfold Noble Truths consist of right views, intention, speech, conduct, livelihood, effort, attention, and meditation.

Buddhism reached China via foreign merchants on the trade routes to the west. By AD 166, Buddhism had a presence in the imperial court, although it remained primarily a religion practiced by foreigners until the beginning of the fourth century. By the end of the fifth century, it had swept across China. In Tibet, Buddhism evolved into Lamaism, also known as Tibetan Buddhism.

Islam

China was introduced to Islam by Arab and Persian merchants, probably during the 8th century. The Muslim God is Allah, and their prophet is Muhammad, who was born in Mecca around AD 570. The revelations of Muhammad were compiled in the Koran, which sets forth the four principle tenets of Islam:

• Faith in the absolute unity of Allah

• Belief in angels as messengers of Allah

• Belief in prophetic messengers (Muhammad being the last of these, following Jesus and the Old Testament prophets)

• Belief in a final judgment which will reward the faithful

Salvation is achieved through the Five Acts of Worship, or the Pillars of Islam:

• Physical and spiritual purification

• Prayer

• Giving of alms

• Fasting during the holy month of Ramadan

• The hajj, or pilgrimage to Mecca

SOCIAL ETIQUETTE

F YOU ARE INTRODUCED TO A GROUP OF PEOPLE (for example, if you tour a factory), you may be greeted with applause. You should also clap in greeting. While bows are the standard greeting, you may see handshakes, especially with foreigners. When greeting someone, follow his or her lead. Men can wait for a Chinese to offer his hand for a handshake or bow in reply to his bow. Women who want to shake hands will generally have to offer their hand first. A Chinese handshake is generally quite soft; don't use your power handshake or pump the other person's hand. You will not see people kissing hello or good-bye.

You may see people of the same gender holding hands; this is merely a sign of close friendship. However, it's unlikely that your Chinese friends will do this with you. Queuing is not common; be prepared to assert yourself in stores, at bus stops, and in post offices.

Expect to be stared at when you are out and about. Most Chinese are extremely curious about Westerners and staring is not considered rude. Privacy and personal space are not held sacred. If your Chinese counterpart stands closer to you than is comfortable, try not to back away, since doing so will send a negative signal.

On a personal level, physical contact between strangers is not appreciated. Don't try to pat someone on the back, or casually touch someone's arm. On an impersonal level, such as in crowded subways, buses, or trains, contact with others cannot be avoided and there is much pushing and shoving. No apology is necessary in these instances. Because it is forbidden for monks and Buddhist priests to have any physical contact with women, women should take care not to bump into or accidentally brush against them.

The Chinese prefer not to display their emotions in public, either verbally or nonverbally. If you are prone to animated gesturing and facial expressions, try to minimize them when speaking with Chinese.

It's considered unclean to put your fingers in your mouth for any reason, so don't lick your fingers! When visiting someone, keep your feet on the floor and off desks, tables, and other furniture.

Your posture is a reflection of your upbringing and education. Don't slouch and keep both feet on the floor; don't cross your legs. If you need to point, use your open hand, not one finger, which is rude. Never use your head or foot to point out a person. Don't offend by beckoning someone with one finger. Use your whole hand, palm down, and make a scratching motion with your fingers. Don't use your foot to move objects.

Spitting on the sidewalk is common in some parts of China, but it is definitely not good manners. You will also see people blowing their noses (without a tissue) onto the street.

"Going Dutch" does not translate into Chinese. If a colleague or friend pays for a meal or even a subway ride, try to pick up the tab the next time.

Ask for permission before taking pictures of a person. Respect your surroundings in terms of dress, decorum, and photography.

Chinese names have the family name first, the given names second. Therefore, Kai Chong Chen's family name is "Kai" and his given name is "Chong Chen." Given names are used only by family and close friends. Always address people by their family names and courtesy title (Miss Xie, Mr. Man, etc.). Use professional titles, such as Doctor, if you know it. Doctor, Mayor, Lawyer, and Professor are professional titles often heard. You will also hear business titles, such as General Manager, Manager, and Engineer. The title can be used without a family name.

Women do not take their husband's name when they marry. Refer to married women by Madam and their own last name.

Don't be surprised if you are asked questions you wouldn't be asked at home, such as "How old are you?," "Are you married?," and even "How much money do you make?" Don't be offended by these questions. If you do not wish to answer, just decline in a friendly tone with humor. For example, to the question about your income, you might say "Just enough to pay the bills, I'm afraid." Do not say how much you make without also mentioning the cost of living in your home country. A salary in the United States is generally several times that of a Chinese salary, and you run the risk of alienating co-workers if they perceive only the difference in salary without appreciating the difference in the cost of living.

There are many things that you will enjoy discussing with Chinese, such as travel, cuisine, art, and family. However, some topics are better left alone, such as politics and government (including the situation with Taiwan), and human rights. Other sensitive issues, such as the 1999 U.S. bombing of the Chinese embassy in Belgrade or the charges of espionage on the part of China, are perhaps best left unaddressed. Avoid negative comments about China and its history. No one likes to have his or her country criticized by outsiders.

Certain gestures and other forms of nonverbal communication are important to know. For example, a laugh or smile is often used to indicate embarrassment or nervousness rather than amusement. A typical expression of displeasure is a quick sucking of air between the teeth. A nod does not always signal agreement. It can be a confirmation that the person has understood you or even a polite gesture if the person has not.

You will have to learn to read between the lines. Chinese are generally uncomfortable communicating negatives, and may respond with a positive to maintain harmony. Negatives might also be communicated in a jesting manner. Humility, patience, and an easy-going nature are all important qualities. Using these skills will ensure harmony, the goal of most interactions. Don't forget the all-important concept of face!

Jokes do not travel well. Puns and double entendres don't translate and references to events or icons of one's home country are often not understood. Avoid sexual or political jokes especially. Avoid the American propensity to jump-start conversation with a joke to break the ice.

DOING BUSINESS

F YOU'RE A BUSINESS TRAVELER IN CHINA, you probably still feel like a pioneer, even though it's been almost 20 years since former leader Deng Xiaoping launched the "open door" policy and started inviting foreign investment into the previously isolated country. "We are learning how to compete in the market economy, and we need foreign expertise," a Chinese official or enterprise manager might tell you. But don't be misled into believing that you can come in with a plan this week and sign a contract next week, or that Western-style efficiency will be welcome in a joint venture with a Chinese company.

The Chinese, as every foreign business traveler quickly learns, have an elaborate, unwritten code of rules that apply to every aspect of business, from negotiating the contract to selling the product. A good way to prepare yourself is to read Sun Tze's *The Art of War*. The true author of this Chinese classic is unknown, but the best guess is that it was written by a brilliant military strategist who lived sometime around the fourth century BC. Sun Tze's basic principle held that moral strength and intellectual faculty were the decisive factors in battle, and today, these are the guiding factors in negotiating business deals. Not that you're dealing with adversaries. But from the days when the first foreign firms began to eye China's vast potential market of 1.2 billion consumers, the Chinese quickly realized that they had something the world wanted, so why not assure themselves a share in the capital that foreign ventures were sure to generate?

Upon joining the World Trade Organization in January 2002, China agreed to gradually open the financial services industry within the country to foreign competition by 2007. In January 2004, Citibank and HSBC became the first foreign banks to get permission for issuing credit cards in China. The move comes as part of a package of reforms China is undertaking to meet its WTO obligations. But foreign businesses can't expect to expand into China without a hitch. The Japanese car-maker Toyota ran into serious problems with Chinese state-run newspapers in late 2003 when it put out two ads: one featured a Toyota vehicle towing a truck that resembled a Chinese military vehicle, and the other showed a stone lion—a traditional Chinese symbol of authority—saluting a Toyota truck. Both ads were considered to imply the superiority of Japanese products over Chinese products. Toyota immediately apologized for the oversight, stating that the two ads were solely commercial and contained no other intention.

According to *The Art of War*, you sometimes have to yield a city or give up ground in order to gain a more valuable objective. Although it might seem a good idea in the short run to bow to ideological pressure from China, it is probably best for a company's long-term goals and international image to hold out. There is dissension today within the ranks of China's government, and attempts to appease the authorities who make demands today may backfire if these people fall out of favor domestically, or if America's political relations with China deteriorate.

Furthermore, though the Chinese authorities may insist that their politics are none of our business, the lack of a clear rule of law in China can work against conducting business here. On a number of occasions business people have found themselves arrested and detained on trumped-up or nonexistent charges following a disagreement with a local partner or government authority over terms. Often the disagreement has to do with a city or provincial ministry's wanting an unreasonable share in the company. It is to the advantage of all foreigners living or spending time in China to push for political reforms that would incorporate due process of law.

This is all part of pioneering. In a country that had almost no modern roads 20 years ago, there are now huge swathes of concrete everywhere—and vehicles to run on them. According to World Bank figures, China's economy grew at a rate of 7% in 2003, despite the lingering effects of the SARS breakout. The forecast for 2004 is an economic growth rate of between 8.4% and 9.5%.

From being a country with virtually no capital, it has moved to among the top six nations in the world in terms of foreign exchange reserves. The people in the cities wear designer fashions, and construction cranes loom above almost every city or village street. Some observers think that as the market economy grows, a measure of democratic reform will come. The Chinese people themselves are likely to demand a freer flow of information, if only to help them make financial decisions. With the Internet more and more accessible to the masses, the Chinese government is having a harder time censoring communications. Nevertheless, China has the most extensive Internet censorship regulations of any nation. In January 2004, Amnesty International urged China to free 54 people jailed for expressing opinions on the Internet; citing a sharp rise in the number of people detained for anything from political speech to spreading news about SARS. Specialists maintain that China must reform its current political system to keep pace with its fast-growing economy. In spite of the economic reforms, this is still a centrally planned system called "socialism with Chinese characteristics." It is still a society with a thousand years of practice at handling foreign traders. Here are some fundamentals you should know before you go:

Your Team: If you're new to the place, retain the services of a China consultant who knows the language and has a strong track record. The nonprofit United States–China Business Council (✉ 1818 N Street NW, Suite 200, Washington, DC 20036 ☎ 202/429–0340 🖷 202/775–2476 ⊕ www.uschina.org), which has additional offices in Hong Kong, Beijing, and Shanghai, is a good source for consulting services, referrals, and other information. Choose your own translator who will look out for your interests.

Know who you'll be meeting with in China, and send people with corresponding titles. The Chinese are very hierarchical and will be offended if you send a low-level manager to meet a minister. All of this ties into the all-important and intricate concept of "face," which can best be explained as the need to preserve dignity and standing.

Don't bring your spouse on the trip, unless he or she is involved in the business. Otherwise the Chinese will think your trip is really a vacation.

Attitudes Toward Women: The Chinese will take a woman seriously if she has an elevated title and acts serious. Women will find themselves under less pressure than men to hang out at the karaoke until the wee hours. This is partly because the party list might include prostitutes. (A woman will also avoid the trap that Chinese local partners sometimes lay to get rid of an out-of-favor foreign manager. They'll have a prostitute pick him up, then get the police to catch him so that he can be banished from the country for a sexual offense.)

Business Cards: Bring more than you ever thought you'd need. Consult a translator before you go and have cards made with your name and the name of your company in Chinese characters on the reverse side.

The Greeting: When you are introduced to someone in China, immediately bow your head slightly and offer your business card, with two hands. In the same ceremonious fashion accept your colleague's business card, which will likely be turned up to show an Anglicized name.

Be there on time. The Chinese are very punctual. When you are hosting a banquet, arrive at the restaurant at least 30 minutes before your guests.

The Meeting: Don't make plans for the rest of the day, or evening, or tomorrow or the next day. And don't be in a rush to get home. Meetings can go on for days, weeks, whatever it takes to win concessions. Meetings will continue over a lavish lunch, a lavish dinner that includes many toasts with mao tai, and a long night at a karaoke, consuming XO cognac from a showy bottle. To keep in shape for the lengthy meetings, learn the art of throwing a shot of mao tai onto the floor behind you instead of drinking it down when your host says "ganbei." (Chances are he is not really drinking either.)

Gifts and Bribes: Yes, a local official might ask you to get his child into a foreign university or buy your venture partner a fleet of BMWs. A few years ago a survey by the Independent Commission Against Corruption in Hong Kong found that corrupt business practices may represent 3%–5% of the cost of doing business in China, a factor that respondents (Hong Kong firms) claimed was bearable and not a disincentive. However, the Chinese government has been campaigning against corruption and business fraud. American companies have the added constraint of the Foreign Corrupt Practices Act, which prohibits offering or making payments to officials of foreign countries. The law can be a good excuse for not paying bribes. However, you may find yourself faced with a great many arbitrary fees to be paid to the city and county for everything from your business license to garbage collection. It is hard to avoid paying these.

To win friends in a small but legal way, give small gifts to the people you meet. Bring a shipment of such items as pens, paperweights, and T-shirts emblazoned with your company logo. And, before you leave town, host a banquet for all of the people who have entertained you.

Communication: Gestures that seem insignificant on the surface will help make or break your efforts to gain entry into China. Escort a departing visitor to the elevator as a way of giving him face, for example. To make a visitor feel particularly esteemed, walk him all the way to the front door of the building. And don't "have other plans" when your Chinese associates invite you out. As in many Asian countries, personal relationships are more important than the contract. The people you are dealing with may not tell you what they really want from a partnership with you until you're out eating and drinking.

There are many ways of saying "no" that may sound like "yes" to foreigners. If you hear that your proposal "is under study" or has arrived at "an inconvenient time," start preparing a new one.

A manager of a local factory in search of a foreign venture partner might tell you that the deal can be done, but that doesn't mean it will be. Make sure you meet with the officials in charge of your sector in the city, those who have the authority to approve the deal. If someone says he has to get the boss's approval, you should have a hearing with the boss—even if it means getting your boss there on the next flight to meet with his counterpart.

Early on, you may be asked to sign a "letter of intent." This document is not legally binding; it serves more as an expression of seriousness. But the principles in the letter, which look like ritual statements to the Westerner because they lack specific detail, may be invoked later if your Chinese partner has a grudge against you. He'll say you have not lived up to the spirit of mutual cooperation and benefit initially agreed upon.

How to Compromise: You will have to give your Chinese partner something he wants. He might, for instance, want your capital to go into lines of business other than what you had in mind. You might have to agree to this if establishing a presence in China is important to your business. Take the example of John C. Portman III, vice chairman of the Atlanta-based architecture firm John Portman & Associates. Portman spent the early 1980s courting the Shanghai government. Besides volunteering suggestions for redeveloping the city, he set up a trading company that brought an exhibition of goods from Shanghai to Atlanta. Not his usual line of business, but in the end the friendships he'd cultivated netted his company the coveted contract to design and develop the $200 million Shanghai Centre, which houses the Portman Ritz-Carlton Hotel, and China now accounts for about half of the company's total business.

Know when to be flexible, but for important details such as who actually has control of the venture and its operations, hold out, even if it takes a year or more. There are ways to make sure of who is really in charge of a joint venture, even though for matters of face and power the Chinese partner will probably want to provide the person with the loftiest title. You will also want to own the controlling share, because it means quality control, profitability, and decision-making power over matters for which your company is legally liable. Often an inside deal is worked out, whereby the foreign party provides the general manager, who actually is in charge of day-to-day operations, while the Chinese partner brings in the chairman, who works with a board of directors and has authority only over broad policy issues.

Don't go to China and tell your prospective partner you want to start production by a certain date. Expect your Chinese associates to drive their hardest bargain just when you thought it was safe to go home. They know that once rumors of a concluded negotiation become public, you will not be able to back down from the deal

without having to make difficult explanations to your investors and headquarters.

Demand that your contract include an arbitration clause, which stipulates that if a dispute arises the matter will be tried by an arbitrator, preferably in the United States or a third country. However, even in China, there are arbitration centers that comply with international standards and are well ahead of the court system.

Being There: Saddled with 50 employees from the state-owned enterprise and you don't even have a customer in China? That's the way things have been done. You will have to make changes slowly and be prepared to train people for new skills. Profits may be equally slow to roll in, but remember the corporate axiom that has become the main China strategy: We're in it for the long haul.

If you're trying to break into the China market with a product or service, learn more about the consumers you're targeting through a focus study. These have become popular among prospective consumers, who have proved willing to sit through sessions lasting as long as three hours. (Focus panels generally last only 40 minutes in the United States.) Test the name in different cities, because meaning can vary according to the local language. As the *Economist Intelligence Unit* once reported, one company had a name for a butter product that meant "yellow oil" in one city, "engine oil" in another, and "cow fat" in a third.

The Law in China: China works on civil law—that is, laws are passed by the National People's Congress and implemented. Quickly. Hong Kong's legal structure is based on common law (the same as Britain's and the United States'), which develops through judicial decisions (case law). The heart of Hong Kong's existence, "One Country, Two Systems," is that both judicial systems exist side by side. But sometimes they clash, particularly when it comes to business. China lacks predictability in its business environment because its laws aren't all consistent. The government that has made a partial transition to a market economy but some laws still protect local firms and state-owned firms from imports, while encouraging exports. There are still remnants of a planned economy, prone to over-investment and overproduction, unrelated to supply and demand.

Will Feng Shui Help Your Prospects? The 7,000-year-old art of placing objects in harmony with the environment and the elements is virtually mandatory in Hong Kong and Taiwan—it always had a stronger influence in southern China. In other areas, it's officially considered feudalist superstitious nonsense, but of course, if it facilitates business. . . . If there's any doubt in your mind, by all means call a geomancer.

While China speeds along toward overtaking the United States as the world's largest economy—the World Bank forecasts that will happen in the year 2020—any number of factors may make or break your efforts to reap some of the benefits of this dizzying growth. Barring serious political upheaval, you'll probably want to stay here and make constant—i.e., day-to-day—adaptations to the changing demands of the market. Like armies, companies in China have to figure out when to advance their presence, when to scale back, when to retreat to another location. And with each new strategy, be prepared to negotiate, feast, and sing karaoke songs.

–By Jan Alexander

Updated by Keming Liu

UNDERSTANDING THE VISUAL ARTS IN CHINA

SINCE THE RENAISSANCE, in Europe and in the Americas the visual arts have generally been defined as works of architecture, painting, and sculpture. In pre-modern China, however, only one visual art held an esteemed status: calligraphy, the art of writing with a brush (*shu fa*). The design and making of buildings, the carving of images, many kinds of pictorial art, and crafts in general were simply not a part of definitions of "art." Their makers had no special status and these things were not the object of aesthetic discourse. In the 20th century, all of this changed. Collectors of Chinese art now amass paintings, hardwood furniture, porcelain, strange-shaped Taihu rocks, clay teapots, tomb figurines, rubbings, and much more. For practical purposes, art in China today is an eclectic mix, corresponding roughly to the concept of "material culture," all those things human beings have made with craft and creativity.

The most important artist in Chinese history was "anonymous." Much ancient art consists of durable objects—jades, ceramics, bronzes, stone carvings, and the like—and for all but recent periods the authorship of these works is simply unknown. Even when history is well documented, material culture emanated from workshops staffed with artisans whose names were rarely recorded. These workshops were often established for the imperial institution, and their quality standards were extraordinarily high. Only in the final century of the Eastern Han dynasty (second century AD) do we start to have names of scholar-officials who were master calligraphers; famous named painters are known from a slightly later period. Outside the realm of calligraphy and painting, however, the makers of buildings, sculpture, and objects remained anonymous. It was not until the 17th and

18th centuries that the court began to recognize renowned ceramic masters, such as Liu Yuan from Henan, and Tang Ying from Shenyang. Thus, unlike the history of recent Western art with its emphasis on famous masters, for much of Chinese art history attention is focused on long-lasting artistic traditions and on the particular periods when they flourished.

The "Son of Heaven," the emperor, was the most important patron in Chinese history. From the time of the Qin First Emperor (c. 221 BC) onwards, the imperial institution was responsible for almost all of the great public works and artistic monuments of China: from the Great Wall to imperial palaces, from Buddhist cave-chapels to pagodas. The emperors, through their court staff, dictated the designs of these sites, and officials charged with carrying out such projects could be held accountable with their life if they failed to satisfy their ruler's demands. In a very real sense, a tour of China becomes an overview of the remains of those strong, long-lasting dynasties—the Han (206 BC–AD 220) and Tang (618–906), the Ming (1368–1644) and Qing (1644–1911)—that left behind notable monuments. Imperial projects are characterized by their scale (the vastness of a Tang tomb), by their quantity (the myriad furnishings of the Forbidden City), by the quality of their materials and work (the images of the Great Buddha niche at the Longmen Grottoes, near Luoyang), and by their symbols of imperial power (most typically, dragons and phoenixes). No other institution or segment of the population in pre-modern China could challenge the imperial institution in the realm of art production and patronage.

Among the earliest arts to flourish in China were jade carving and pottery. These traditions have roots in Neolithic cultures of the fifth through third millennia BC; jade, for example, was especially notable in the Hongshan Culture of modern-day Inner Mongolia and Liaoning and in the Liangzhu Culture of modern-day Shanghai, Jiangsu, and Zhejiang. The workmanship evident in Neolithic jades is displayed to great effect at the Liangzhu Culture Museum near Hangzhou (Zhejiang). The minute designs worked on the surfaces of these stones seem impossible in an age before sophisticated magnification and power tools. The Guan Porcelain Museum, also near Hangzhou, displays a Southern Song (12th–13th centuries AD) imperial kiln and tells the story of celadons (greenwares), one of China's most important ceramic traditions. The high volume and high quality of this and other imperial kilns anticipates the achievements of sophisticated modern-day production. With both jade and ceramics there is a living connection to the remote past: the materials and processes of modern Chinese workshops and factories (often a part of tours) are not fundamentally different from their pre-modern antecedents. Jade carving continues to flourish in China today, using a great variety of hardstones and other attractive minerals. Many celadons offered for sale today—including Longquan, Guan, and Yaozhou wares—use the same clay sources and glaze recipes as their imperial-era prototypes. While excavated artifacts are not for sale and true antiques are very pricey, affordable replicas of both hardstones and ceramics are widely available.

The worlds of ancient and medieval China may be lost, but they are not utterly beyond our experience. Tombs from the Han Dynasty (206 BC–220 AD) were made mainly of brick and stone, and were buried very deeply; they are thus very well preserved. To date, more than 40 Han mausoleums have been unearthed, of which the Tomb of Liu Sheng in Mancheng (Hebei), the Tomb of the Southern Yue King in Guangzhou (Guangdong), and the Tomb of Lu King in Rushan (Shandong) remain

intact. A visit to a tomb or the Forbidden City in Beijing affords the visitor an experience akin to time travel. At such sites you can begin to appreciate the setting and context for objects now displayed in museum cases. Dragon robes take on new meaning once you have stood in the vast courtyard before the Hall of Supreme Harmony within the Forbidden City, where the Ming and Qing emperors presided over pre-dawn court gatherings. There you can begin to understand the role of the dragon as a symbol for the unity of the Chinese people. Tombs, temples, and cave-chapels offer the richest experiences of art in context for ancient and medieval times, while the former imperial palaces at Beijing, Chengde (Hebei), and Shenyang (Liaoning) are the most complete repositories for many of the arts of late imperial eras, after the 15th century.

In late medieval times, with the Northern Song (10th–12th centuries) period, scholar officials came to dominate Chinese society through their unique social status and the perquisites of rank they enjoyed. They created their own arts for personal expression and relaxation. Calligraphy was preeminent, but painting, garden design, the collecting of antiquities and of objects for the scholar's studio were also significant. Modern-day museums display much calligraphy and painting by scholar artists ("literati," *wenren*)—men like Ni Zan, Shen Zhou, or Dong Qichang who were self-styled amateurs in the sense that they did not obtain their social identity through their artistic skills. Garden design of the Ming and Qing is also largely a scholar's taste, designed to engage all the senses and to be savored in different ways at all times of the day and year. The many fine gardens in cities like Suzhou, Yangzhou, Nanjing, Hangzhou, and Shanghai were aped by imperial patrons in Beijing (as at Bei Hai and the Summer Palace). Idealized views of the Chinese past derived from the exquisitely harmonized settings of scholar's gardens (as in the 18th-century novel, *The Dream of the Red Chamber*) should be taken with the proverbial grain of salt. Only a small percentage of the population actually lived in such idyllic precincts.

* * *

E VOCATIONS OF THE NATURAL WORLD, especially the "mountains and waters" (*shan shui*) of the diverse Chinese continent, played an exceptionally large role in later Chinese arts. Paintings, garden design, porcelain decoration, and scholars' objects all took the eternal and ever-changing natural environment as their theme. This does not mean that Chinese artists or scholar-amateurs actually lived in nature or were devoted to the great outdoors. It does suggest the importance of the natural world as a source of Taoist and Buddhist imagery about life and the human condition. And because it can be appreciated without a specialist's knowledge of history or literature, landscape—both the real and the artistic—offers many rewards for the traveler. A tour of the Huangshan mountains (Anhui) or Li River (Guilin) is a quintessential artistic experience as well as a nature-lover's delight. The images of the natural world that you see from your train window are evoked in the gardens or museums you visit.

Because calligraphies and paintings were mounted as scrolls that were rolled up when not on view, it is very difficult to see the great works of the most acclaimed Chinese artists. Unlike the Mona Lisa, which is dependably on view in the Louvre, Chinese paintings are shown for limited periods only once or twice a year. The superb Shanghai Museum, with its modern galleries and strong holdings in painting and calligraphy, is something of an exception. Painters of the Southern Song (1127–1279), Yuan (1279–1368), Ming, and Qing dominate Chinese museum holdings. If you are a fan of Ma Yuan's "one-corner" compositions (Ma was the scion of a whole family of Southern Song court painters), you will be able to see works of his period and style, if not necessarily works of his hand. Your chances to see the great names of later dynasties will increase considerably. The "Four Great Masters" of the Yuan, of the Ming, and of the Qing—artists who constitute one of the backbones of scholar painting—are regularly on display because they produced large numbers of works that in turn were collected avidly in later periods. With an artist like Shen Zhou (1427–1509) the lifetime output was so great and so diverse that, with diligent looking in museums, you can probably encounter the master repeatedly. Many literati works are ink monochrome and something of an acquired taste, like prints and drawings. Brilliantly colored works on silk produced for the Qing court—such as a large, impressive portrait of the Qianlong emperor (18th century) in armor on horseback—are well represented in Chinese museums. Until recently these were scorned by western art historians.

For the last thousand years or more, rulers and scholars in China have collected certain objects primarily for their historical value. The most prized objects, such as bronze ritual vessels and stone monuments, could be compared with the received historical record and Confucian classics because they carried inscriptions. Antiquarian study of relics preoccupied collectors, leading to the compilation of extensive illustrated catalogues of their holdings, and, not surprisingly, to a flourishing art market as well as considerable fakery. The collections of the Palace Museum (within the Forbidden City, Beijing) reflect these traditional interests and practices. Rich in archaic bronzes and jades, but poor in sculpture, the Palace collection was amassed by art-loving emperors starting in the Northern Song period (10th–12th centuries). Today it is not only one of the world's strongest collections of calligraphy and painting, it also houses the extensive furnishings of the Qing imperial court, from dragon robes to cloisonné and mechanical clocks sent as gifts by European powers. A fraction of the collections was moved to the island of Taiwan in 1949, but the bulk of its holdings remains intact and has been augmented by donations and discoveries in the 1990s. Visiting the Palace Museum can serve as a quick introduction to the kinds of things regarded as art in pre-modern China, as well as an immersion in the luxurious lifestyle of the ruling class.

A wider range of objects fills the many other museums in China. Most museums focus on history, using objects to tell the story of Chinese civilization from prehistory to modern times (c. 1840). These displays generally bring to mind exhibits in natural history and science museums, with their educational graphics, dioramas, models, and reproductions. Original works, including ancient jades, bronzes, ceramics, and other art, are installed amid these pedagogical aids. (Such display practices horrify some non-Chinese art curators, who place great weight on the unencumbered aesthetic experience of authentic art objects.) The preeminent example of this kind of presentation is the Museum of Chinese History, on Tiananmen Square in Beijing. The museum staff has gathered together many important new acquisitions, such as a blue glazed lamp of the Six Dynasties period (222–589), Tang stone figurines, and a Ming embroidered silk portrait of the Heavenly Kings. The exhibits interpret the objects, which is useful both for the local population and for viewers who cannot read labels written in Chinese. Thus a visit to the Museum of Chinese History can provide a useful overview of Chinese civilization, albeit with history diced into neat dynastic segments under an overall Marxist framework ("primitive society, slave society, feudal society"). Most city and provincial museums depict the history of their own region, so the periods emphasized and the material displayed reflect the strengths and weaknesses of each area. The Shaanxi History Museum in Xian, an imperial capital for many dynasties, is thus correspondingly rich in tomb treasures and

luxury goods from those epochs, and has some of the most modern facilities in all of China. Similarly, the Yunnan Provincial Museum in Kunming reflects the ethnic diversity of its peoples, both historically and in the present day.

Since 1950, the national government has made a notable commitment to archaeology, rescuing sites and artifacts from the path of bulldozers and carrying out extensive surveys and excavations in every province and region. The artistic and artifactual heritage as it is known today, a half century later, has caused scholars to rewrite the history of China from earliest times to the early imperial periods (beginning 221 BC). Virtually any volume written prior to the 1970s has been seriously compromised by information gathered in more recent decades. Books and journals can be found in museums and bookstores, but most of them are in Chinese. Many of the finest discoveries are, however, presented comprehensively through site museums—such as the Banpo Neolithic Village and the Qin First Emperor's Terra-cotta Army, both a short drive east of Xian, or the tomb of the Nanyue King in downtown Canton (Guangzhou). In these you can actually walk into an ancient site and see the artifacts in place, much as the archaeologists first encountered them. Many museums have galleries devoted exclusively to important local discoveries, such as the chime of 65 musical bells in the Hubei Provincial Museum (Wuhan) or the desiccated corpses in the Xinjiang Museum (Ürümqi). Don't be surprised if the most famous objects from a particular museum are not on display; they may be on loan to Beijing or abroad in a traveling exhibition.

Many fine art titles are now available at Chinese museums, sites, and bookstores, generally at bargain prices, although only a small fraction have English texts. Recent archaeology and expanding definitions of what constitutes serious topics for study have greatly enlarged the purview of "Chinese art history," and no one can command it all. Some of the most useful guides to discoveries of the late 20th century are exhibition catalogues: *The Golden Age of Chinese Archaeology: Celebrated Discoveries from the People's Republic of China* (National Gallery of Art, 1999), *The Great Bronze Age of China* (Metropolitan Museum of Art, 1980), *The Quest for Eternity* (Los Angeles County Museum, 1987), *Son of Heaven: Imperial Arts of China* (Seattle, 1988), *Mysteries of Ancient China* (British Museum, 1996), *China: Five Thousand Years* (Guggenheim Museum, 1997), and *The Golden Age of Archaeology* (National Gallery, 1999).

Two recent volumes also make good use of art and archaeology to introduce Chinese history and culture: Patricia Buckley Ebrey, *The Cambridge Illustrated History of China* (Cambridge, 1996), and Robert E. Murowchick, ed., *Cradles of Civilization: China* (University of Oklahoma, 1994). Laurence Sickman and Alexander C. Soper's *The Art and Architecture of China* (Pelican History of Art, Yale University Press, many editions) remains the best one-volume text, but covers only architecture, painting, and sculpture. Jessica Rawson, ed., *The British Museum Book of Chinese Art* (British Museum, 1992) is especially broad in its coverage.

BOOKS & MOVIES

Books

History

For general overviews of Chinese history from the 1600s to the present, start with *Modern China: A Guide to a Century of Change* (Graham Hutchings, Harvard University Press, 2000) or *The Search for Modern China* (Jonathan Spence, Norton, New York, 1990). To explore deeper roots, with essays on specific cultural topics, read *An Introduction to Chinese Civilization* (John Meskill, ed., D.C. Heath, 1973) or *Anglo-China: Chinese People and British Rule in Hong Kong 1841–1880* (Christopher Munn, Curzon Press, 2001). To get a a better understanding of the rise of Mao and his archrival, Chiang Kaishek, pick up *Before Mao* (Patrick Lescot, Ecco, 2004) or *Chiang Kai-Shek* (Jonathan Fenby, Carroll & Graf, 2004). *Chinese Lives: An Oral History of Contemporary China* (ed. by W. J. F. Jenner and Delia Davin, Pantheon, 1987), by the Chinese journalists Sang Ye and Zhang Xinxin, though dated makes an interesting read. *One China, Many Paths* (Chaohua Wang, Verso Books, 2003) is a collection of essays that paint a vibrant panorama of the contemporary intellectual scene in the People's Republic.

Excellent books on Tibet include *High Peaks, Pure Earth: Collected Writings on Tibetan History and Culture* (Hugh Richardson, Serindia, 1998) and *Amdo Tibetans in Transition: Society and Culture in the Post-Mao Era* (Toni Huber, Brill Academic Publishers, 2002).

Memoir

A number of memoirs provide not only personal stories, but also intimate windows on China's vast socioeconomic changes. *The Lost Daughters of China: Abandoned Girls, Their Journey to America, and the Search for a Missing Past* (Karin Evans, J. P. Tarcher, 2001) is part memoir, part travelogue, part East–West cultural commentary that weaves the author's experience of adopting a Chinese infant with observations about Chinese women's history and that country's restrictive reproductive policies. *The Private Life of Mao Zedong: The Memoirs of Mao's Personal Physician* (Zhisui Li, with Anne Thurston, Random House, 1994) combines the doctor's personal history and an intimate, controversial focus on the PRC's founding father. For a portrait of modern China, try *Behind the Wall* (Colin Thubron, Penguin Books, 1989) and *China Wakes* (Nicholas D. Kristof and Sheryl Wudunn, Vintage Press, 1995). For light reading about the Chinese techno generation, *Shanghai Baby* (Weihui Zhou, Simon & Schuster, 2001) is a Chinese version of *Bright Lights, Big City*. It portrays a young urban woman, Coco, who explores the intoxicating but at times cruel underbelly of China's most Westernized city, Shanghai. Coco represents a new generation in China whose search for moral grounding in a country of shifting values is complicated by issues of sexuality, feminism, and material desire.

Economics and Policy

Capitalist China: Strategies for a Revolutionized Economy (Jonathan R. Woetzel, John Wiley & Sons, 2003) discusses the new wave of major companies doing business in China. *Internationalizing China: Domestic Interests and Global Linkages* (David Zweig, Cornell University Press, 2002) analyzes the effect of the open market in urban centers and rural regions. Zweig notes that China's future depends on the extent to which corruption, which can disrupt development tremendously, can be controlled by government policies. *China's New Order: Society, Politics, and Economy in Transition* (Hui Wang, Harvard University Press, 2003) proffers an objective view on China's political structure and the direction of its reform.

Fiction

For a taste of historical Chinese literature, spend some time with *Story of the Stone*; it's also known as *Dream of the Red*

Chamber (Xueqin Cao, trans. by David Hawkes, Penguin Books, 1973). Any book or essay by author Lu Xun will give you a taste of China's painful path from dynastic rule through early Communist rule; try *Diary of a Madman and Other Stories* (trans. by William Lyell, University of Hawaii Press, 1990). *Bolshevik Salute* (Meng Wang, University of Washington Press, 1989) is one of China's first modern novels translated into English. Of the collections of Chinese literature and poetry both ancient and modern, check out *An Anthology of Chinese Literature: Beginnings to 1911* (Stephen Owen, ed. and trans., Norton, 1996) and *From May Fourth to June Fourth: Twentieth Century Chinese Fiction and Film* (David D. W. Wang and Ellen Widmer, eds., Cambridge University Press, 1993).

A number of the works of Gao Xianjian, the Nobel Laureate for Literature, have been translated into English, including *Buying a Fishing Rod for My Grandfather* (HarperCollins, 2004), a collection of short stories that depict the fragility of love and life, and the haunting power of memory. Anchee Min, known for her bestselling memoir, *Red Azalea* (Berkley Books, 1995), has since published several novels, including *Wild Ginger* (Houghton Mifflin, 2002) and *Empress Orchid* (Houghton Mifflin, 2004). The novel *Waiting* (Ha Jin, Vintage Books, 2000) won the 1999 National Book Award and the 2000 PEN/ Faulkner Award for Fiction. The story tells of one man's frustration at the hands of the bureaucracy as he tries to marry the woman he loves.

Movies

Among Chinese directors, Chen Kaige captures the beauty of the Chinese countryside in his mysterious, striking *Life on a String* (1991). He also directed an epic story of the artistic and personal commitment of two Peking opera stars, *Farewell,*

My Concubine (1993) and *Temptress Moon* (1997). Tian Zhuangzhuang directed the controversial *The Blue Kite* (1994), a story of the travails of a young schoolteacher under communism in the 1950s and '60s. (It is currently not allowed to be shown in China). The outstanding films of director Zhang Yimou, such as *Red Sorghum* (1987), *Ju-Dou* (1990), *Raise the Red Lantern* (1991), *Shanghai Triad* (1995), *The Story of Qiu Ju* (1992), and *To Live* (1994) all star the excellent actress Gong Li, whose roles range from a glamorous mob mistress in 1930s Shanghai to a rural worker.

The director Ang Lee was celebrated for his 2001 *Crouching Tiger, Hidden Dragon,* which won four Academy Awards. Lee's earlier films are also worth seeing; *Eat Drink Man Woman* and *The Wedding Banquet* are amusing looks into modern-day Chinese relationships.

An American filmmaker of Chinese descent, Peter Wang, looks wryly at contemporary China in *A Great Wall* (1986). Director Ann Hui's *Song of the Exile* (1990) follows a young woman returning home to Hong Kong after graduating from a British university.

A Western take on Chinese history is presented in Bernardo Bertolucci's *The Last Emperor,* filmed in China. Three documentary films by Ambrica Productions (New York), *China in Revolution 1911–1949* (1989), *The Mao Years 1949–1976* (1994), and *Born under the Red Flag 1976–1997* (1997), depict the political and social upheavals that followed the death of the last emperor. They are available from Zeitgeist Films (☎ 800/ 255–9424). The Long Bow Group (Boston) has produced *The Gate of Heavenly Peace* (1996), a documentary film about the Tiananmen Square protests; it is available from Naata (☎ 415/552–9550).

CHINA: A CHRONOLOGY

400,000–200,000 years ago	Early Paleolithic age: Fossil remains date Peking Man, which exhibits characteristics of modern Mongoloids. Evidence of use of stone tools.
8000–5000 BC	Neolithic age: Beginnings of agriculture.
2205–1766 BC	Purported reign of Xia Dynasty; no archaeological proof of its existence. Noted for use of fire, houses, and silk.
1766 BC–1122 BC	Shang Dynasty: Beginnings of concept of "mandate of heaven," emphasizing good conduct of government and right of the populace to rebel against wicked leaders. Noted for highly developed bronze castings, carved jade ritual objects, and oracle bones.
1027BC–770BC	Zhou Dynasty establishes capital near present-day Xian. Development of the feudal system. Writing used to keep records and for history and poetry books. Usage of coin currency.
607 BC–487 BC	Lifetime of Lao-tzu, philosopher who sought truth (dao) and utmost virtue in political relations and human nature, believing power should be in hands of people. Advisor to emperor. Purported author of *Tao Te Ching*. Founder of Taoism.
551 BC–479 BC	Lifetime of K'ung Fu-tzu (Confucius), teacher of moral principles of conduct and princely rule. Author of the *I Ching,* or Book of Changes. Stressed importance of humanity, courtesy, uprightness, honesty, and knowledge. Beginnings of Iron Age.
476–221 BC	Warring States period.
372 BC–289 BC	Lifetime of Meng-tzu (Mencius), proponent of living in proper relationships based on duty defined in social terms.
220 BC–206 BC	Despotic Qin Shi Huang Di (self-named "First Emperor") unites China and divides country into present-day 48 commanderies. Establishes capital and underground tomb with terra-cotta soldiers at Changan (Xian). Work begun on Great Wall to keep out nomadic tribes of north. Civil service exams instituted. Script, weights and measures, and coinage standardized. Books burned and Confucian scholars persecuted. Beginning of overland trade with Roman Empire.
206 BC–AD 220	Han Dynasty. Gao-zu (202–195 BC) prevents attack from Huns by marrying daughter to Hun emperor. Wu Di (141–87 BC) encourages revival of Confucian studies; expands Chinese power to almost present-day position. Beginnings of papermaking. Collapse of Han Dynasty and dissolution of the empire.
AD 25–AD 220	Introduction of Buddhism from India. Silk Route developed.
265–420	Xin Dynasty.
420–589	Division of China into Northern and Southern dynasties.
589–618	Empire reunified under the Sui Dynasty. Grand Canal constructed, connecting northern and southern China. Development of gentry class. Reinstatement of civil service exams.

618–907   Tang Dynasty. China's "Golden Age"; great flowering of arts and sciences under Xuan Zong (712–756). Notable poets: Du Fu, Wang Wei, Gao Shi, Bo Juyi, and Yuan Zhen. Coexistence of foreign religions. Rise of scholar-officials. Expansion of Buddhism and Confucian ethics. Paper and printing exported to West. Expansion of Buddhism and Confucian ethics. Only empress ever to rule China, Empress Wu (627–705), concubine to previous emperors, declares herself emperor in 690; orders ruthless persecution of opponents.

907–960   Instability following collapse of Tang Dynasty leads to division of rule into Five Dynasties in north and Ten Kingdoms in south. Empire collapses and Barbarians invade north China. Beginnings of urban life and neo-Confucianism. Paper money and a primitive printing press are introduced, as well as the foot binding of women. First military use of gunpowder.

960–1280   China reunited under Song Dynasty, capital established at Kaifeng. Coexistence with Jurchen, Khitan, and Jin rule. Flourishing of landscape painting. Genghis Khan defeats Jin in northwestern China in 1215.

1260   Mongol leader Kublai Khan, grandson of Genghis Khan, establishes Peking as his capital.

1279–1368   Mongol conquest of all of China and Tibet; founding of Yuan (original) Dynasty under "foreign" rule. Marco Polo reputed to visit China; serves under Kublai Khan (1275–1292). Rebellion instigated by White Lotus and Red Turbans groups leads to collapse of empire.

1368–1644   Ming (Brilliant) Dynasty is marked by consolidation of power and institutional foundations of Chinese state. Capital moved to Nanjing until 1403. Beijing becomes capital again and Forbidden City constructed in 1421. Maritime expeditions across Indian Ocean.

1550   Europeans come to China seeking trade and Christian converts; Macau established as first European settlement in 1553.

1644   Manchu (Jurchen) conquest and founding of Qing Dynasty. Capital returns to Peking. Pigtail forced on Chinese as sign of submission.

1662–1722   Kangxi Emperor, strong supporter of Confucian morality, consolidates the dynasty militarily. Taiwan reclaimed by China from Dutch.

1736–96   Qianlong Emperor presides over glorious period of pre-modern history. Emphasis on literature and scholarship in history, philosophy, and classics. Novels of the period include *Dream of the Red Chamber* (Cao Xueqin) and *The Romance of the Three Kingdoms* (Luo Guanzhong).

1794   First American ship arrives at Chinese port. Beginnings of Sino-American trade.

1773   To offset growing British demand for tea, and in response to restrictions on foreign trade, British begin exporting opium to Canton.

1839–42 Opium War. China orders complete halt of opium trade. British naval forces capture Fujian and Zhejiang.

1842 Qing emperor is forced to sign Treaty of Nanjing, which permits full resumption of British drug trade and exacts payments of indemnities from China.

1843 Treaty ports, allowing growth of Western commerce and culture and legal extraterritoriality for foreigners, grow from 5 eventually to 80 sites. Hong Kong ceded to Great Britain and China opened to Christian missionaries.

1853 Taiping Rebellion. The Taipings (Heavenly Kingdom of Great Peace), a peasant organization founded on Christian beliefs, take Nanjing and declare it their capital.

1856–60 Second Opium War. In retaliation against Chinese acts of protest against British and French, Treaty of Tianjin opens additional ports to foreign traders and grants extraterritorial privileges to foreigners.

1860 Chinese refuse ratification of Treaty of Tianjin. Anglo-French troops enter Peking and destroy Old Summer Palace.

1864 Final defeat of Taipings by combined Chinese and European forces.

1877 First group of Chinese students sent to Europe to study.

1883–85 Sino-French War, resulting in French control of Vietnam. Extravagant Empress Dowager Cixi (1835–1908), mother of the successor to the Qing throne, advises and exploits following three emperors. Under her direction, naval funds are squandered on reconstruction of Summer Palace.

1893 Birth of Mao Zedong to upper-level peasants in Hunan.

1894–95 China loses Korea, Taiwan, and Pescadores Islands in Sino-Japanese War.

1898 Hundred Days Reform seeks to remake the examination system, the administration, and government institutions in order to inaugurate a system of modern government.

1900–01 Boxer Rebellion, led by fanatical peasant secret societies, suppressed by Eight-Power allied invasion (English, French, American, Japanese, Russian, and other forces). The Empress Dowager forced to flee, palace occupied. Russia invades Manchuria.

1901–11 Qing reforms: establishment of college system, introduction of modern government departments, and abolition of old examination system.

1908 Death of Empress Dowager Cixi. Her son, two-year-old Emperor Pu Yi, inherits the throne.

1911 Republican revolution led by Sun Yat-sen (1866–1925) leads to fall of the Qing Dynasty.

1912 Nationalist party (Guomindang; GMD) is formed. Yuan Shikai becomes president of the Republic and Beijing is declared capital.

1916 Death of Yuan Shikai. Beginnings of Warlord Era, during which Japanese, military commanders, and Communists compete in seeking to reform China.

1917 China declares war on Germany.

1919 China refuses to sign Treaty of Versailles, which cedes former German territories in Shandong province to Japan. Anti-imperialist sentiments give way to the May Fourth Movement, characterized by liberal thinking reflected in literature, political participation by women, and educational reform.

1921 Chinese Communist Party (CCP) founded in Shanghai.

1925 Death of Sun Yat-sen. May 30th Movement marked by anti-imperialist student demonstrations in Shanghai.

1926 GMD armies in the Northern Expedition, from Guangzhou to Yangzi valley, defeat warlord forces, including Japanese, in south China.

1927 GMD turns against CCP. Chiang Kai-shek establishes GMD capital in Nanjing.

1928 U.S. recognizes government of Chiang Kai-shek in Nanjing.

1931 Japan occupies Manchuria.

1934 Communists driven out of base in Jiangxi province by GMD and begin Long March, arriving in Yanan, Shaanxi province, some 6,000 mi and one year later. Only one-fourth of the 90,000 people survive the cross-country expedition.

1935 Mao Zedong becomes chairman and undisputed leader of CCP at Zunyi Conference.

1936 With encouragement from some Communist officers, Chiang Kai-shek is kidnapped by one of his generals in the Xian Incident and is released only when GMD agrees to cooperate with Communists against Japanese.

1937–45 Sino-Japanese War. GMD and CCP join forces against Japanese, but alliance ends by 1941.

1945 U.S. General George Marshall arrives in China to try to put together a coalition government between Communists and Nationalists.

1946 Full-scale civil war between GMD and CCP breaks out.

1949 People's Republic of China is established under Mao Zedong in Beijing. Nationalists, led by Chiang Kai-shek, flee with national treasures and entire gold reserves to Taiwan, leaving China bankrupt.

1950 China enters Korean War against United States. Marriage and agrarian reform laws passed. Sino-Soviet Treaty of Friendship, Alliance, and Mutual Assistance is signed.

1951–52 Three Antis Campaign against corruption, waste, and bureaucratism and the Five Antis Campaign against bribery, tax evasion, theft of state assets, cheating, and stealing of economic intelligence.

1952 Land Reform completed. Violent measures against landlords and local despots.

1953 Korean armistice. Beginning of First Five-Year Plan inaugurating transition to socialism by subordinating agriculture to industry.

1954 First National People's Congress adopts PRC state constitution. U.S. signs Mutual Defense Treaty with Nationalist government on Taiwan.

1955 Setting up of agricultural producers' cooperatives begins, in which peasants cultivate land together and share a common product in proportion to their pooled contributions.

1956 Mao Zedong makes Hundred Flowers speech inviting criticisms of cadres and the bureaucracy.

1957 Anti-Rightist Campaign purging erstwhile critics of regime who dared to speak out during Hundred Flowers period.

1958 Commune system established by amalgamating former agricultural producers' cooperatives. Great Leap Forward aimed at economic transformation in industry and agriculture. Chinese shell Nationalist offshore islands of Quemoy and Matsu.

1959 Resistance to occupation of Tibet suppressed. Dalai Lama flees to India. Chinese Defense Minister is dismissed for speaking out against Great Leap Forward.

1960 Soviet withdrawal of experts. Overambitious and misguided industrial targets of Great Leap result in devastating famine with an estimated 30 million deaths.

1960–62 Three years of natural disasters.

1962 Sino-Indian border war.

1964 China's first nuclear explosion.

1965 First signs of Cultural Revolution erupt in literary sphere in nationwide criticism of play, *Hai Rui Dismissed from Office.*

1966 Eleventh Plenum of Eleventh Central Committee formalizes the Cultural Revolution in move against Mao's critics, which leads to ousting of head of state Liu Shaoqi and general secretary of party Deng Xiaoping. Reign of terror and massive destruction ensue.

1967 Military is called in to restore order.

1968 Millions of urban youth sent to countryside to learn from peasants.

1969 Border clashes with Soviet Union. Ninth Party Congress names Defense Minister Lin Biao as Mao Zedong's closest comrade-in-arms and successor.

1971 Head of a powerful military faction, Lin Biao dies in mysterious plane crash over Mongolia. U.S. State Department abolishes travel restrictions to China, and U.S. table tennis team visits Beijing. Taiwan is expelled from UN, and China takes its seat on UN Security Council.

1972 President Nixon and Prime Minister Tanaka of Japan visit China. Shanghai communiqué is signed beginning process of normalization of relations between China and United States.

1975 Premier Zhou Enlai outlines program of four modernizations in agriculture, industry, science and technology, and national defense. Death of Chiang Kai-shek in Taiwan.

1976 Death of Zhou Enlai. First Tiananmen demonstrations against radical political line of Cultural Revolution. Severe earthquake measuring 7.5 demolishes city of Tangshan. Death of Mao Zedong is followed by arrest of Cultural Revolution protagonists, the "Gang of Four," led by Mao's wife.

1977 Deng Xiaoping returns to power.

1978 Sino-Japanese Treaty of Peace and Friendship is signed. Third Plenum of Eleventh Central Committee inaugurates socialist modernization and liberalized agricultural policies.

1978–79 Wall poster movement attacking Cultural Revolution and Mao Zedong evolves into Democracy Wall Movement.

1979 Resumption of formal diplomatic relations with United States. Deng Xiaoping visits United States. Sino-Vietnamese war. Democracy Wall is closed down and leading dissident Wei Jingsheng is arrested and sentenced to 15 years' imprisonment.

1980 Trial of "Gang of Four" and former military figures associated with Lin Biao. Opening of four special economic zones.

1981 Campaign against spiritual pollution and Western influences.

1983 Anti-crime campaign resulting in thousands of executions and deportations to countryside.

1984 Third Plenum of Twelfth Central Committee endorses broad economic and urban reforms.

1986 Student demonstrations begin in Hefei, Anhui province, and spread to Shanghai, Beijing, and 17 other cities.

1987 Party General Secretary Hu Yaobang is dismissed for failure to crack down on students. Anti-bourgeois liberalization campaign ensues against Western values and institutions.

1989 Death of Hu Yaobang leads to massive demonstrations in Beijing on Tiananmen Square for six weeks. Declaration of martial law does not quell crowds in Square. Military is brought in on June 4, resulting in thousands of deaths. General Secretary Zhao Ziyang is dismissed from office.

1992 Fourteenth Party Congress endorses concept of socialist market economy. First free elections in China.

1995 Chinese test-fire missiles off northern coast of Taiwan.

1997   Paramount leader Deng Xiaoping dies. Upon expiration of 99-year lease, sovereignty over Hong Kong reverts to China. Jiang Zemin becomes president of the Republic.

2000   China attains "normal" trade status with the United States.

2001   Beijing is chosen as the site of the 2008 Olympic Games. Also, China officially joins the World Trade Organization.

2003   Severe Acute Respiratory Syndrome (SARS) is first diagnosed in February. The disease infects more than 8,000 people and kills roughly 10% of victims. Treatment and quarantines end the outbreak in June. Hu Jintao suceeds Jiang Zemin as president. China's first manned space mission is completed successfully.

— Mielikki Org

LANGUAGE NOTES

PRONUNCIATION & VOCABULARY

CHINESE PLACE NAMES

ESSENTIAL CHINESE SIGNS

PRONUNCIATION & VOCABULARY

	Chinese	English Equivalent	Chinese	English Equivalent
Consonants				
	b	boat	p	pass
	m	mouse	f	flag
	d	dock	t	tongue
	n	nest	l	life
	g	goat	k	keep
	h	house	j	and yet
	q	chicken	x	short
	zh	judge	ch	church
	sh	sheep	r*	read
	z	seeds	c	dots
	s	seed		
Vowels				
	ü	you	ia	yard
	üe	you + e	ian	yen
	a	father	iang	young
	ai	kite	ie	yet
	ao	now	o	all
	e	earn	ou	go
	ei	day	u	wood
	er	curve	ua	waft
	i	yield	uo	wall
	i (after z, c, s, zh, ch, sh)	thunder		

Word Order
The basic Chinese sentence structure is the same as in English, following the pattern of subject-verb-object:

He took my pen.	Tā ná le wǒ de bǐ.
s v o	s v o

Nouns
There are no articles in Chinese, although there are many "counters," which are used when a certain number of a given noun is specified. Various attributes of a noun—such as size, shape, or use—determine which

counter is used with that noun. Chinese does not distinguish between singular and plural.

a pen	yìzhī bǐ
a book	yìběn shū

Verbs

Chinese verbs are not conjugated, and they do not have tenses. Instead, a system of word order, word repetition, and the addition of a number of adverbs serves to indicate the tense of a verb, whether the verb is a suggestion or an order, or even whether the verb is part of a question. *Tāzaì ná wǒ de bǐ.* (He is taking my pen.) *Tā ná le wǒ de bǐ.* (He took my pen.) *Tā you méi you ná wǒ de bǐ?* (Did he take my pen?) *Tā yào ná wǒ de bǐ.* (He will take my pen.)

Tones

In English, intonation patterns can indicate whether a sentence is a statement (He's hungry.), a question (He's hungry?), or an exclamation (He's hungry!). Entire sentences carry particular "tones," but individual words do not. In Chinese, words have a particular tone value, and these tones are important in determining the meaning of a word. Observe the meanings of the following examples, each said with one of the four tones found in standard Chinese: *mā* (high, steady tone): mother; *má* (rising tone, like a question): fiber; *mǎ* (dipping tone): horse; and *mà* (dropping tone): swear.

Phrases

You don't need to master the entire Chinese language to spend a week in China, but taking charge of a few key phrases in the language can aid you in just getting by. The following supplement will allow you to get a hotel room, get around town, order a drink at the end of the day, and get help in case of an emergency.

Listen to the phrase and repeat what you hear in the space provided.

Common Greetings

Hello/Good morning.	Nǐ hǎo/Zǎoshàng hǎo.
Good evening.	Wǎnshàng hǎo.
Good-bye.	Zàijiàn.
Title for a married woman or an older unmarried woman	Tàitai/Fūrén
Title for a young and unmarried woman	Xiǎojiě
Title for a man	Xiānshēng
How are you?	Nǐ hǎo ma?
Fine, thanks. And you?	Hěn hǎo. Xièxie. Nǐ ne?
What is your name?	Nǐ jiào shénme míngzi?
My name is . . .	Wǒ jiào . . .

Nice to meet you.	Hěn gāoxìng rènshì nǐ.
I'll see you later.	Huítóu jiàn.

Polite Expressions

Please.	Qǐng.
Thank you.	Xièxiè.
Thank you very much.	Fēicháng gǎnxiè.
You're welcome.	Bú yòng xiè.
Yes, thank you.	Shì de, xièxiè.
No, thank you.	Bù, xièxiè.
I beg your pardon.	Qǐng yuánliàng.
I'm sorry.	Hěn baòqiàn.
Pardon me.	Dùibùqǐ.
That's okay.	Méi shénme.
It doesn't matter.	Méi guānxi.
Do you speak English?	Nǐ shuō Yīngyǔ ma?
Yes.	Shì de.
No.	Bù.
Maybe.	Huòxǔ.
I can speak a little.	Wǒ néng shūo yī diǎnr.
I understand a little.	Wǒ dǒng yì diǎnr.
I don't understand.	Wǒ bù dǒng.
I don't speak Chinese very well.	Wǒ Zhōngwén shūo de bù haǒ.
Would you repeat that, please?	Qǐng zài shūo yíbiàn?
I don't know.	Wǒ bù zhīdaò.
No problem.	Méi wèntí.
It's my pleasure.	Lèyì er wéi.

Needs and Question words

I'd like . . .	Wǒ xiǎng . . .
I need . . .	Wǒ xūyào . . .
What would you like?	Nǐ yaò shénme?
Please bring me . . .	Qǐng gěi wǒ . . .
I'm looking for . . .	Wǒ zài zhǎo . . .
I'm hungry.	Wǒ è le.
I'm thirsty.	Wǒ kǒukě.
It's important.	Hěn zhòngyào.
It's urgent.	Hěn jǐnjí.
How?	Zěnmeyàng?

How much?	Duōshǎo?
How many?	Duōshǎo gè?
Which?	Nǎ yí gè?
What?	Shénme?
What kind of?	Shénme yàng de?
Who?	Shuí?
Where?	Nǎli?
When?	Shénme shíhòu?
What does this mean?	Zhè shì shénme yìsi?
What does that mean?	Nà shì shénme yìsi?
How do you say . . . in Chinese?	. . . yòng Zhōngwén zěnme shūo?

At the Airport

Where is . . .	. . . zài nǎr?
customs?	Hǎigūan
passport control?	Hùzhào jiǎnyàn
the information booth?	Wènxùntái
the ticketing counter?	Shòupiàochù
the baggage claim?	Xínglǐchù
the ground transportation?	Dìmìan jiāotōng
Is there a bus service to the city?	Yǒu qù chéng lǐ de gōnggòng qìchē ma?
Where are . . .	. . . zài nǎr?
the international departures?	Guójì hángbān chūfā diǎn
the international arrivals?	Guójì hángbān dàodá diǎn
What is your nationality?	Nǐ shì něi guó rén?
I am an American.	Wǒ shì Měiguó rén.
I am Canadian.	Wǒ shì Jiānádà rén.

At the Hotel, Reserving a Room

I would like a room . . .	Wǒ yào yí ge fángjiān.
for one person	dānrén fáng
for two people	shuāngrén fāng
for tonight	jīntīan wǎnshàng
for two nights	liǎng gè wǎnshàng
for a week	yí ge xīngqī
Do you have a different room?	Nǐ hái yǒu bié de fángjiān ma?
with a bath	dài yùshì de fángjiān
with a shower	dài línyù de fángjiān
with a toilet	dài cèsuǒ de fángjiān
with air-conditioning	yǒu kōngtiáo de fángjiān

| How much is it? | Duōshǎo qián? |
| My bill, please. | Qǐng jiézhàng. |

At the Restaurant

Where can we find a good restaurant?	Zài nǎr kěyǐ zhǎodào yìjiā hǎo cānguǎn?
We'd like a(n) . . . restaurant.	Wǒmen xiǎng qù yì ge . . . cānguǎn.
elegant	gāo jí
fast-food	kuàicān
inexpensive	piányì de
seafood	hǎixiān
vegetarian	sùshí
Café	Kāfēi diàn
A table for two	Liǎng wèi
Waiter, a menu please.	Fúwùyuán, qǐng gěi wǒmen càidān.
The wine list, please.	Qǐng gěi wǒmen jiǔdān.
Appetizers	Kāiwèi shíwù
Main course	Zhǔ cài
Dessert	Tiándiǎn
What would you like?	Nǐ yào shénme cài?
What would you like to drink?	Nǐ yào hē shénme yǐnliào?
Can you recommend a good wine?	Nǐ néng tūijiàn yí ge hǎo jiǔ ma?
Wine, please.	Qǐng lǎi diǎn jiǔ.
Beer, please.	Qǐng lǎi diǎn píjiǔ.
I didn't order this.	Wǒ méiyǒu diǎn zhè gè.
That's all, thanks.	Jiù zhèxie, xièxiè.
The check, please.	Qǐng jiézhàng.
Cheers!/Bottoms Up! To your health!	Gānbēi! Zhù nǐ shēntì jiànkāng.

Out on the Town

Where can I find . . .	Nǎr yǒu . . .
an art museum?	yìshù bówùguǎn?
a museum of natural history?	zìránlìshǐ bówùguǎn?
a history museum?	lìshǐ bówugǔan?
a gallery?	huàláng?
interesting architecture?	yǒuqù de jiànzhùwù?
a church?	jiàotáng?
the zoo?	dòngwùyuán?

I'd like . . .	Wǒ xiǎng . . .
to see a play.	kàn xì.
to see a movie.	kàn diànyǐng.
to see a concert.	qù yīnyuèhuì.
to see the opera.	kàn gējù.
to go sightseeing.	qù guānguāng.
to go on a bike ride.	qí dānchē.

Shopping

Where is the best place to go shopping for . . .	Mǎi . . . zuì hǎo qù nǎr?
clothes?	yīfu
food?	shíwù
souvenirs?	jìniànpǐn
furniture?	jiājù
fabric?	bùliào
antiques?	gǔdǒng
books?	shūjí
sporting goods?	yùndòng wùpǐn
electronics?	diànqì
computers?	diànnǎo

Directions

Excuse me. Where is . . .	Duìbùqǐ . . . zài nǎr?
the bus stop?	Qìchēzhàn
the subway station?	Dìtiězhàn
the rest room?	Xǐshǒujiān
the taxi stand?	Chūzū chēzhàn
the nearest bank?	Zùijìn de yínháng
the hotel?	Lǚguǎn
To the right	Zài yòubiān.
To the left.	Zài zuǒbiān.
Straight ahead.	Wǎng qián zhízǒu.
It's near here.	Jiuzài zhè fùjìn.
Go back.	Wǎng húi zǒu.
Next to . . .	Jǐnkào . . .

Numbers

Cardinal

0	Líng	5	Wǔ
1	Yī	6	Lìu
2	Er	7	Qī
3	Sān	8	Bā
4	Sì	9	Jǐu

10	Shí	30	Sānshí
11	Shíyī	40	Sìshí
12	Shí'èr	50	Wǔshí
13	Shísān	60	Lìushí
14	Shísì	70	Qīshí
15	Shíwǔ	80	Bāshí
16	Shílìu	90	Jǐushí
17	Shíqī	100	Yìbǎi
18	Shíbā	1,000	Yìqiān
19	Shíjǐu	1,100	Yìqiān yìbǎi
20	Ershí	2,000	Liǎngqiān
21	Ershíyī	10,000	Yíwàn
22	Ershí'èr	100,000	Shíwàn
23	Eshísān	1,000,000	Bǎiwàn

Ordinal

first	Dì yī	seventeenth	Dì shíqī
second	Dì èr	eighteenth	Dì shíbā
third	Dì sān	nineteenth	Dì shíjǐu
fourth	Dì sì	twentieth	Dì èrshí
fifth	Dì wǔ	twenty-first	Dì èrshíyī
sixth	Dì lìu	twenty-second	Dì èrshí'èr
seventh	Dì qi	thirtieth	Dì sānshí
eighth	Dì bā	fortieth	Dì sìshí
ninth	Dì jǐu	fiftieth	Dì wǔshí
tenth	Dì shí	sixtieth	Dì lìushí
eleventh	Dì shíyī	seventieth	Dì qīshí
twelfth	Dì shí'èr	eightieth	Dì bāshí
thirteenth	Dì shísān	ninetieth	Dì jǐushí
fourteenth	Dì shísì	hundredth	Dì yìbǎi
fifteenth	Dì shíwǔ	thousandth	Dì yìqiān
sixteenth	Dì shílìu		

Time

What time is it?	Xiànzài shénme shíjiān?
It is noon.	Zhōngwǔ.
It is midnight.	Bànyè.
It is 9:00 A.M.	Shàngwǔ jǐu diǎn.
It is 1:00 P.M.	Xiàwǔ yì diǎn.

It is 3 o'clock.	Sān diǎn (zhōng).
5:15	Wǔ diǎn shíwǔ fēn.
7:30	Qī diǎn sānshí (bàn).
9:45	Jǐu diǎn sìshíwǔ.
Now	Xiànzài
Later	Wǎn yì diǎnr
Immediately	Mǎshàng
Soon	Hěn kuài

Days of the Week/Months of the Year

Monday	Xīngqī yī
Tuesday	Xīngqī èr
Wednesday	Xīngqī sān
Thursday	Xīngqī sì
Friday	Xīngqī wǔ
Saturday	Xīngqī lìu
Sunday	Xīngqī rì (tiān)
What day is today?	Jīntiān shì xīngqī jǐ?
January	Yí yuè
February	Eňr yuè
March	Sān yuè
April	Sì yuè
May	Wǔ yuè
June	Lìu yuè
July	Qī yuè
August	Bā yuè
September	Jǐu yuè
October	Shí yuè
November	Shíyī yuè
December	Shí'èr yùe
What is the date today?	Jīntiān shì shénme rìzi?
Today is Thursday, September 22.	Jīntīan shì jǐu yuè èrshí'èr hào, xīngqī sì.
Yesterday was Wednesday, September 21.	Zuǒtiān shì jǐu yùe èrshíyī hào, xīngqī sān.
Tomorrow is Friday, September 23.	Míngtiān shì jǐu yuè èrshísān hào, xīngqī wǔ.

Modern Connections

Where can I find . . .	Zài nǎr kěyǐ shǐ yòng . . .
a telephone?	dìanhuà?
a fax machine?	chuánzhēnjī?
an Internet connection?	guójì wǎnglù?

How do I call the United States?	Gěi Měiguó dǎ diànhuà zěnme dǎ?
I need . . .	Wǒ xūyào . . .
a fax sent.	fā chuánzhēn.
a hookup to the Internet.	yǔ guójì wǎnglù liánjiē.
a computer.	diànnǎo.
a package sent overnight.	liányè bǎ bāoguǒ jìchū.
some copies made.	fùyìn yìxiē wénjiàn.
a VCR and monitor.	lùyǐngjī he xiǎnshìqì.
an overhead projector and markers.	huàndēngjī he biāoshìqì.

Emergencies and Safety

Help!	Jiùmìng a!
Fire!	Jiùhuǒ a!
I need a doctor.	Wǒ yào kàn yīshēng.
Call an ambulance!	Mǎshàng jiào jiùhùchē!
What happened?	Fāshēng le shénme shì?
I am/My wife is/My husband is/My friend is/Someone is . . .	Wǒ/Wǒ qīzi/Wǒ Zhàngfu/Wǒ péngyǒu/Yǒu rén . . .
very sick.	bìng de hěn lìhài.
having a heart attack.	xīnzàngbìng fāzuò le.
choking.	yēzhù le.
losing consciousness.	yūndǎo le.
about to vomit.	yào ǒutù le.
having a seizure.	yòu fābìng le.
stuck.	bèi kǎ zhù le.
I can't breathe.	Wǒ bù néng hūxī.
I tripped and fell.	Wǒ bàn dǎo le.
I cut myself.	Wǒ gē shāng le.
I drank too much.	Wǒ jiǔ hē de tài duō le.
I don't know.	Wǒ bù zhīdào.
I've injured my . . .	Wǒ de . . . shòushāng le.
head	tóu
neck	bózi
back	bèi
arm	shǒubèi
leg	tuǐ
foot	jiǎo
eye(s)	yǎnjīng
I've been robbed.	Wǒ bèi qiǎng le.

CHINESE PLACE NAMES

	Pinyin	English	Chinese Character
Chapter 1, Beijing			
	Běijīng	Beijing	北京
	Gùgōng	Forbidden City	故宫
	Tiānānmén Guǎngchǎng	Tiananmen Square	天安门广场
	Yíhéyuán	Summer Palace	颐和园
Chapter 2, Side Trips from Beijing			
	Bādálǐng Chángchéng	Badaling Great Wall	八达岭长城
	Jiètāisì	Temple of the Altar	戒台寺
	Lúgōuqiáo	Lugouqiao (Marco Polo Bridge)	芦沟桥
	Míng Shísānlíng	Ming Tombs	明十三陵
	Mùtiányù Chángchéng	Mutianyu Great Wall	慕田峪长城
	Qīngdōnglíng	Eastern Qing Tombs	清东陵
	Sīmǎtái Chángchéng	Simatai Great Wall	司马台长城
	Yúnjūsì	Yunju Temple	云居寺
	Zhōukǒudiàn Běijīng Yuánrén Yízhǐ	Zhoukoudian Peking Man Site	周口店北京猿人遗址
Chapter 3, Shanghai			
	Chén Xiàng Gé	Chen Ziang Ge	陈香阁
	Dàjìng Gé	Old City Wall	大境路老城墙
	Dōngtaí Lù Gǔdaì Chǎng	Dongtai Road Antiques Market	东台路古代场
	Shànghǎi Pǔdōng Fázhǎn Yínháng	Former Hongkong & Shanghai Bank	上海浦东发展银行
	Fúyóu Lù Gǔdaì Chǎng	Fuyou Road Antiques Market	富有路古代场
	Hǎiguān Lóu	Customs House	海关楼
	Hépíng Fàndiàn	Peace Hotel	和平饭店
	Huángpu Gōngyuán	Huangpu Park	黄埔公园
	Waì Tān	The Bund	外滩
	Yùyuán	Yu Garden	豫园
	Húxīntīng Cháshì	Midlake Pavilion Teahouse	湖心亭茶室

Zhōngguo Yínháng	Bank of China	中国银行
Dà Jù Yuàn	Grand Theatre	上海大剧院
Dà Shìjiè	Great World	大世界
Guójī Fàndiàn	Park Hotel	国际饭店
Huā Niǎo Shìchǎng	Bird and Flower Market	花鸟市场
Jǐngān Gu Sì	Jingan Temple	静安古寺
Rénmín Gōngyuán	People's Park	人民公园
Rénmín Guáng Chǎng	People's Square	人民广场
Shànghaǐ Bówūguǎn	Shanghai Museum	上海博物馆
Shànghaǐ Meǐshūguǎn	Shanghai Art Museum	上海美术馆
Shànghaǐ Zhánlán Zhōngxīn	Shanghai Exhibition Center	上海展览中心
Yúfó Sì	Jade Buddha Temple	玉佛寺
Fúxīng Gōngyuán	Fuxing Park	复兴公园
Lónghuá Gu Sì	Longhua Temple	龙华古寺
Lánxīng	Lyceum Theatre	兰心大剧院
Shànghaǐ Gōngyì Meǐshù Yànjiūsuǒ	Shanghai Arts and Crafts Research Institute	上海工艺美术研究所
Sóng Qìnglíng Gùjū	Soong Chingling's Former Residence	宋庆龄故居
Sūn Zhōngshān Gùjū	Song Yat-sen's Former Residence	孙中山故居
Yàndàng Lù	Yandan Lu Pedestrian Street	雁荡路
Xújiāhuì Dàjiàotǎng	Xujiahui Cathedral	徐家汇教堂
Zhōnggòng Yīdàhuìzhi	Site of the First National Congress	中共一大会址
Bīngjiāng Dà Dào	Riverside Promenade	冰江大道
Dōngfāng Míngzhū	Oriental Pearl TV Tower	东方明珠
Jīnmào Dàshà	Jinmao Building	金茂大厦
Pudōng Mǎtóu	Pudong Ferry Terminal	浦东码头
Shànghaǐ Lìshi Bówūguǎn	Shanghai History Museum	上海历史博物馆
Shànghaǐ Zhèngquàn Jiāoyīsuo	Shanghai Securities Exchange Building	上海证券交易所
Lu Xùn Gōngyuán	Lu Xun Park	鲁迅公园
Móxī Huìtáng	Moshe Synagogue	摩西会堂
Huǒshān Gōngyuán	Huoshan Park	火山公园

Chapter 4, Side Trips from Shanghai

Jiāngsū	Jiangsu	江苏
Nánjīng	Nanjing	南京
Sūzhōu	Suzhou	苏州
Wúxī	Wuxi	无锡
Zhènjiāng	Zhenjiang	镇江
Ānhuī	Anhui	安徽
Zhèjiāng	Zhejiang	浙江
Hángzhōu	Hangzhou	杭州

ESSENTIAL CHINESE SIGNS

Doctor	Yīshēng	医生
Entrance	Dàmén	大门
Exit	Chūkǒu	出口
Gas station	Jiāyóuzhàn	加油站
Hospital	Yīyùan	医院
Hotel	Lǚgǔan	旅馆
Parking	Tíngchēchǎng	停车场
Police	Jǐnchá	警察
Rent-a-car	Zūchēchǎng	租车场
Restaurant	Cāngǔan	餐馆
Rest rooms	Cèsǔo	厕所
Taxi	Chūzūchē	出租车

INDEX

NOTES

Arrive Monday

Tuesday

WEDNESDAY

THURSDAY

NOTES

NOTES

NOTES

NOTES